The Julien Site

AMERICAN BOTTOM ARCHAEOLOGY
FAI-270 Site Reports
Volume 7

Series Editors:

Charles J. Bareis (Principal Investigator and Program Coordinator)
and
James W. Porter (Project Director)

Technical Editors:

Carolyn L. Handell-McElrath
and George R. Milner

Investigations conducted under the auspices of the Illinois Archaeological Survey in cooperation with:

The United States Department of Transportation
Federal Highway Administration

The United States Department of the Interior
National Park Service

The State of Illinois
Department of Transportation

J. Paul Biggers (Chief of Environment)
Earl H. Bowman (Chief of Environment, retired)

John A. Walthall, Ph.D. (Chief Archaeologist)

The Julien Site

(11-S-63)

George R. Milner

assisted by

Joyce A. Williams

with contributions by

Paula G. Cross and Sissel Johannessen

Published for the Illinois Department of Transportation
by the University of Illinois Press
Urbana and Chicago
1984

Manufactured in the United States of America

Library of Congress Cataloging in Publication Data

Milner, George R., 1953-
The Julien site (11-S-63)

(American Bottom archaeology ; v. 7)
Bibliography: p.
1. Julien Site (Cahokia, Ill.) 2. American Bottom
(Ill.) — Antiquities. 3. Cahokia (Ill.) — Antiquities.
I. Illinois. Dept. of Transportation. II. Title.
III Series.
E78.I3A58 1984, vol. 7 970s [977.3'89] 84-602
ISBN 0-252-01070-1 (vol. 7)
ISBN 0-252-01061-2 (set)

CONTENTS

Section 1: Archaeology

by George R. Milner

Section 2: Ancillary Research

PREFACE

In June of 1977, the University of Illinois at Urbana-Champaign signed an agreement with the Illinois Department of Transportation for the mitigation of archaeological resources within the right-of-way of Federal Aid Interstate 270 (redesignated 255) in the American Bottom in Monroe, St. Clair, and Madison Counties, Illinois. As part of this agreement, the University, in cooperation with the State and the Illinois Archaeological Survey, has the right to publish the results of these archaeological investigations. This volume by George R. Milner is a revised version of Report 31 originally submitted by the FAI-270 Archaeological Mitigation Project to the Illinois Department of Transportation in partial fulfillment of contractual obligations of the agreement. This volume also represents one of a series of major site reports that have been selected by the Project for publication by the University of Illinois Press. Each of the descriptive site reports will present a detailed summary of the archaeography of particular sites investigated by the Project. These volumes will not attempt to make regional comparisons or interpretations, since such syntheses are presented in a summary volume of the FAI-270 Archaeological Mitigation Project, entitled "American Bottom Archaeology," edited by Charles J. Bareis and James W. Porter, and published by the University of Illinois Press (March, 1984).

For the Department of Anthropology, University of Illinois at Urbana-Champaign, I would like to acknowledge the support and cooperation of the United States Department of Transportation, Federal Highway Administration; the State of Illinois, Illinois Department of Transportation; the Illinois Archaeological Survey; and the University of Illinois Press.

Charles J. Bareis
Principal Investigator and
Program Coordinator

ACKNOWLEDGMENTS

The author would like to thank those who made the archaeological investigations of the Julien site possible. Mr. Chapman and Mr. Matloob permitted excavations to proceed prior to state ownership of the site area. Many people spent long and arduous hours completing the field and laboratory investigations of the Julien site and recovered material. I would like to mention by name just a few whose efforts contributed much to the successful completion of the Julien site field investigations: William Woods, the 1978 SIUE Site Director; and Charles Bentz, Thomas E. Emerson, and Ann B. Stahl who served at different times as the 1979 Field Supervisors. In addition, Andrew C. Fortier, Steven J. Ozuk, Michael E. Morelock, Dale L. McElrath, and Fred A. Finney served as Field Supervisors for varying lengths of time at the site. The hard work of all these individuals is appreciated. I would like to especially thank several field crew members for their hard work, including Joyce A. Williams, Carol Gerdt, Mary J. Weismantel, Pat Anderson, Kelly R. Cox, John Duncan, Lise Marx, Ken Nekola, Debra Schindler, Alison Towers, and Roger Williamson. The long hours spent by Roger Williamson on following heavy machinery is especially appreciated.

Special thanks go to Connie Bodner (FAI-270 Laboratory Director) for her work in overseeing the initial processing and organizing of material recovered from the field investigations, and to Michael Morelock and Denise Steele for supervising much of the flotation work. Cindy Balek, Cora St. Martin-Bentz, John Duncan, Joan Ecker, Carol Gerdt, Ken Nekola, Mike Meinkoth, and Christy Wells all spent many hours preparing the inventory of materials and assisting with analysis. A special thanks goes to Joyce A. Williams who worked tirelessly during the period when the site records and materials were analyzed. Her knowledge of lithic materials and current research contributed much to the Julien site analysis. Our many requests for computer output kept Merrily Shaw very busy, particularly during the final months of analysis.

The Zooarchaeologist would like to thank Lucretia Kelly, who read initial drafts and offered many helpful suggestions, and Diane Ladner, who spent many days sorting and weighing bone. A special thanks goes to Sarah Neusius at the University of Missouri-Columbia Osteology Laboratory and the staff of the Illinois State Museum for permission to use their comparative collections.

The Paleoethnobotanist would like to acknowledge the contributions of Deborah Pearsall, who established the FAI-270 Paleoethnobotany Laboratory, and Lucy Whalley, who helped in sampling and identifying the Julien site floral material. Eric Voigt, Anne Price, Gail Snyder, Lisa Carlsen, Lisa Griffith, Gerry Wait, Mike Lawrence, Guinivere Joy, and Alvin Hishinuma processed the flotation samples.

The many fine illustrations in the report were prepared by R. E. Smith; the graphs and maps by Guy Prentice, Mary Engbring, and

Ruth Krochock. Kelly R. Cox assisted in arranging figures and illustrations in the early drafts of this volume. Jeff Abrams assisted in the field photography, the preparation of plates in this volume, and by photographing individual specimens for subsequent illustration. Final photographic touch-up and paste-up work were performed by Dean Meador. Final touch-up and paste-up work on maps and illustrations were performed by Scott Wade.

Overall editorial supervision and content editing were provided by the Project Editor, Carolyn McElrath, assisted by Judith Jablonski, George R. Milner, and additional Project editorial staff. Editorial comments were provided by John E. Kelly, who also provided information pertaining to a recently discovered hematite outcrop in the American Bottom region. Typing the manuscript into the University of Illinois text editor (ICE) and formatter (RNF) was performed by Luann White and Judith Jablonski, assisted by Project editorial staff. The author gratefully acknowledges the contributions of these individuals for the completion of this volume.

11-S-63 1978 Field Crew

Kenneth Williams, Site Director*
Keith A. Brandt, Field Supervisor*

William Woods, Site Director**
George R. Milner, Field Supervisor**

Crew Members

Jay Eberle
Cathy Fladung
John Fox
Carol Gerdt
Brad Koldenhoff
Steve McAllister
Mike Scales
Paul Sergio
Elaine Svezja
Mary J. Weismantel

*Original supervisory staff
**Replacement supervisory staff

11-S-63 1979 Field Crew

George R. Milner, Site Director
Charles Bentz, Supervisor
Thomas E. Emerson, Supervisor
Ann B. Stahl, Supervisor
Andrew C. Fortier, Field Supervisor*
Steven J. Ozuk, Field Supervisor*
Michael E. Morelock, Field Supervisor*
Dale L. McElrath, Field Supervisor*
Fred A. Finney, Field Supervisor*

*These individuals served on short-term bases as supervisors.

Crew Members

Pat Anderson
John Arnold
Cindy Balek
Cora St. Martin-Bentz
Kelly R. Cox
Paula G. Cross
Helen Deluga
John Duncan
Debra Fields
Carol Gerdt
Sheryl Goodnick
Marie Hackett
Nick Hakiel
Kathy Hesterberg
S. Madonna Horcher
Sue Jelly
Denise Knight
Robin Kozloff
Larry A. Kritis
Richard B. Lacampagne
Gareth Lewis
Melissa Marshall
Lise Marx
Ken Nekola
Donna (Howard) O'Connor
Keith Powers
Guy Prentice
Jackie Riechmann
Becky Schaefer
Debra Schindler
Peter W. Stahl
Marilyn Staehle
Alison Towers
Craig Volkert
Mary J. Weismantel
Joyce Williams
Roger Williamson

Section 1: Archaeology

American Bottom Chronology

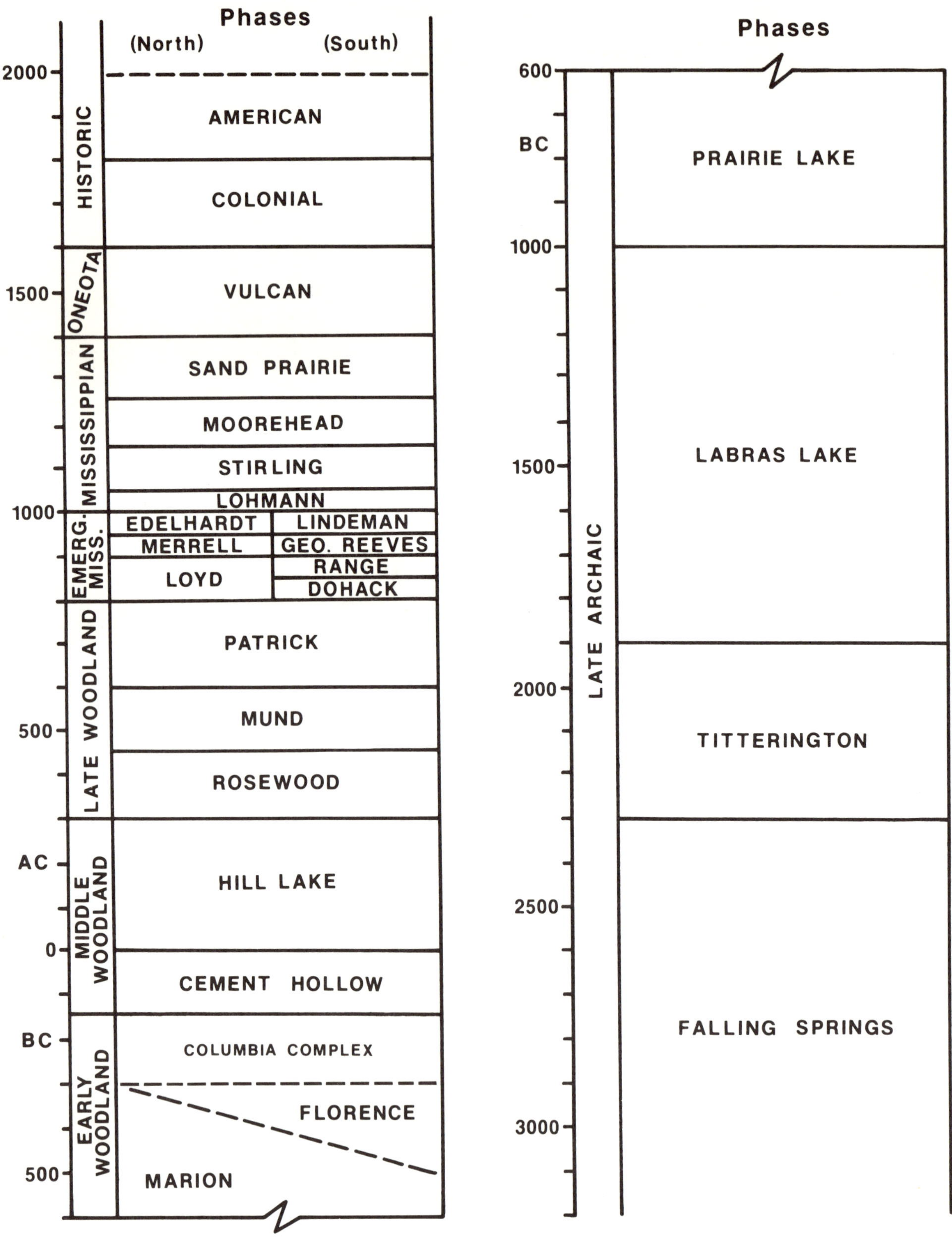

INTRODUCTION

Construction of Federal Aid Interstate 270 (FAI-270) affected several prehistoric sites near the Goose Lake meander scar. Julien (11-S-63), the largest of these sites, consisted of an extensive area of low density surface debris that covered several locally prominent bottomland ridges. These ridges were located within the corporate limits of Cahokia, Illinois.

This volume presents the results of field investigations carried out at the Julien site during 1976, 1978, and 1979. These field investigations were conducted at various times by archaeologists from the Illinois Department of Transportation (IDOT), Southern Illinois University-Edwardsville (SIUE), and, most recently, the University of Illinois at Urbana-Champaign (UIUC).

Test excavations in 1976 and subsequent work in 1978 located Mississippian features in a small portion of the right-of-way area. In 1979, the UIUC assumed the SIUE contract obligations for archaeological work at the site. An excavation strategy was implemented that was compatible with what was then known about small Mississippian settlements (Prentice and Mehrer 1981; Smith 1978c) in general and the Julien site in particular. That excavation strategy was designed to facilitate accurate delineation of discrete, areally circumscribed, and spatially isolated clusters of features of the sort that typified the Julien site. These clusters of features consisted primarily of structures, pits, and posts. Such feature groupings tended to represent discrete Mississippian occupational components, which are here called households.

The areally extensive 1979 excavations confirmed that the principal occupation of the Julien site occurred during the Mississippian period. There was also a Late Woodland occupation, discussed below in this volume. However, the focus of this volume is on the later, and much more extensive, Mississippian period occupation of the Julien site locality.

Site Significance and Investigative Approach

As a region, the American Bottom is of considerable significance to midwestern culture history and to the investigation of processes that resulted in the development and maintenance of complex prehistoric cultural systems. All archaeological sites, which can range from small, single-purpose activity areas to large, internally complex centers, are integral components of prehistoric cultural systems. In complex, hierarchically organized societies, there is often considerable diversity in settlement size and function. The prehistoric cultures of eastern North America that are known to archaeologists as "Mississippian" are examples of such complex systems. Sites of all sizes and functions should be included in regional studies of settlement patterns. Yet, small sites have often been overlooked in past archaeological work in the American Bottom. That work focused primarily on the large and spectacular mound centers.

This volume, however, focuses on the nature and spatial extent of a series of small Mississippian households known collectively as the Julien site. An appreciation of small Mississippian settlements as elements of a complex settlement pattern is not possible without understanding their internal organization and function. The Julien site field and laboratory investigations were directed toward describing specific aspects of such small Mississippian settlements as they occurred in the American Bottom. Included are contributions to available information on the size, areal extent, and relative permanence of these small settlements. Most importantly, perhaps, are the contributions of this volume to an understanding of the level of participation that these small settlements had within the larger regional Mississippian cultural system.

The Julien site investigations are perhaps best described as exploratory and this volume as descriptive. The initial chapters describe the excavated features and the recovered artifacts. Information is presented in a manner that contributes to the archaeological reconstruction of prehistoric life. The final chapter is a discussion of the nature of prehistoric adaptation to the Julien site bottomland locality. Although this volume focuses specifically on data derived from the Julien site field and laboratory investigations, it serves as a basis for future studies of small Mississippian settlements in the American Bottom.

Site Description and Locale

The Julien site was located in St. Clair County, Illinois, within the limits of the present-day village of Cahokia. The site limits, as defined by the IDOT archaeological investigations of the highway alignment lay between the UTM coordinates E748000-748600 and N4270600-4271350 (Kelly et al. 1979). On the surface, the site was represented by a scatter of prehistoric debris covering 25.8 ha. The scatter was neither uniformly distributed nor especially heavy. Approximately 5.7 ha of the site as defined by surface survey was located within the FAI-270 highway right-of-way. Preliminary IDOT investigations indicated that the area was to be directly and adversely affected by highway construction (Kelly et al. 1979).

The surface debris scatter designated as the Julien site was located on a series of sandy ridges that ran in a northeast to southwest direction. The ridges, which for the most part were parallel to one another, formed part of the Goose Lake point bar. Abandoned and presently drained, the Goose Lake channel scar lay ca. 0.8 km southeast of the excavation area. A particularly prominent ridge in the series was included within the highway alignment; it had been truncated at both its northeastern and southwestern ends by subdivisions. The soil of this ridge was classified as a Landes fine sandy loam. Lower swale areas flanking this and other nearby ridges contained soils classified as Riley silty clay loam (Wallace 1978). The field where the Julien site was located was cultivated during the period when archaeological investigations were conducted at the site.

The excavation area was located on a well-drained ridge (Plate 1). Archaeological work on the ridge during the 1979 field season was only rarely hampered by drainage problems. In contrast, a swale immediately to the northwest of the southern half of the excavation area remained full of standing water until late in the spring of 1979. These alternating wet and dry areas were presumably important factors affecting prehistoric settlement of the Julien site locality, as explained later in this volume.

The bluff area closest to the site was located ca. 2 km to the south-southwest. At that point, the bluffline abruptly changed course, and the floodplain width increased considerably. Directly east of the site, the bluffline was further away, ca. 4.5 km. The Mississippi River was located ca. 7.3 km due west of the site.

Several other prehistoric sites were located within several kilometers of the Julien site (Figure 1). Closest were the Florence Street (11-S-458), Sandy Ridge Farm (11-S-660), Marcus (11-S-631), and Byron (11-S-432) sites. All of these sites were situated on the same point bar complex as the Julien site and were recently excavated by UIUC archaeologists as part of the FAI-270 Archaeological Mitigation Project. Of particular significance were the Stirling phase occupation at the Sandy Ridge Farm site (Jackson 1980) and the Sand Prairie phase occupation at the Florence Street site (Emerson 1980a). These sites were located on the same ridge as the Julien site. Other nearby sites with Mississippian occupations similar to those encountered at Julien include Lily Lake (Norris 1978), Labras Lake (11-S-299) [Yerkes 1980], East St. Louis Stone Quarry (11-S-468) [Milner 1981a], and Range (11-S-47) [J. Kelly 1979, 1980a]. In a broader regional perspective, the Julien site is only one of many areas of extensive, but low density, debris scatter that cover alluvial ridges in the American Bottom. Larger sites in the area include Cahokia and its several satellite town-and-mound complexes. Julien and several well-known sites are indicated in Figure 2.

History of Archaeological Investigations

A site designated as Julien was first recorded in 1961 by Alan Harn during a survey of American Bottom sites jointly sponsored by the Illinois Archaeological Survey (IAS) and the National Science Foundation. Flakes were collected from a small area ca. 350 m north of the Illinois Route 157 and Triple Lakes Road intersection, although it was noted that the site might cover a larger area. This portion of

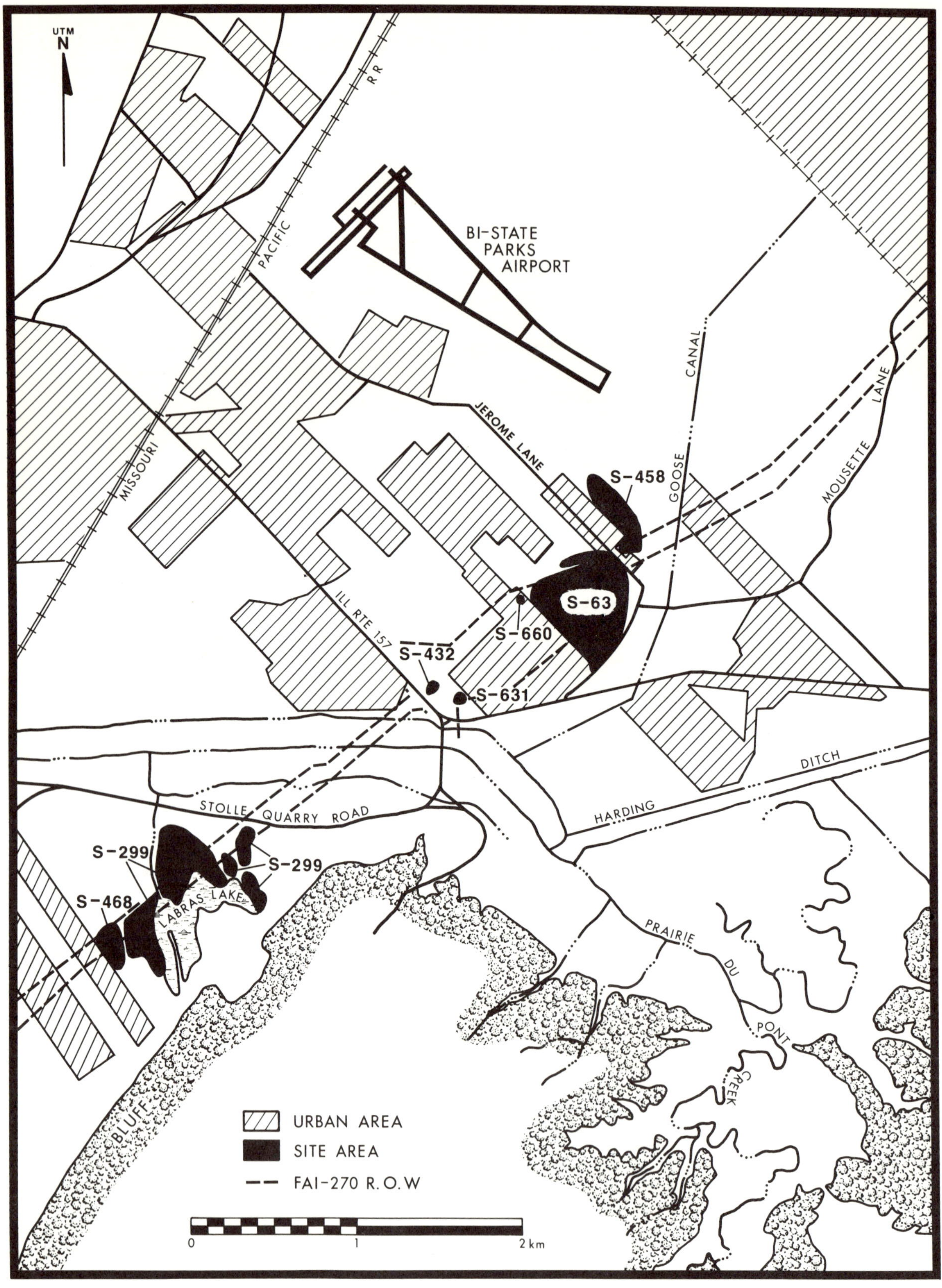

Figure 1. Julien and Nearby Sites

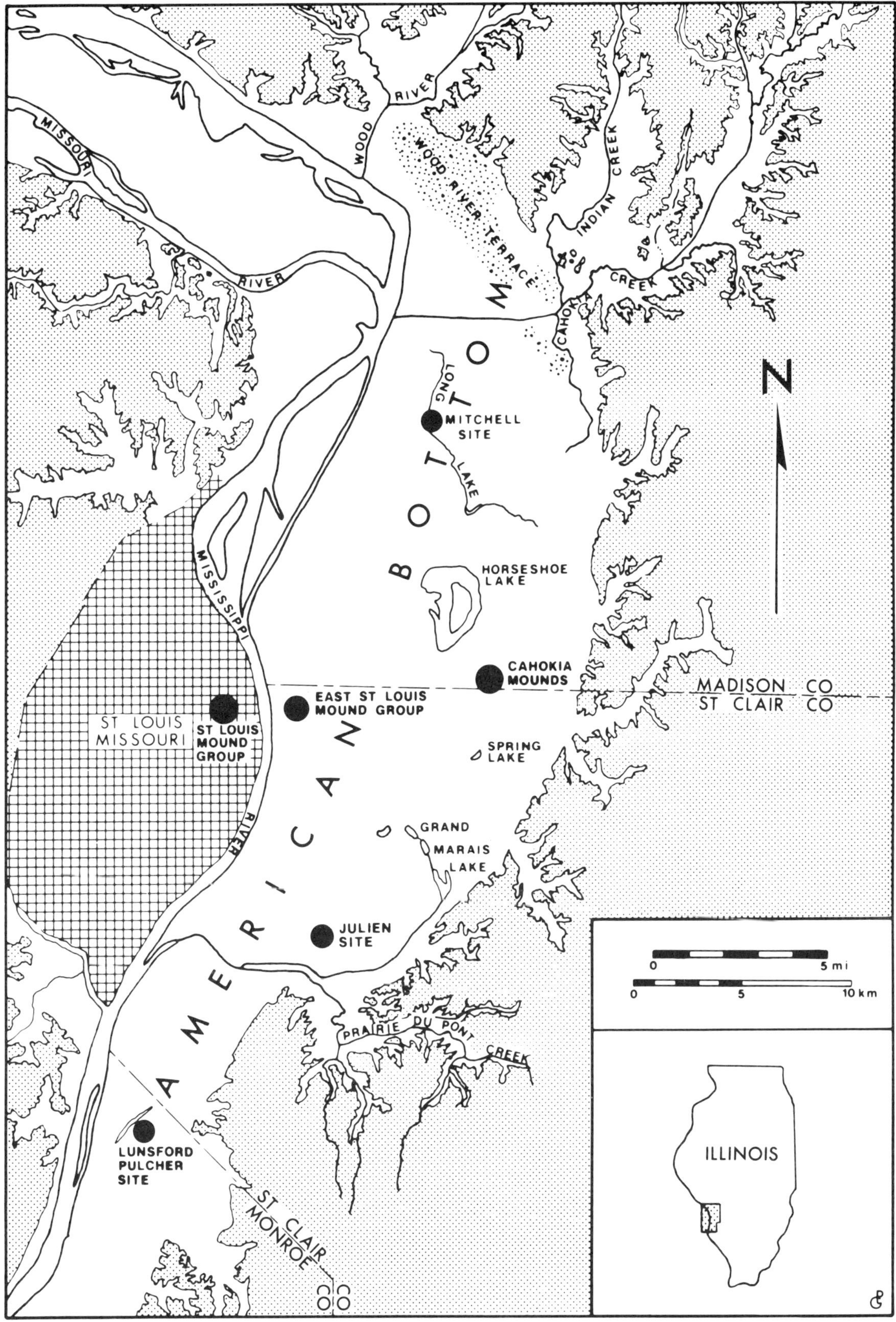

Figure 2. American Bottom

present-day Cahokia was later visited by Dennis Hammer as part of the Blue Waters Survey (Denny 1974). Materials indicating a Mississippian occupation were reported and included with those from the site previously recorded as Julien (11-S-63). The area was again examined in 1974 by Freimuth and Dickinson as part of a preliminary survey of the proposed FAI-255 (later designated FAI-270) highway alignment; they reported a site with Late Woodland and Mississippian components and assigned a new IAS number (11-S-436) to the site.

As part of the FAI-270 site survey, IDOT archaeologists checked both the site locality and the IAS records to clarify the by then somewhat confusing site designations. Apparently, the flakes Harn had collected were actually found in the vicinity of the newly designated Charles Julien site (11-S-469), a site reported by IDOT archaeologists. The Julien site subsequently discussed in this volume was located in a large field surrounded by subdivisions ca. 1 km northeast of the Illinois Route 157 and Triple Lakes Road junction. Collections of the Blue Waters and preliminary FAI-255 surveys were made in the Julien site area as defined by the IDOT archaeologists. Additional information concerning the various field designations and site numbers can be found in Kelly (et al. 1979).

Test excavations at the Julien site were conducted by IDOT archaeologists and the SIUE field school under the direction of Dr. Sidney Denny. The 1976 investigations of subsurface archaeological remains included phosphate testing by IDOT personnel with hand-held soil probes and test excavations by both SIUE field school and IDOT personnel. Phosphate testing procedures were designed to locate likely areas of subsurface features (Kelly et al. 1979). The testing was conducted at 4-m intervals, using a grid based on the highway centerline. Several plowzone soil stains in the central portion of the site were noted during the phosphate and surface survey work. Subsequent test excavations revealed a burned structure (Feature 3) that corresponded to one of the stains.

Test excavation units were placed primarily in the central portion of the ridge, a location of consistently high phosphate readings. Twenty-two randomly placed units, each measuring 1 m x 1 m, were excavated; several of these were later expanded into larger units. Four trenches were also dug. Trenches 1 and 2 transected Feature 3, a large burned structure. Trench 3 exposed several areas of fill, and three features (Features 1, 2, and 4) were recognized during the testing operations. Trench 4, situated on a ridge southeast of the other test units, was outside the present right-of-way limits. It was located to test a topographically high area, a possible mound. Prehistoric features were not recognized in the fourth trench. The excavation of Features 1 and 4, both pit features, was completed during 1976. Work was initiated, but not completed, on two structures (Features 2 and 3). The excavation units were backfilled at the close of the field season.

Mitigation phase excavations were initiated in 1978 by SIUE with the

UIUC as prime contractor. During the period from June to October, SIUE archaeologists conducted another surface collection of the right-of-way, piece-plotted recovered materials, removed plowzone from 1791 m2 with heavy machinery, shovel scraped the exposed area, and completed the excavation of seven features (for additional details, see Woods 1978). The areas cleared of plowzone were numbered Blocks 1, 2, and 3 (Plate 1). The partially excavated Feature 2 was located in Block 1; Feature 3, also partially excavated, was located in Block 3.

By the fall of 1978, it had become apparent that the prime contractor (UIUC) would have to assume direct responsibility for managing the SIUE contract effort (Letter from Bareis to Bowman, 4 October 1978). The supervisory structure of the SIUE field crew was consequently altered, and a Field Supervisor was loaned to SIUE for the period from 17 October to the end of the field season in December. During the closing weeks of October, methodical excavation techniques and a rigorous recording format were introduced. By the end of the season, the excavation pace had increased to a level commensurate with contract obligations.

A total of 5579.5 hours were spent at the site during 1978. During that period, the excavations concentrated on features located within the three excavation units already cleared of plowzone. Seventy-seven features were excavated. The two structures partially excavated in 1976 were left sealed with backdirt for the following season.

Prior to the start of the 1979 field season, SIUE withdrew from participation in the project, and the UIUC assumed responsibility for their work (Letter from Denny to Bareis, 8 March 1979). At that point, the land where the Julien site was located was still privately owned. Two of the landowners wished to remove soil from the ridge within the right-of-way for use as fill in adjacent low-lying areas. One landowner had started that work in the previous season, but it had been quickly halted by deteriorating weather conditions. In 1979 he agreed to permit the archaeologists to work before soil was removed.

Work during the 1979 season concentrated on the removal of the remaining plowzone, extending the grid system for mapping purposes, and defining and excavating prehistoric features. Plowzone was removed from a 38,403 m2 area, designated Blocks 4 and 5. Block 4 was that area northeast of the centrally located Block 1; Block 5 was located to the southwest. Removal of plowzone was completed in Block 4 during May, with the exception of the June excavation of a residential yard at the northeastern end of the excavation area. Plowzone removal in Block 5 was completed in June. In addition, two deep trenches in Block 5 were excavated to facilitate the geomorphological investigations of the site area.

A total of 7766 hours were spent at the site during the 1979 season. Shovel scraping (1890 m2) was restricted to areas of feature concentration, and 231 features were completely excavated. Feature

Plate 1. Julien Site Area: upper, Block 1 (view to northwest); lower, Blocks 1 and 2 (view to southeast)

excavation focused first on the unfinished 1976 work and on features within Block 4, the area which was to be leveled by the landowner. One of the structures tested in 1976 (Feature 2) proved quite complex, and considerable time was spent completing it during the 1979 season. By the end of June, excavations had been completed on all features except for the superimposed complex in Block 5 that included four structures (Features 208, 215, 231, and 241). The excavation of archaeological features at the site was completed by the middle of July 1979.

Excavation Methods

The following discussion of field methods pertains to the excavations conducted after the UIUC assumed direct management of the SIUE contract obligations in October 1978. This was the period during which over 95% of the plowzone was removed and about 97% of the feature excavations were completed.

Archaeological investigations conducted by the UIUC at the Julien site were oriented toward evaluating the nature and extent of prehistoric occupations on bottomland sand ridges. The excavation strategy had several primary objectives: clearing as large an area as possible of plowzone; defining and excavating features to examine variation in their form and interpreted function; and delineating complexes of contemporaneous or associated features. The feature clusters distinguished at the site represent occupational components that varied in size and, possibly, temporal duration. These relatively inclusive feature groupings permitted a more complete interpretation of prehistoric behavior, especially in its spatial aspects, than that allowed by the treatment of features as single and isolated units devoid of all but perhaps general functional and broad temporal meaning.

An extensive area was cleared of plowzone to realize these research objectives (Figure 3; Plate 2). Samples of material from the plowzone had been recovered through repeated surveys of the site surface, so the plow-disturbed soil was removed by heavy machinery without screening. Plowzone depth usually varied from 0.2 m to 0.3 m; it was deeper in the low-lying areas than in the adjacent ridge crest and slopes. Variation in plowzone depth presumably was a result of erosional wash from high to low elevations. The area cleared of plowzone included the topographically high area within the right-of-way and portions of low swales bordering the ridge. This encompassed an area where most of the surface material was concentrated. A paddlewheel, backhoe, and bulldozer were used to remove plowzone from 40,194 m2 (ca. 10 acres); this area was then examined carefully for evidence of features, such as pits and structures. Plowzone removal with the paddlewheel, when there was enough room to maneuver, was cost efficient and usually produced a smooth surface ideal for recognizing disturbances in the subsoil. The backhoe and bulldozer were employed in more restricted areas, primarily around existing excavation units. A backhoe with a special wide and toothless bucket was especially useful in rechecking apparent gaps in

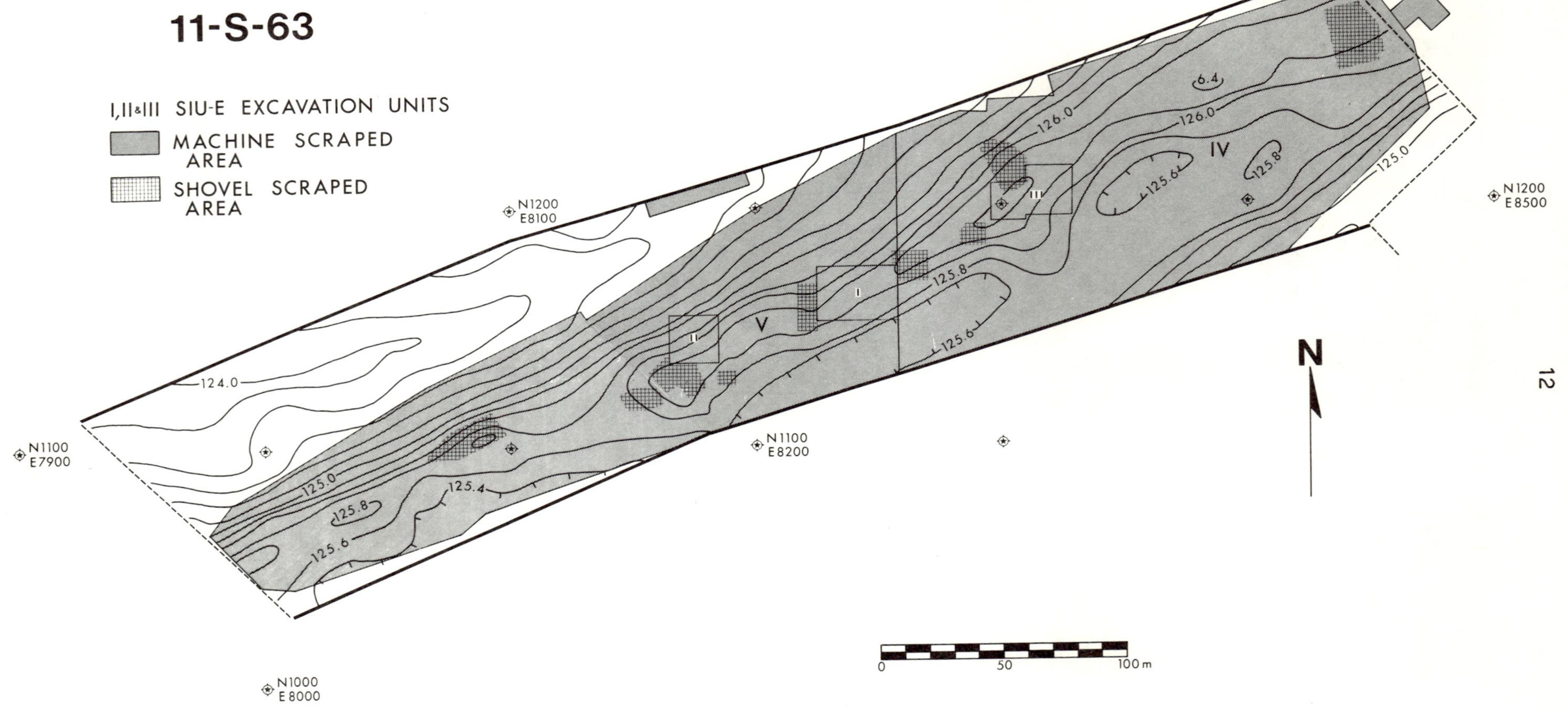

Figure 3. Plowzone Removal

Plate 2. Excavations: upper left, Block 4; upper right, Block 4 structures; lower left, Block 4 feature definition; lower right, isolated feature definition

the distribution of features within the central site area. It was encouraging that features were not found during such rechecking operations, which involved the removal of several additional centimeters of subsoil.

The judicious use of machinery permitted a reduction in the amount of time and effort needed for feature recognition and definition at the base of plowzone (Plate 2). Only areas of feature concentration were shovel scraped, a total of 3681 m2. That amounted to ca. 9.2% of the total area cleared of plowzone. Additional shovel scraping was necessary only in the immediate vicinity of features for definition purposes.

The excavation of features at the Julien site closely followed the general procedures used at other sites by UIUC personnel, fully discussed in Finney (1979). The grid employed was based on the Universal Transverse Mercator (UTM) system. It was established at the site by IDOT surveyors and extended by the archaeologists throughout the site area. Once features were identified and defined, their shapes were recorded in plan view using right angle mapping procedures. The features also were cross-sectioned, and the resulting profiles mapped to record the various filling episodes. If the features were oval, they were profiled along their long axes; rectangular pits or structures were profiled across their widths.

The materials recovered from feature contexts were separated according to major filling episodes. The vertical and horizontal proveniences of items occurring on definable surfaces, such as on feature floors, were also recorded. Flotation samples were likewise separated by the major fill episodes recognized in the field. Early in June, it became necessary to alter the flotation sampling strategy to reduce the number and volume of samples obtained from each feature. Prior to that time, flotation samples, usually 10 l each, were taken from approximately every 10 cm of fill in the first half of the feature excavated. Different fill units, when distinguished, were removed separately from that half. The procedure was repeated in the second half of a feature except that the collection units were often subdivided according to the fill episodes appearing in the profile. Larger samples were taken from structures rather than from pits because the fill volumes in structure basins were greater. From June on, the usual practice was to take a 10 l sample from every 10 cm of each fill only in the second half of each feature. Larger or more frequent samples were taken from fills that were especially rich in floral or faunal remains.

The soil from feature contexts was not screened, except for soil retained as flotation samples. Trowels and shovels were both employed in feature excavation; shovels were typically used on the large-volume structure fills and on pit fills that appeared to be sterile.

Casual examination of feature backdirt indicated that the excavators missed some material, although the amount missed appeared to be low.

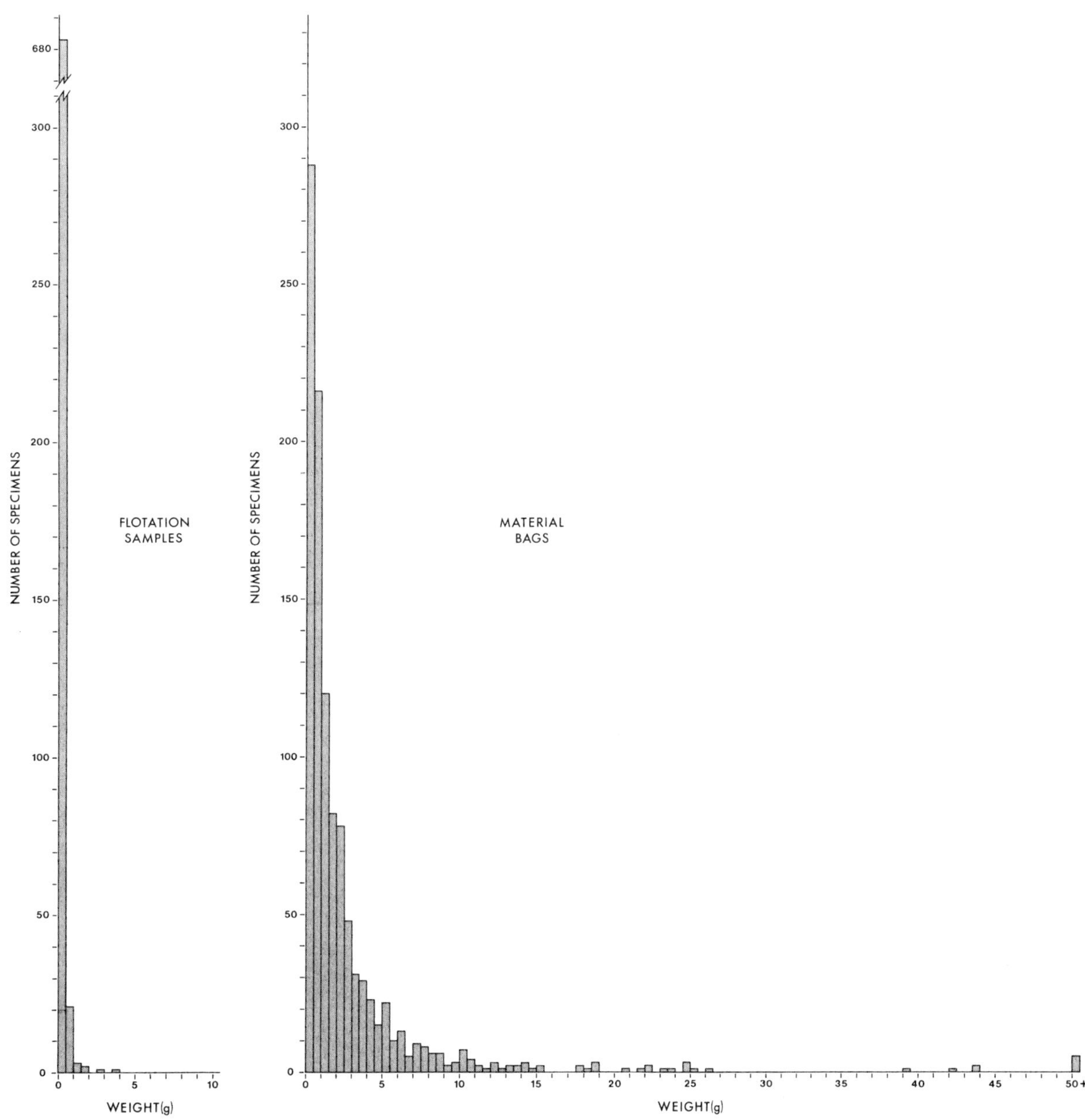

Figure 4. Weight Distribution of Chert by Flotation Samples and Material Bags

That observation prompted a closer inspection of biases introduced by not floating entire feature fills; floating entire feature fills would have been a prohibitively expensive and time consuming task. Chert artifacts and debris were selected in order to examine this sampling problem, since items of that particular raw material are abundant and not easily broken. The latter is an important property, since the selection of fragile material would contribute to overnumeration in small size categories due to postexcavation accidents in transporting and processing recovered objects. The weight of a single raw material can be expected to correlate closely with size, the dimension presumably discriminated by the excavators. A 10% random sample was selected of all features excavated during the period of UIUC management; the particular excavators involved had no effect on the selection process. A replacement feature was selected in the several cases where the initial feature chosen did not contain chert. The weights of chert items from material lots and flotation samples were then compared (Figure 4).

It is important to note that excavators typically pulled material for inclusion in a material bag while taking a flotation sample; therefore,the flotation samples can be regarded as representative of soil that contained artifacts overlooked by the excavators. Large items should have been excluded from the flotation samples. This was clearly apparent in the histograms. Few pieces of chert from flotation samples weighed more than 0.5 g. In fact, most of the ca. 700 flakes recovered from the flotation samples were very small and would easily have passed through a 1/4 inch mesh had the soil been screened in the field. Floating a variable amount of soil from different features (thereby altering the proportion of total fill volume subjected to more thorough recovery techniques) would, therefore, affect analyses based on counts, but have considerably less effect on analyses based on weights.

FEATURES

The most striking aspect of the Julien site was the nature of the feature distribution. [The five section maps in Figures 5 to 10 are numbered from southwest to northeast.] Features were generally located on the higher portions of the ridge, yet they were not uniformly distributed along its length. Features were concentrated in the central area where numerous examples of feature superpositioning also occurred. The prehistoric occupation was represented by Late Woodland and Mississippian features, although most features were affiliated with the Mississippian period. The Mississippian occupation represented a series of spatially and temporally discrete occupational components, each composed of one or more structures and associated features.

The subsurface feature distribution generally conformed to the surface debris scatter, materials which would have been churned for years in the plowzone. Figure 11 is based on the controlled surface collection conducted by SIUE archaeologists early in the 1978 season.

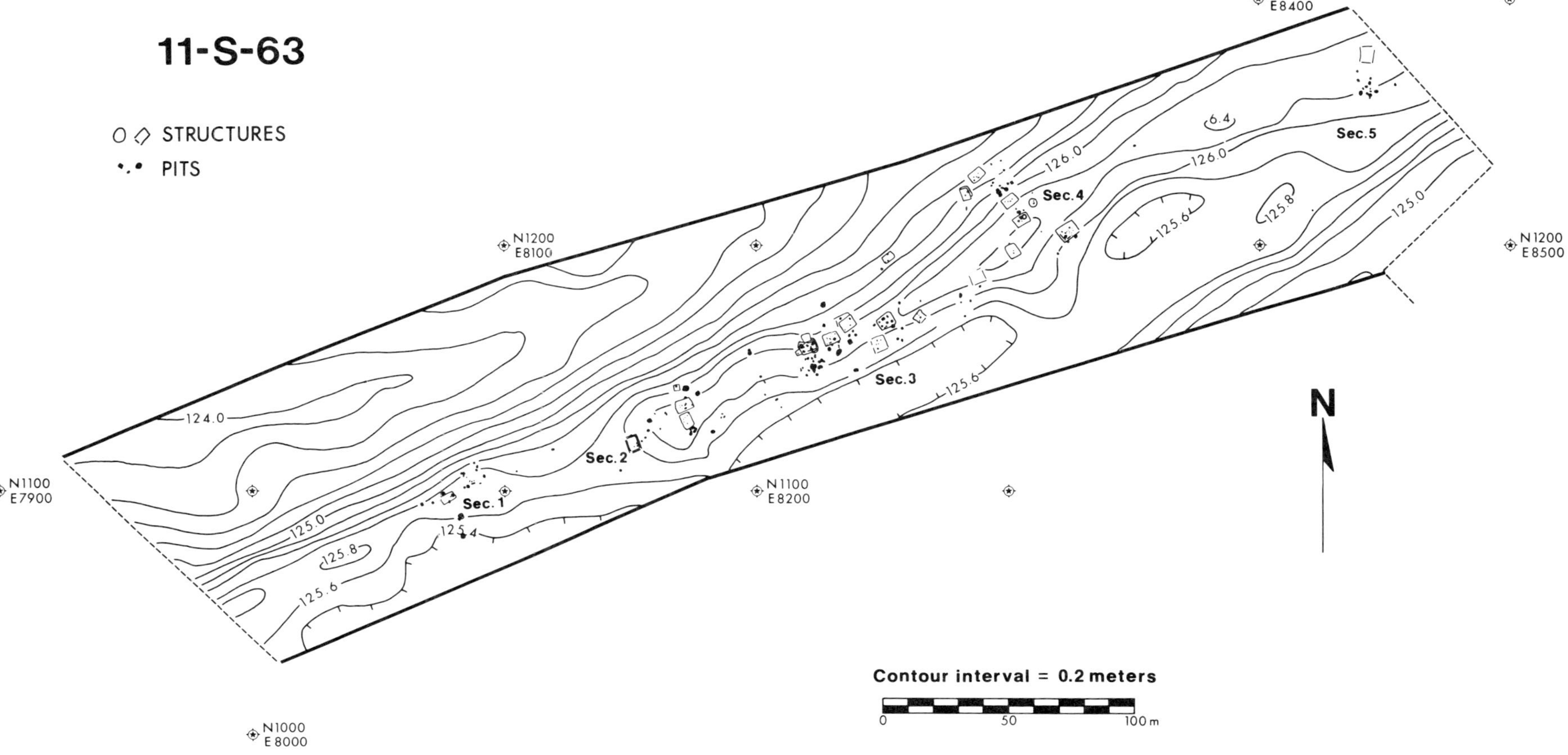

Figure 5. Feature Distribution (see pocket map)

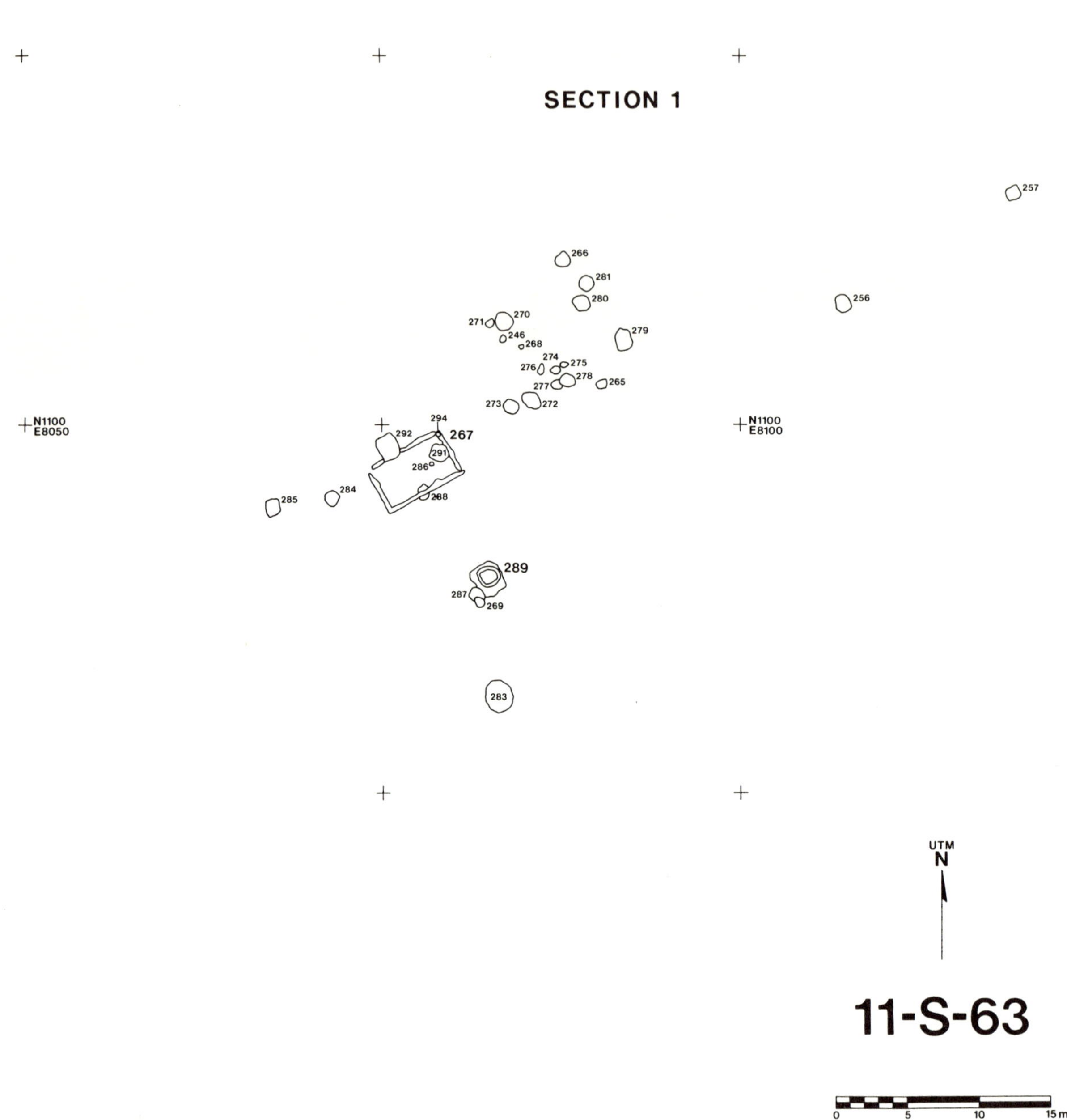

Figure 6. Feature Distribution, Section 1

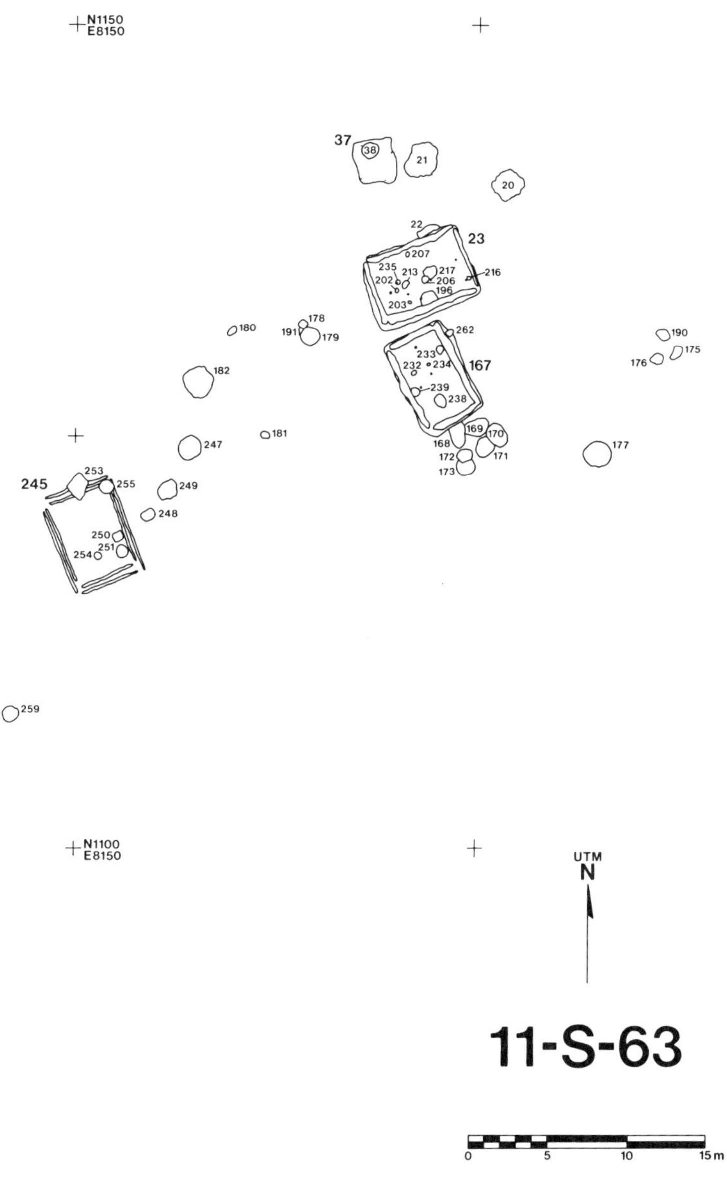

Figure 7. Feature Distribution, Section 2

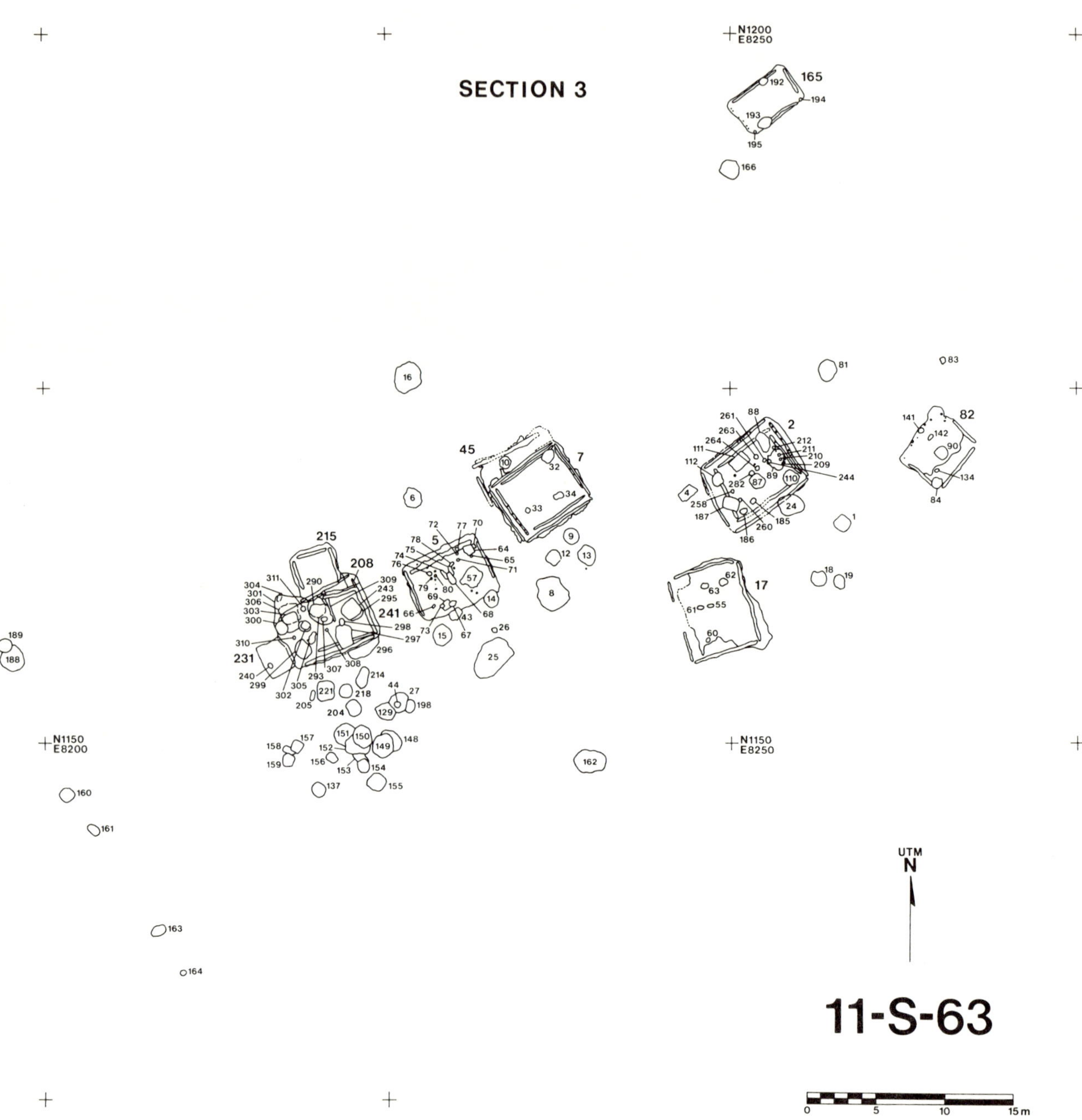

Figure 8. Feature Distribution, Section 3

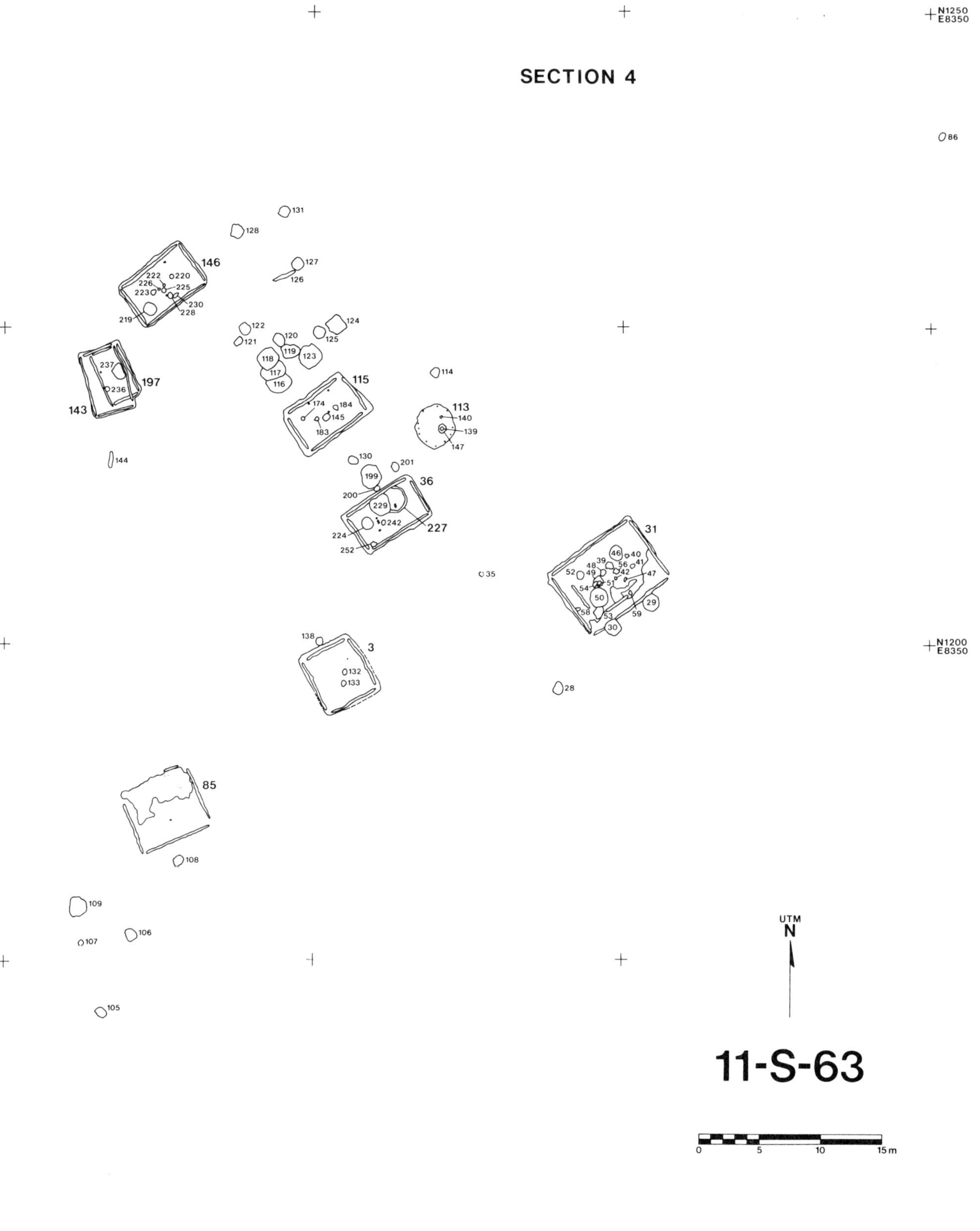

Figure 9. Feature Distribution, Section 4

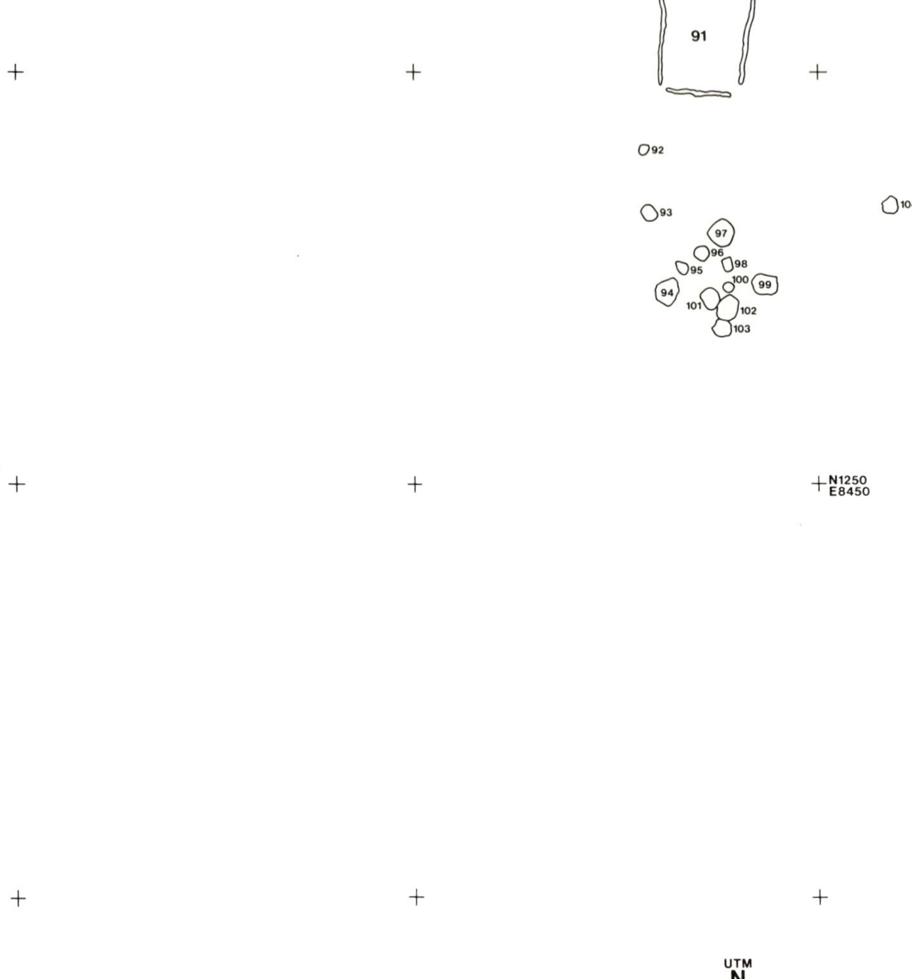

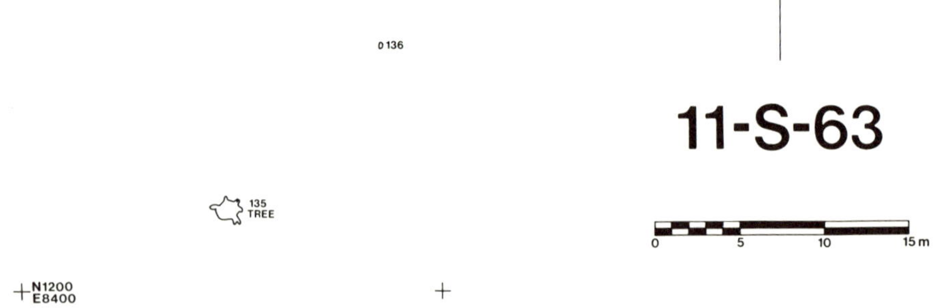

Figure 10. Feature Distribution, Section 5

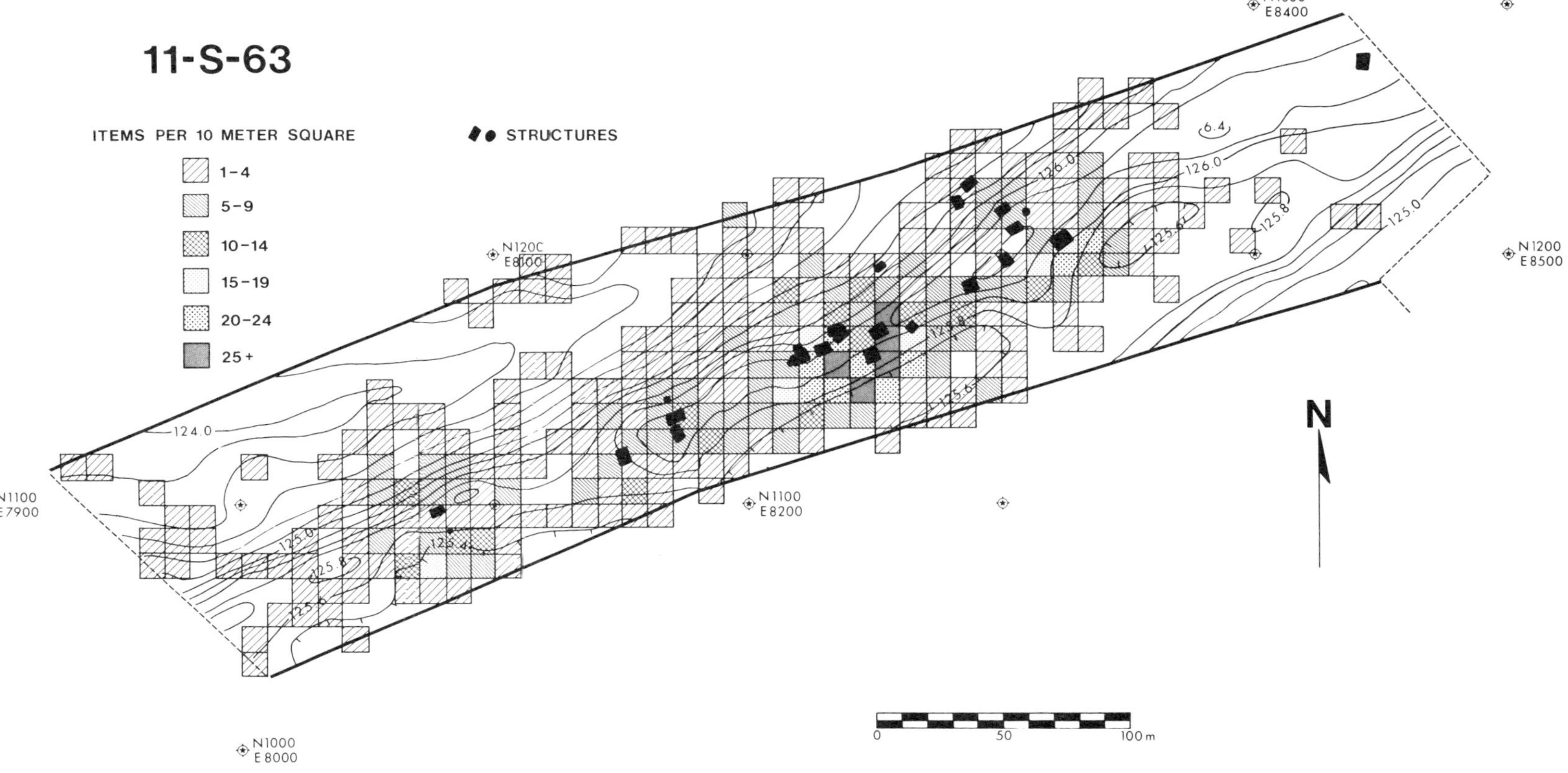

Figure 11. Relationship of Surface Material Density to Subsurface Structures

The SIUE inventory notes were used to identify the material, and the surface debris was not reexamined by UIUC personnel. Items of certain prehistoric affiliation, e.g., chert, pottery, and various artifacts, were mapped according to 10 m x 10 m squares using provenience information obtained by the controlled survey. The nature of the surface material scatter corresponded generally to the location of subsurface features. In addition, the amount of surface material increased in the immediate vicinity of some, but not all, of the features. Notable exceptions to the general association of surface debris and subsurface features were a Mississippian structure and a nearby group of Late Woodland pits, which were located at the northeastern end of the excavation area. Some prehistoric items were found in that area, however, during plowzone removal by the landowner in 1978 and by the archaeologists in 1979. It is important to note that these particular features would have been excluded from the excavation area had its limits been drawn according to the distribution of material derived from the controlled surface collection. This omission of features would have been rather significant, since it included all Late Woodland features and the only Mississippian structure excavated by the Project that had not been cleaned by its occupants prior to abandonment.

A sequence of numbers (from 1 to 311) was assigned in the field to the Julien site features (Appendix 1). The designation Feature 11 was assigned by SIUE personnel to what was apparently a fill variation within the Feature 7 structure basin. Since it was not actually a separate feature, there were a total of 310 features within the excavated portion of the site.

Cultural disturbances less than 0.2 m in diameter (all posts) were assigned postmold numbers. All but one of the postmolds were located within structures and represented either wall or internal posts. Each set of postmolds associated with a structure was assigned a separate number sequence (Appendix 1). The very sandy soil and extensive rodent activity at the site made it difficult to recognize small-diameter postmolds. Undoubtedly, additional small posts were once distributed throughout the site area, but evidence of shallow posts had been destroyed by the 0.2 m to 0.3 m deep plowzone.

Of the 310 features at the site, 309 were the result of human activity. One (Feature 135) was a tree disturbance. Thirteen features were assigned to the Late Woodland occupation on the basis of recovered materials. These features were clustered at the northeastern end of the excavation area. The greatest number, 290 features, were assigned to the Mississippian occupation. These features usually contained diagnostic materials within their fills. In fact, the rim segments described in a subsequent section were from 121 different features, although, as usual, more body sherds were recovered than rim sherds. Most of the other features were assigned to the Mississippian period on the basis of their association as internal features to Mississippian structures. A Mississippian affiliation was assumed for five features because they were situated in the central site area close to many others that belonged to the same period. Six spatially isolated features were excavated that did not contain diagnostic materials. However, given the nature of the site, those features were probably also Mississippian in age.

The sizes and shapes of the Late Woodland, Mississippian, and unidentified features are provided in Appendix 1. A variety of categories and terms pertaining to feature characteristics are used throughout the following descriptive sections and in Appendix 1. Most conform to those discussed in Finney (1979) and need only brief explanation.

The dimensions of length, width, and depth were recorded for all features. When necessary, additional measurements were taken to document particular aspects of feature morphology. Measurements of length and width were recorded in the field to the nearest centimeter; that is how they are presented in this volume. Depth was recorded by the excavators to the nearest half centimeter, but for consistency and computational simplicity the depth measurements in this volume have been rounded to the next higher whole number, unless otherwise noted.

Several shapes describe the feature orifices, including circles, ovals, rectangles, and irregular shapes. The first two describe a continuous series with the circular orifice dimensions of length and width being more nearly equal than they were for the oval features. In plan view, the rectangular features were angular with parallel opposing sides. The corners of all rectangular features were somewhat rounded. In profile, most features fell into one of the following descriptive classes: continuous arcs, the basin and conical forms; nearly vertical sides with distinctly differentiated and relatively flat bases; and various irregular shapes. Most features were modified cylinders with insloping, vertical, outsloping, or bell-shaped walls. The bell-shaped forms were distinguishable from the outslanting forms by a distinctive, lateral flaring of the basal sections of the walls. Feature bases tended toward the following shapes: flat; slanting, where the margin of one side was distinctly higher than the other; and convex, sometimes referred to as rounded. Distinctive post pits with associated insertion or extraction ramps were also found; occasionally, the features had two separate ramps. The irregular category, regardless of whether it pertains to the profile or plan views, represents shapes that defied description by simple geometric forms.

Data describing the shape and size of each feature are found in Appendix 1. Unfortunately, information relevant to those descriptive attributes was not available for two features excavated prior to UIUC involvement at the site. The plan shape of an additional feature (Feature 191) was not determined, since it was almost completely superimposed by two other features. Profile characteristics were not determined for structures lacking basins or for hearths in the surface hearth feature category. The latter feature category represented restricted areas of burning on structure floors, the only intact living surfaces present at the site. Except for the discolored, burned soil subjacent to what was once a fire, the surface hearths had no archaeologically preserved vertical dimension.

The Julien site feature fills displayed considerable variation in color, texture, and mottling; these characteristics were described in the field for each fill. For the purposes of this analysis, however, the feature fills were reduced to four principal categories. The color designations refer to verbal descriptions found on the Munsell (1971) soil color 10YR page. The most common fill category consisted of silty sands or sandy loams that tended to range from dark brown to dark yellowish-brown. This soil often contained inclusions, such as additional soil mottles; charcoal flecks; burned soil, usually oxidized; and cultural debris, such as pottery, chert, and limestone. It represented soil from upper soil horizons or midden-like soil that had accumulated on the now missing original ground surface. Both soils would have accumulated in open and abandoned features. Another common soil category found in features included the sterile-like fills. These light colored, silty sands or fine sands closely resembled the surrounding sterile soil; these fills and the subsoil were often difficult to distinguish in the field. Zones such as these were usually devoid of cultural materials; however, mixing with other fills was occasionally indicated by darker colored mottles. The frequent inclusion of large quantities of sterile-like fill apparently resulted from a slumping of feature walls. Indeed, excavators found that the friable sands at the site were prone to collapse; exposed surfaces frequently gullied during heavy rains.

Two additional soils were represented infrequently at the site. One was a soil that usually ranged in color from dark brown to very dark brown or dark gray. It had a distinctive loamy texture and was more compact than the brown fills mentioned previously. These dark soils closely resembled those flanking the sand ridge after the plowzone had been removed. As mentioned previously, the soil series within the Julien site area corresponded closely to the local ridge and swale topography. The last of the fill categories included burned lenses of soil. In some instances, actual burned surfaces were recognized. These included the bases and sides of hearths and the floors of several burned structures. Lenses of burned soil were also occasionally included in the feature fills. Presumably, these burned lenses were soils from nearby fires that had either been eroded or dumped into features.

Late Woodland

All features assigned a Late Woodland affiliation were pits. Thirteen Late Woodland (Patrick Phase) features (Features 92-104) were located in a group at the northeastern end of the excavation area (Figures 5 and 12). A nearby structure (Feature 91) belonged to a later Mississippian (Sand Prairie phase) occupation.

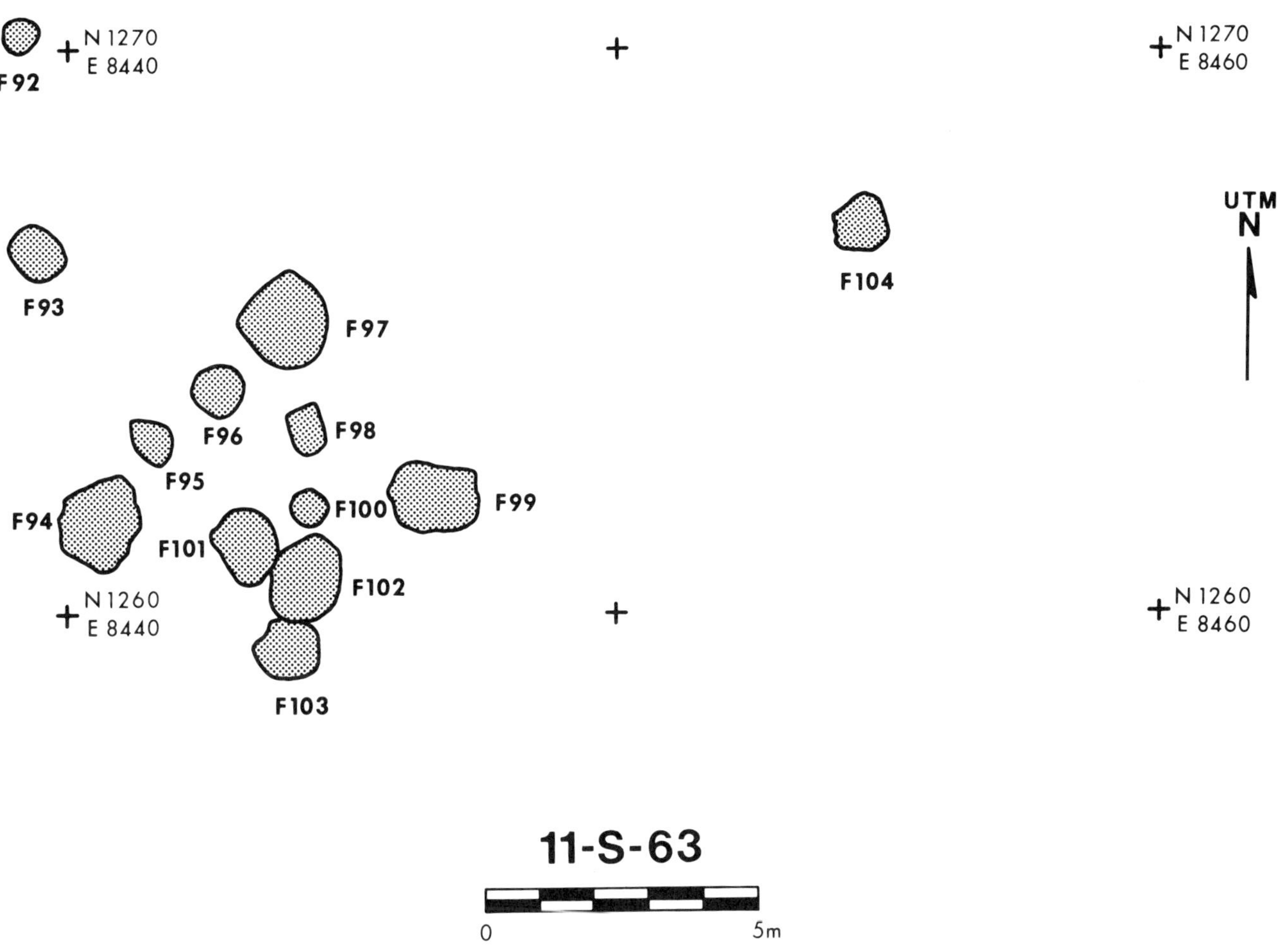

Figure 12. Late Woodland Feature Distribution

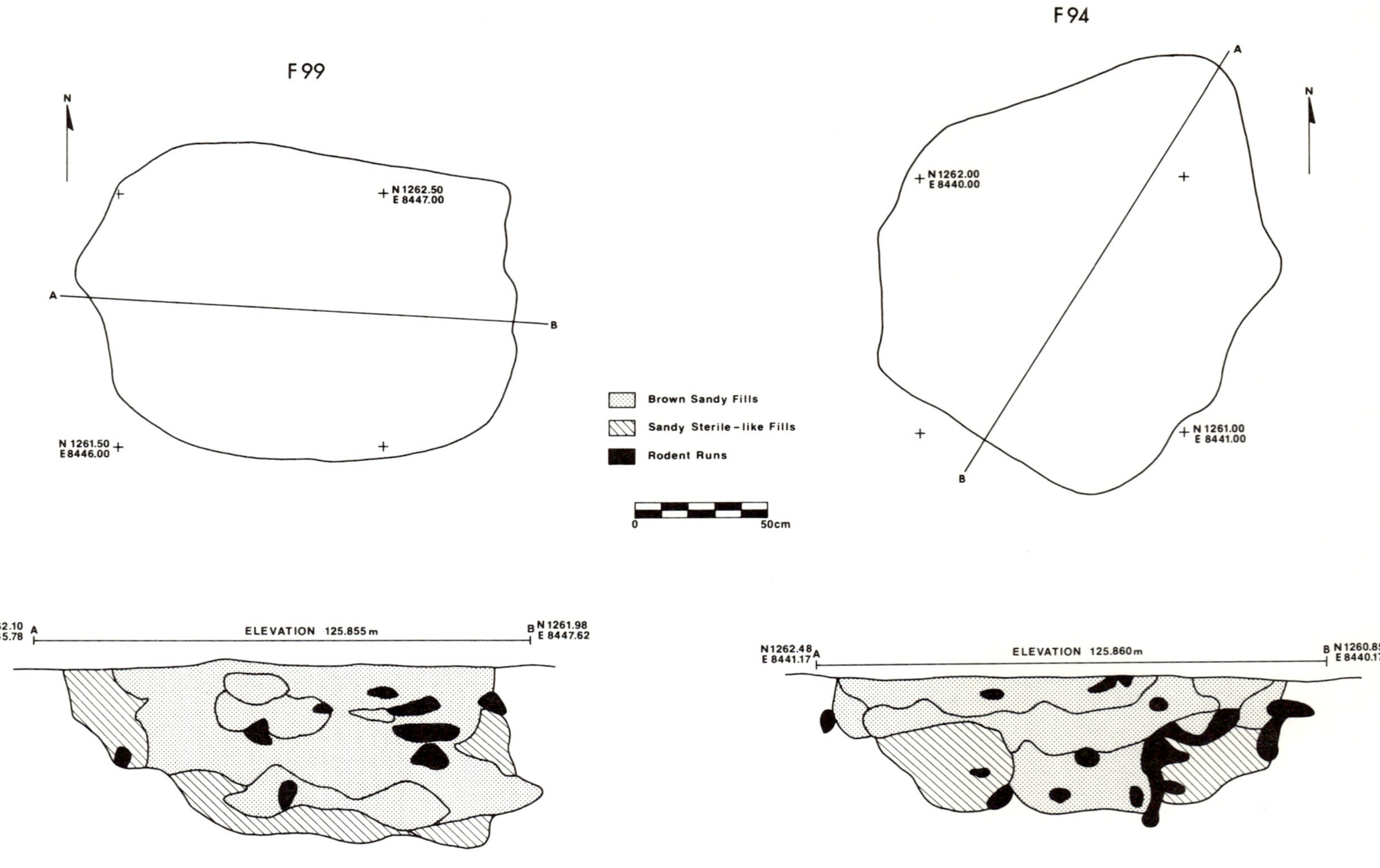

Figure 13. Late Woodland Features 94 and 99, Plan and Profile Views

Most of the Late Woodland pits were roughly cylindrical. Six were oval in plan view; of the remainder, four were circular and three were rectangular. Their maximum diameters ranged from 0.66 m to 1.69 m (mean=1.19 m, s=0.37). In profile, nine had vertical walls and flat, irregular, or slanting bases. One pit was bell-shaped, and three had inslanting walls with relatively flat bases. Maximum feature depths ranged from 0.16 m to 0.76 m (mean=0.43 m, s=0.21).

The plan views and profiles both usually exhibited irregularities attributable to a slumping of their sides (Figure 13); the slumped, sterile-like fills were, at times, very conspicuous parts of the feature profiles. Five profiles had portions of one side that slanted irregularly toward the feature bases. These uneven side contours represented areas where feature walls had collapsed. Both sides of two feature profiles were similarly slumped.

The extent of slumping indicated by the feature profile shapes was consistent with the nature of the major filling episodes. About 25% of the soil zones visible in the feature profiles were light-colored, sandy, sterile-like fills. Slumped fills in individual features ranged from "not present" to 63.9% of the total soil visible in profile.

The clustered nature of this isolated group of pits suggested that they were indeed associated with one another, although they were not necessarily strictly contemporaneous. The same restricted area was probably selected repeatedly for the construction of pits. In fact, body sherds from two separate pits (Features 94 and 99) were found to fit together. These two features were separated by about 6 m.

Presumably, the Late Woodland pits were not immediately filled following abandonment, thus permitting the sometimes extensive slumping to occur. Observations of feature filling at various Project sites, including Julien, indicate that the processes of slumping and filling would have proceeded rapidly, perhaps filling the pits in just a few seasons.

Mississippian

A total of 290 features were assigned to the Mississippian period. These were grouped into several principal categories: structures, pits, posts, hearths, isolated wall trenches, a smudge pit, and unidentified fill areas. Structures not only were well-represented; they were the basis for subsequent discussions of Mississippian feature and artifact associations.

Twenty-eight Mississippian structures were excavated. They were quite varied in terms of overall size, shape, basin depth, as well as type and number of enclosing walls. The structures were associated with varying numbers of internal features. These associated features are discussed more fully in following sections of this volume. At least four structure categories were present; these categories were based on some of the above-mentioned morphological characteristics. These categories include structures with three or more enclosing wall trenches; square basin structures without wall trenches; circular wall trench structures; and one circular structure with peripherally located wall posts.

Circular Wall Trench Structures

The structures with the smallest internal dimensions (Features 227 and 289) were those with roughly circular wall trenches. In Feature 227 the floor area was 3.06 m2, and in Feature 289 it was 1.08 m2. Feature 227 was superimposed by a large rectangular structure (Feature 36) so the size and shape of its basin were unknown (Figure 18). The basin for Feature 289 was an irregular rectangle measuring 2.3 m x 2.01 m; the basin size was much larger than the wall trench dimensions. There was a considerable amount of limestone in the fill of this feature; much of it was grouped together and lying flat. Only a few pieces of limestone were located on top of the wall trench fill; the trench, of course, was distinguished after the basin excavation had been completed. The majority of the recovered limestone was located within the area enclosed by the circular wall trench.

The sizes of the Feature 227 and 289 wall trenches indicated that these were relatively substantial, although small, structures. The wall trench for Feature 227 averaged 0.15 m in width and at its deepest point measured 0.21 m. The Feature 289 trench was wider and deeper, averaging 0.2 m in width and 0.45 m in depth. These wall trench dimensions approximate those of the much larger rectangular buildings at the site. It should be noted, however, that a portion of the Feature 227 trench was removed when a superimposed rectangular structure (Feature 36) was constructed. The function of these two circular structures was undetermined, but their small size and substantial construction suggested use as above-ground storage facilities, perhaps for maize.

Circular Post Structure

There was another circular structure located within the area excavated, but it was considerably larger than those discussed previously. Feature 113 had a roughly circular and shallow basin (Figures 14 and 15). The internal floor area was 6.38 m2, a measurement obtained through using available wall posts. The walls had been supported by at least 11 posts, which were represented by individual postmolds. These postmolds were relatively small and shallow. In plan view, their maximum diameters ranged from 0.1 m to 0.14 m (mean=0.12 m, s=0.01), and they extended from 0.12 m to 0.19 m (mean=0.16 m, s=0.02) into the sterile soil.

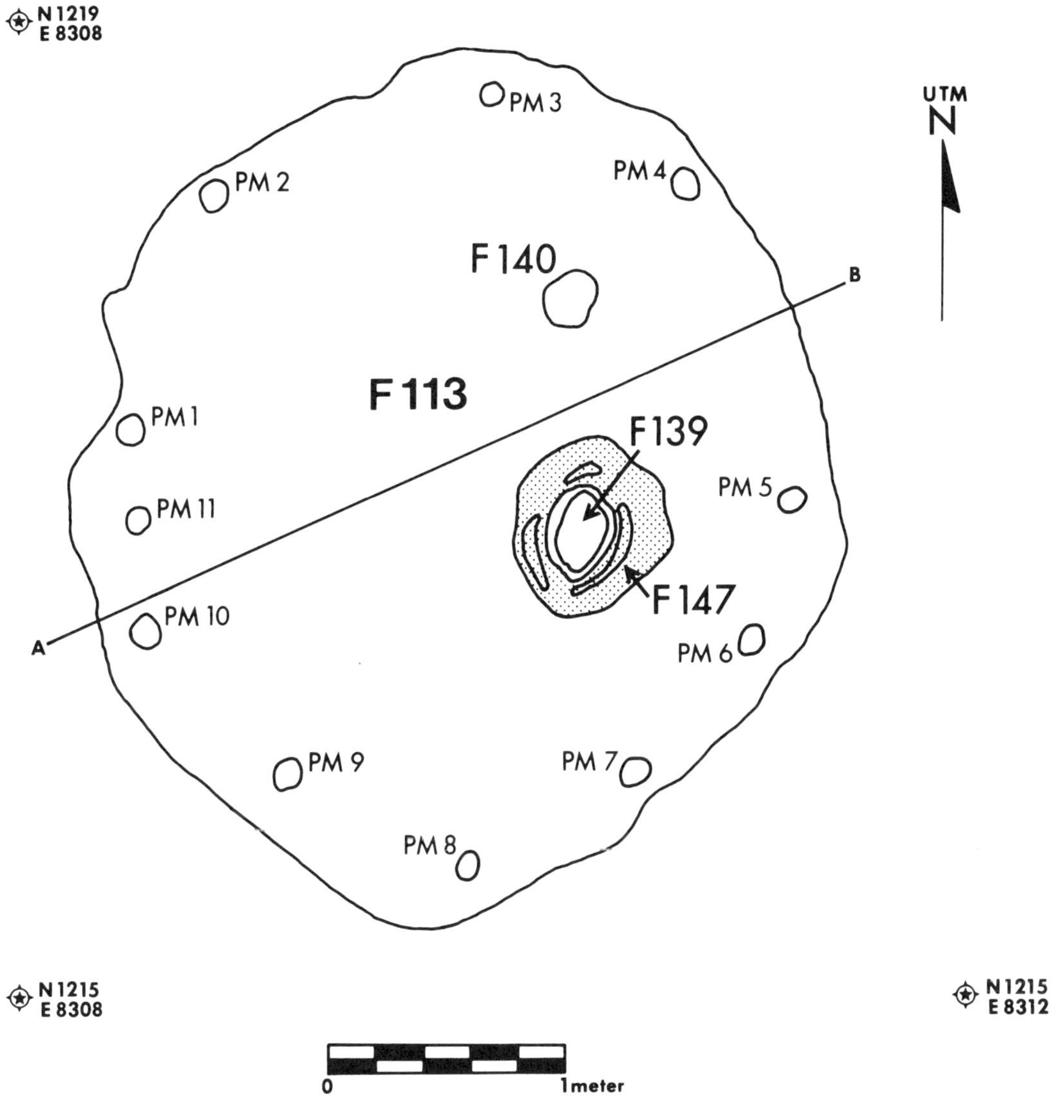

Figure 14. Mississippian Structure Feature 113, Plan View

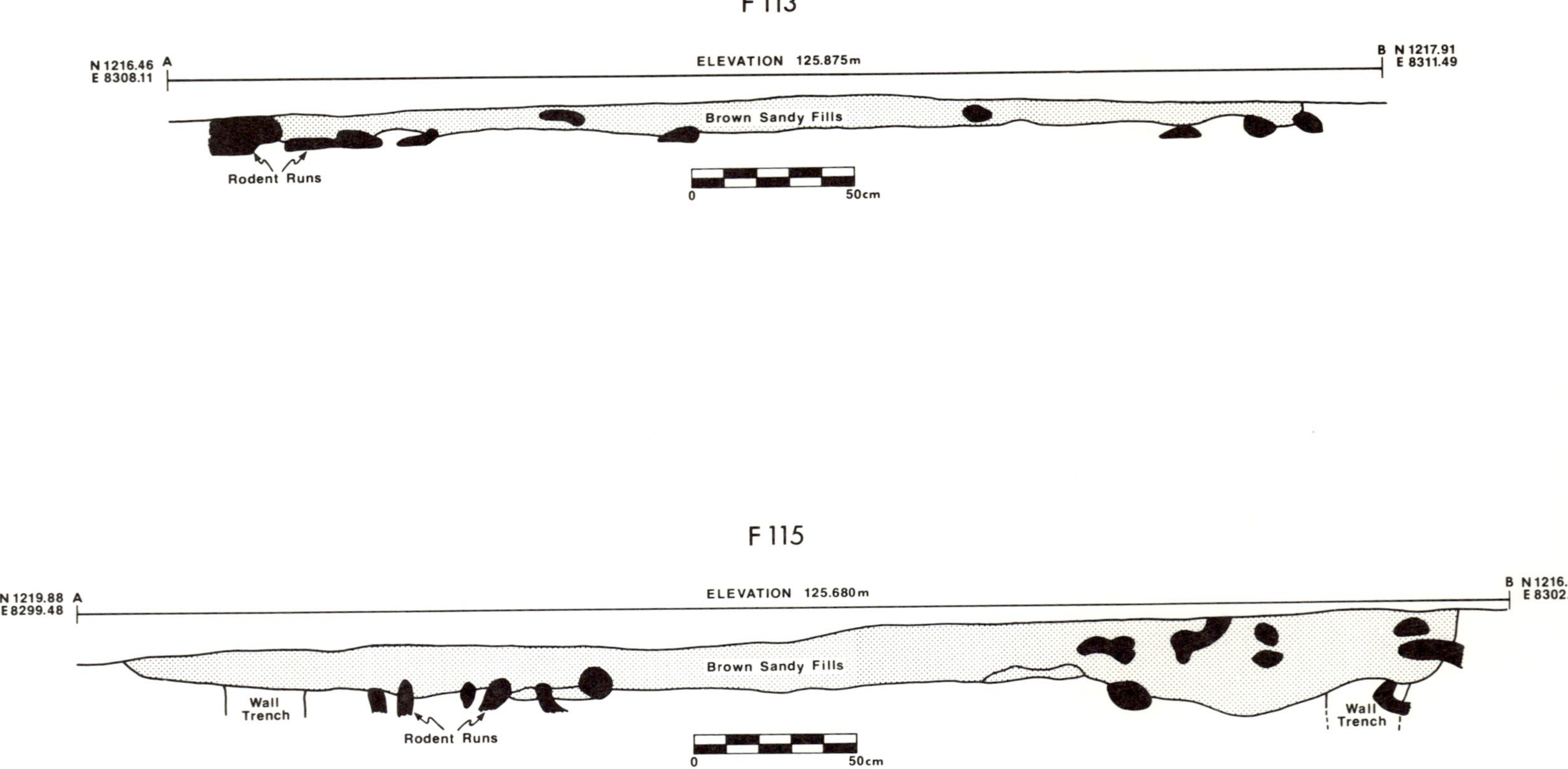

Figure 15. Mississippian Structure Features 113 and 115, Profiles

Inside this structure were located a rebuilt hearth and a smudge pit; both were presumably associated with the structure as internal features. The hearth had been reused on at least two occasions, and separate feature numbers (Features 139 and 147) were assigned to the two distinct episodes of use. These two features and the smudge pit (Feature 140) are discussed more fully later in this volume. Both the rebuilt hearth and smudge pit were located to one side of the structure midpoint. Presumably, this structure was a sweatlodge.

Rectangular Structures without Wall Trenches

Two rectangular (nearly square) structures lacking enclosing wall trenches were excavated. Feature 37 was an isolated feature; the other (Feature 231) was associated with a superimposed feature concentration that also included structure Features 208, 215, and 241. Features 37 and 231 were both rather small when compared with other rectangular structures at the site. Feature 37 measured 2.6 m x 2.45 m; the Feature 231 basin was 2.48 m long and 2.22 m wide. Internal supports were not visible in Feature 231, but the walls presumably consisted of a series of individually set posts. Postmolds, as indicated previously, were difficult to distinguish at the site, and the rodent activity in this area was particularly heavy. Within this structure was located a small, oval pit (Feature 240) that contained a large lump of clay; the clay had been possibly cached for future use in manufacturing ceramic vessels. Feature 231 superimposed a much larger rectangular wall trench structure designated Feature 241 (Figure 25).

Four small, peripherally located wall posts were identified in Feature 37. Others were presumably present, but were not recognized in the rodent-disturbed, fine sandy subsoil at the basin floor. The fill was relatively sterile; most of the material from the feature was recovered from a small ceramic concentration that measured 0.09 m x 0.2 m; apparently, it was a rodent disturbance.

Rectangular Wall Trench Structures

Twenty-three structures were rectangular and had three or four of their sides enclosed by posts set into wall trenches. This grouping of structures did not necessarily imply functional uniformity; it only implied that from an archaeologist's perspective, these structures shared certain readily distinguishable characteristics of shape and construction technique. Of these structures, 18 had wall trenches that completely enclosed their floors. Individual trenches usually did not connect at the structure corners. The other five structures had three trenches each; the fourth side either remained open, was enclosed by partial wall trenches, or was enclosed by posts set in individually dug postholes.

The structures varied considerably in overall size. This is

illustrated in Figure 16 by the distribution of internal floor areas. One structure (Feature 31), was much larger than the rest. Feature 31 is discussed in more detail below, but it should be noted here that size was only one of several characteristics indicating that this structure had served a specialized function.

The basins of most structures extended below the base of plowzone. Only Features 245 and 267 (Plate 3) did not have basins, although those of several other structures had been partially destroyed by plowing. In eight structures, a thin, dark, silty, compact fill was located on the floor. This dark, packed fill appeared to be a soil that had been tracked into the structures by the original occupants. In no structure did this soil layer extend completely across the floor. A similar zone was perhaps present on the floor of Feature 2 before it burned; its presence would account for a very hard, brick-like soil that covered portions of the structure floor.

Various posts, pits, and other features were located inside the structures. There were up to 8 pits, 20 internal posts, and 5 hearths per structure. Two structures had internal wall trenches as partitions; Feature 208 had one such wall trench and Feature 31 had two.

Several of the Julien site structures were burned. Features 2, 3, 82, 85, and 91 contained charred log segments that had been wall or roof members. Portions of each floor were burned, but only Feature 91 contained an appreciable amount of in situ cultural debris. Apparently, the other structures had been abandoned and cleaned before they burned.

Two other structures (Features 143 and 146) burned after they had been abandoned and their basins had started to collect fill. Irregular, discontinuous clumps of burned soil and charcoal were present in the fills of these two structures. Charred remains were located primarily around the basin edges over the wall trenches. The location of the burned material indicated that what remained of a decaying wall had burned in abandoned and partially filled structure basins.

Five structures at the site had been rebuilt. Three of these five structures had double sets of four wall trenches each (Features 2, 7, and 245). In each structure, the trenches of the later buildings were aligned parallel to the earlier set. In two features (Features 23 and 167), the posts in the wall trenches had apparently been replaced with no change in overall structure size. The trenches of both structures were relatively wide in plan view. The wall trenches belonging to Feature 167 (Plate 3) were V-shaped or T-shaped in cross section; wall trenches typically had vertical sides. These unusual cross section shapes might be due to digging around the base of an existing wall to remove, and possibly to replace, wall posts. The wall trenches in Feature 23 were also relatively wide, but the sides were more nearly vertical than those of Feature 167. Of particular interest was the southern wall of Feature 23 in which the later trench diverged slightly from the earlier trench.

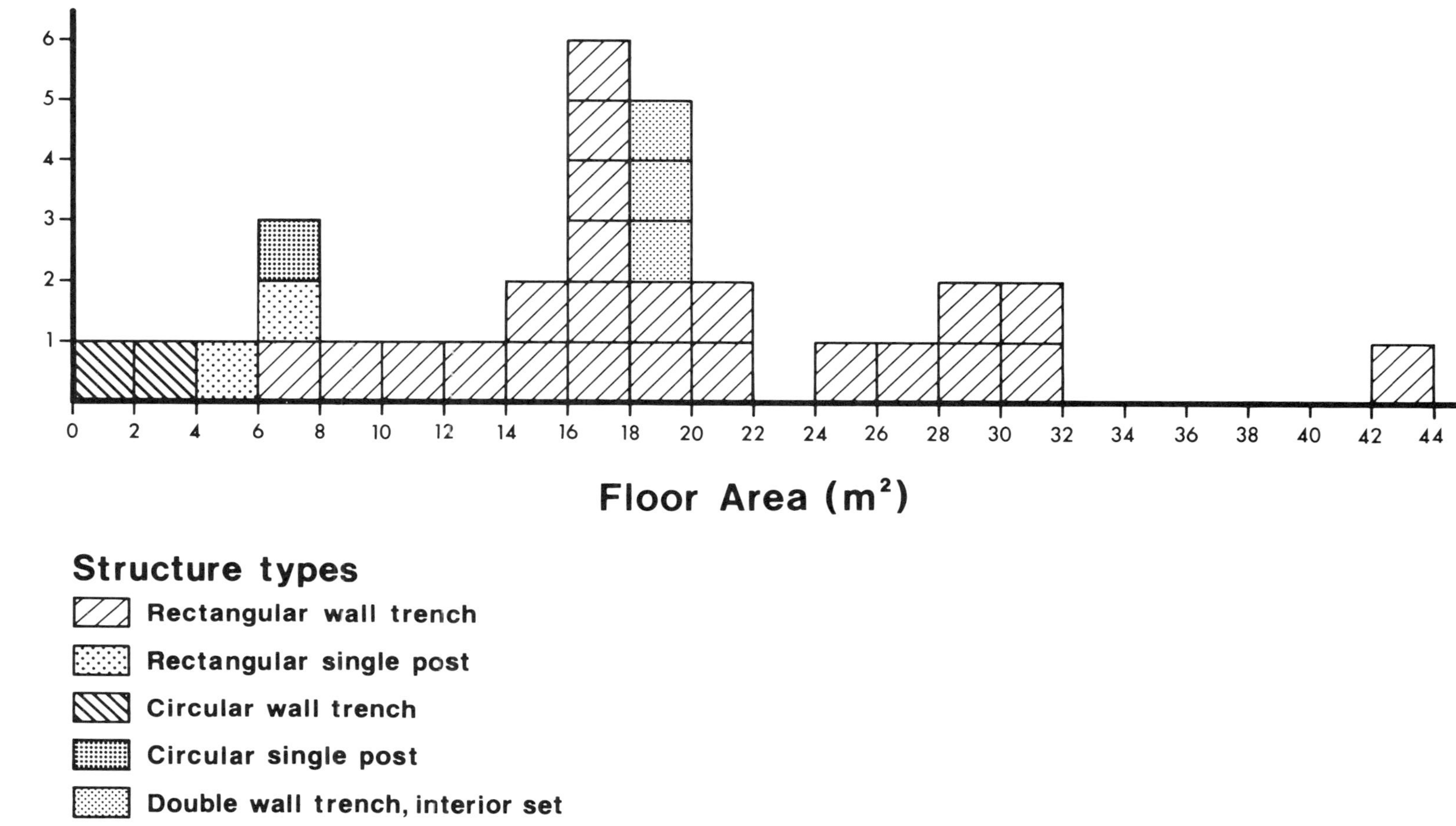

Figure 16. Internal Floor Area Distribution for Mississippian Structure Types

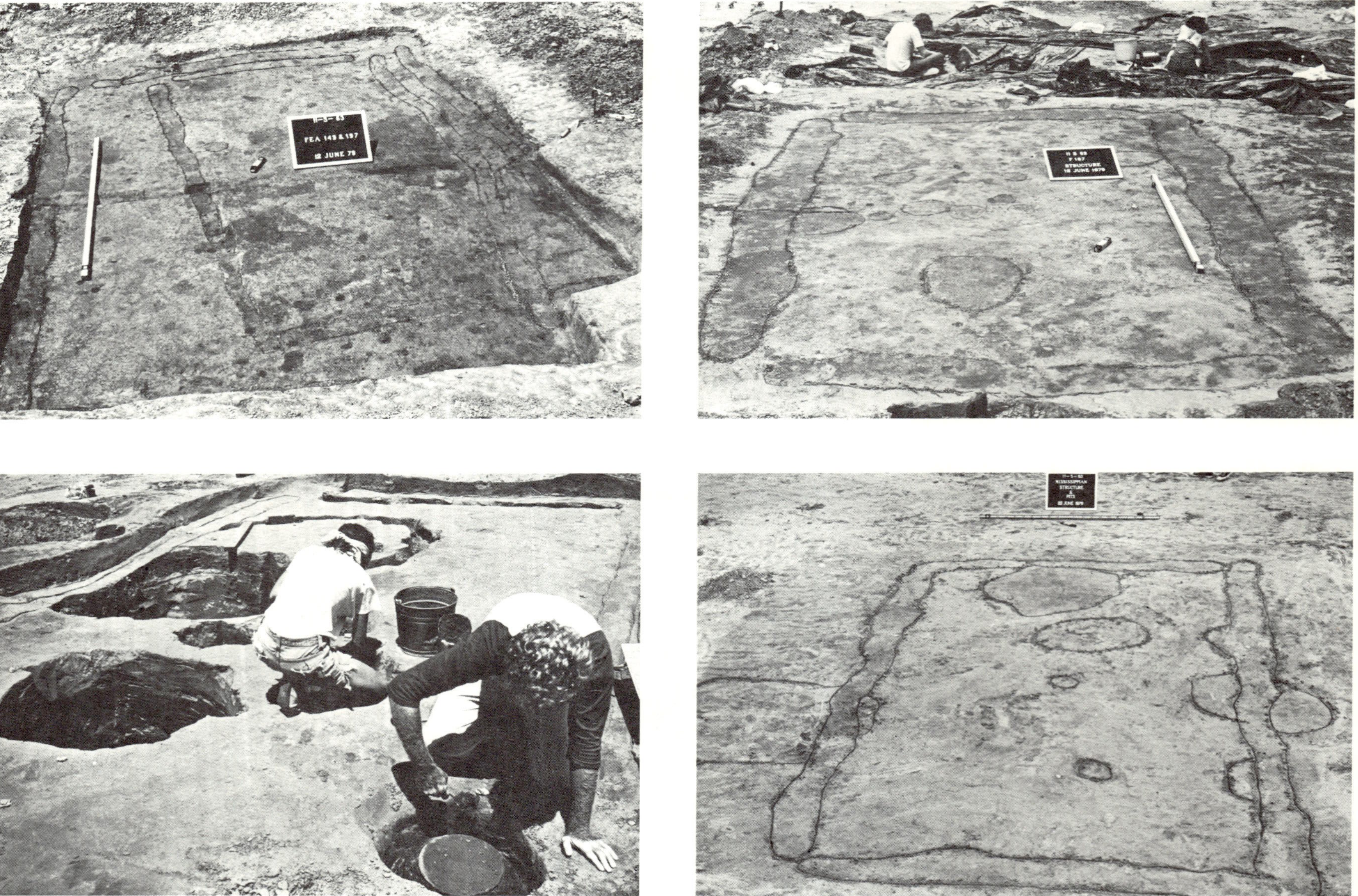

Plate 3. Structures: upper left, Features 143 and 197; upper right, Feature 167; lower left, Feature 36 with vessel in Feature 252; lower right, Feature 267

Several other structures superimposed earlier structures, but were not aligned precisely with them. The reuse of a single area for construction was well-demonstrated in the Feature 208, 215, 231, and 241 complex. This feature concentration is discussed below in more detail; however, it is important to note here that this particular area served as the focus of a complicated cycle of construction and abandonment. Two additional sets of structures were superimposed: Features 7 and 45, and Features 143 and 197 (Plate 3). The later structures in each sequence (Features 7 and 143) were oriented at somewhat oblique angles to the initial structures. Perhaps a previously existing depression was chosen as a convenient place to construct a later, but unrelated, structure. These structure sequences would not be considered rebuildings in the sense of the term used previously to describe the activities in Features 2, 7, 23, 167, and 245. In those five structures, buildings had been dismantled and rebuilt immediately thereafter.

The Julien site structures were aligned generally parallel or perpendicular to the ridge axis. All orientations of rectangular wall trench construction structures are included in Figure 17. Apparently, the prominent, and at times markedly sloping, ridge influenced the choices made when orienting structures.

Selected Structure Descriptions

Four structures or structure complexes are discussed in the following pages in more detail. Each illustrates either aspects of structure construction or the manner in which structures were used.

Individual Structures

If any single structure could be chosen as typical of the early Mississippian (Stirling phase) occupation at the Julien site, it would be Feature 36 (Figure 18; Plate 3). The basin of this structure was rectangular with a length of 6.52 m and a width of 4.07 m. The 0.31 m deep basin was filled throughout most of its depth with a relatively homogeneous, dark yellowish-brown, silty sand containing a moderate amount of cultural debris. A discontinuous, 0.05 m thick band of dark, silty, and compact soil covered portions of the structure floor. Occasionally, chert flakes or pieces of pottery were found either within this zone or at its base, i.e., on the basin floor. The largest items recovered from this particular soil zone included a hammerstone and a shell-tempered sherd weighing 83.7 g. This soil zone represented a packed floor similar to those found in a few other structures. The compact soil zone did not cover one of the large internal pits (Feature 229), but did continue across two pit features in the structure (Features 224 and 252). This indicated that the internal features in this building were not all used simultaneously.

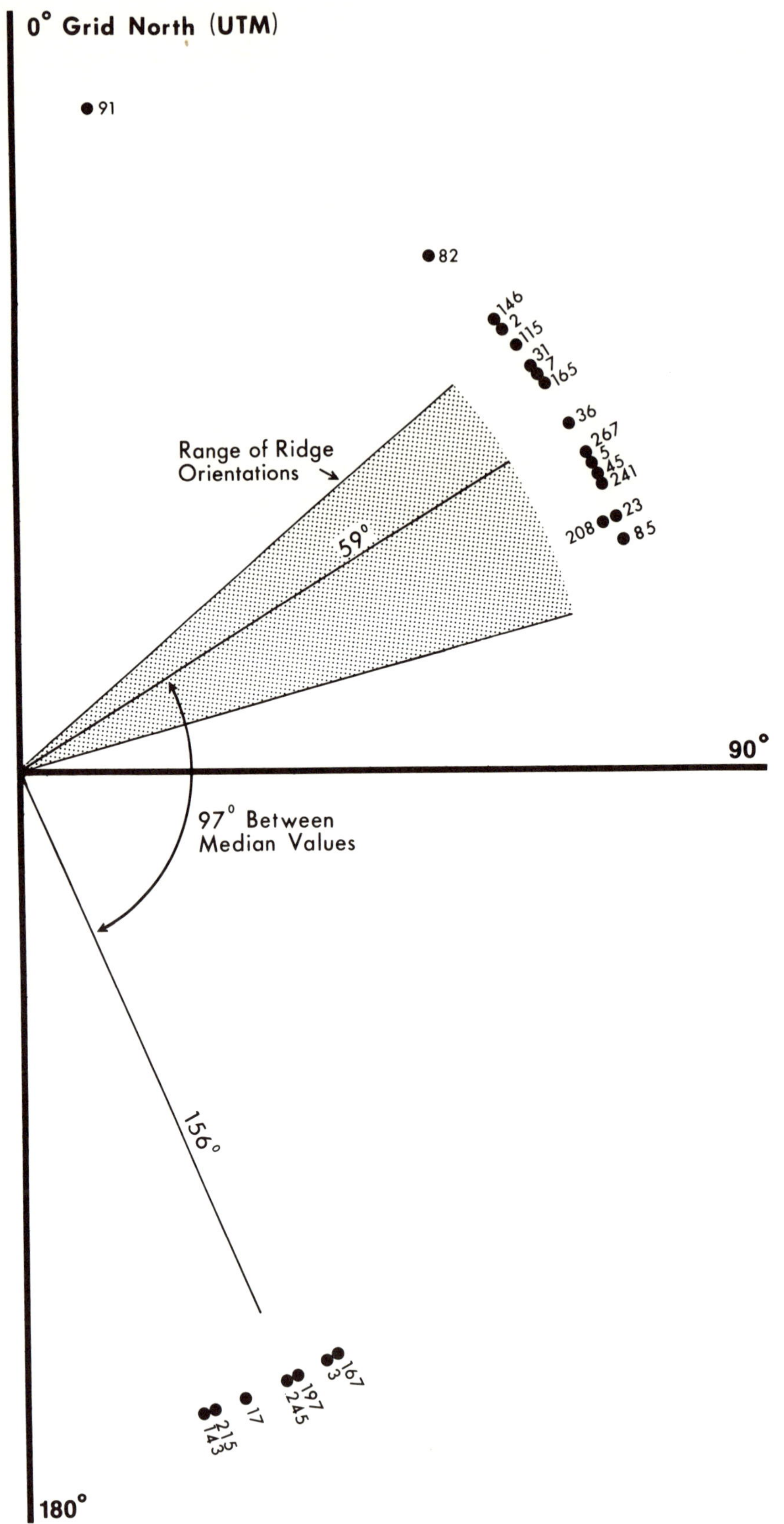

Figure 17. Orientations of Mississippian Wall Trench Structures

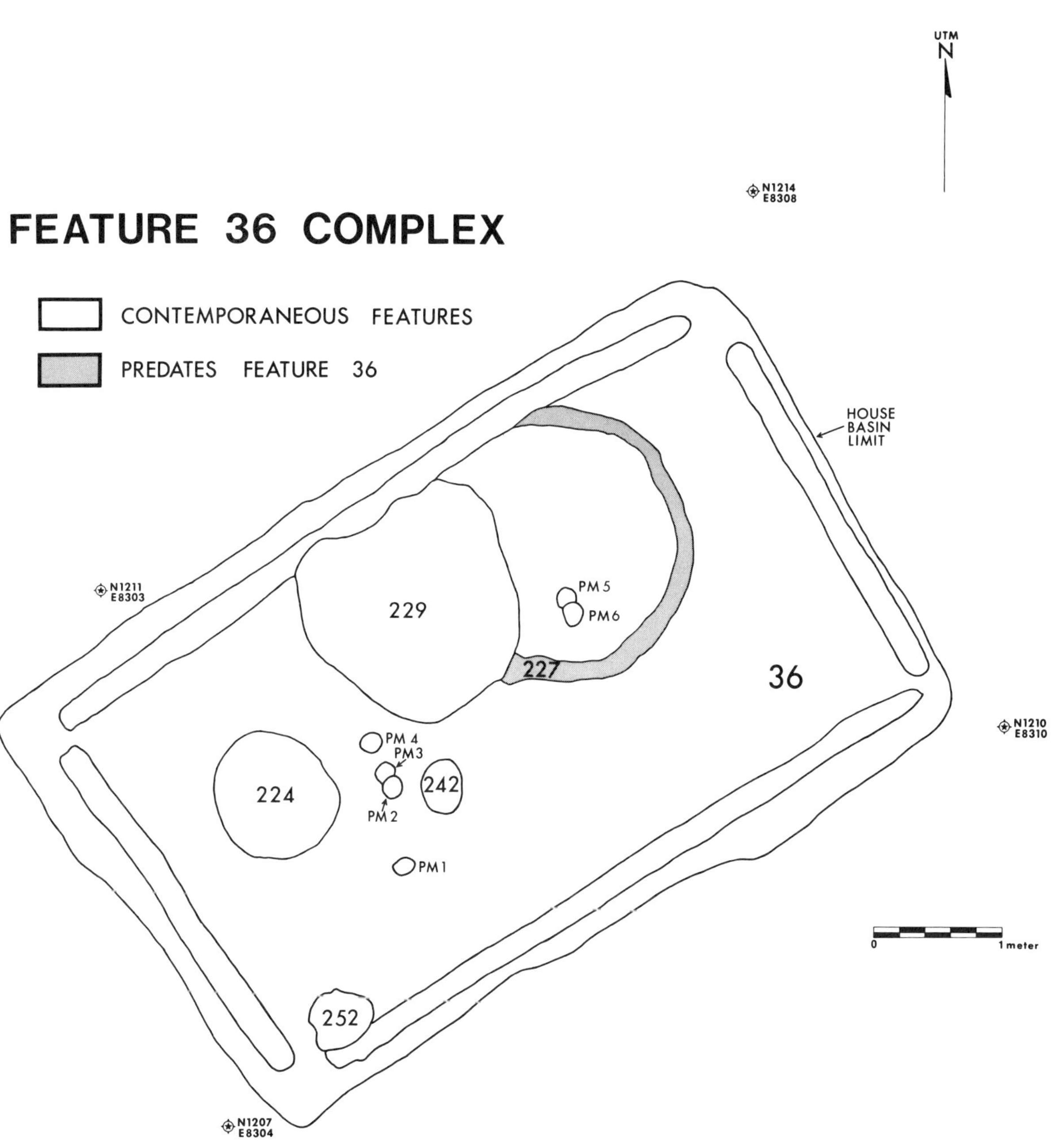

Figure 18. Mississippian Structure Features 36 and 227, Profiles

The wall trenches of Feature 36, first visible when the basin fill had been removed, were long, relatively straight, and contained a sterile-like fill. The midpoint widths of the four trenches had a mean of 0.19 m; the mean of their maximum depths was 0.41 m.

Several pits and posts were associated with structure Feature 36 as internal features. Two (Features 224 and 229) were large and deep, presumably used for storage (Figures 18 and 19). Feature 224 had apparently been reexcavated, indicating its use on at least two separate occasions. Large storage facilities, similar to those in Feature 36, were frequently found along the walls of other Julien site structures. Feature 252 serves as an example of the small orifice, typically shallow features frequently found in Julien site structures. This particular pit (Feature 252) apparently was excavated to hold a sizable, shell-tempered jar. It was only slightly larger and deeper than necessary to contain this vessel (Figure 20; Plate 3). Vessels such as the one recovered from Feature 252 might have been sealed with a perishable material like rawhide. Several postmolds were also scattered across the structure floor; these were designated Postmolds 1 to 6 and Feature 242. The maximum diameters of the six postmolds ranged from 0.12 m to 0.18 m (mean=0.16 m, s=0.02), and they extended from 0.08 m to 0.3 m into the subsoil (mean=0.19 m, s=0.10). The post designated Feature 242 was considerably larger in plan, measuring 0.41 m x 0.32 m. It had a maximum depth of 0.4 m. While their function was not determined, these posts probably supported the roof or internal partitions.

Feature 31, a Moorehead phase structure, with an internal floor area of 42 m2, was by far the largest of the Julien site structures (Figure 16 and 21). This structure was situated on the ridge slope, and its 0.27 m deep basin had been partially truncated by plowing along its southeastern edge. There was an irregular, shallow layer of dark, compact silty soil around all but the southeastern wall. The general appearance of this soil and its location suggested that it may have been an unintentional deposit tracked into the structure by the occupants. Clumps of the dark floor soil were present as occasional inclusions in 7 of the 12 features containing fills within the structure (The four surface hearths were excluded from that total).

Structure Feature 31 had four wall trenches with a mean midpoint width of 0.17 m and a mean maximum depth of 0.41 m. Internal supports or partitions consisted of two short wall trenches and four internal post features (Features 51, 54, 56, and 59). The post features had a mean depth of 0.27 m. Three were centrally located: Feature 56 was on one side of the structure's midpoint, and Features 51 and 54 were on the other side. Feature 49, a hearth, superimposed Feature 51 and part of Feature 54. Post Features 51 and 54, therefore, were not used throughout the period when this structure was used.

There were five hearths in structure Feature 31. Feature 49 was the shallow, prepared hearth mentioned above that superimposed two post

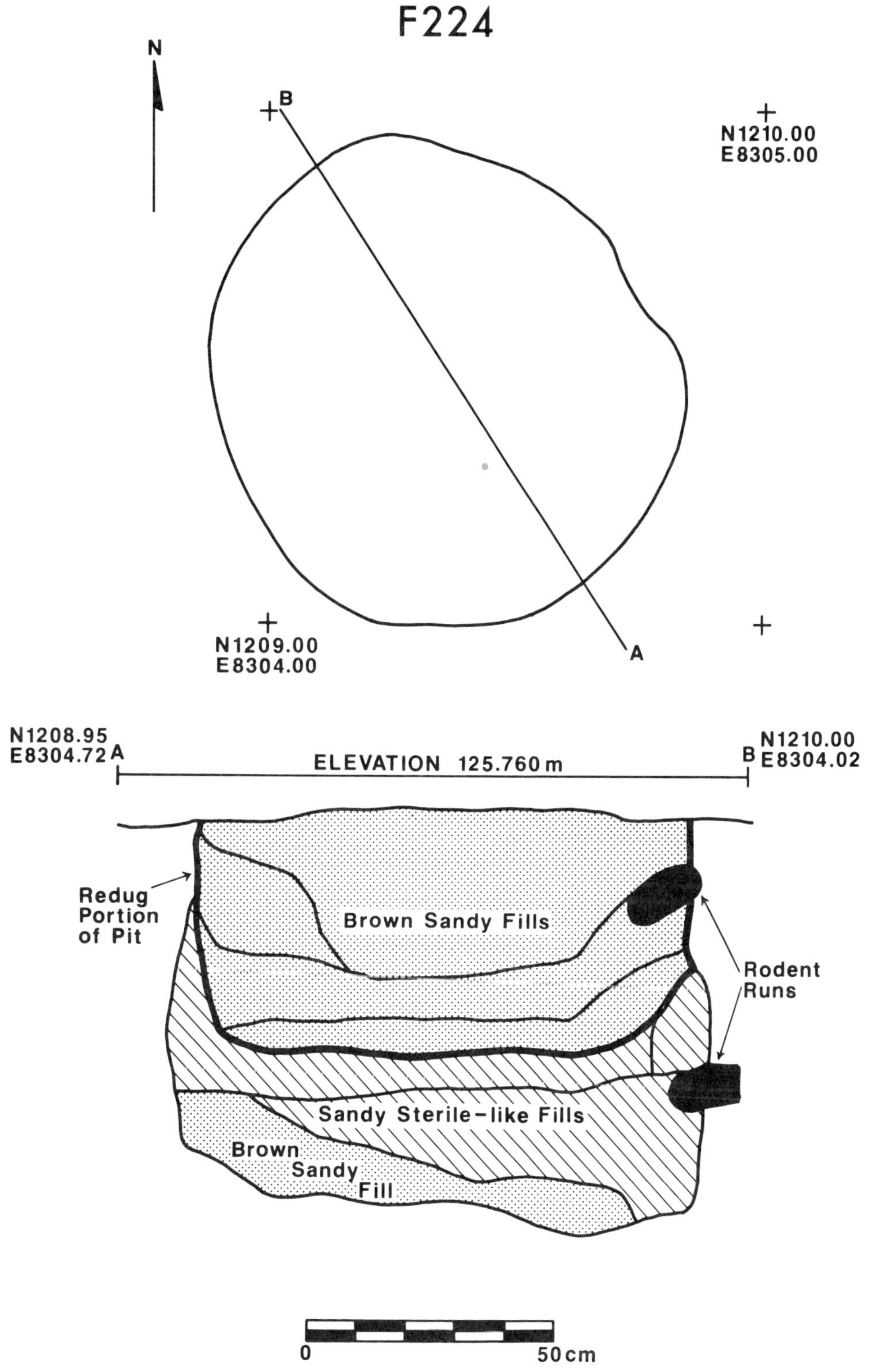

Figure 19. Redug Mississippian Pit Feature 224, Plan and Profile Views

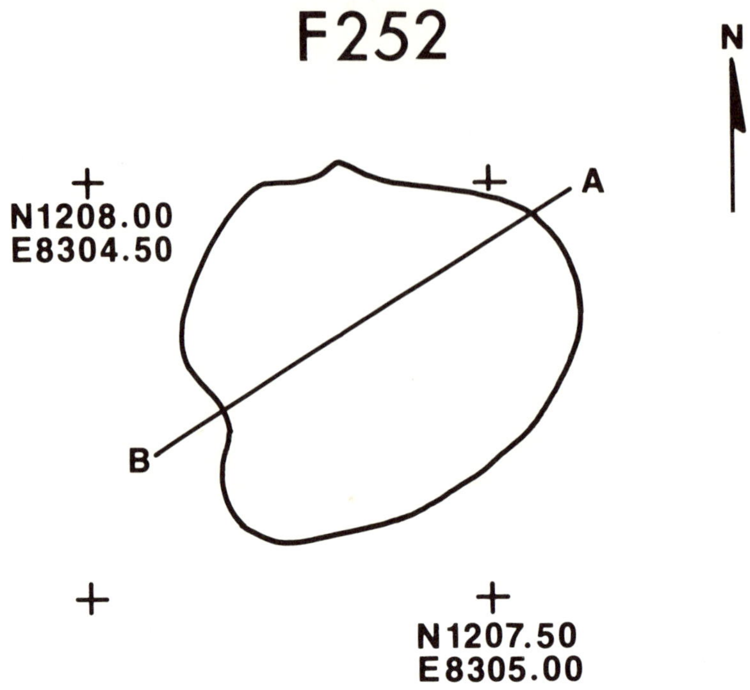

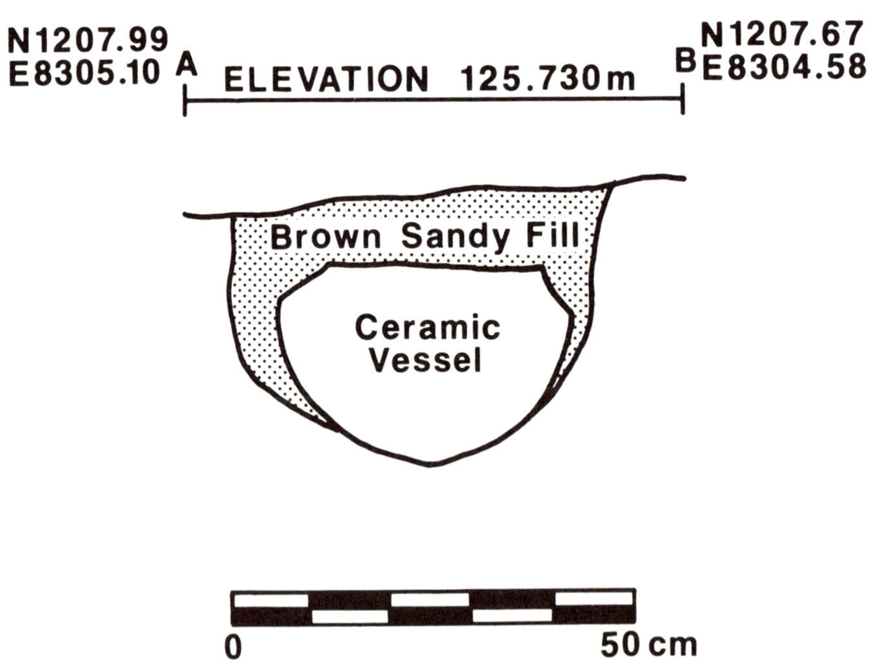

Figure 20. Mississippian Storage Pit Feature 252 with Complete Vessel, Plan and Profile Views

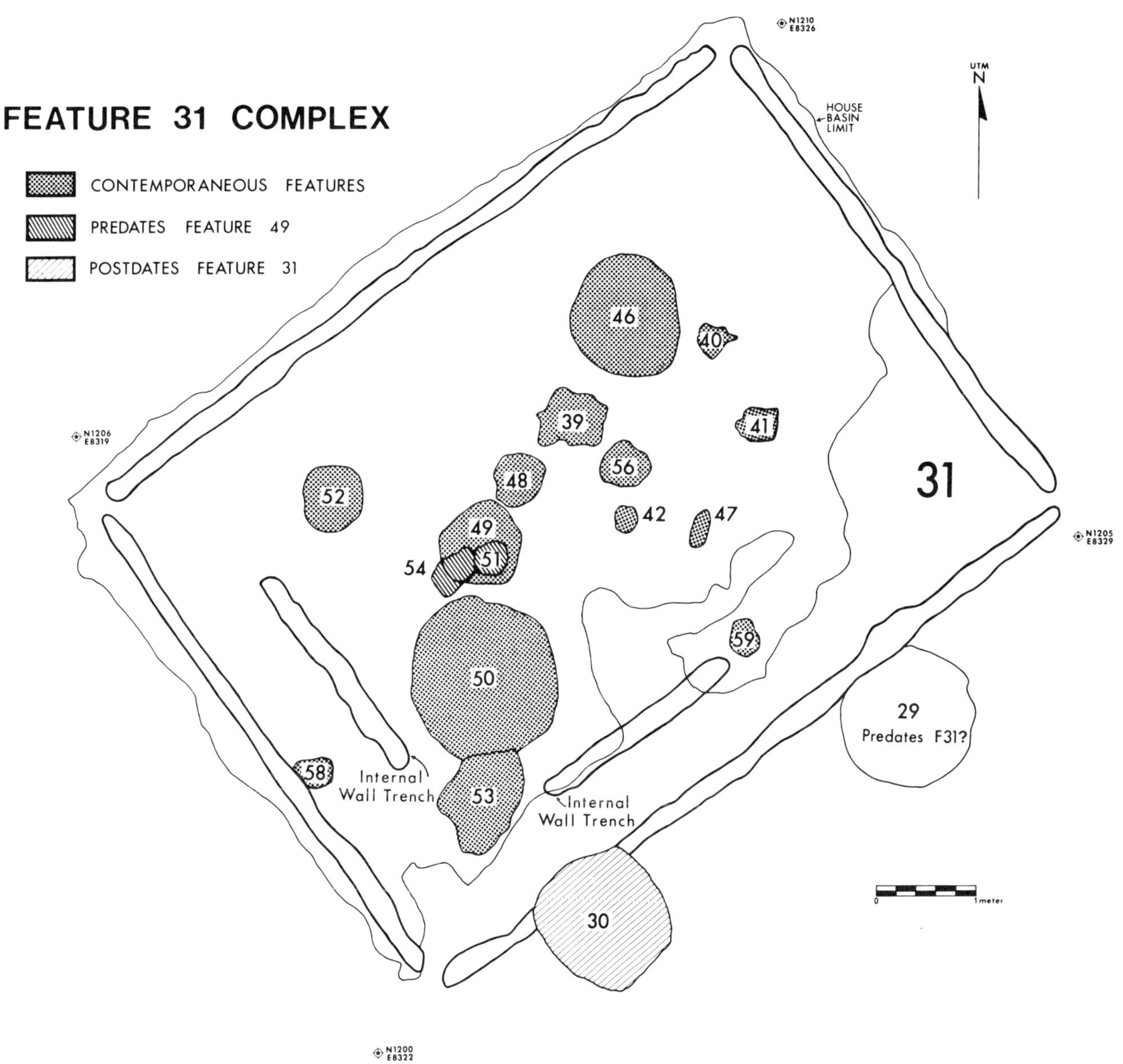

Figure 21. Mississippian Structure Feature 31, Plan View

features. The other four hearths were thought to be paired features: Feature 39 with 42 and Feature 40 with 41. All of the hearths represented areas of the structure floor that had been burned. The dark, packed floor soil had been burned in two of these features (Features 39 and 40). The large number of hearths in Feature 31 was unusual; in fact, 35.7% of all hearths at the site occurred within this structure.

Seven of the internal features in structure Feature 31 were classified as pits (Features 46, 47, 48, 50, 52, 53, and 58). These ranged from very small pits or depressions to some that were quite sizable, such as Feature 50. Three of the pits exceeded 0.5 m in both maximum diameter and depth. The largest pit in the structure (Feature 50) was roughly circular in plan view. Its orifice measured 1.6 m by 1.5 m in plan and it was 0.9 m deep. This feature was especially noteworthy, since 72 projectile points were scattered throughout its various fills. Illustrated in Figure 22 are the pit profile and the proportion of points obtained from each of the fills that were removed separately in the second half of the feature. Note that two of the fill zones contained appreciably more projectile points than the others. Most of the points were found near the bottom of the pit. The number of points per zone did not reflect the amount of soil within each of the several filling episodes visible in profile.

Clearly, Feature 31 was an unusual structure. Its overall size, two internal partitions, large number of hearths, and many associated projectile points distinguished this particular structure from the remainder at the site. It may have served in a public context; the large number of projectile points indicates that it was perhaps a men's house.

Feature 91 was one of the latest structures at the site; it was affliated with the Sand Prarie phase. It was relatively large with an internal floor area of 31.75 m2. The wall trenches, which were irregular in plan view, had a mean midpoint width of 0.27 m. The mean maximum depth of the wall trenches was 0.29 m. The basin fill in this particular structure was truncated around its margins by the plowzone. The floor itself was somewhat irregular, but it was generally lower in the middle of the structure. Portions of the floor were burned, primarily oxidized; the extent of burning is indicated in Figure 23.

The floor of Feature 91 represents the only intact living surface at the Julien site that contained an appreciable amount of in situ debris. Three activity areas were apparent. Most of the materials were located in the northern half of the structure, particularly in the northeastern quadrant. Here were located a sandstone metate, a pottery trowel, and three broken vessels (probably used as small containers). Two of these vessels, designated 91-3 and 91-4, were broken bowls (Plate 4). The third vessel, 91-1, was a small water bottle that was broken and partially buried in a shallow depression in the floor. All three vessels were apparently used after they had been broken. Buried as it

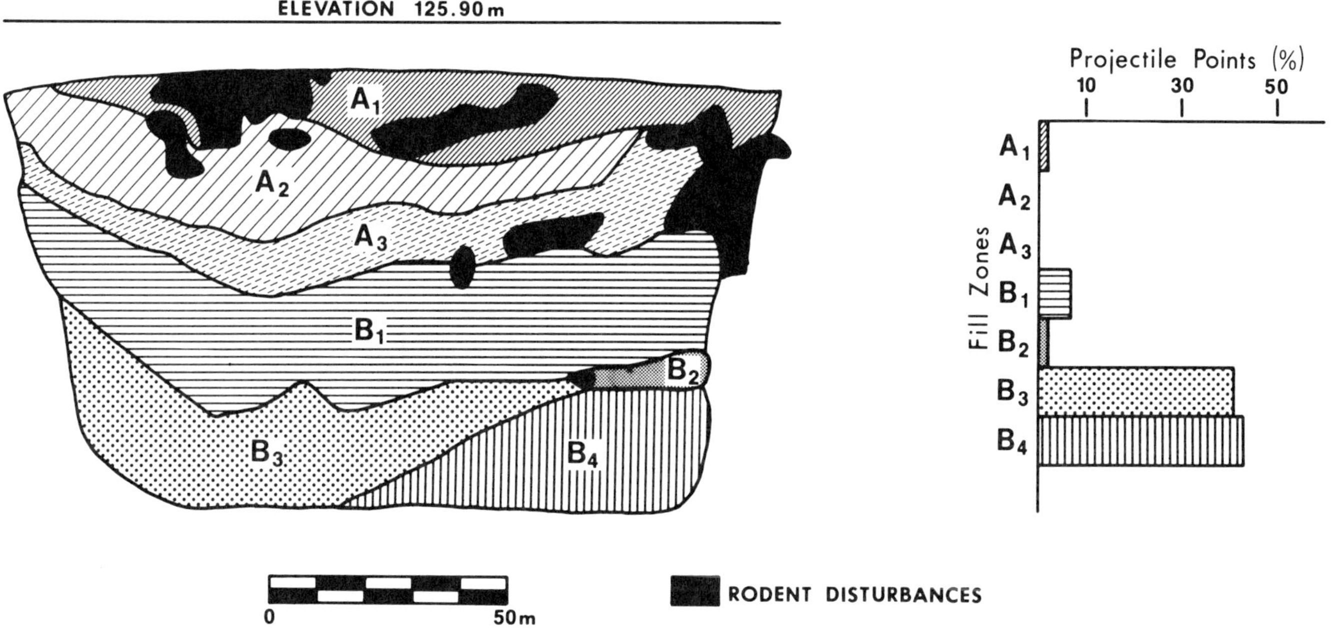

Figure 22. Mississippian Projectile Point Distribution by Zones in Feature 50

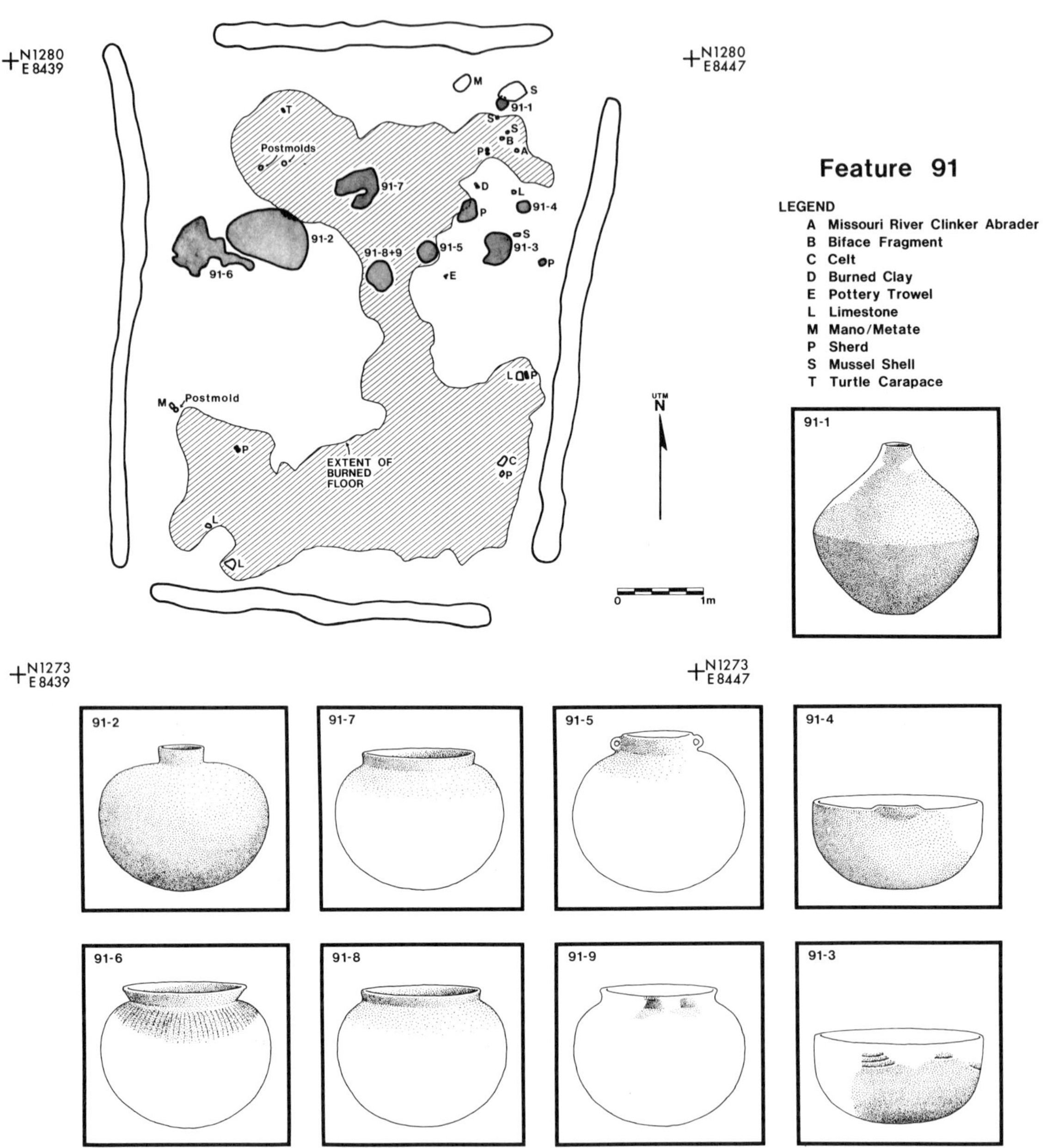

Figure 23. Mississippian Structure Feature 91, Plan View and Material Distribution

Plate 4. Feature Materials: upper left, burned twine in Feature 91; upper right, bowl fragment (91-4) on floor of Feature 91; lower left, excavating tool cache in Feature 187; lower right, limestone slab floor in Feature 221

was, the water bottle would have been a shallow, bowl-like container. A concentration of mussel shell was located partially over and around the water bottle. These shells may have been in a perishable container when the structure burned. Just west of this activity area were two additional water bottles and three large jars. The vessels were designated 91-2, 91-5, 91-6, 91-7, and 91-8. Within one jar (91-8) were found the fragmentary sherds of another vessel (91-9), which was poorly preserved. The available segments resembled a jar, but that identification is uncertain. It appears as if the two vessels were stacked on top of each other. This portion of the structure may have been a storage area. Three distinct areas of Feature 91 have been, therefore, identified. They include a relatively clean southern half, a special activity area in the northeastern quadrant distinguished by abundant debris, and an area opposite that activity area where large vessels were used for storage.

Rebuilding Activities

The following descriptions of Feature 2 and the feature complex that included structure Features 208, 215, 231, and 241 illustrate the nature of the rebuilding activites that took place in certain areas of the Julien site. Feature 2, considered first, was a rebuilt structure with eight wall trenches. The second group of structures comprised part of a complex series of superimposed features, including the four structures and numerous associated features, mostly pits.

Much of the Feature 2 basin fill was excavated during the 1976 testing at the site. The remaining basin fill and internal features were excavated during the 1979 field season. The structure was relatively large, and it was associated with the Sand Prarie phase occupation of the site (Figure 24). Significantly, it was one of only three structures with a double set of wall trenches, one of only five structures with burned floors, and it had more internal posts and pits than any other structure at the site. The second set of trenches enclosed a larger floor area than the earlier set, 31.02 m2 and 18.36 m2, respectively. The earlier wall trench mean midpoint width was 0.21 m; the mean maximum depth of those trenches was 0.42 m. The later wall trenches had a mean midpoint width of 0.19 m, and a mean maximum depth of 0.43 m. Evidence of eleven wall postmolds were found in the trench fills; all but one were located in the wall trenches of the later set. Eight of the outer wall trench postmolds had small portions of charred logs remaining upright within them. These represented the only in situ remains of wall support posts found at the site. The maximum depth of the structure basin was 0.33 m. Apparently, the later basin was either the same depth or deeper than that of the earlier structure. A packed, burned zone partially covered the floor in the northeastern portion of the structure. Its full extent in the southwestern portion of the structure was not determined; much of that area had been partially excavated during the testing of the site. The hard-packed, burned zone was 0.03 m thick and extended across several of the early wall trenches

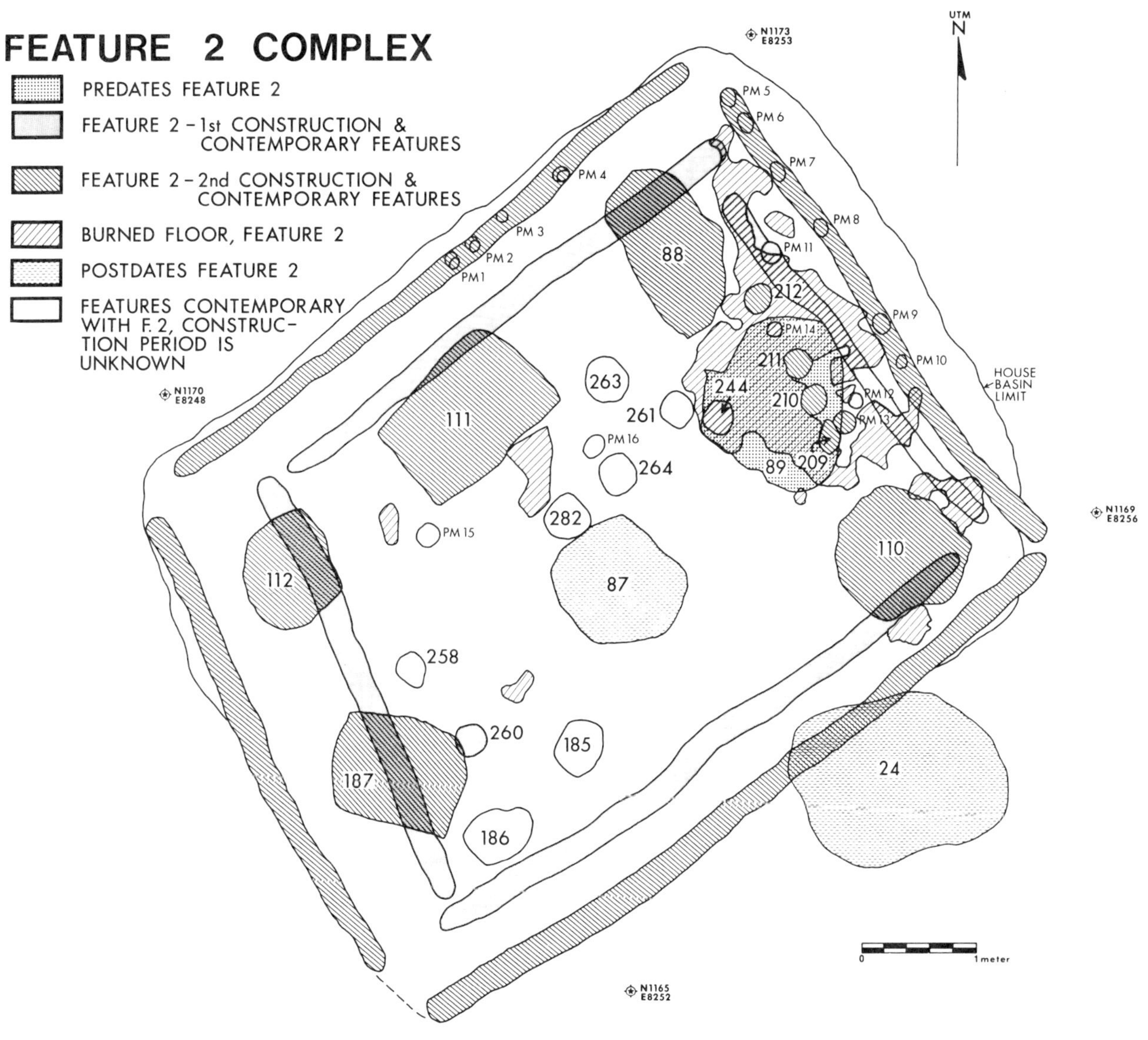

Figure 24. Mississippian Structure Feature 2 Complex, Plan View

and features. There were occasional gaps in the zone through which posts associated with the later of the two structures must have extended. This compact, burned zone was probably one of the dark, silty fills that were occasionally found on the floors of Julien site structures. The packed floor in Feature 2 was presumably fired to its brick-like consistency when the structure burned.

None of the pits could be definitely associated with the earlier of the two structures. There were, however, three internal posts (Feature 244 and Postmolds 12 and 14) that were superimposed by the hard, burned floor zone of the later structure. An additional postmold (Feature 260) was superimposed by a pit associated with the later structure. These four postmolds presumably supported posts that belonged to the earlier structure.

Five internal postmolds were associated with the second set of wall trenches; (Features 209, 210, 211, and 212, and Postmold 13). These postmolds were aligned in a row paralleling the northeastern wall trench. These postmolds were first noticed as gaps in the hard, burned floor; apparently, the floor soil zone had accumulated around the bases of the posts placed in these postmolds.

Five internal pits were associated with the later structure (Features 88, 110, 111, 112, and 187). Each pit was relatively large and deep, and all of them superimposed wall trenches belonging to the earlier structures. Two pits contained cached artifacts. In pit Feature 88, an excavating tool rested in the fill near its base; a cache of excavating tools and other items were found resting on the bottom of Feature 187. One of these five pits (Feature 110) had a rectangular base and, probably, a similarly shaped orifice. The orifice, however, had eroded into an irregular circle. Two of the pits (Features 88 and 110) were apparently open, but partially filled with soil, when the structure burned. Feature 88 had a lens of burned fill ca. 0.2 m thick extending across the center of the profile. This pit must have been half-full of soil when the structure burned. The filling history of Feature 110 was somewhat more complex. The basal zones of pit Feature 110 had accumulated prior to the burning of structure Feature 2. The upper ca. 0.15 m of soil in Feature 110 were reduced, contained charcoal, and probably related to the burning of the structure. Above these zones was an irregular, ca. 0.25 m thick, lens of burned soil that contained pieces of the previously discussed Feature 2 floor zone. This lens extended only partially across the pit; it had evidently washed into the feature after the structure had burned. Such erosion apparently contributed to the previouslu mentioned irregular orifice of this pit. The uppermost soil zones in both Features 88 and 110 were composed of the brown, debris-laden fills commonly found at the site. These fills, and those of the Feature 2 basin, apparently washed into the feature depressions after the structure had burned.

The remaining posts and small pits within Feature 2 were not assigned to either rebuilding episode. Most of these features were located in the western two-thirds of the structure, which had been excavated during the testing work.

The most complicated sequence of superimposed features at the Julien site involved a relatively small, 8 m by 9 m area where 25 features and 2 postmolds were identified (Figure 25). The major elements of this superimposed group of features consisted of four structures that were oriented roughly parallel to one another. They differed from one another in a number of respects, including their size, shape, nature of wall supports, and number of internal features. Feature 231 has been previously discussed as one of two rectangular structures lacking wall trenches. Rectangular structure Features 208, 215, and 241 each had sets of three or four enclosing wall trenches.

The internal floor area of Feature 215 was 6.49 m2. Evidence of enclosing wall supports was not discovered in the similarly shaped Feature 231; the area encompassed by the basin of Feature 231 measured 5.37 m2. The internal floor areas of the two larger structures (Features 208 and 241) were difficult to accurately calculate, since each had only three walls. The approximate size of Feature 208 was 16.56 m2 and of Feature 241 was 21.28 m2. The means of the wall trench midpoint widths for Features 208, 215, and 241 were 0.22 m, 0.21 m, and 0.25 m, respectively. Corresponding means for the wall trench maximum depths were 0.34 m, 0.33 m, and 0.40 m.

Feature 208 was the initial structure in this feature sequence. It consisted of a 0.35 m deep basin and three wall trenches. It was associated with a single internal postmold (Postmold 1) and a large pit (Feature 293). Both the postmold and pit were located adjacent to the northwestern wall of the structure. A grinding object covered with red pigment was found along the wall of pit Feature 293. Feature 309, a wall trench, may have been associated with this particular structure. If the two were indeed associated, the wall trench may have been some kind of internal partition. Two additional features, a pit (Feature 307) and a postmold (Feature 308), were associated with the basins of either structure Feature 208 or 241.

The second structure in the sequence was Feature 215. The southeastern wall trench of this structure superimposed the northwestern wall trench of Feature 208. The earlier trench was possibly reexcavated in order to place posts belonging to the Feature 215 wall. A Kaolin chert excavating tool was recovered at the level of the floor from the eastern end of the northwestern wall trench of Feature 215. Like other such artifacts at the site, it had been placed along the wall, presumably between the upright wall supports. The floor of Feature 215 was partially covered by a layer of dark and silty soil; perhaps this packed zone was deposited while the structure was occupied. Internal features were not found within this small structure.

Most of the features in the superimposed sequence were associated with the structure designated Feature 241. That structure had a maximum

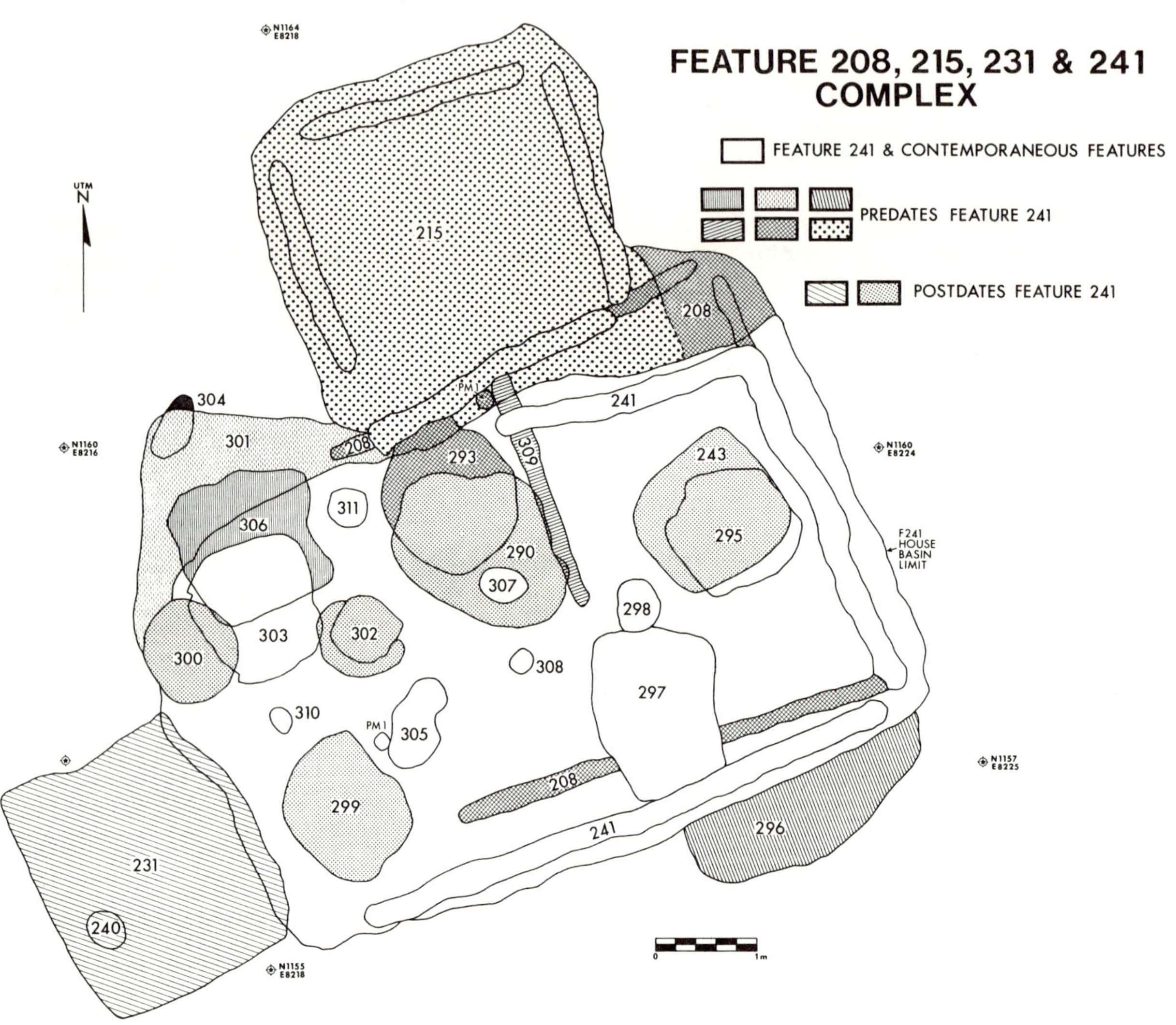

Figure 25. Mississippian Structure Feature Complex: Features 208, 215, 231, and 241

basin depth of 0.54 m, and wall trenches were located along three of its sides. It contained one associated postmold (Postmold 1) and seven pits (Features 295, 297, 298, 303, 305, 310, and 311). The pits varied in size, but three were relatively large, over 1 m wide and over 0.7 m deep.

The floor of Feature 241 was not uniformly level. In the southeastern portion of the structure the floor sloped noticeably toward the orifices of pit Features 297 and 298. There may once have been considerable activity around these pits, but the friable sand surrounding them had eroded to produce an uneven, sloping floor. When the two pits were no longer in use and had filled, a dark, silty soil accumulated in the low area of the structure floor. This soil eventually covered both features, reaching a depth of ca. 0.2 m. The top of this zone was relatively flat and approximated the level of the rest of the floor of the Feature 241 basin. This packed soil zone was restricted to the southeastern portion of the structure in the vicinity of Features 295, 297, and 298.

After Feature 241 was abandoned, a portion of its northwestern corner was burned. This area was designated Feature 302, and the burning occurred early in the basin filling process. The burned soils included the edge of a pit (Feature 303), a small amount of the Feature 241 basin fill, and the floor of Feature 241.

The fills in the northwestern portion of the Feature 241 basin generally contained numerous charred nutshells. The charcoal-laden fill dipped down somewhat in the vicinity of pit Feature 311; perhaps the fill in this small pit was once loosely consolidated and has since settled, displacing the overlying sediments. Like the Feature 241 fills, the upper zones of a pit designated Feature 303 contained many nutshells. This pit may have been only partially filled with soil when the structure was abandoned. Its upper soil zones and those of the structure basin may have resulted from a continuous deposition with fills that contained an unusually large amount of charred plant remains.

Structure Feature 241 superimposed two amorphous fill areas (Features 296 and 301) and a pit (Feature 306). This structure was, in turn, superimposed by pit Features 243, 290, 299, 300, and structure Feature 231.

Feature 231 was one of two small, rectangular structures lacking wall trenches discussed previously in greater detail. It superimposed the western margin of structure Feature 241, and was, therefore, the latest structure in the feature concentration. One small, internal pit (Feature 240) was located within this structure.

General Structure Characteristics

All of the Julien site structures were different. This variability defied efforts to define a representative structure archetype. The 23 rectangular wall trench structures, however, shared several characteristics. In general, the structures had been relatively large, substantial, semisubterranean buildings, with three or four enclosing walls. The number of internal features associated with structures varied greatly. Internal pits, when present, apparently had a shorter use-life than that of the structures themselves. This is indicated by the internal pits that were covered by thin, compact layers of soil, distinctive soil zones that had been deposited while the structures were occuppied. In addition, one internal pit (Feature 224) in structure Feature 36 had been reexcavated after having been previously used, abandoned, and filled with soil. Building orientations were relatively consistent. Most structures were oriented either parallel to the ridge or perpendicular to it. Several structures had been rebuilt by replacing posts in existing wall trenches, while others had been rebuilt by excavating new trenches parallel to an older set. In addition, later structures were sometimes constructed where an earlier building had stood. Partially filled structure basins were presumably noticed by later Mississipain inhabitants of the site and these depressions were selected as the locations for new semisubterrean structures. Most of the large rectangular structures were probably used for a variety of domestic purposes. Only one of these structures (Feature 31) has been identified as a public facility.

Pits

Most of the Julien site pits were assigned to the Mississippian period. Of 197 pits, 34% were located within structures.

The maximum orifice dimensions of the pits ranged from 0.26 m to 3.24 m; the mean diameter was 1.06 m (s=0.49). The pits ranged in depth from 0.05 m to 1.07 m; the mean depth was 0.34 m (s=0.22). While a variety of pit shapes were present, the predominate form was a modified cylinder (Table 1; Figures 26 and 27).

In general, deep pits had more fill zones than shallow pits (Figure 28). The strength of that relationship is described by a correlation coefficient (r) of 0.68; the SPSS scattergram subprogram was used in calculating this correlation coefficient (Nie et al. 1975). Brown, silty sand and sterile-like slumps were the most abundant pit fill categories. The fills of internal pits resembled those of external pits. Brown, sandy fills comprised 78.2% of the total fills in internal pits. The remaining fills included sterile-like slumps (17.5%); very dark brown, silty soils (2.0%); and burned lenses (2.4%). Corresponding figures for external pits were 82.2%, 16.8%, 0.9%,and 0.1%. These figures were based on the fills visible in the profiles of large pits, those pits with maximum dimensions in plan and profile that exceeded 0.5 m. The similarities between these two sets of figures indicated similar filling processes.

Table 1. Mississippian Pit Features

Plan View

Shape	N
Circular	36
Oval	139
Rectangular	21

Profile View

Shape	N	Shape*	N
Basin	15	Inslanting Walls	76
Conical	6	Vertical Walls	73
Bell	3	Outslanting Walls	3
		Irregular	11
		Sides Unknown	8

* Variable bases.
Note: missing observations not included.

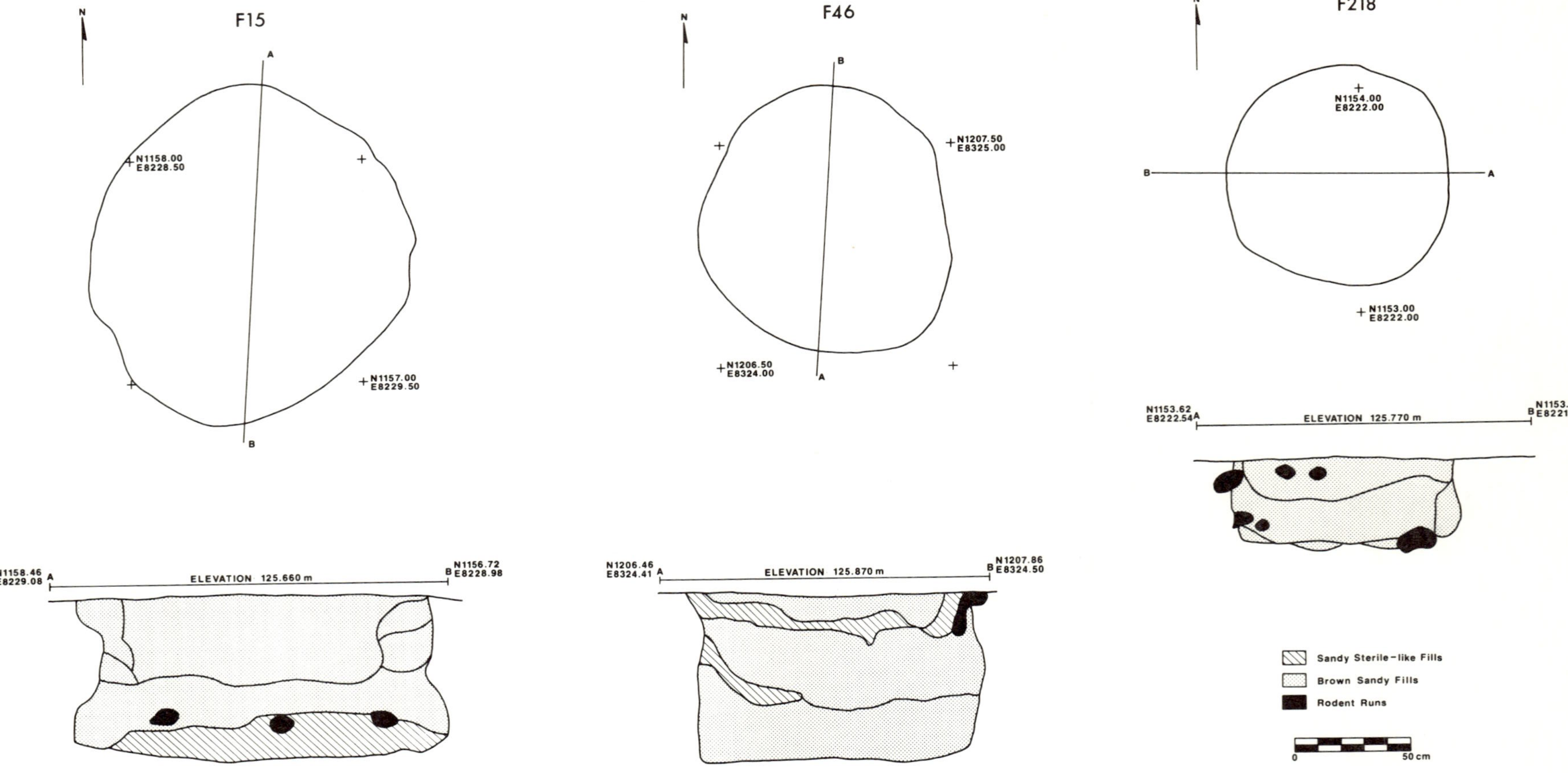

Figure 26. Mississippian Pit Features 15, 46, and 218; Plan and Profile Views

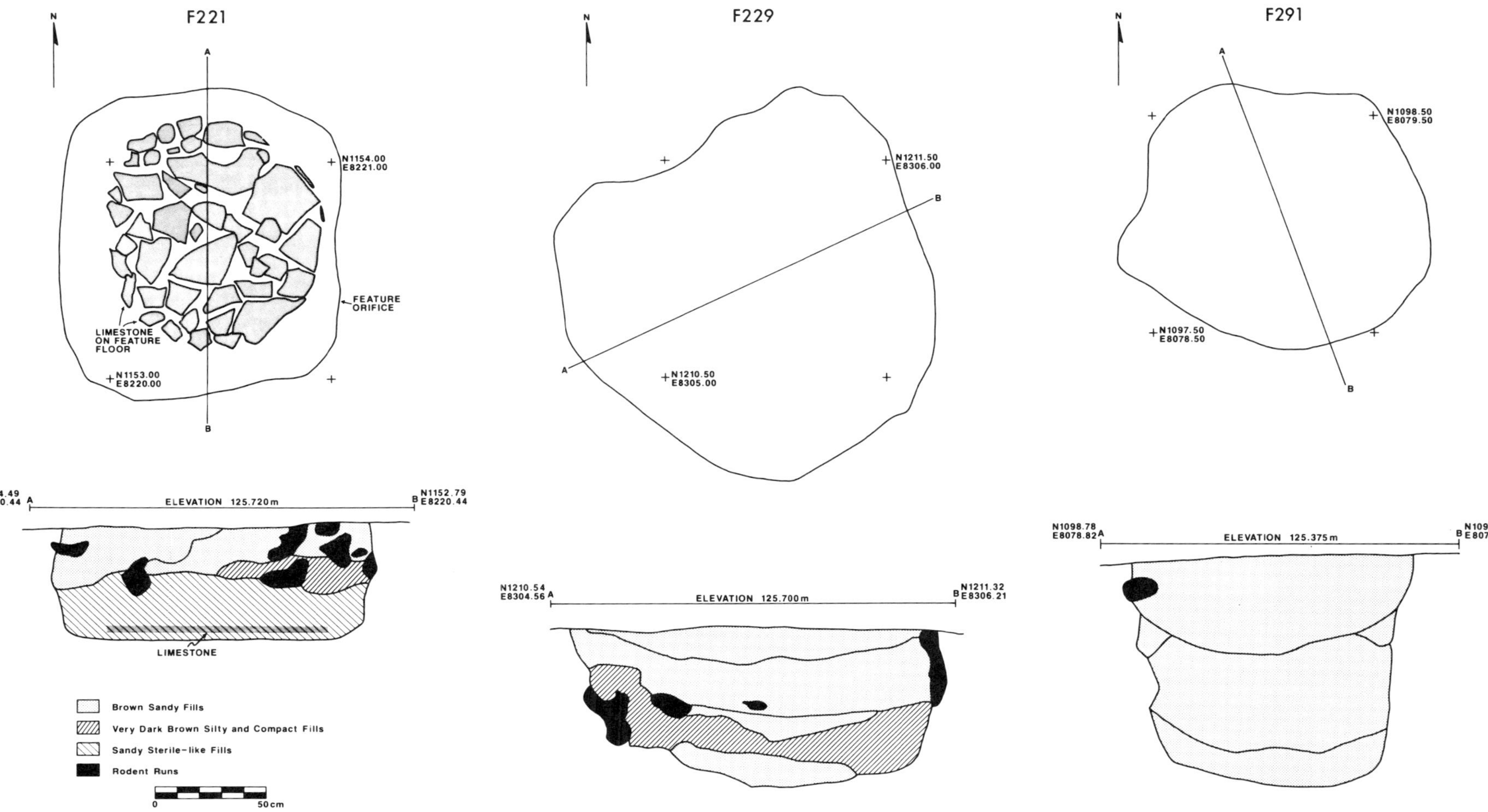

Figure 27. Mississippian Pit Features 221, 229, and 291; Plan and Profile Views

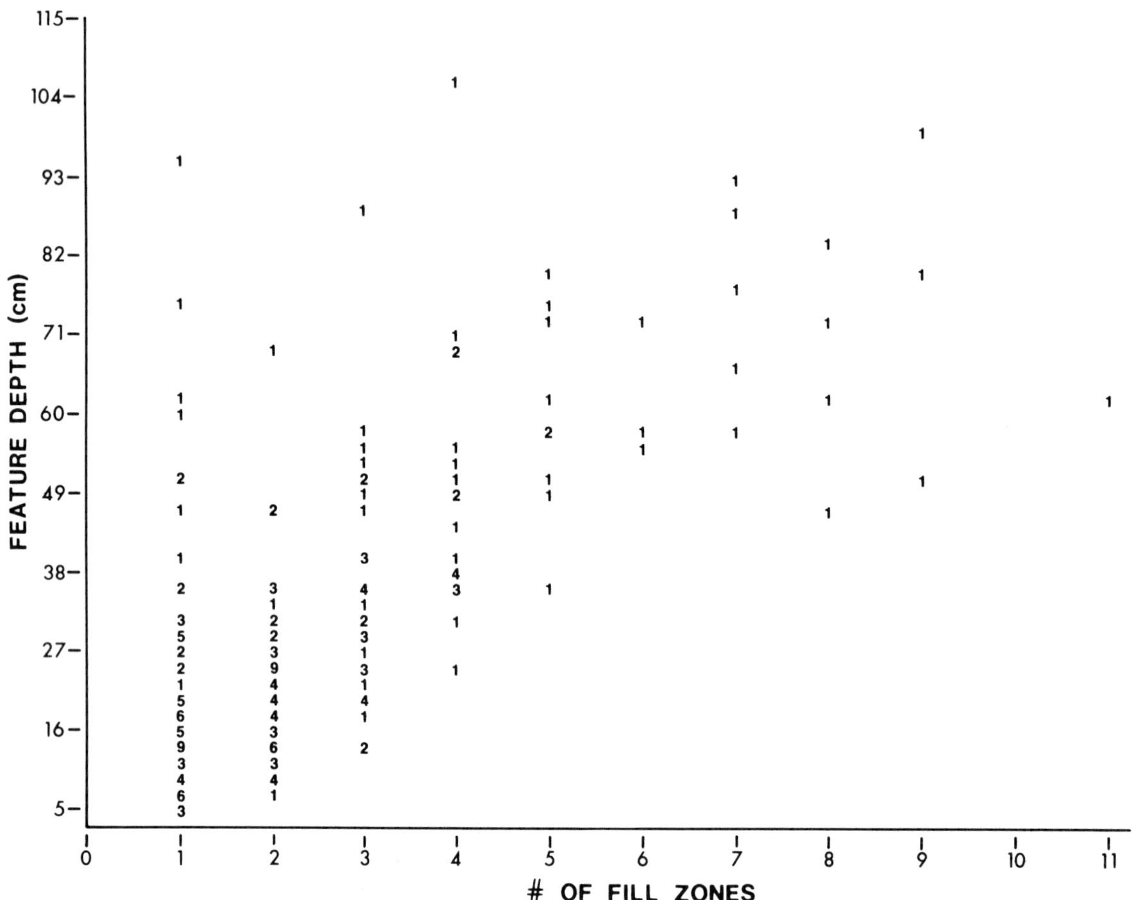

Figure 28. Scattergram of Mississippian Pits by Fill Zones and Feature Depths

The pits associated with structures as internal features were presumably used for storage. However, with the notable exception of Feature 252, there was little direct evidence to support this inference. Feature 252 was located in the southwestern corner of structure Feature 36, and it contained a complete jar, which was sitting upright (Plate 3). Other pits also contained items that had been intentionally placed within them. An example was the large piece of potter's clay in Feature 240, a small pit within Feature 231. Caches of artifacts occasionally were found that rested on the bases or along the walls of large pits (Plate 4). However, the primary function of large pits was probably for the storage of large-volume and bulky materials, presumably foodstuffs like maize.

More small, shallow pits were found in structures than were large pits (Figure 29). In Figure 29, the maximum depths are recorded to the nearest 0.5 cm. Note that Feature 252, which had a maximum diameter of 0.47 m and depth of 0.33 m, fell within the small pit category. There was a continuous size gradient from the numerous small pits to the largest of the internal pit features. Individual pits were probably made no larger than necessary to store the intended materials. That would account for the great range in pit capacity. One of the large internal pits (Feature 224) had been reexcavated, and the second episode of use was considerably less than the first (Figure 19).

The externally located pits were probably also used for storage. Two pits, Features 221 (Figure 27 and Plate 4) and 287, were lined with limestone. Perhaps the linings were related to the storage functions of these particular pits. The base of Feature 221 was covered with 64 pieces of limestone that weighed 27.6 kg. Smaller pieces of limestone were scattered over the floor of Feature 283. Many of thsese pieces of limestone were large slabs. In this feature there were 56 pieces of limestone that weighed 17 kg.

Although the externally located pits were scattered throughout the excavation area, the majority occurred in four clearly distinguishable clusters (Figures 5-10). One cluster was located near Feature 267, a structure at the southwestern end of the excavation area. This particular cluster consisted of 15 pits and 1 postpit. Two smaller clusters were located near structure Features 167 and 115. Six pits comprised the cluster located near structure Feature 167; 10 pits comprised the cluster located near structure Feature 115. The largest group of externally located features occurred south of the superimposed feature complex that contained structure Features 208, 215, 231, and 241. This particular group of external features consisted of 21 pits and 1 hearth. Portions of several ceramic vessels that linked these pits to the nearby structure complex were found in the fills of separate features. The clustering of pits within areally restricted portions of the site reflects the use of particular locations within the site for specialized activities. Without exception, the clusters of pits were located near structures.

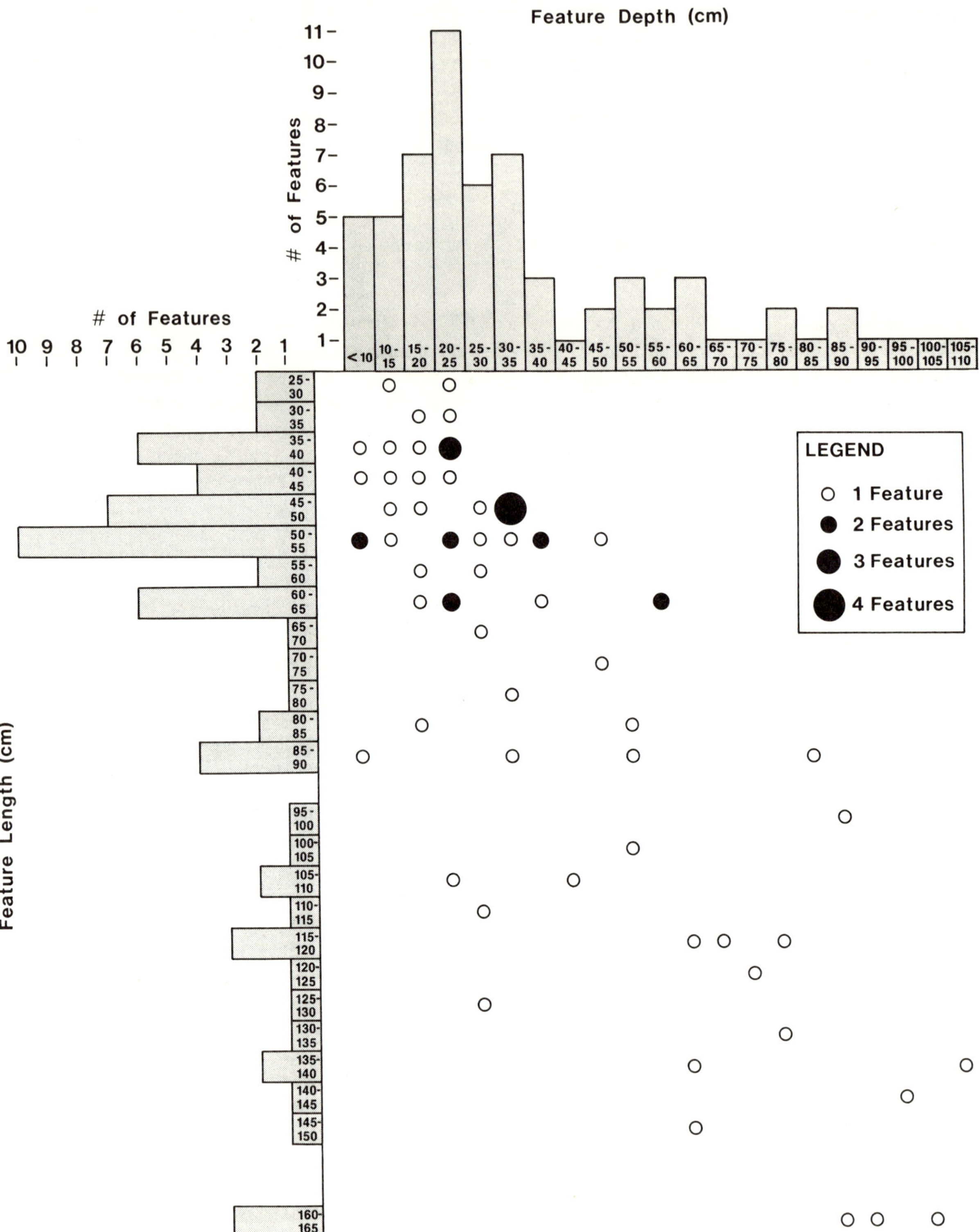

Figure 29. Distribution of Mississippian Internal Pits by Length and Depth

Posts

Evidence for posts was abundant; 144 postmolds and postpits were recognized. Posts exceeding 0.2 m in diameter were assigned feature numbers; smaller posts were given postmold numbers (Figure 30). Of both categories, 5 were located outside structures, while 139 occurred either in the structure walls or inside the structures.

Most of the post features had relatively straight or insloping sides and rounded bases, including posts that received postmold numbers and the features described as postmolds in Appendix 1. Post features that had one or two insertion, or extraction, ramps were called postpits.

There were 15 postpits with either one or two associated ramps. Most of the ramps were probably used for the extraction of posts. The fills, when differentiated, usually appeared to have been deposited in open depressions. Such depressions might have resulted from digging posts out of the ground when it became necessary to remove or replace posts. The postpit fills were not consistent with those expected if ramps were used for the insertion of posts, i.e., exhibiting distinct zones of packing and an organically stained zone where a post had decayed.

The postmolds and post pits associated with structures ranged in depth from 0.03 m to 0.57 m (mean=0.19 m). Those located within structures were presumably used to support the roof, walls, or internal partitions. The function of the posts located outside of structures was not determined. Those post features extended 0.17 m to 0.57 m (mean=0.39 m) below the plowzone. They would, therefore, have supported sizable posts. The exterior posts probably once supported constructions like windbreaks, canopies, or drying racks.

Hearths

Fourteen hearths were excavated at the Julien site. All were Mississippian, and the majority (12) were associated with various structures. The hearths consisted either of burned surfaces, presumably resulting from fires built on the ground or were prepared depressions that contained fires.

Six hearths were of the surface variety. All were found within structures, including Features 23, 31, and 241. Four surface hearths in structure Feature 31 were of particular interest, since they were arranged in two paired sets. The westernmost pair included Features 39 and 42; the other pair included Features 40 and 41. It was not determined whether these hearth pairs were used simultaneously or sequentially. There was an additional hearth in Feature 31, but that hearth (Feature 49) had a basin-shaped profile and it was larger than the four nearby surface hearths.

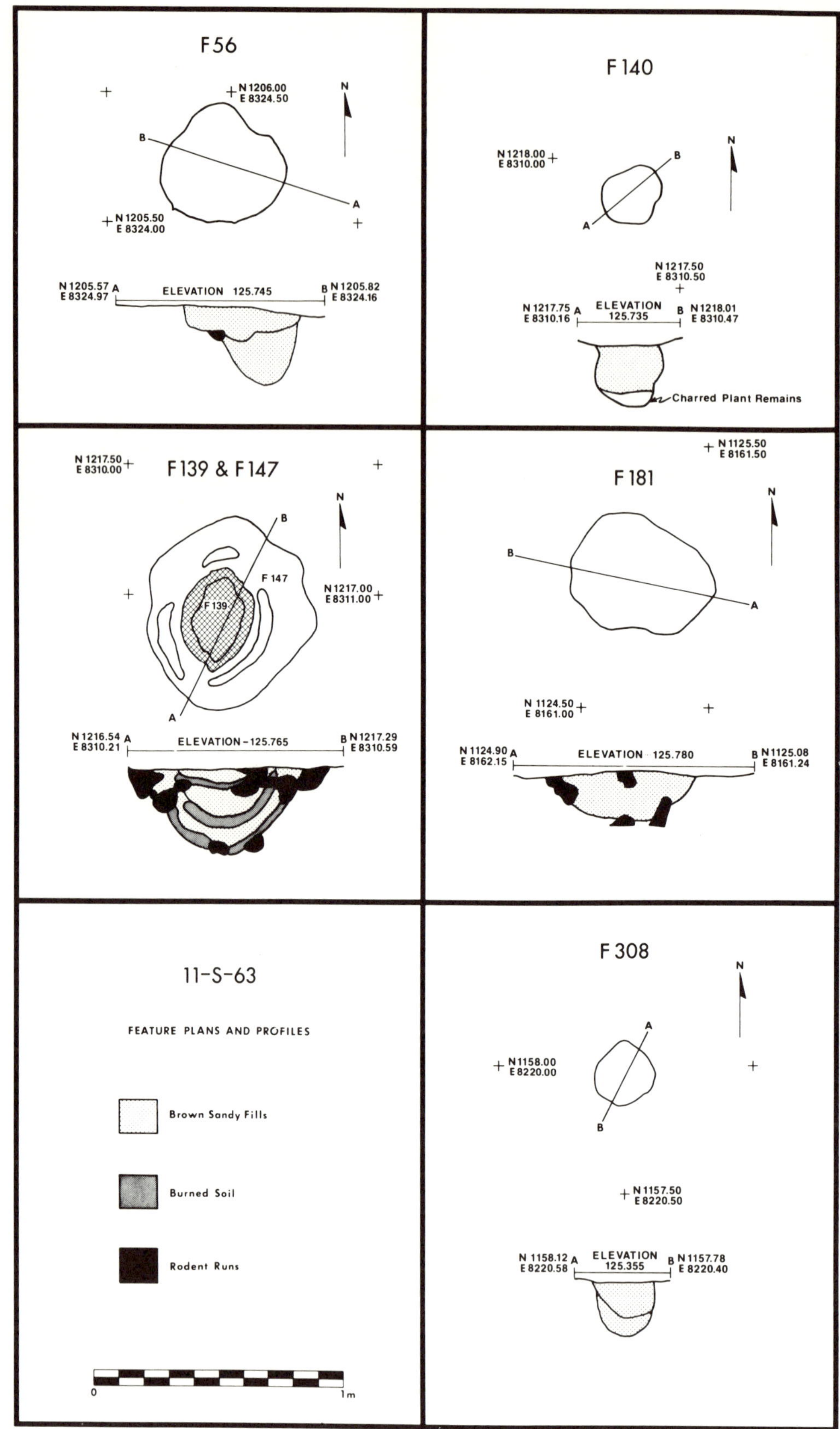

Figure 30. Mississippian Features (clockwise from upper left): Post Pit Feature 56, Smudge Pit Feature 140, Pit Feature 181, Postmold Feature 308, and Hearth Features 139 and 147; Plan and Profile Views

The burned area (Feature 302) in the northwestern corner of structure Feature 241 was also of interest, since it related to the filling of that particular structure basin. Feature 302 was an oval area of burned soil that had an oxidized central area and an arc of reduced soil around its southwestern margin. The burned and discolored soil included sterile subsoil, fill from an earlier pit (Feature 303), and a little of the Feature 241 basin fill. This area had apparently been burned while the structure basin remained open, but after the structure had been abandoned and soil had begun to collect in the basin.

Of the eight prepared hearths, six were located in structures. Half of the structure hearths were oval in plan view; the others were circular. The long axes of these features ranged from 0.40 m to 0.97 m (mean=0.63 m, s=0.24). The sides of five internal prepared hearths were insloping, and the bases were either convex or irregular. The exception was Feature 225, which was located within structure Feature 146. This hearth had vertical walls and a convex base. The depth of these six internal hearths ranged from 0.11 m to 0.30 m (mean=0.2 m, s=0.07).

Separate feature numbers (Features 139 and 147) were assigned to zones of fired soil within one hearth feature (Figure 30). Separate feature numbers were assigned because these zones represented two distinct firing episodes. The hearth was located within the only sweatlodge at the site (Feature 113). The two zones of fired soil were oval in plan view and conical in profile. Feature 147 was the first of the two burning episodes, Feature 139 was the second. The two burned soil zones were separated by about 0.05 m of unburned fill. There was also a small, indistinct, 0.02 m to 0.03 m thick layer of burned soil very near the top of the feature profile. That soil may represent yet another burning episode, and would, of course, have postdated the firing episodes designated as Features 139 and 147. The most recent, but, minor, burned zone was not assigned a separate feature number.

Only two hearths were located outside the Julien site structures. Features 44 and 178 were of moderate size with long axis diameters of 0.45 m and 0.60 m, respectively. These two features must once have been relatively deep, since they extended below the base of the plowzone 0.12 m and 0.20 m, respectively. Both hearths occurred in the central site area in the vicinity of numerous pits. Additional hearths were undoubtedly once present outside of structures, but have been destroyed by recent plowing of the site area.

Isolated Wall Trenches

Five isolated wall trenches were excavated at the site. Three were assigned feature numbers; two of these trenches were partitions within a structure (Feature 31) and were designated as internal wall trenches and not given separate feature numbers.

Three of the five isolated wall trenches served as internal

partitions. One trench may have been associated with structure Feature 208; two belonged to structure Feature 31. The two partitions in Feature 31 flanked the western and southern walls in the southwestern corner of the structure. These two partitions were very similar to one another. The southern trench was 2.2 m long, and the western was 2.3 m long. Both trenches were 0.22 m wide and 0.36 m deep.

The wall trench designated Feature 309 was associated with the previously described complex of four superimposed structures (Features 208, 215, 231, and 241). The trench was used early in the structure sequence, and it was perhaps associated with Feature 208 as an internal partition. Feature 309 was superimposed by the northernmost wall trench of a later structure (Feature 241). The Feature 309 trench was 2.35 m long, 0.22 m wide, and 0.28 m deep.

The two isolated wall trenches (Features 126 and 144) located outside of structures were found near the majority of features in the central site area. Feature 126 was longer than Feature 144; the former measured 1.96 m and the latter 1.35 m. They closely resembled each other in terms of their widths (0.32 m and 0.29 m) and depths (0.16 m and 0.17 m). It was not determined how they were used, but the trenches may have supported some sort of windbreak, a rather substantial drying rack, or a similar construction.

Smudge Pit

One Julien site feature was interpreted as a smudge pit (Figure 30). This pit, Feature 140, was first identified at the base of Feature 113, the sweatlodge. The smudge pit presumably longed to the sweatlodge; it is unlikely that the apparent association is entirely fortuitous. The smudge pit was circular in plan view, measuring 0.23 m x 0.21 m. This 0.23 m deep feature had somewhat irregular walls and base, but otherwise it resembled the profiles of many postmolds. Much of the fill was a brown, silty sand containing occasional fragments of charcoal. A distinctive characteristic of this particular feature was the 6 cm lens of charred plant material at its base. Recognizable remains within the lens included small twigs and corn cobs. Cultural materials were not found in the charred remains and overlying fill.

This feature closely matched criteria established by Binford (1967) for the identification of a smudge pit feature class. However, the sides near the orifice of the Julien site feature were not oxidized, a characteristic of many smudge pits at midwestern sites.

Fill Areas

Two features can be described only as amorphous fill areas. Features 296 and 301 were relatively shallow (0.12 m and 0.13 m, respectively). Both were located adjacent to the edges of the superimposed feature complex composed of structure Features 208, 215, 231, 241, and their associated internal features (Figure 25). Features 296 and 301 may have been portions of partially destroyed features or shallow borrow areas where soil was removed for adjacent, and extensive, rebuilding activities.

In plan view, the basin of Feature 301 appeared to resemble the basin of nearby structure Feature 231. Unfortunately, feature definition in this particular portion of the superimposed feature complex was complicated considerably by the presence of numerous irregularly shaped, superimposed fills with similar colors and textures. Therefore, while it was possible that Feature 301 may represent part of a structure basin, supporting evidence in the form of wall postmolds or trenches was not found.

Radiocarbon Dating

Wood charcoal samples were obtained from five burned structures. The dates, which ranged from 960 A.C. to 1390 A.C., were obtained from samples from logs that were part of structural supports (Table 2). Four fourteenth-century dates from three structures were consistent with recovered ceramic assemblages that were clearly affiliated with the Sand Prairie phase. A 960 A.C. date from structure Feature 2 was definitely too early. Artifactual materials from the other two structures were limited, but those found in Feature 3 were consistent with an early

Table 2. Radiocarbon Dates

Feature	ISGS #	Date
2	589	1320 ± 75 A.C.
	758	960 ± 75 A.C.
3	587	1240 ± 75 A.C.
82	581	1360 ± 75 A.C.
85	586	1120 ± 110 A.C.
91	579	1345 ± 75 A.C.
	760	1390 ± 75 A.C.

thirteenth century date, especially given the time range implied by the standard deviation. A fifth date of 1120 A.C., from structure Feature 85, appeared somewhat early given the kinds of items recovered from the structure and, especially, the structure's general morphology. A Moorehead or Sand Prairie phase affiliation is suggested for this particular structure; the former phase would be included within the upper 110 years range of the date.

RAW MATERIALS AND ARTIFACTS

The artifacts from the Julien site are discussed in terms of categories of presumed functional significance, e.g., projectile points, excavating tools, and ceramic vessels. Categories familiar to archaeologists are employed to organize the considerable collection of items from feature contexts. Admittedly, such categories are based on the time-honored classification of items by an intuitive mix of artifact morphology, raw material type, inferred function, and even a measure of "common sense". Inferred artifact functions were not checked by any of the several time-consuming analytical techniques available for evaluating shape, edge wear, and the like. The categories employed here are, however, sufficiently precise to permit statements to be made about prehistoric life at the site, one of the research goals of this study.

Only materials recovered from feature contexts are described here. However, numerous items from disturbed contexts, e.g., the surface, plowzone, and backdirt, have been catalogued for future researchers. All materials derived from the 1978 and 1979 site excavations, regardless of their original contexts, have been cleaned, labeled, inventoried, and are retrievable in a computerized format on both bag and feature bases. Materials from the 1976 testing of features are similarly available.

Raw Materials

Artifacts and debris from Late Woodland and Mississippian features comprised many different raw materials. This discussion pertains to both cultural components; however, the primary concern is with the Mississippian occupation from which a wide variety of raw materials were recovered. Feature provenience is given below only when a particular raw material was represented by only occasionally occurring, small, and usually unmodified fragments.

Local Raw Materials

Many raw materials in the Julien site collection were from sources located near the site. These were recovered as broken artifacts, whole artifacts, and debris. Limestone, calcite crystals, and sandstone would have been available in the bluffs east of the site. Limestone, when present, usually had been burned. Several artifacts had been fashioned from limestone, including excavating tools and two unusually shaped objects. Sandstone generally occurred in the form of grinding implements; its coarse texture was well-suited for grinding and smoothing a variety of softer materials, such as wood and bone. Glacial till exposed by creeks in the uplands bordering the floodplain would have been a nearby source for igneous and metamorphic cobbles, as well as sedimentary rocks. Cobbles generally had been used as hammerstones, various grinding implements, and ground stone tools. Grover gravel, with its distinctive red cortex, also occurs in deposits in the American Bottom area. The source of Missouri River clinker is located far from the American Bottom, but pieces float down the Missouri River and are deposited on the Mississippi floodplain (Porter 1974). Therefore, this material would have been locally available to the Julien site inhabitants.

Chert was a common material in the Julien site collection; for purposes of this analysis, it was divided into ten varieties. Six varieties of chert were locally available. The so-called "local" category includes the white chert found in the Burlington limestone formation. Chert from the well-known Crescent Hills quarry area was also included in this category. Three other recognizable chert types are thought to outcrop in limestone formations located in St. Clair and adjacent counties. These are the Fern Glen, Root Beer, Ste. Genevieve, and Old Blue cherts. These three chert categories, as they have been used here, are described in Kelly (1980b) and Emerson (1980b). A miscellaneous chert category includes unidentified varieties. Often these were poor grade cherts, presumably obtained from creek beds and gravel bars located in the vicinity of the site. Grover Gravel also occurs in deposits in the American Bottom area.

Bone, shell, and wood, of course, would have been readily available materials. Comparatively few bone and shell artifacts were recovered, however, since preservation at the site was generally poor. Items of bone and shell are described in the accompanying faunal report. The several burned Mississippian structures at the site provided abundant samples of charred plant remains.

Nonlocal Raw Materials

Materials from distant sources occurred infrequently in the Julien site collection. Southern Illinois chert varieties, including Mill Creek, Dongola or Cobden Ball, and Kaolin, were well represented by tools, but represented by comparatively little debitage. Usually, these artifacts occurred as large tools. An exotic, poor grade, fossiliferous chert, described as Mansker in Emerson (1980b), was occasionally present.

Other exotic materials, such as galena, hematite, bauxite, and quartz crystals, were present, but in small quantities. The first three

Table 3. Presence of Exotic Materials by Feature

Feature	Copper	Mica	Bauxite	Quartz	Galena	Hematite	Whelk Shell
2				X	X	X	
3						X	
5	X				X	X	
7				X	X	X	
9						X	
15					X		
17					X	X	
23					X		X
24				X		X	
31					X	X	
43						X	
50					X	X	
57					X		
84						X	
87					X	X	X
88			X			X	
89						X	X
109							X
111						X	
114						X	
116						X	
146		X			X		
149					X		
152					X		
155			X				
157						X	
185					X		
188						X	
220					X		
221						X	
241				X	X	X	
243				X		X	
249					X		
255						X	
267			X		X		
293		X	X		X	X	X
295			X				
298						X	
299			X				
300			X				
303						X	

Key
X indicates presence

apparently were employed as pigments, but, occasionally, artifacts were made of these materials. Both galena and hematite occur in southeastern Missouri, a likely source for most, or all, of the Julien site materials. Two pieces of galena from the Julien site were subjected to a trace element analysis; apparently, they are from the Potosi Formation in southeastern Missouri (Walthall 1981). Although the Julien site hematite probably came from Missouri, there are localized deposits of poor grade hematite in the bluffs bordering the American Bottom. Quartz crystals occur in the Missouri Ozark region; they were only represented by small fragments in five features at the Julien site. During the Historic period, quartz crystals were sometimes used for divining purposes (Hudson 1976). Bauxite occurs in several southern states.

Occasionally, items were recovered from Mississippian features that indicated contact with distant portions of the midcontinental United States (Table 3). Such specimens include a 0.2 g piece of copper from Feature 5, small fragments of mica from Features 146 and 293, and several whelk shell artifacts.

Late Woodland

Materials from 13 Late Woodland pits represent only a small proportion of the total debris recovered from Julien site features. Explanations of terms used below, such as utilization and heat treatment, are found in the description of Mississippian period materials.

Lithic Materials

Lithic raw materials from Late Woodland features included limestone, sandstone, siltstone, igneous cobbles, and chert. Local varieties dominated the chert assemblage; only two polished Mill Creek flakes were recovered. Most of the chert appeared to be heat treated. In all, there were 171 chert flakes that weighed 466.6 g. Slightly less than half, 74 (43.3%), showed evidence of utilization, yet they collectively weighed 363.5 g, or 77.9% of the total. Of these, the large flakes appear to have been selected for various cutting or scraping tasks. Several relatively large utilized flakes were blade-like and displayed edge wear along their lateral margins. One utilized flake was evidently used in a manner similar to the Mississippian flake perforators described in a subsequent section. The various Late Woodland artifacts are listed in Table 4.

Vessels

Ceramic sherds were recovered from all Late Woodland features. Two body sherds from different features fit together, one from Feature 94 and the other from Feature 99. Rim segments, considered as 18 separate vessels, were recovered from seven Late Woodland features.

Table 4. Late Woodland Artifacts and Polished Flakes by Raw Material

Material	Flat Surfaced Sandstone Abraders		Hammerstones		Cores		Biface Fragments		Projectile Point Fragments		Polished Flakes	
	N	Wt(g)	N	Wt(g)	N	Wt(g)	N	Wt(g)	N	Wt(g)	N	Wt(g)
Sandstone	3	90.3	-	-	-	-	-	-	-	-	-	-
Igneous	-	-	1	483.4	-	-	-	-	-	-	-	-
Mill Creek Chert	-	-	-	-	-	-	-	-	-	-	2	1.1
Local Chert	-	-	-	-	1	21.6	1	3.2	1	1.3	2	2.4

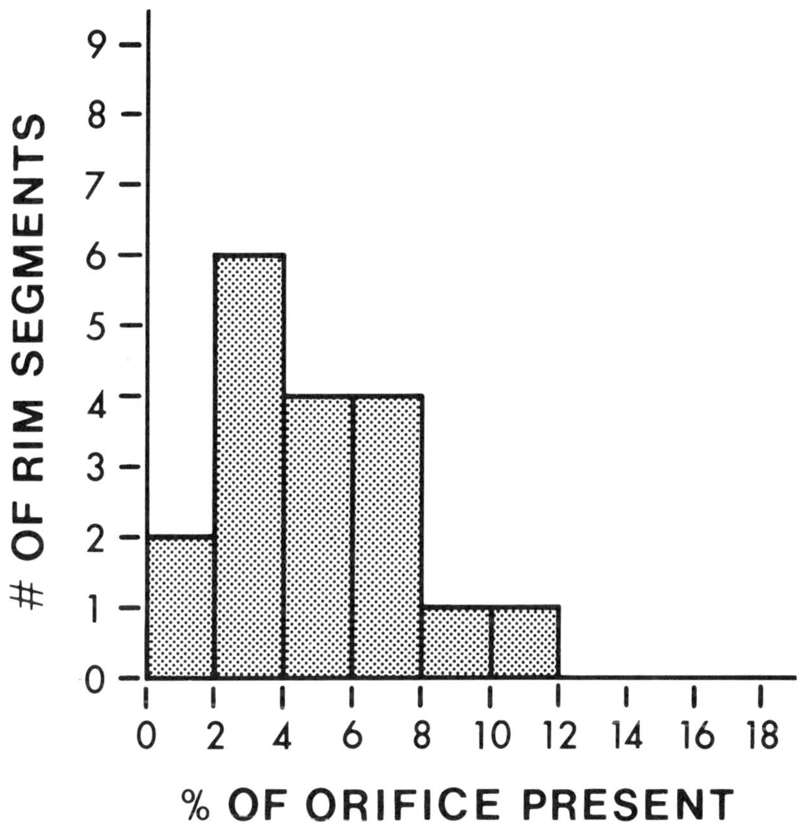

Figure 31. Late Woodland Ceramics, Percent of Orifice Present

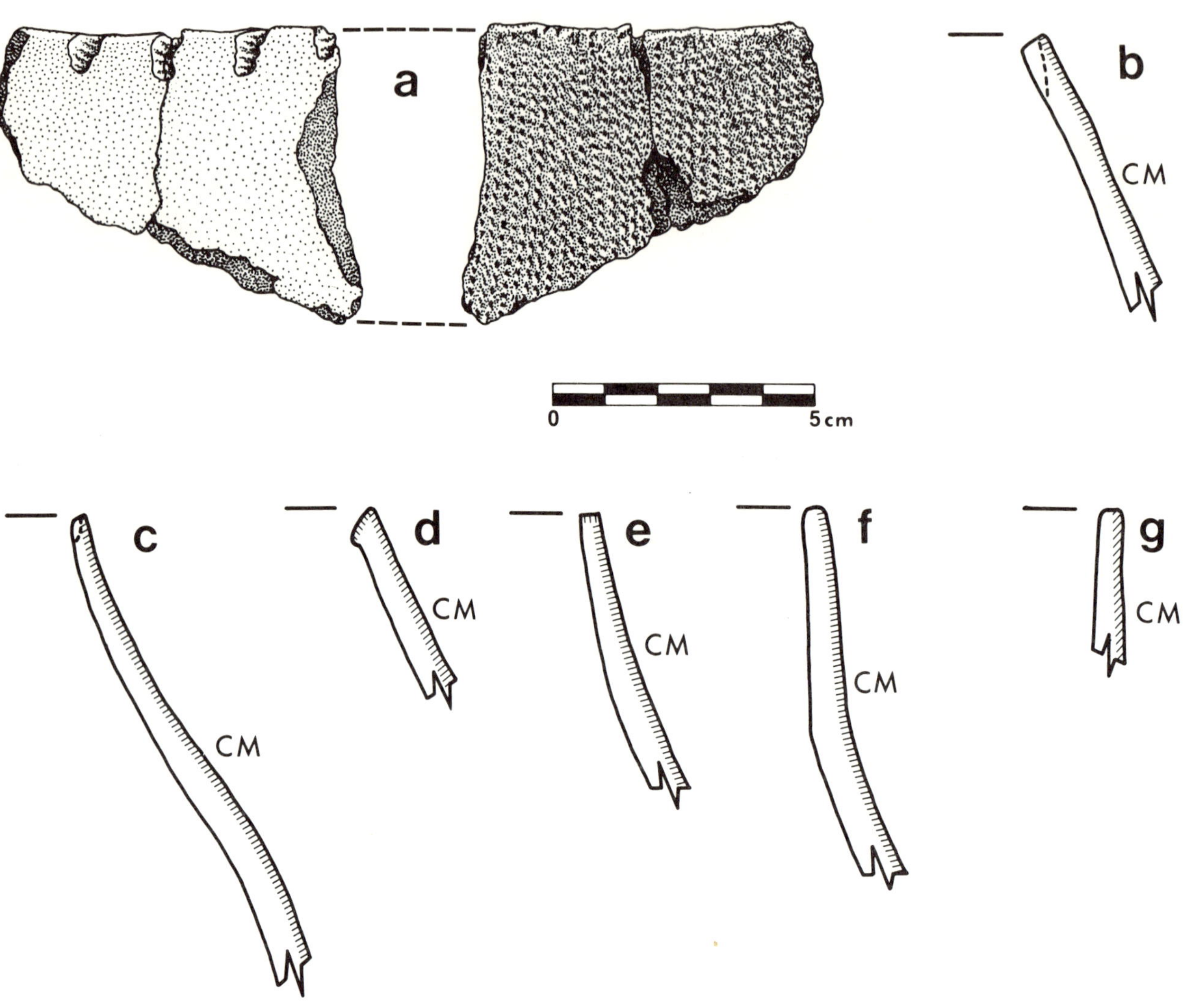

Figure 32. Late Woodland Jar Rims: a, 101-1, interior and exterior; b, 101-1, profile; c, 93-1, profile and interior lip impressions; d, 97-3, profile; e, 97-2, profile; f, 101-4, profile; and g, 101-5, profile

Table 5. Late Woodland Ceramics

		Interior Notching		Lip Cord Impressed		Cordmarking Below Rim			Observable Cord Twist		
		+	-	+	-	Vertical (+)	Diagonal (+)	Crossed (+)	S (+)	Z (+)	S and Z (+)
Jars	N	4	13	5	12	14	1	2	13	1	1
	%	23.5	76.5	29.4	70.6	82.4	5.9	11.8	86.7	6.7	6.7
Bowls	N	-	1	-	1	1	-	-	1	-	-
	%	-	100.0	-	100.0	100.0	-	-	100.0	-	-
Total	N	4	14	5	13	15	1	2	14	1	1
	%	22.2	77.8	27.8	72.2	83.3	5.6	11.2	87.5	6.3	6.3

Key
+ indicates presence
- indicates absence

The Late Woodland ceramics were tempered with grog, although some pastes contained variable amounts of well-rounded grit particles. The paste colors ranged from light orange -brown to brown-black. The reconstructed rim segments ranged in weight from 1.3 g to 80.5 g. Each segment represents only a small proportion of the original vessel circumference (Figure 31).

The majority of vessels represented by rim segments were jars (Table 5). None could be completely reconstructed, but the vessels probably were once globular with rounded or concoidal bases. Most of the rims were slightly insloping; the rest were vertical (Figure 32). The jar lips were rounded or angular; the latter were horizontal or sloped toward the vessel interior. Occasionally, the superior lip surface was decorated with cord impressions.

The exterior jar surfaces were finished with cordmarks or smoothed over cordmarks. Usually, the cords were S-twist. Cordmarks immediately below the rim were often vertically oriented.

Interior notches were sometimes present on the jar rims. In three of four vessels with notches, the impressions had been made with a cord-wrapped stick. The cord-wrapped stick impressions on two specimens were oriented in a counterclockwise direction from the lip to the vessel interior. The third rim segment with cord-wrapped stick impressions was too small and eroded to determine the orientation of notching. The remaining rim section with notching had narrow, vertical, single cord impressions ringing the interior lip surface.

The ceramics resemble those of the Patrick phase as described by Fowler and Hall (1972). Similar vessels have been described by Vogel (1975) as belonging to what are called Early Bluff assemblages by American Bottom archaeologists.

Mississippian

Debitage

The single most abundant nonceramic material recovered from Mississippian features was chert. It was found in the form of tools, cores, and flakes.

Fifty-four chert cores were recovered. Several chert types were present, although most cores had been made from locally available materials (Table 6). Core sizes varied widely, with the smallest specimen weighing 4.0 g and the largest 283.8 g. Many cores had been battered along one or more edges to prepare a striking platform. Scars on most cores indicated that flakes had been removed in many different directions, a process that produced an irregular core shape. A few cores had been specifically prepared for blade production. One small

Table 6. Mississippian Cores

Chert Types	N	%	Wt(g)	%
Kaolin	1	1.9	42.2	1.7
Dongola	1	1.9	49.6	1.9
Root Beer	2	3.7	81.4	3.2
Old Blue	2	3.7	45.5	1.8
Local	46	85.1	2240.3	87.8
Miscellaneous	2	3.7	91.9	3.6
Total	54		2550.9	

5.1 g core of local chert from Feature 2 bore flake scars where microdrills had been removed; apparently, microdrills were only infrequently produced at the site. Only two microdrills were recovered from feature contexts (Figure 33).

A 10% random sample of chert flakes from the Mississippian component was analyzed to determine the types of raw materials present in the collection, their abundance, and the nature of that debris (Table 7). Materials were selected for examination on a per feature basis. If a feature was selected for analysis that contained no chert, another was substituted.

The chert flakes from Mississippian features included the varieties of chert discussed previously. Each flake was examined to see if any of the original cortex remained. Flakes displaying any of the original cortical surface were classified as cortical flakes.

Each flake was also examined for heat treatment and edge wear. Thermally-altered chert flakes were further divided into intentionally heat-treated and accidentally burned categories. The heat-treated chert in the collection tended to display a distinctive "waxy" surface texture and often a distinctive color. Exposed surfaces of chert in the burned category usually were blackened and occasionally displayed pot-lid fractures. The flakes were also examined with a 10X hand lens to determine whether the edges had been altered. Included in the utilized category were flakes that had been intentionally retouched to produce a working edge and those that displayed minute chipping from use.

In addition to the flakes in the general utilized category, several flakes had been worked to produce recognizable tools. The following discussion of flake tools and polished flakes involves specimens from the entire collection, except the flake projectile points, which are discussed separately in a later section.

Two flake scrapers were recovered from Mississippian feature contexts (Features 2 and 243). They were differentiated from the numerous utilized flakes by their large size and steep edge retouch. Both scrapers had been fashioned from local chert. One weighed 41.4 g, the other 34.4 g. The smaller of the two specimens is illustrated in Figure 33.

Ten utilized flakes classified as gravers were recovered from Mississippian features (Table 8; Figure 33). One or more of their edges had been altered to produce a small, sharp, unifacially flaked tip. These tools were probably used to score or scrape material like bone. Two gravers had been reused and displayed multiple cutting tips.

Polished flakes broken off large bifacially worked tools were well represented in the Mississippian features. Flakes with polish were recognized macroscopically during the inventorying process. The flakes were later separated into high and low gloss categories using a 10X hand

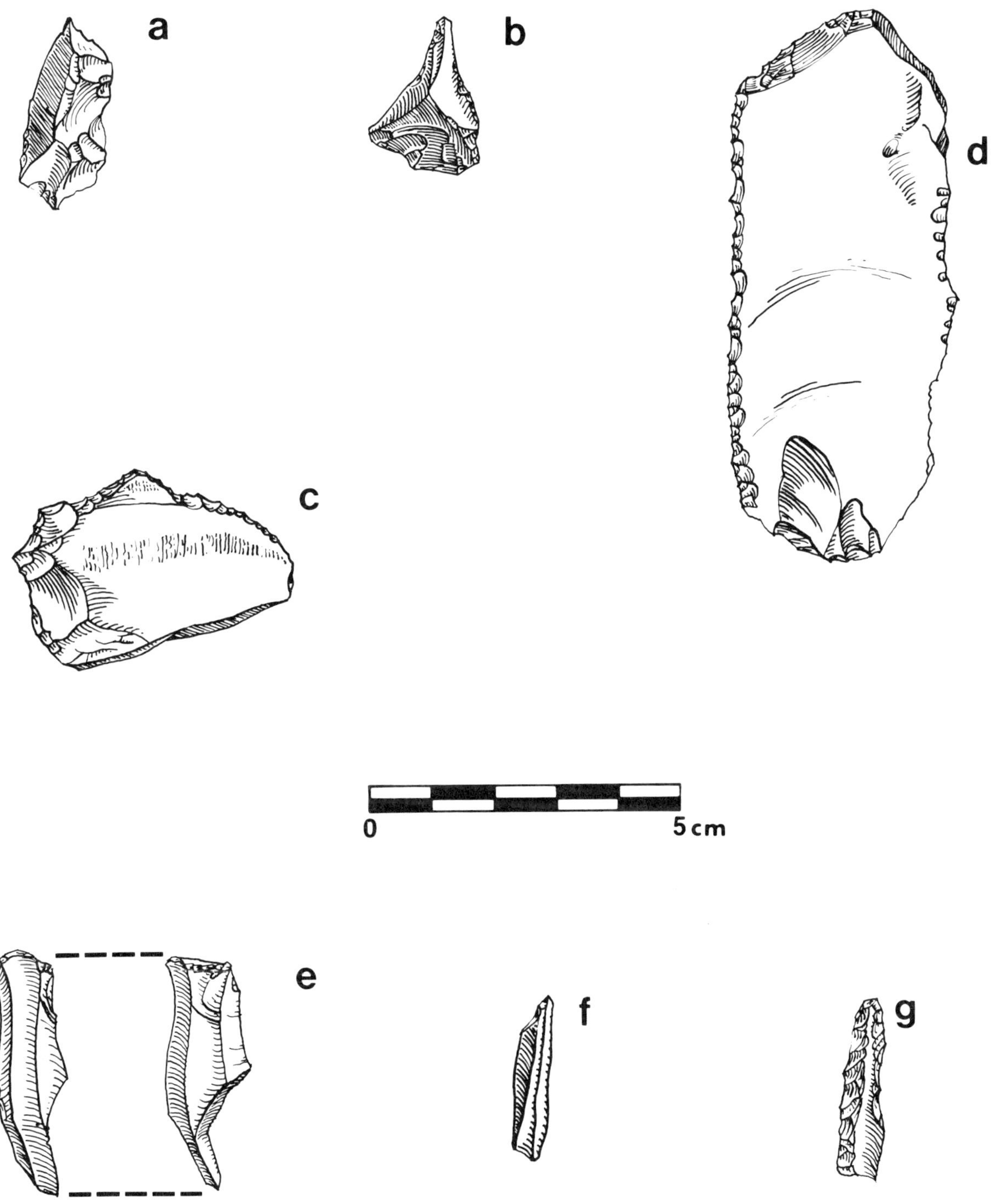

Figure 33. Mississippian Debitage Tools: a-c, flake gravers; d, flake scrapers; e, microdrill core; f-g, microdrills

Table 7. Chert from Mississippian Features (10% Sample) by Type

	Utilized Flakes				Thermally Altered Flakes								Cortical Flakes				Total Flakes	
					Heat-treated				Burned									
Chert Type	N	%	Wt(g)	%	N	%	Wt(g)	%	N	%	Wt(g)	%	N	%	Wt(g)	%	N	Wt(g)
Mill Creek	11	10.4	18.2	22.1	4	3.8	2.1	2.5	2	1.9	2.2	2.7	5	4.7	11.3	13.7	106	82.5
Kaolin	1	50.0	3.5	81.4	1	50.0	0.8	18.6	-	-	-	-	-	-	-	-	2	4.3
Dongola	-	-	-	-	-	-	-	-	1	50.0	0.5	25.0	1	50.0	0.5	25.0	2	2.0
Root Beer	4	36.4	16.6	61.9	3	27.3	6.2	23.1	1	9.1	0.9	3.4	6	54.5	17.0	63.4	11	26.8
Old Blue	3	10.3	7.6	29.2	-	-	-	-	3	10.3	2.7	10.4	4	13.8	15.9	61.2	29	26.0
Fern Glen	1	16.7	2.3	20.0	-	-	-	-	2	33.3	5.8	50.4	-	-	-	-	6	11.5
Grover Gravel	1	100.0	5.7	100.0	-	-	-	-	-	-	-	-	1	100.0	5.7	100.0	1	5.7
Mansker	-	-	-	-	-	-	-	-	-	-	-	-	1	50.0	4.1	95.3	2	4.3
Local	201	35.5	827.5	58.7	320	56.5	743.2	52.7	67	11.8	312.4	22.2	18	3.2	275.6	19.5	566	1409.8
Miscellaneous	73	16.7	365.3	42.9	77	17.6	246.1	28.9	230	52.5	362.7	42.6	32	7.3	112.0	13.1	438	852.4
Total	295	25.4	1246.7	51.4	405	34.8	998.4	41.2	306	26.3	687.2	28.3	68	5.8	442.1	18.2	1163	2425.3

Note: % figures are computed separately for each chert type category and express the quantities (by count and weight) that are utilized, heat-treated, burned, or are cortical flakes.

Table 8. Mississippian Gravers by Chert Type

Chert Type	N	%	Wt(g)	%
Local	9	90.0	34.0	99.0
Miscellaneous	1	10.0	0.5	1.0
Total	10		34.5	

Table 9. Mississippian Polished Flakes by Chert Type

	High Gloss				Low Gloss			
Chert Type	N	%	Wt(g)	%	N	%	Wt(g)	%
Mill Creek	220	69.2	332.1	69.4	102	69.9	241.5	70.0
Kaolin	15	4.7	29.1	6.1	8	5.4	23.9	6.9
Local	80	25.1	111.3	23.3	36	24.7	79.5	23.1
Miscellaneous	3	1.0	6.2	1.2	-	-	-	-
Total	318		478.7		146		344.9	

Table 10. Mississippian Polished Tools and Tool Fragments by Chert Type

	High Gloss				Low Gloss			
Chert Type	N	%	Wt(g)	%	N	%	Wt(g)	%
Mill Creek	30	81.1	7608.4	92.6	14	53.9	1019.0	51.7
Kaolin	2	5.4	375.4	4.6	1	3.8	38.7	2.0
Local	5	13.5	232.3	2.8	11	42.3	913.8	46.3
Total	37		8216.1		26		1971.5	

lens. The high gloss flakes displayed a continuous high sheen across the flake surface, reflected a bright light, and striations were readily recognizable. The low gloss flakes did not exhibit a continuous, polished area, and sheen was absent in deep chert imperfections and flake scars. Overall, low gloss flakes appeared rather dull, and striations were difficult to recognize.

The high gloss flakes were generally easier to recognize macroscopically than those with a low gloss. That was particularly true when the polished area represented only a small proportion of the flake surface. This may have contributed to an underenumeration of small low gloss flakes, seen in Figure 34.

High gloss flakes were undoubtedly derived from excavating tools, the hoes or spades. The bit ends of those tools typically displayed a high siliceous polish that extended several centimeters back from the cutting edge. The low gloss flakes may have been from interior areas of excavating tools, as well as from knives, woodworking tools, or portions of other tools subjected to abrasion, such as hafting areas.

Mill Creek chert dominated both the high and low gloss categories of flakes (Table 9). That pattern was duplicated when high gloss, polished tools and tool fragments were compared (Table 10). The local chert comprised a larger proportion of the total chert in the low gloss category than it did in the high gloss category.

Excavating Tools

Twelve complete excavating tools and 42 fragments were recovered from Mississippian features. Excavating tools are often referred to as hoes and spades. Mill Creek chert was the predominate material utilized for these tools (Table 11). This thin, tabular chert naturally lends itself to the manufacture of large stone tools. A specimen from Feature 246, weighing 1417.0 g, was, in fact, the largest tool in the Mississippian assemblage. Portions of the easily recognized cortex characteristic of Mill Creek chert were present on both sides of four of the seven complete Mill Creek chert tools identified. Only one tool was completely devoid of cortex on both surfaces.

The excavating tools were plano-convex in longitudinal section (Figure 36). The bit ends tended to be broad, sometimes flared, while the poll ends were narrow. The wide ends were usually polished to a high sheen, and the cutting edges were worn and rounded. The poll ends occasionally were battered, with large flakes removed; when polished, they did not display the extreme shine that was characteristic of the bit ends.

The tools were divided into five morphological types (Table 12). The function of Types 1, 2, and 3 as digging tools was clear; the other two tool categories may have been used for some other purpose. The

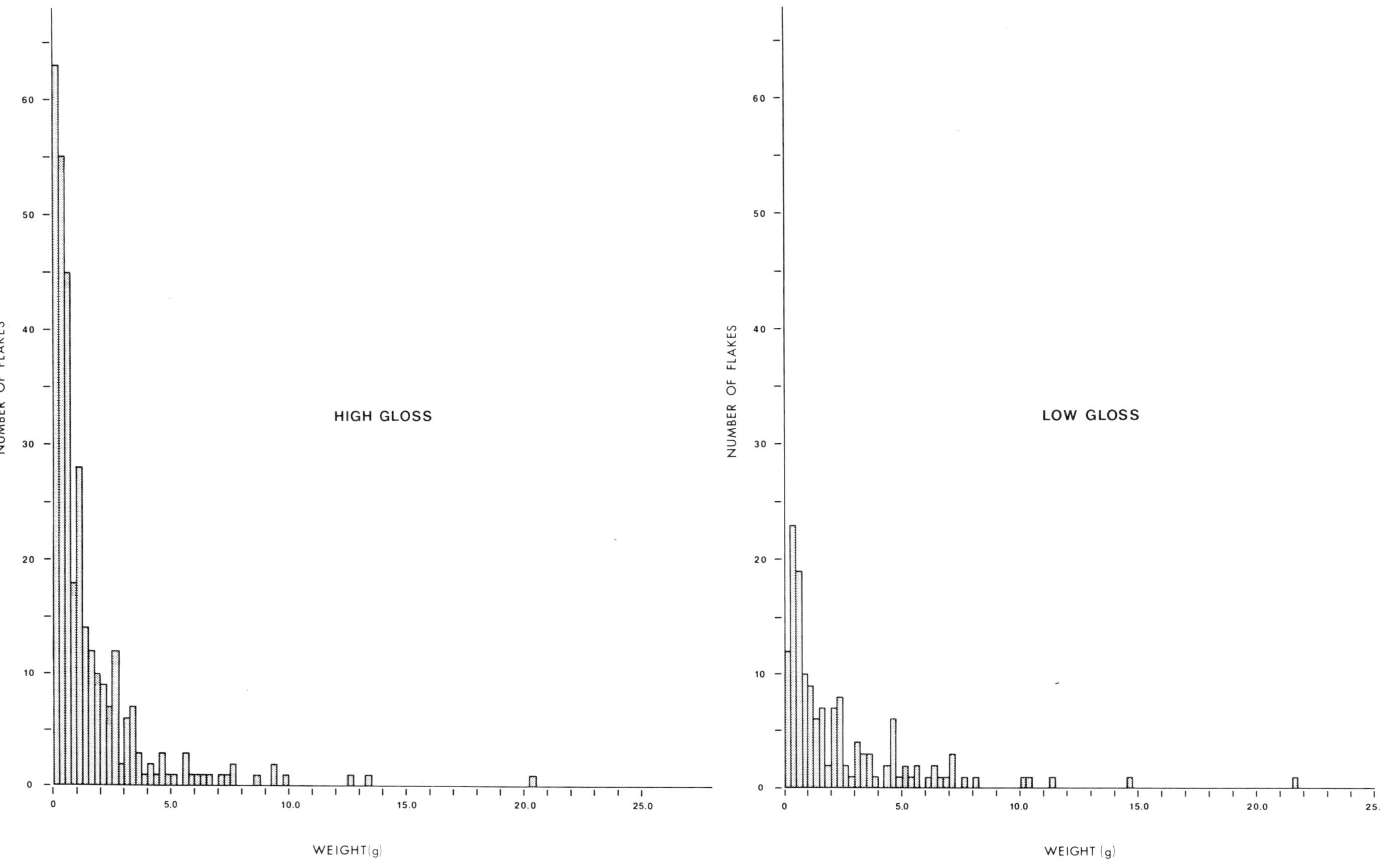

Figure 34. Mississippian High and Low Gloss Polished Flakes, Distributed by Weight

Table 11. Mississippian Excavating Tool Types by Raw Material

	Type 1				Type 2				Type 3		Type 4		Type 5		Misc.					
	Whole		Fragments		Whole		Fragments		Whole		Fragments		Whole		Fragments		Total			
Material	N	Wt(g)	N	Wt(g)	N	Wt(g)	N	Wt(g)	N	Wt(g)	N	Wt(g)	N	Wt(g)	N	Wt(g)	N	%	Wt(g)	%
Mill Creek Chert	6	3279.2	2	475.8	1	1417.0	2	986.9	-	-	2	199.7	-	-	26	1825.5	39	72.2	8184.1	75.1
Kaolin Chert	-	-	-	-	-	-	-	-	1	323.5	-	-	-	-	2	90.9	3	5.6	414.4	3.8
Local Chert	-	-	-	-	1	370.0	-	-	-	-	1	145.0	1	240.5	3	75.8	6	11.1	831.3	7.6
Miscellaneous Chert	-	-	-	-	-	-	-	-	-	-	-	-	1	277.4	1	60.1	2	3.7	337.5	3.1
Limestone	1	372.5	-	-	-	-	-	-	-	-	-	-	-	-	3	758.2	4	7.4	1130.7	10.4
Total	7	3651.7	2	475.8	2	1787.0	2	986.9	1	323.5	3	344.7	2	517.9	35	2810.5	54		10898.0	

Table 12. Mississippian Excavating Tool Morphology

Tool Type	Length (cm) N	Mean	s	Width (cm) N	Mean	s	Weight (g) N	Mean	s
1	7	20.7	2.9	8	11.8	1.1	7	521.8	115.5
2	2	26.3	-	4	10.5	-	2	893.5	-
3	1	13.5	-	1	11.9	-	1	323.5	-
4	-	-	-	2	6.9	-	-	-	-
5	2	14.1	-	2	6.4	-	2	259.0	-

Note: Standard deviation calculated if five or more specimens are present.

Table 13. Excavating Tools from Mississippian External Pits and Structures with Associated Pits

	Whole				Fragments				Total			
	N	%	Wt(g)	%	N	%	Wt(g)	%	N	%	Wt(g)	%
Structures with Associated Pits	9	75.0	4213.2	67.1	33	78.6	3800.4	82.3	42	77.7	8013.6	73.5
External Pits	3	25.0	2066.9	32.9	9	21.4	817.5	17.7	12	22.3	2884.4	26.5
Total	12		6280.1		42		4617.9		54		10898.0	

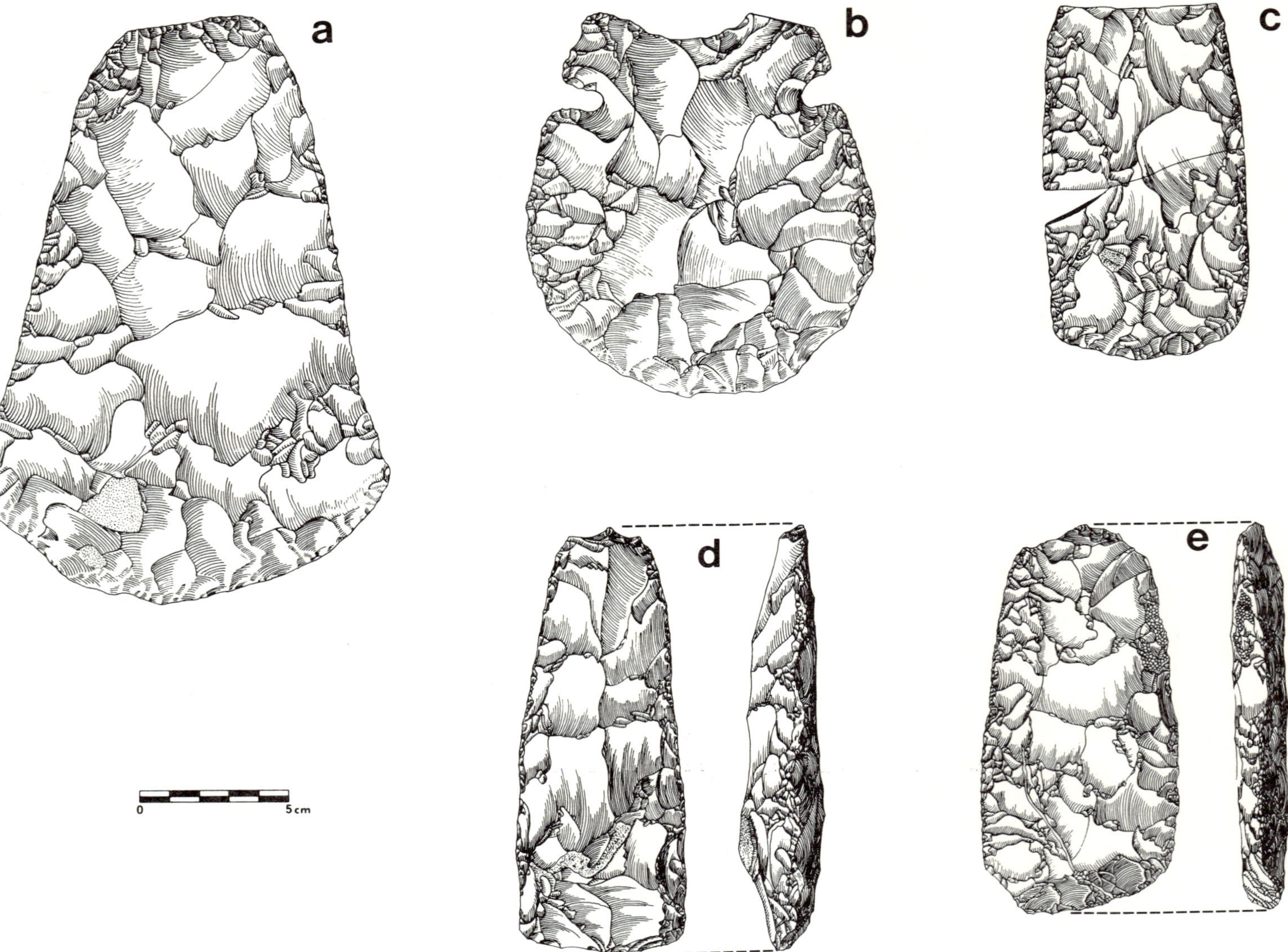

Figure 35. Mississippian Excavating Tools: a, Type 1; b, Type 3; c, Type 4 fragment; d-e, Type 5

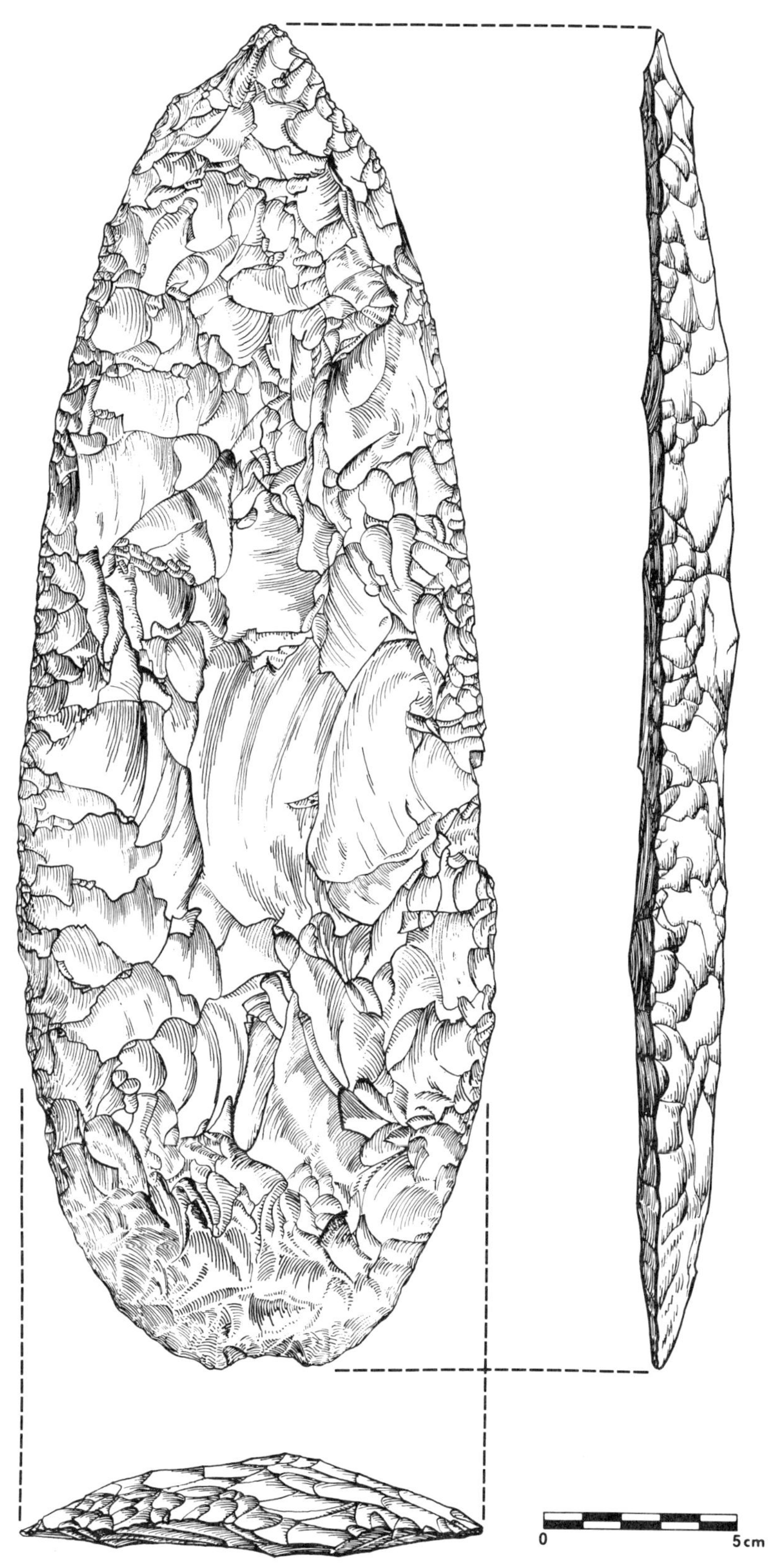

Figure 36. Mississippian Excavating Tool, Type 2

distinctive morphology of Types 1, 2, and 3, as well as their use as general purpose excavating tools have been recognized by archaeologists since the late nineteenth century (Rau 1876).

The Type 1 category comprised the largest number of tools. These tools were distinguished by flared bits and incurving sides (Figure 35). All of the complete Mill Creek chert Type 1 tools were recovered from two internal pits of Feature 2, a structure.

The Type 2 category included two whole tools and two fragments. These tools were oval with bit ends that were somewhat broader than their proximal ends. The widest point of the tools was off-center and located toward the larger of the two ends. The largest chert tool at the site was included in this category. Both ends of that specimen exhibited a high polish (Figure 36).

The Type 3 category included a single complete specimen of Kaolin chert (Figure 35). The bit end was curved and the other end was notched. The notching suggested a different hafting technique than that used for the larger Type 1 and Type 2 tools. The notching may reflect a need to haft a tool made from a small piece of chert. For example, one of the broken, oval, Type 2 excavating tools exhibited sides that had been reworked to form opposing, irregular, and shallow hafting notches. The Kaolin notched tool came from a wall trench in Feature 215.

The Type 4 tool category was represented by three chert fragments, two of which fit together. Both artifacts were narrow and had slightly convex bit ends with angular margins. The tool represented by two fragments was found in a wall trench of Feature 7, lying on top of a chert core (Figure 35). The other artifact was also found in Feature 7 but in basin fill.

The Type 5 category was represented by two complete specimens. That type had relatively straight sides with bits reworked by steep retouching (Figure 35). Except for the retouching, they were similar to Type 4 tools. One of the Type 5 tools was heavily battered along its sides. Although relatively large and resembling in many respects the other excavating tools, the Type 5 tools could have been used for working a material such as wood, rather than soil. The high degree of polish often found on the other tools was not present on the two Type 5 specimens.

Most of the whole tools (75.0%) and tool fragments (78.6%) were recovered from structures or from their internal features (Table 13). In fact, Feature 187, a pit within structure Feature 2, contained four complete Type 1 tools and a broken Type 2 tool (Plate 4). The large number of excavating tools from structure-related contexts may have resulted from caching these presumably highly valued tools and large broken fragments.

There was a near perfect segregation of excavating tool types among the various structures. This was particularly apparent in the Feature 187 cache where there were four complete Type 1 tools and only one broken tool of another type. The significance of this distributional pattern was not determined, although it may reflect differential access at various times during the Mississippian period to groups of specialists who manufactured only one style of excavating tool.

Celts and Adze

Celts, celt fragments, and one adze had all been fashioned from ground stone. Chips of polished ground stone, presumably derived from similar artifacts, are also listed in Table 14 with the ground stone tools.

The celt and adze tool classes closely approximate standard type definitions (Figure 37). The Julien site celts were bilaterally symmetric in both longitudinal sections. Polished, somewhat laterally flared and relatively sharp cutting edges were found at the bit ends. Poll ends tapered slightly to rough and blunt ends. One of the celts displayed a shallow groove that had been cut across the side closest to the bit edge. The significance of this groove remains unknown. The adze was asymmetric along the longitudinal section perpendicular to the cutting edge. One of the opposing surfaces was flat, while the other was convex. The bit had been fashioned into a polished, sharp cutting edge; the opposite end was blunt and rough.

Two small, celt-like artifacts were polished over their entire surfaces; presumably, these were not utilitarian objects. One had been the poll end of a celt; it was recovered from Feature 208. A miniature celt weighing 153 g was found in Feature 9. In addition to being highly polished, this small celt had numerous fine scratches distributed over its entire surface. The marks were concentrated near the bit end where they primarily were oriented parallel to the cutting edge. The marks presumably were a by-product of the polishing process.

Knives

Large, bifacial specimens called knives were finely worked, elongated artifacts with tapered ends (Figure 39). The proximal ends were blunt, while the distal ends, unless broken, tended to be pointed and sharp. The maximum widths of these artifacts were located at their midpoints or toward their distal ends. Two dimensions of shape (length and width) strongly (r=0.94) covaried (Table 15 and Figure 38). On one knife fragment, the entire surface was polished; this polish may indicate that the knife was kept in some sort of wrapping. The knives correspond to the artifact form locally known as the Ramey knife.

Mill Creek and local chert varieties were usually employed in manufacturing the Julien site knives (Table 16). Kaolin chert,

Table 14. Mississippian Celts and Adze

	Celts	Adze	Celt Fragments	Other Ground Stone Fragments	Total
N	3	1	4	4	12
Wt(g)	1091.3	608.4	944.2	22.7	2666.6

Table 15. Mississippian Knife Morphology (N=6)

	Length (cm)	Maximum Width (cm)	Weight (g)
Mean	16.68	5.17	111.43
s	1.74	0.50	26.09

Table 16. Mississippian Knives by Raw Material

	Knives				Knife Fragments				Combined Total			
Chert Type	N	%	Wt(g)	%	N	%	Wt(g)	%	N	%	Wt(g)	%
Mill Creek	2	33.3	231.8	34.7	6	100.0	176.5	100.0	8	66.7	408.3	48.3
Kaolin	1	16.7	129.6	19.4	-	-	-	-	1	8.3	129.6	15.3
Local	3	50.0	307.2	45.9	-	-	-	-	3	25.0	307.2	36.4
Totals	6		668.6		6		176.5		12		845.1	

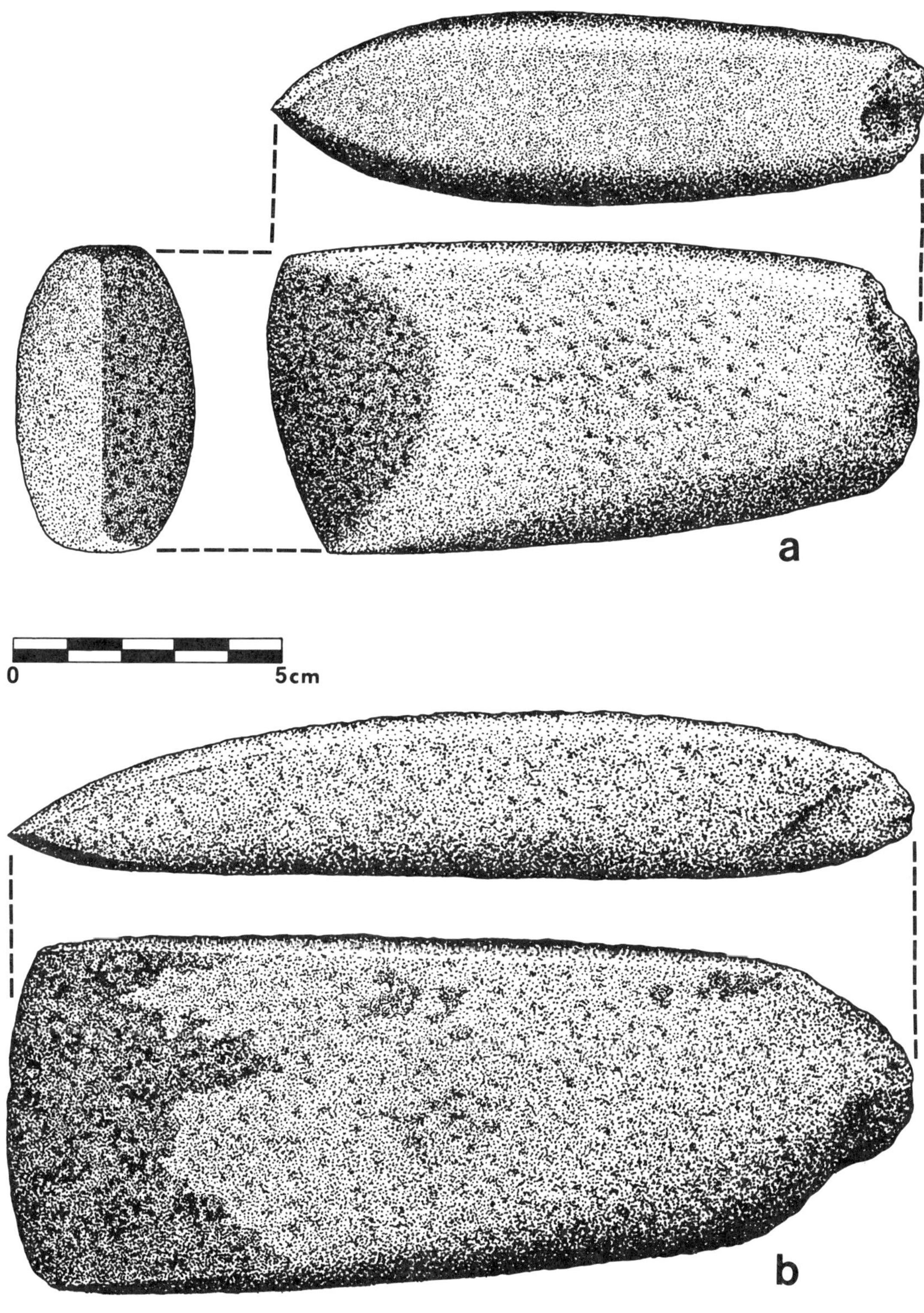

Figure 37. Mississippian Lithics: a, celt; b, adze

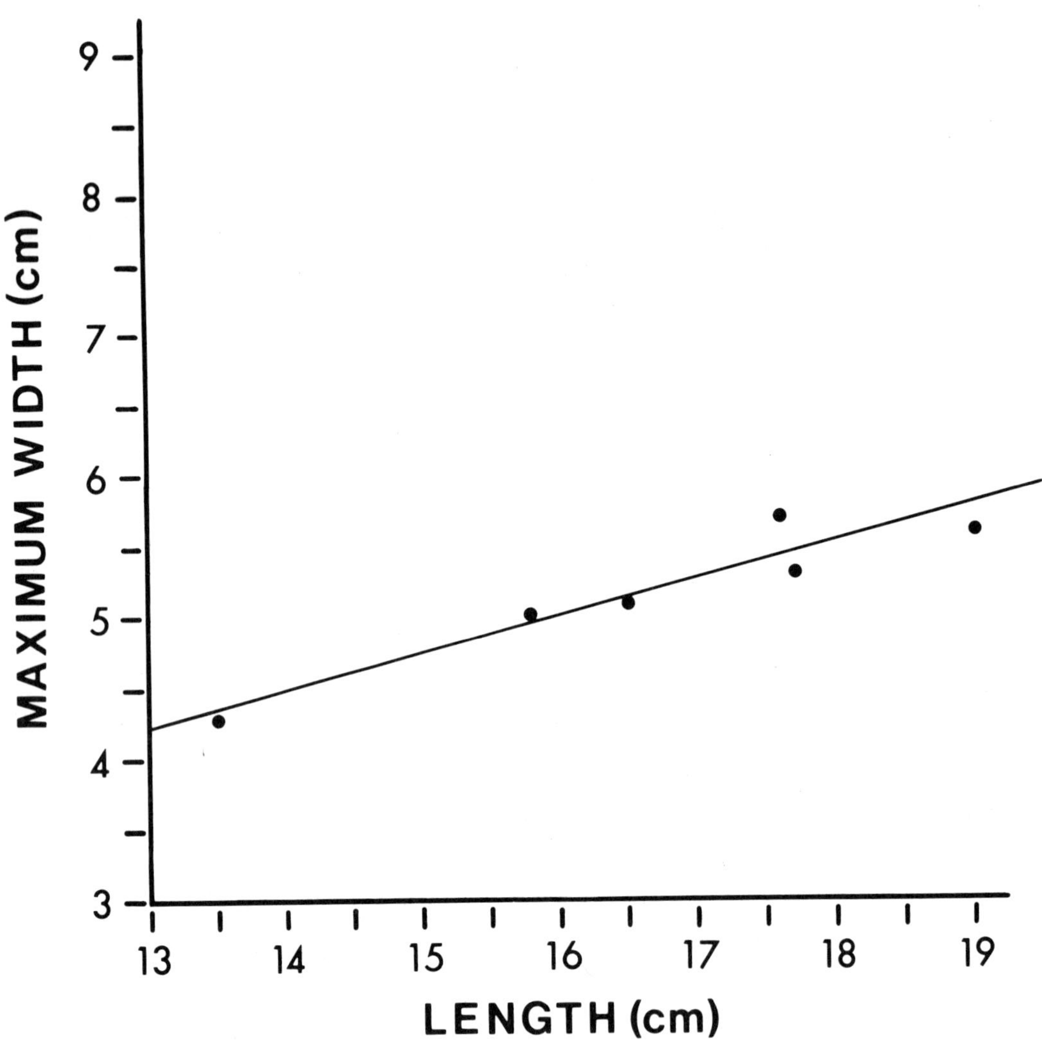

Figure 38. Mississippian Knife Morphology

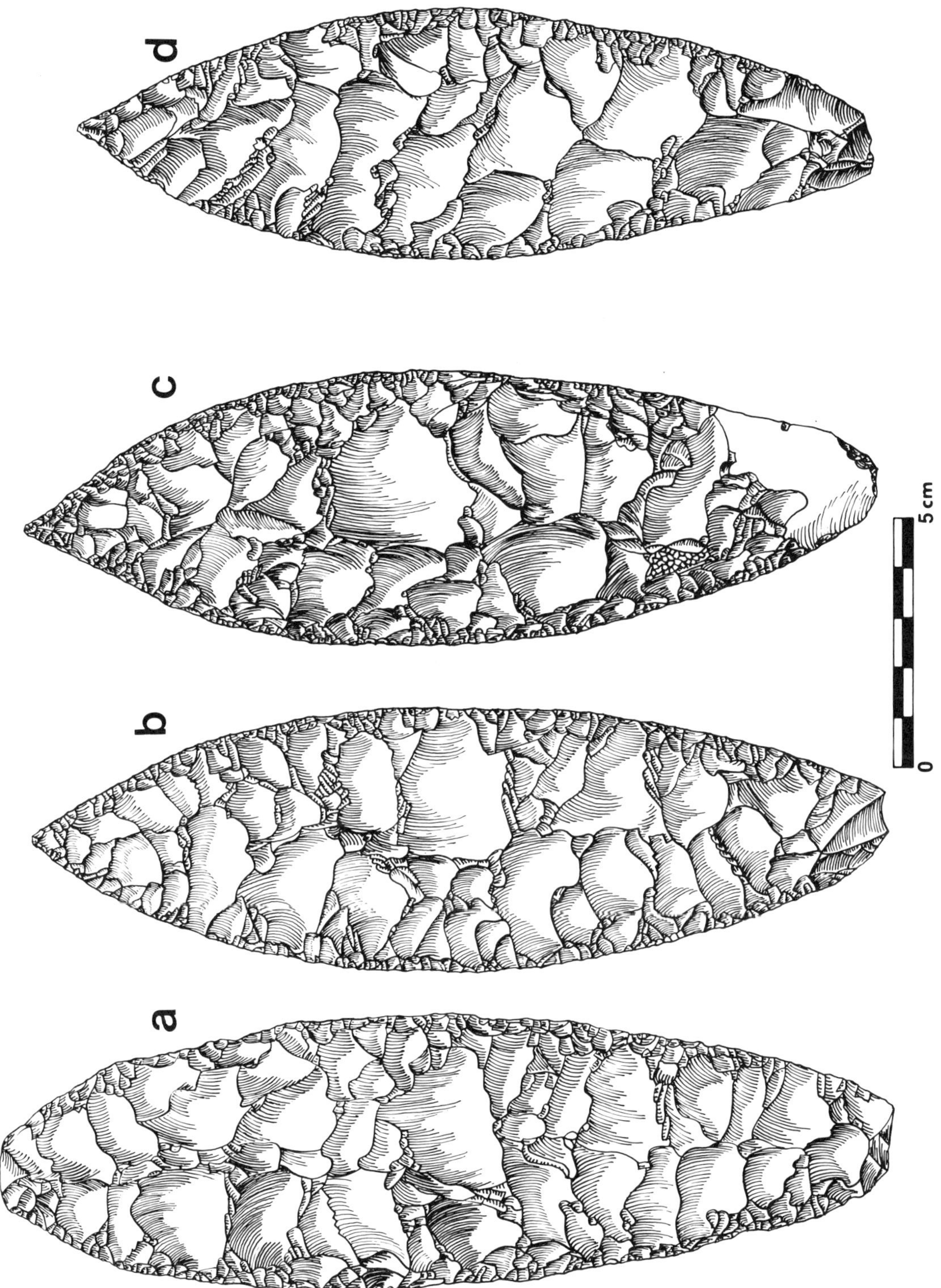

Figure 39. Mississippian Knives from Feature 2 Cache

represented by a single knife, was rarely used as a raw material. Four of the six whole knives were found in a single cache of artifacts in Feature 2, a structure. Two of the knives in that cache had been fashioned from Mill Creek chert, the other two from the local white chert.

Projectile Points

Two major classes of projectile points were recovered from Mississippian features: large, bifacially worked points reminiscent of "earlier" point styles; and small Mississippian point forms. The large, bifacial points were usually broken; they probably represent accidental inclusions in later features or the opportunistic reuse of tools that had been found by Mississippian period Indians. Mississippian points were generally small, isosceles triangles that were often modified by corner or side notching.

Five fragmentary, expanding-stemmed projectile points were present in the collection (Table 17). One of these specimens had been reworked, apparently for use as a scraper (Figure 40). This tool was 2.3 cm long and 2.1 cm wide. There were three contracting stemmed projectile point bases and one complete point (Table 17). The contracting stemmed point was 5.9 cm long and 3.3 cm wide (Figure 40). An additional point with a concave base and basal grinding was recovered that may have been reused, perhaps as a perforating tool (Figure 40). That point was 5.5 cm long and 2.7 cm wide.

The features yielded 153 complete and fragmentary Mississippian projectile points. These points displayed certain attributes of shape that permitted separation into nine distinctive varieties. The differences in these points were little more than variations on a basic triangular theme. For descriptive purposes the nine types represent an adequate partitioning of a form continuum; for other research purposes, different categories might be desired. For example, it would be possible to further subdivide the numerous and variably shaped Type 2 points into additional categories. Alternatively, side-notched varieties distinguished as separate types might be combined into an all-encompassing, and very heterogeneous, supercategory. Membership within a category merely implies a shared set of characteristics considered to be distinctive and possessed by some, but not all, of the points in a category.

The techniques employed to manufacture Mississippian points ranged from modest chipping of a flake edge to extensive bifacial working of all point surfaces. The points in the nine categories were subdivided into a "flake" variant, when 50% or more of either the dorsal or ventral surfaces remained unmodified by retouching, and a more heavily worked "bifacial" variant. Most of the types were represented by both bifacial and flake points (Table 18). Generally, flake points appear as poorly worked versions of the bifacial varieties. Specimens conforming to the

Table 17. Large, Bifacially Worked Projectile Points from Mississippian Features by Chert Type

	Contracting-stemmed				Expanding-stemmed							
	Whole		Fragments		Fragments		Miscellaneous		Total			
Chert Type	N	Wt(g)	N	Wt(g)	N	Wt(g)	N	Wt(g)	N	%	Wt(g)	%
Dongola	-	-	-	-	1	5.1	-	-	1	10.0	5.1	6.9
Local	-	-	1	6.3	2	5.7	-	-	3	30.0	12.0	16.2
Miscellaneous	1	14.8	2	18.1	2	7.9	1	16.1	6	60.0	56.9	76.9
Total	1	14.8	3	24.4	5	18.7	1	16.1	10		74.0	

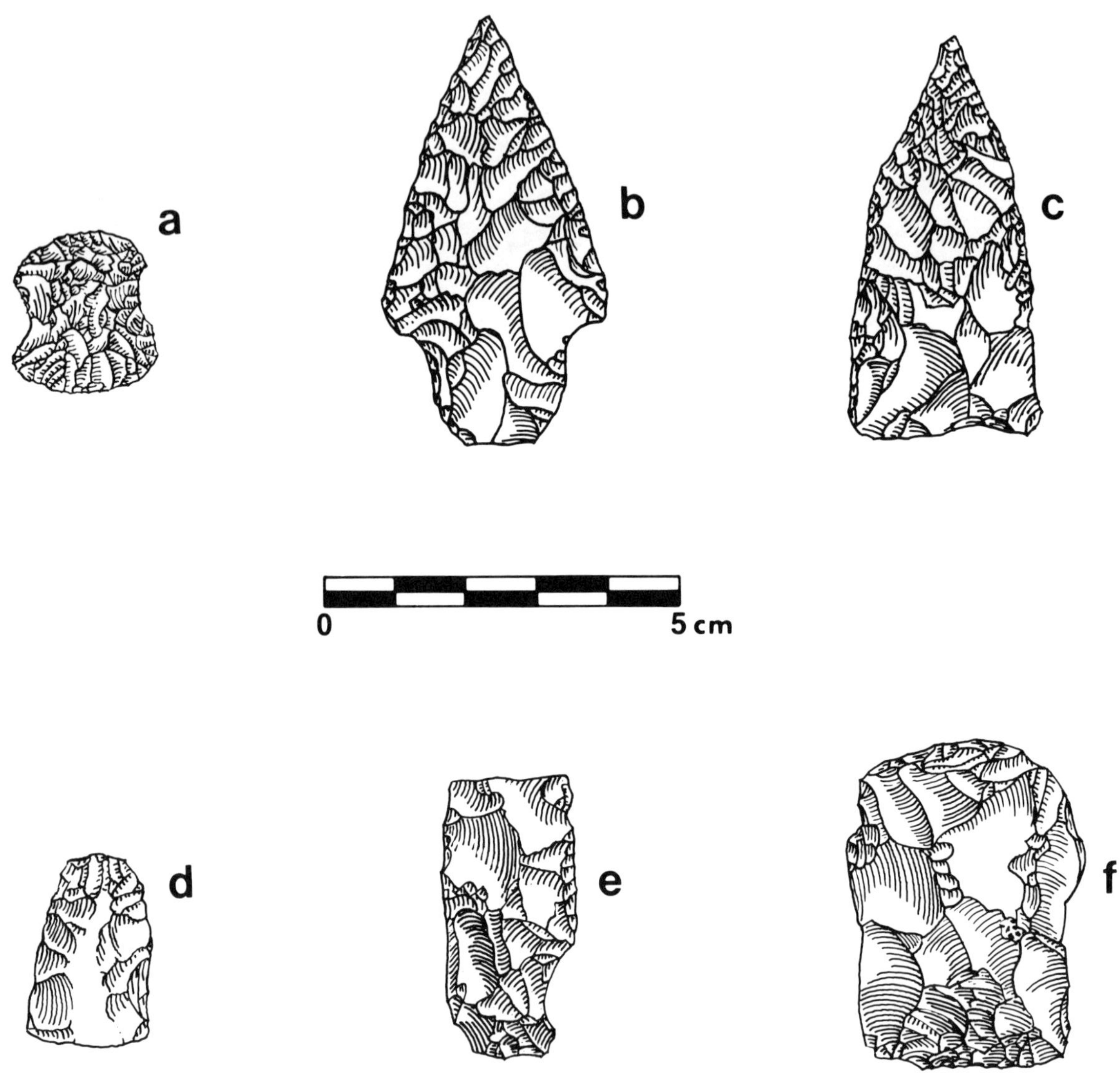

Figure 40. Mississippian Lithics: a, reworked point scraper; b, contracting-stemmed point; c, reworked point perforator; d, polished tool; e, spokeshave; f, wedge

nine point categories as well as the flake and bifacial point variants are illustrated in Figures 41, 42, and 43; point characteristics are listed in Tables 19 and 20.

Table 18. Small Mississippian Point Types Occurring as Flake Points and as Bifacially Worked Points

	Point Types								
	1	2	3	4	5	6	7	8	9
Flake Points	+	+	+	-	+	+	+	+	+
Bifacially Worked Points	+	+	+	+	+	-	-	+	+

Key
+ indicates presence
- indicates absence

The Type 1 point form displayed a conspicuous, expanding stem where flakes had been removed from basal corners. These points tended to be long in relation to their width.

Type 2 points were essentially triangular with shallow notches produced by retouching on their sides near their bases. The bases of these points were flat or slightly convex; the convex bases were probably attributable to manufacturing accidents rather than to design. The length/width ratio distribution was skewed to the right (Figure 44). Individual flake points occasionally displayed remarkable bilateral asymmetry. One of nine bifacially worked points had been rubbed with a red pigment, presumably hematite or bauxite (Figure 45). This point was from Feature 295.

The Type 3 point form was similar to the Type 2 point form, except that its base was somewhat concave. Apparently, the basal portions were intentionally thinned by the removal of flakes.

Points in the Type 4 category were trinotched. Notches were found in the two long sides near the basal end; a third was present in the base. One of the Type 4 points, from structure Feature 31, was

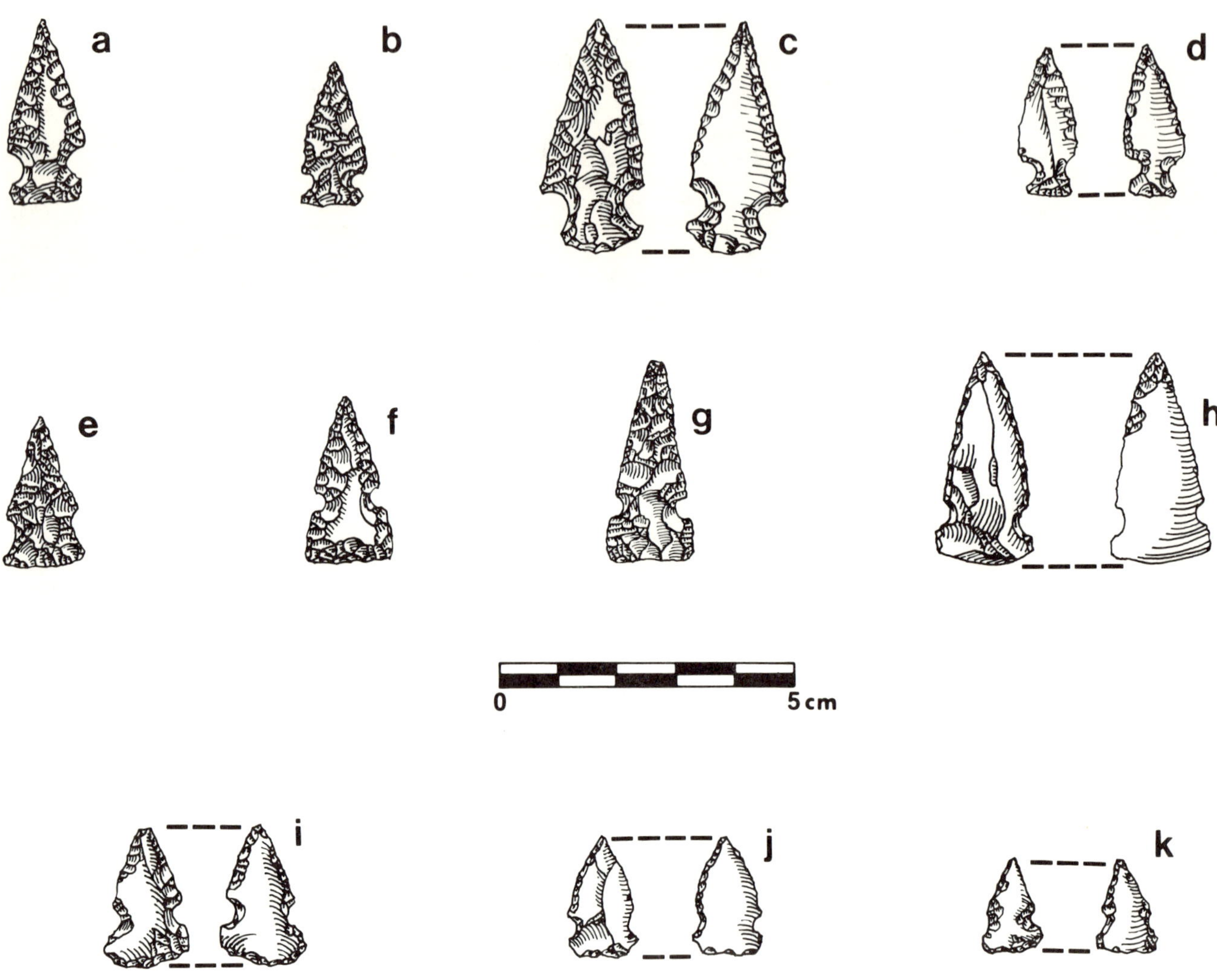

Figure 41. Mississippian Projectile Points: a-b, Type 1 bifacial points; c-d, Type 1 flake points; e-g, Type 2 bifacial points; h-k, Type 2 flake points

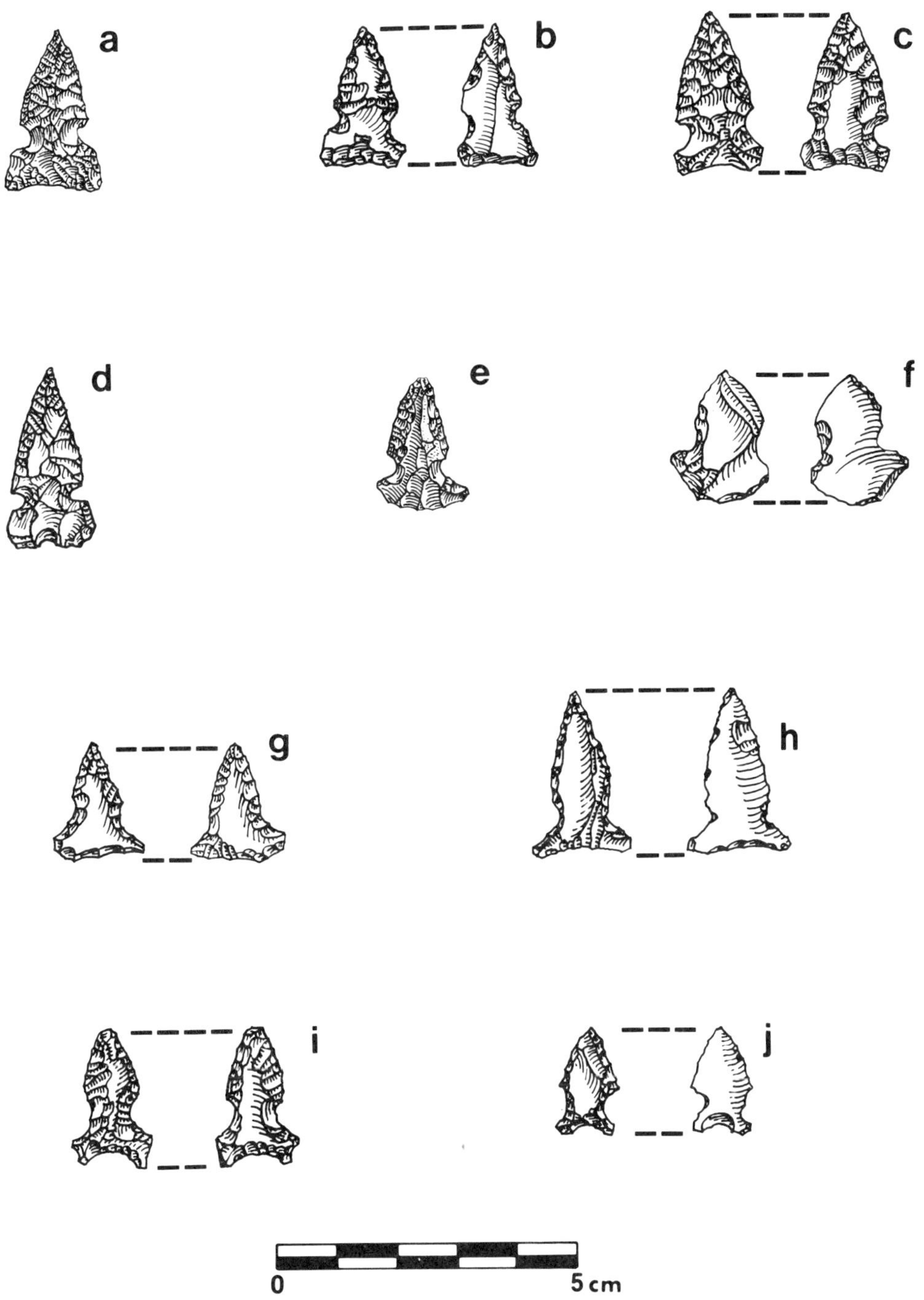

Figure 42. Mississippian Projectile Points: a, Type 3 bifacial point; b-c, Type 3 flake points; d, Type 4 bifacial point; e, Type 5 bifacial point; f-g, Type 5 flake points, h-j, Type 6 flake points

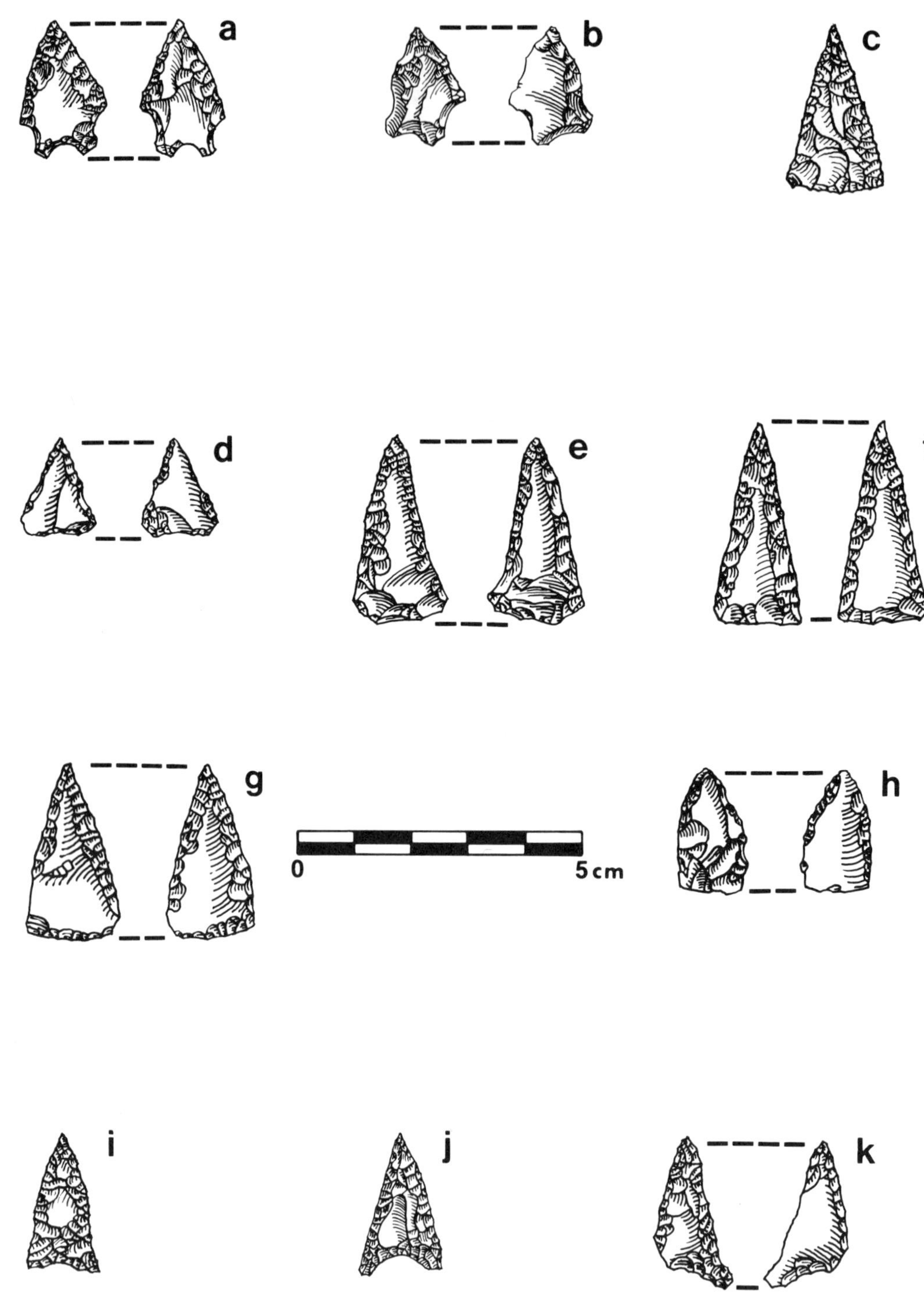

Figure 43. Mississippian Projectile Points: a-b, Type 7 flake points; c, Type 8 bifacial point; d-h, Type 8 flake points; i-j, Type 9 bifacial points; k, Type 9 flake point

Table 19. Small Mississippian Bifacial Points

					Length (cm)		Width (cm)		Weight (g)		
Point Type	N	%	Wt(g)	%	Mean	s	Mean	s	Mean	s	r*
1	3	12.0	3.7	9.3	2.71	-	1.21	-	0.95	-	-
2	9	36.0	12.7	31.8	2.96	0.51	1.52	0.16	1.41	0.33	0.64
3	1	4.0	1.1	2.8	2.61	-	1.61	-	1.10	-	-
4+	2	8.0	11.6	29.0	7.70	-	2.43	-	10.50	-	-
					2.96	-	1.53	-	1.10	-	-
5	2	8.0	1.4	3.5	2.15	-	1.35	-	0.70	-	-
8	4	16.0	6.4	16.0	3.05	-	1.55	-	1.60	-	-
9	2	8.0	2.0	5.0	2.39	-	1.64	-	1.00	-	-
Fragments	2	8.0	1.1	2.8							
Total	25		40.0								

+ Dimensions of the two Type 4 points are listed separately.

* Correlation coefficient (r) measures the point length and width association.

Table 20. Small Mississippian Flake Points

Point Type	N	%	Wt(g)	%	Length (cm) Mean	s	Width (cm) Mean	s	Weight (g) Mean	s	r*
1	7	5.5	10.6	9.0	2.71	0.70	1.42	0.27	1.51	1.09	.883
2	65	50.8	49.1	41.5	2.15	0.41	1.21	0.20	0.76	0.42	.610
3	7	5.5	8.5	7.2	2.53	0.44	1.32	0.16	1.21	0.67	.518
5	5	3.9	4.2	3.6	1.92	0.48	1.65	-	0.84	0.44	-
6	7	5.5	6.8	5.8	1.93	0.46	1.36	0.22	0.97	0.50	.535
7	2	1.6	2.9	2.5	2.02	-	1.46	-	1.45	-	-
8	22	17.2	21.1	17.9	2.26	0.55	1.31	0.23	0.96	0.55	.530
9	2	1.6	2.2	1.9	2.44	-	1.48	-	1.00	-	-
Fragments	11	8.6	12.8	10.8							
Total	128		118.2								

* Correlation coefficient (r) measures the point length and width association.

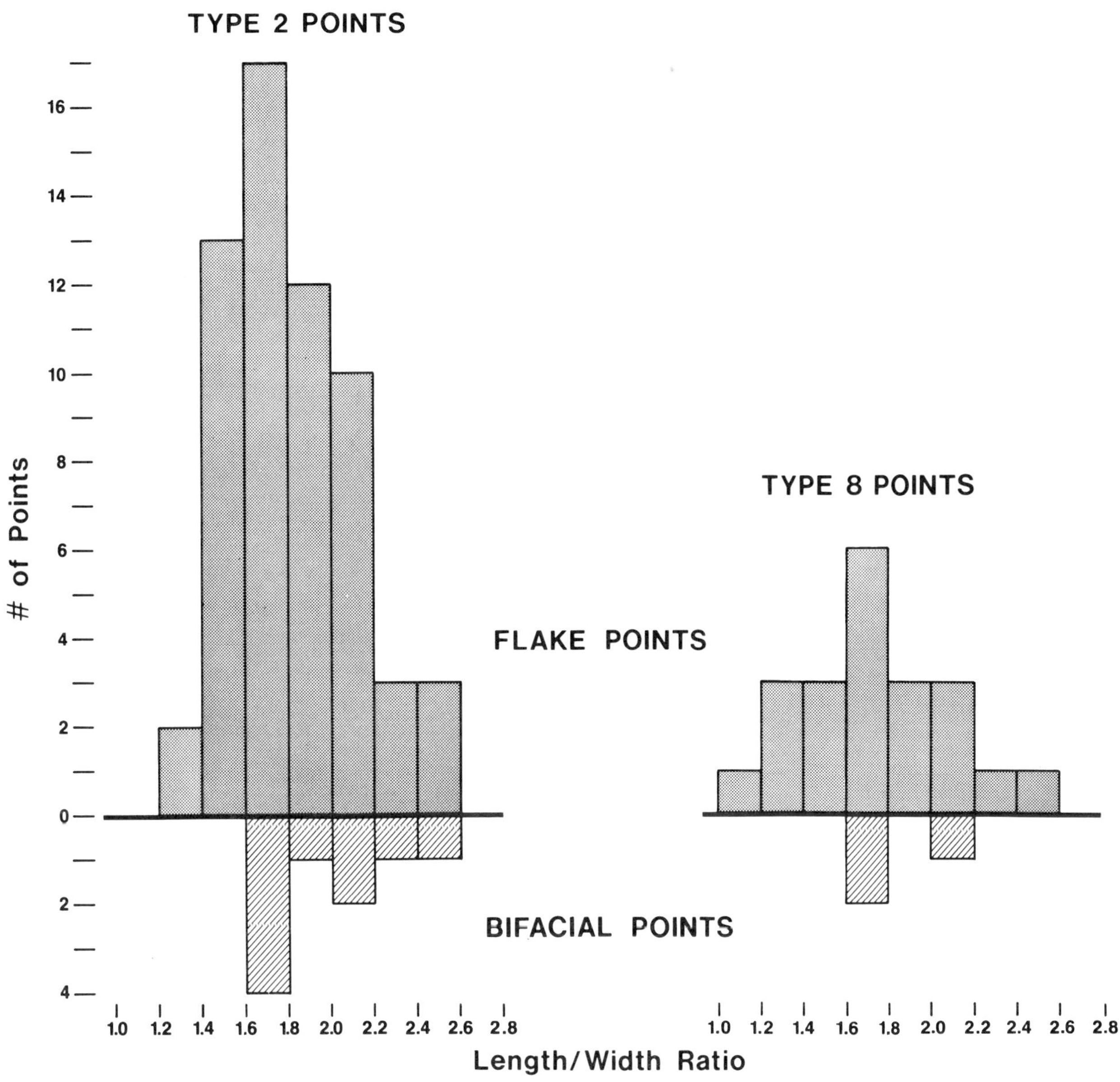

Figure 44. Mississippian Projectile Points: Length/Width Ratio of Types 2 and 8

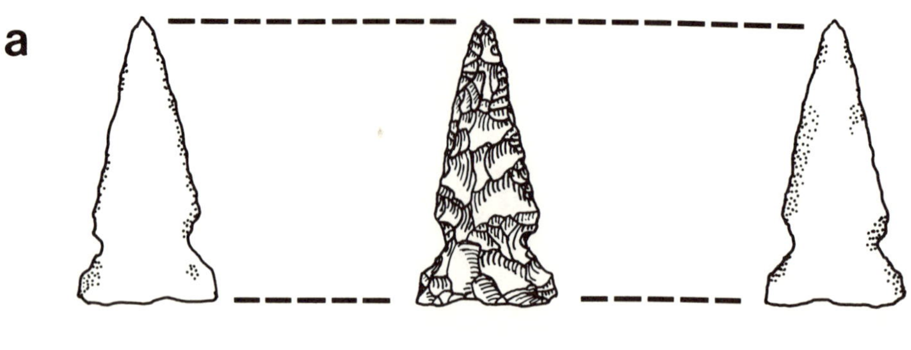

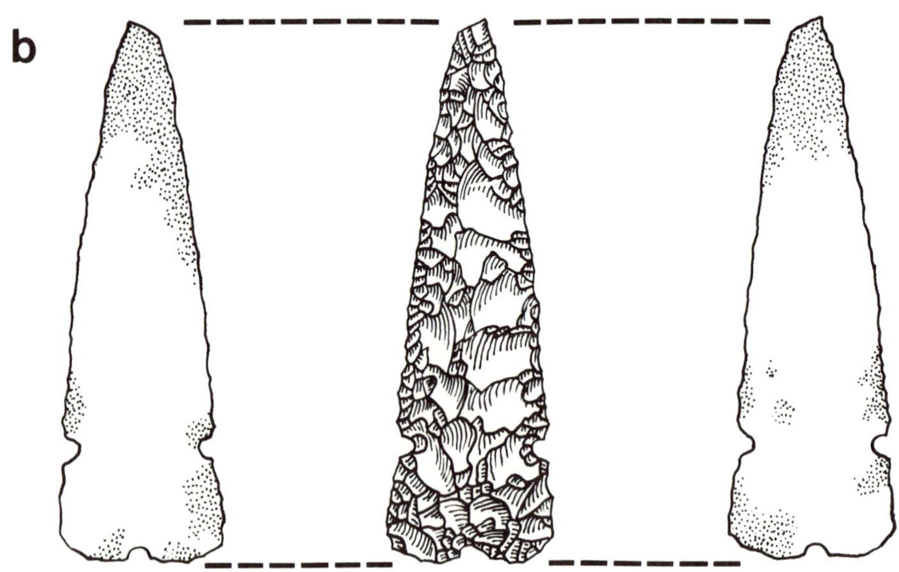

Figure 45. Mississippian Projectile Points with Red Pigment: a, Type 2 bifacial point from Feature 295; b, Type 4 bifacial point from Feature 31

exceptionally large. It was one of only two points in the collection that was covered with a red pigment (Figure 45).

The Type 5 point form was side notched with a lateral extension of the base that projected far beyond the maximum width of the blade. The bases of these points were flat or slightly convex.

The Type 6 point form had a decidedly concave base. Otherwise, it was similar to the Type 5 point form.

Type 7 points were corner-notched with distinctive, concave bases. The bases were so incurved that their lateral margins were unusually conspicuous.

Type 8 points were triangular and lacked modifying hafting or decorative notches. The points ranged from equilateral to isosceles triangles. The distribution of their length/width ratios approximates a normal distribution (Figure 44).

Type 9 points resemble Type 8 points in most respects. However, they have distinctly concave bases.

The flake and bifacial points within each type displayed remarkable similarities in gross morphology; however, their mean dimensions were sometimes different (Tables 19 and 20). Sample sizes were too small to examine dimension inequalities between the flake and bifacial manufacturing categories of all but the Type 2 points. When subdivided by manufacturing technique, the mean lengths and widths of the Type 2 points were found to be significantly different (length, df=71, $p <.001$; width, df=68, $p <.001$) [t-tests calculated by SPSS subprograms (Nie et al. 1975)]. Bifacial points of the Type 2 variant were generally longer and broader than their flake point counterparts.

It is apparent from the summary figures in Tables 19 and 20 that the sizes of the flake points within each of the nine morphological types varied considerably. In addition, the length and width ratios for flake points were not uniform. Of the flake points with sample sizes large enough for comparison, only the stemmed Type 1 variety exhibited a relatively strong measure of association. That lack of uniformity supports the general impression that flake points were the result of inconsistent and relatively crude workmanship where irregularly shaped flakes were used. Frequently, the chert was of poor quality; also, a broad range of chert varieties were used for point manufacture (Table 21). In addition, three flake projectile points were fashioned from polished flakes that originally were from much larger tools, such as hoes. Evidently, the raw materials and the particular flakes used in manufacturing flake points were relatively unimportant. Yet the differences noted in size and shape do not necessarily imply that these points were any less effective as projectile points.

While the small Mississippian flake and bifacially worked projectile

Table 21. Small Mississippian Projectile Points and Fragments by Chert Type

	Bifacial Points				Flake Points			
Chert Type	N	%	Wt(g)	%	N	%	Wt(g)	%
Mill Creek	2	8.0	2.7	6.8	1	0.8	1.0	0.8
Kaolin	-	-	-	-	2	1.6	1.5	1.3
Dongola	4	16.0	4.2	10.5	3	2.3	3.5	3.0
Root Beer	-	-	-	-	7	5.5	9.2	7.8
Old Blue	-	-	-	-	4	3.1	2.9	2.5
Local	11	44.0	22.0	55.0	68	53.1	66.5	56.3
Miscellaneous	8	32.0	11.1	27.8	43	33.6	33.6	28.4
Total	25		40.0		128		118.2	

points could be divided into numerous categories of varying levels of inclusiveness, the importance of such morphological categories derives from their functional or stylistic meaning in terms of past cultural systems. It is doubtful that the variations described here in projectile point morphology represent significant functional differences or improvements from one type to the next. These variations may instead reflect the generally poor quality of the chert used for manufacturing points, or, perhaps, the passing whims of the knappers.

The distributions of the nine point types did not coincide well with those of individual features or feature complexes (Table 22). In fact, eight of the nine types were represented among 80 projectile points that were recovered from a single structure (Feature 31) and its associated internal features. As many as 72 points were found distributed throughout the fill of one of those internal features (Feature 50).

The sheer number of points in Feature 31 and its associated features is perhaps significant. The unusual nature of this structure was previously discussed; presumably it served as some sort of public facility. The numerous projectile points may relate to its special function, perhaps as a men's house.

Only one point style, Type 9, may have some temporal significance. Several of the features where these points occurred were associated with the later Mississippian occupation of the site, including structure Features 2, 3, and 17. However, the stemmed Type 1 points were also associated with the later structures, and they are commonly referred to as "Late Woodland" forms.

It is difficult to imagine that another classificatory scheme would better differentiate the variability in the Julien site projectile point series and permit a closer approximation to archaeologically significant units, i.e., complexes of spatially discrete features. The various projectile points, whether stemmed, side-notched, or triangular, simply seemed to be scattered throughout the spatial and temporal dimensions of the Mississippian occupation at the Julien site.

Perforators

Thirty-eight perforators, used as awls and drills, were recovered from Mississippian features (Table 23). Utilization damage suggested that these tools were used with a rotatory motion. The majority (33 specimens) had been fashioned from chert flakes with one or more edges shaped through minimal retouching into points (Figure 46). The working points were variably shaped, with tips ranging from sharp to blunt. Bifacially worked perforators include the specimen illustrated in Figure 46; a base fragment and three midsections were also bifacially worked.

Table 22. Provenience of Small Mississippian Projectile Points Listed by Structure Associated Context

	Point Types																	
	1		2		3		4		5		6		7		8		9	
Structure	N	%	N	%	N	%	N	%	N	%	N	%	N	%	N	%	N	%
2	2	28.6	2	28.6	-	-	-	-	-	-	-	-	-	-	2	28.6	1	14.3
3	3	25.0	4	33.3	1	8.3	-	-	-	-	-	-	-	-	2	16.7	2	16.7
5	1	33.3	2	66.7	-	-	-	-	-	-	-	-	-	-	-	-	-	-
7	-	-	1	25.0	1	25.0	-	-	1	25.0	-	-	-	-	1	25.0	-	-
17	1	12.5	3	37.5	1	12.5	-	-	-	-	1	12.5	-	-	1	12.5	1	12.5
31	3	4.2	37	51.4	2	2.8	1	1.4	5	6.9	5	6.9	2	2.8	17	23.6	-	-
36	-	-	1	100.0	-	-	-	-	-	-	-	-	-	-	-	-	-	-
82	-	-	1	50.0	-	-	-	-	-	-	-	-	-	-	1	50.0	-	-
85	-	-	1	100.0	-	-	-	-	-	-	-	-	-	-	-	-	-	-
146	-	-	-	-	-	-	1	100.0	-	-	-	-	-	-	-	-	-	-
208	-	-	1	100.0	-	-	-	-	-	-	-	-	-	-	-	-	-	-
241	-	-	11	73.3	-	-	-	-	1	6.7	1	6.7	-	-	2	13.3	-	-

Table 23. Mississippian Chert Perforators by Chert Type

Chert Type	Flake Perforators				Bifacial Perforators				Total			
	N	%	Wt(g)	%	N	%	Wt(g)	%	N	%	Wt(g)	%
Root Beer	4	12.1	4.9	6.7	1	20.0	2.2	13.5	5	13.2	7.1	7.9
Old Blue	1	3.0	1.2	1.6	-	-	-	-	1	2.6	1.2	1.3
Fern Glen	1	3.0	1.2	1.6	1	20.0	4.7	28.8	2	5.2	5.9	6.6
Local	17	51.5	35.5	48.2	1	20.0	1.4	8.6	18	47.4	36.9	41.0
Miscellaneous	10	30.3	30.8	41.8	2	40.0	8.0	49.1	12	31.6	38.8	43.2
Total	33		73.6		5		16.3		38		89.9	

Table 24. Mississippian Bifaces by Chert Type

Chert Type	Ends or Midsections				Edge Fragments				Biface Fragments				Total			
	N	%	Wt(g)	%	N	%	Wt(g)	%	N	%	Wt(g)	%	N	%	Wt(g)	%
Mill Creek	4	30.8	50.2	14.7	-	-	-	-	1	10.0	3.3	1.3	5	18.5	53.5	8.1
Local	7	53.8	191.0	56.1	4	100.0	62.0	100.0	7	70.0	196.6	77.3	18	66.7	449.6	68.5
Miscellaneous	2	15.4	99.2	29.2	-	-	-	-	2	20.0	54.4	21.4	4	14.8	153.6	23.4
Total	13		340.4		4		62.0		10		254.3		27		656.7	

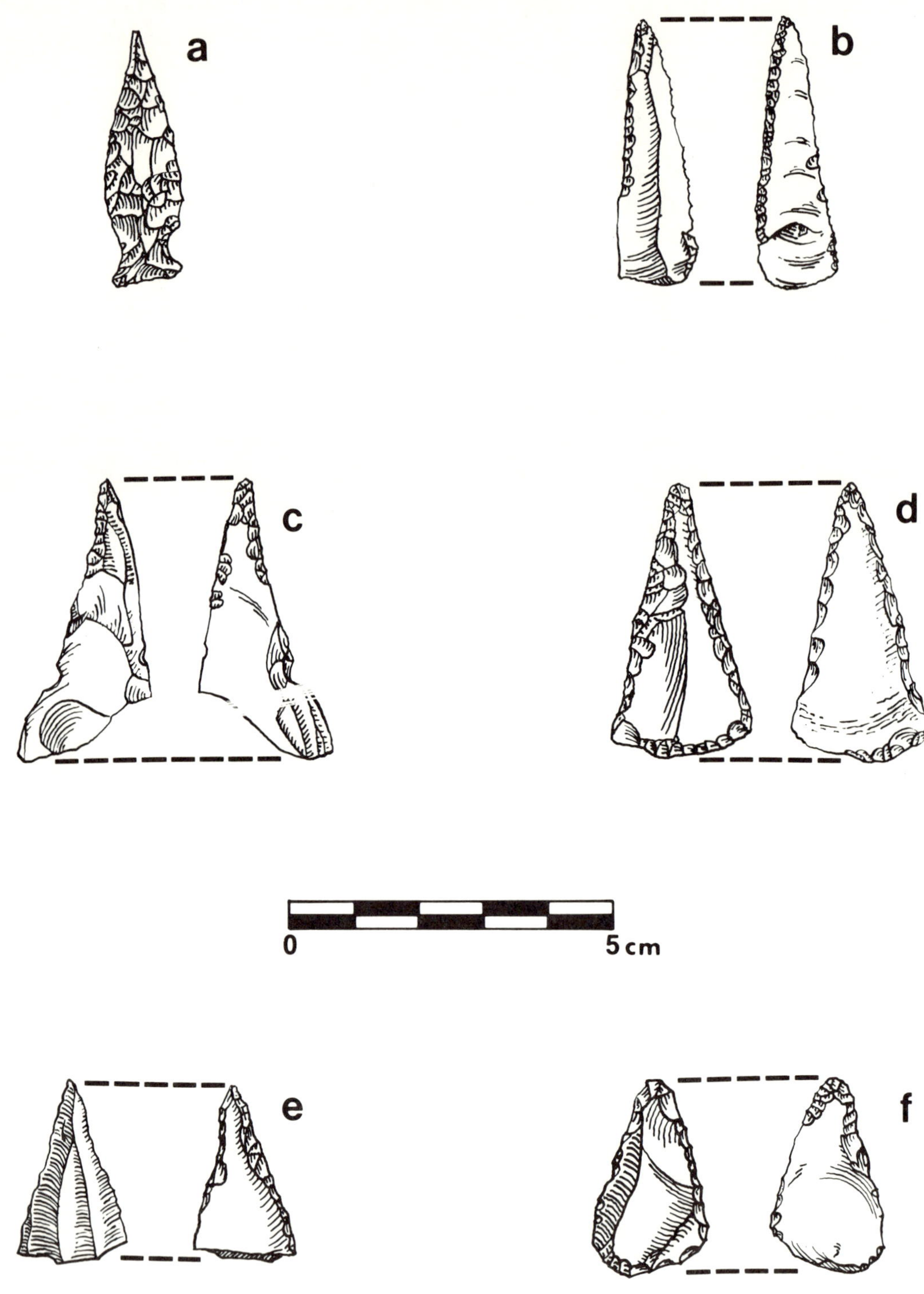

Figure 46. Mississippian Perforators: a, bifacial perforator; b-f, flake perforators

Bifaces

Twenty-seven bifacially worked chert fragments that could not be assigned to specific tool categories were recovered from Mississippian features. Seventeen were defintely tool fragments. The rest were irregularly flaked pieces of chert (Table 24). Eight items displayed a low sheen polish; presumably, these were fragments of large tools. Several bifacial fragments had been reworked for various purposes; these items are described below.

One tool fragment, which was recovered from Feature 7, had been reused as a graver. It was of local chert and weighed 3.3 g. A small 2.5 mm engraving tip had been created by reworking a broken end of an existing bifacial edge. Another biface fragment, from a mixed feature context, had been reused as a spokeshave (Figure 40). This Mill Creek chert artifact weighed 5.7 g. One irregular bifacial specimen of an unidentified chert, from Feature 243, had been used as a wedge (Figure 40). It weighed 26.9 g, was 4.4 cm long, 3.3 cm wide, and 1.7 cm thick.

Hammerstones

Fifty-four hammerstones were recovered from Mississippian features (Table 25). Hammerstones were recognized by their battered surfaces, a result of having been used on many hard surfaces. The majority were igneous cobbles, and many fragments of ground stone tools had been reused as hammerstones (Figure 47). Twenty-one igneous specimens were oval cobbles, and their entire circumferences had been heavily battered. In addition to battered edges, many igneous hammerstones had pecked depressions on their sides. Possibly these artifacts were also used as anvil or nutting stones. The chert hammerstones displayed extensive battered areas, which were much larger than the roughened edge areas of cores, which had presumably resulted from the preparation of striking platforms.

Grinding Objects

Several raw materials were used for grinding or abrading. They included sandstone, igneous cobbles, and Missouri River clinker. Fragments of other raw materials, including hematite, bauxite, and galena, exhibited one or more flat, ground surfaces. Pieces of the last three materials were generally small and may have been ground to produce pigments.

The ground objects were divided into two categories: those with relatively flat or concave surfaces, and those with deep lines or grooves. The two categories undoubtedly reflect functional differences, with the relatively flat objects having been used for grinding, and those with slots for working small-diameter objects. Among other uses, specimens with the relatively flat surfaces could have been employed to process foods. Flat-surfaced abraders included both manos and metates (Figure 47). Individual specimens may have been used for various

Table 25. Mississippian Hammerstones by Raw Material Type

	Hammerstones		Reutilized Tools		Total			
Raw Material	N	Wt(g)	N	Wt(g)	N	%	Wt(g)	%
Igneous	34	10,624.8	7	2,617.4	41	75.9	13,242.2	84.2
Sandstone	1	185.5	-	-	1	1.9	185.5	1.2
Limestone	1	304.5	-	-	1	1.9	304.5	1.9
Chert	5	816.8	-	-	5	9.3	816.8	5.2
Quartzite	5	1,021.5	-	-	5	9.3	1,021.5	6.5
Siltstone	1	149.4	-	-	1	1.9	149.4	1.0
Total	47	13,102.5	7	2,617.4	54		15,719.9	

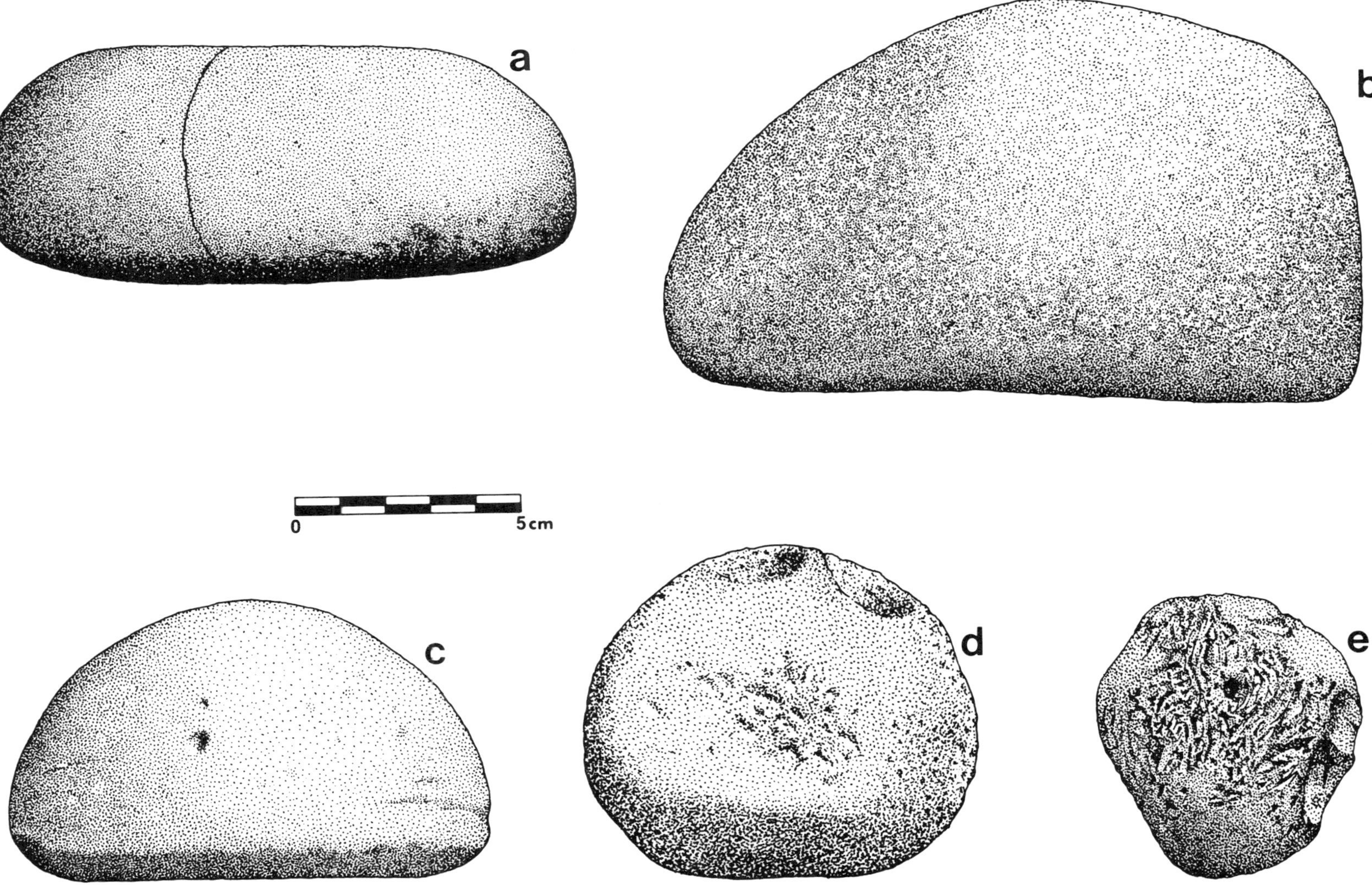

Figure 47. Mississippian Hammerstones and Manos: a-c, manos; d, igneous hammerstone; e, chert hammerstone

purposes. The slotted abraders were used for shaping and smoothing materials such as wood, bone, and shell (Figure 48).

Most of the flat grinding objects had been fashioned from sandstone; 125 were recovered from Mississippian feature contexts (Table 26). One large specimen with a concave grinding surface was recovered from the floor of a burned structure (Feature 91), where it had been used as a metate. That particular specimen also had several slots on its edges.

Three varieties of readily distinguishable grooves were recognized among the slot abraders. Of all the grooves on sandstone abraders, 20.1% were broad and shallow; 29.2% were deeper, with rounded, U-shaped bottoms; and 50.7% had sharply defined V-shaped slots (Table 27). Those differences presumably relate to the types and sizes of the materials being worked with the abraders. The slots often covered entire surfaces of the abraders, and individual grooves occasionally intersected.

Eleven sandstone grinding objects had red pigment partially covering their smooth surfaces. One specimen, from Feature 115, had a peculiar white and red deposit caked on its surface (Figure 48). The white material was probably galena; the red was probably hematite.

Nine igneous cobbles had been used for grinding purposes. One had also functioned as a hammerstone. Four specimens had the remnants of red pigment adhering to their surfaces. One of these four items was cached in pit Feature 293.

Nine abraders had been fashioned from Missouri River clinker. Most of these were slot abraders. In cross section, 59% of the slots were V-shaped, 25% were U-shaped, and 16% were broad, shallow grooves.

Twenty-five pieces of hematite had been used as abraders or had been rubbed to produce pigment. Three specimens were relatively large and may have been manos. Four U-shaped slots were present on one of these specimens.

Twenty-two pieces of galena had flat, ground surfaces. Again, those pieces were probably rubbed to produce pigment. Four pieces had an adhering red residue, suggesting either a purposeful application of a red material like hematite to the pieces or a close association of the two minerals, perhaps in a pouch.

Seven pieces of rubbed bauxite were recovered. The bauxite fragments were apparently from relatively large artifacts; several showed both the original surface and newly smoothed areas. All were recovered from features located near or within the superimposed complex that includes structure Features 208, 215, 231, and 241.

Most of the grinding objects were found either in structures or in their associated features. Of the specimens with slots, 70.2% were found in structure-related contexts; 74.4% of the specimens with flat grinding surfaces were found in similar contexts.

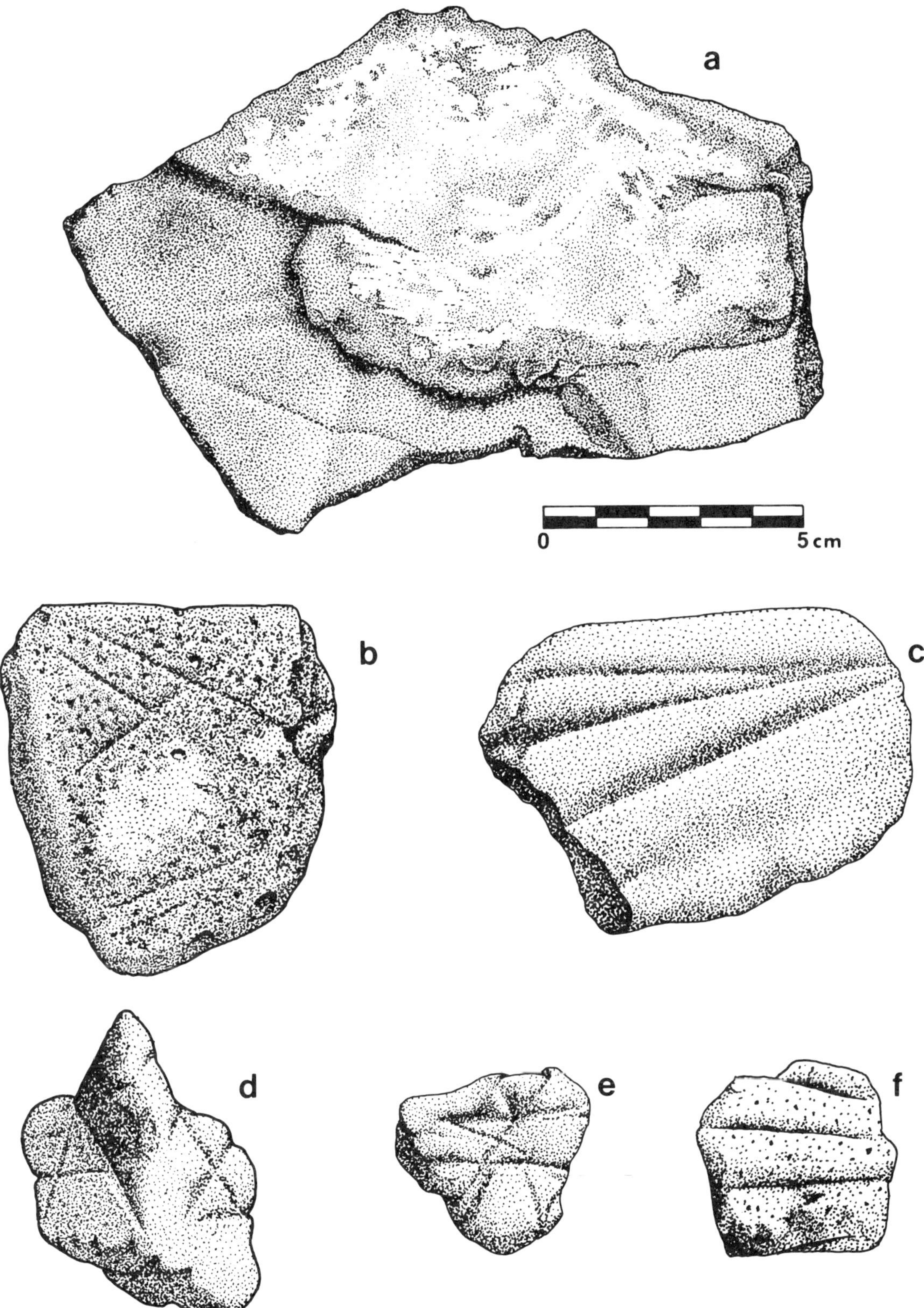

Figure 48. Mississippian Grinding Objects: a, flat abrader with pigment; b, hematite slot abrader; c-e, sandstone slot abraders; f, clinker slot abrader

Table 26. Mississippian Grinding Objects by Raw Material Type

Material	Flat-surfaced Abraders				Slot Abraders				Abraders with Slots and Flat Surfaces				Total Grinding Objects	
	N	%	Wt(g)	%	N	%	Wt(g)	%	N	%	Wt(g)	%	N	Wt(g)
Sandstone	47	37.6	2900.9	30.8	58	46.4	3482.4	37.0	20	16.0	3029.4	32.2	125	9412.7
Igneous	9	100.0	9780.3	100.0	-	-	-	-	-	-	-	-	9	9780.3
Clinker	1	11.1	34.7	13.2	7	77.8	192.2	73.3	1	11.1	35.4	13.5	9	262.3
Hematite	24	96.0	873.8	73.7	-	-	-	-	1	4.0	312.3	26.3	25	1186.1
Bauxite	7	100.0	38.5	100.0	-	-	-	-	-	-	-	-	7	38.5
Galena	22	100.0	206.9	100.0	-	-	-	-	-	-	-	-	22	206.9
Total	110	55.8	13835.1	66.2	65	33.0	3674.6	17.6	22	11.2	3377.1	16.2	197	20886.8

Note: % figures are computed separately for each raw material category and express the quantities (by count and weight) that have flat surfaces or slots.

Table 27. Slot Categories on Mississippian Abraders

	Broad Concave		V-shaped		U-shaped		Total Slots
Material	N	%	N	%	N	%	N
Sandstone	60	20.1	151	50.7	87	29.2	298
Clinker	7	16.1	26	59.0	11	25.0	44
Hematite	-	-	-	-	4	100.0	4
Total	67	19.4	177	51.2	102	29.4	346

Note: % figures are computed separately for each raw material category and express the proportion of each of the slot categories.

Table 28. Mississippian Beads

		Weight (g)	
Material	N	Total	Mean
Ceramic (Whole)	3	5.7	1.9
Ceramic (Fragment)	1	1.0	1.0
Crinoid	3	11.0	3.7
Galena	1	1.0	1.0
Total	8		

Discoidals

Three fragmentary discoidals, two of stone and one of clay, were recovered from two Mississippian features. The ground stone discoidals, from Features 177 and 241, were similarly shaped. Both had rounded margins with concave sides. One was made of quartzite and weighed 43.2 g, was ca. 8 cm in diameter, and was 2.7 cm thick. The other stone discoidal was made from a dark, igneous stone. This fragment weighed 51.4 g, its diameter was 5.7 cm, and it was 1.2 cm thick. A relatively crude clay discoidal, from Feature 241, had grooves on both sides flanking its rounded margin. These were produced by deeply scoring the clay while the discoidal was being manufactured. The clay discoidal weighed 16.0 g, measured 4.6 cm in diameter, and was 1.2 cm thick. The last two discoidal fragments are illustrated in Figure 49.

Beads

Beads were recovered from six features (Table 28, Figure 49). A ground galena bead, from Feature 87, measured 0.46 cm in length and 0.7 cm in diameter. The bore diameter of this bead measured 0.2 cm. Three ceramic beads were found in Feature 279 and one in Feature 150. These beads had a mean diameter of 1.39 cm and a mean bore diameter of 0.29 cm. Three fossil crinoid beads were recovered, one each from Features 241, 291, and 303. The beads consisted of from two to seven crinoid segments.

Unusual Artifacts

Several unusual, nonceramic objects were recovered from Mississippian feature contexts. They are described below.

A 47.5 g piece of Missouri River clinker, which had been ground into a hemisphere, was recovered from Feature 230 (Figure 50). This radially symmetric object was 3.7 cm high and had a flat base that was 5.3 cm in diameter.

Two small pieces of limestone had been ground into geometric forms. One, which was from Feature 17, weighed 59.5 g and had been shaped to form an isosceles triangle (Figure 50). It was 5.1 cm long, measured 4.7 cm at its base, and was 2.1 cm thick. The surface was eroded, so manufacturing marks were not evident. Another worked limestone artifact, which weighed 45.7 g, was recovered from a different feature (Feature 31) [Figure 50]. It was roughly triangular in shape, measured 8.0 cm in length, was 4.1 cm wide, and 1.1 cm thick. The surface exhibited minute traces of red pigment. Presumably, the pigment once covered the entire artifact.

Two pieces of bauxite had been worked into small artifacts. One, an ear spool weighing 13.1 g, was recovered from the wall trench of Feature

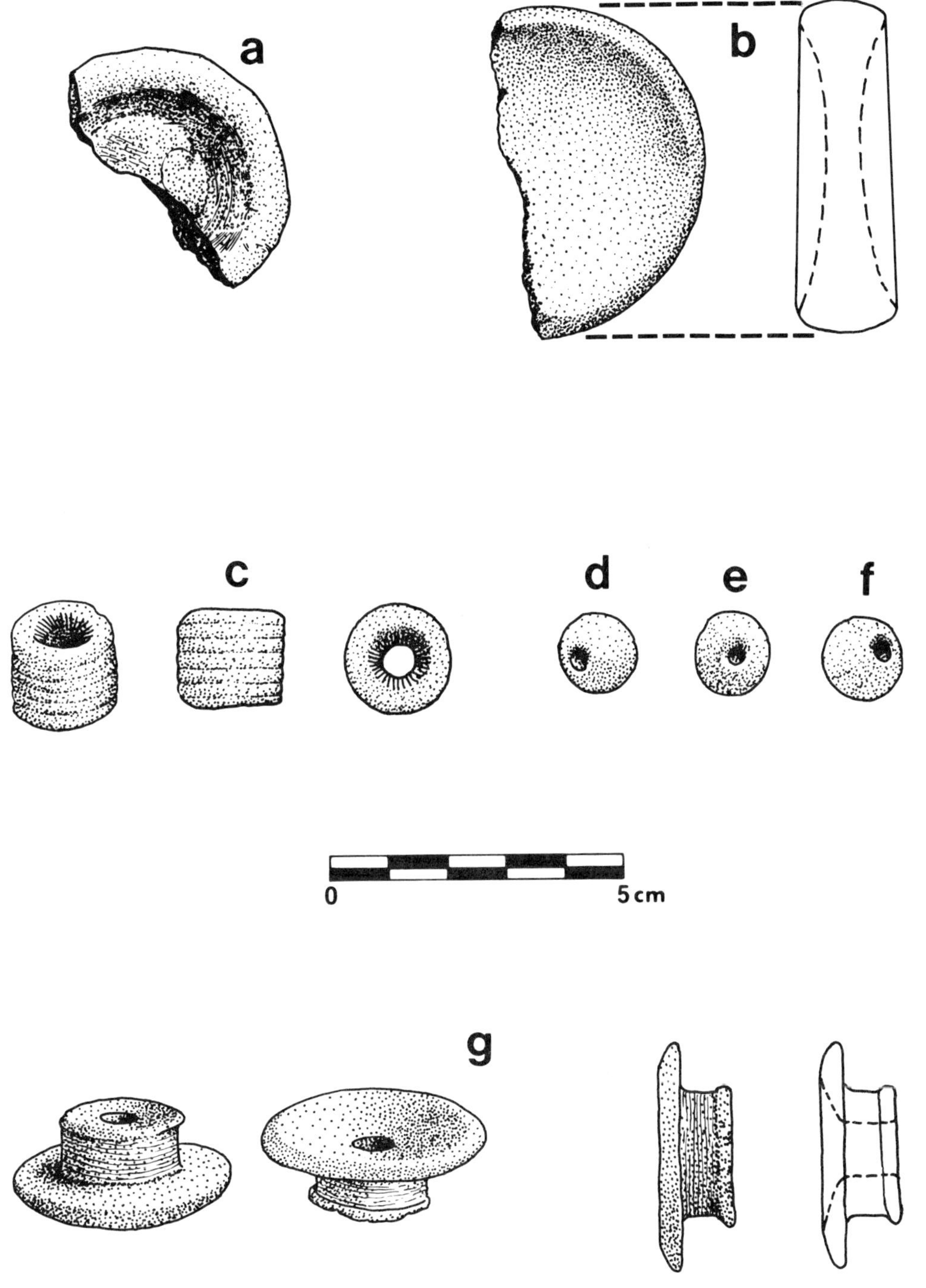

Figure 49. Mississippian Artifacts: a, clay discoidal; b, stone discoidal; c, large crinoid bead; d-f, ceramic beads; g, ear spool

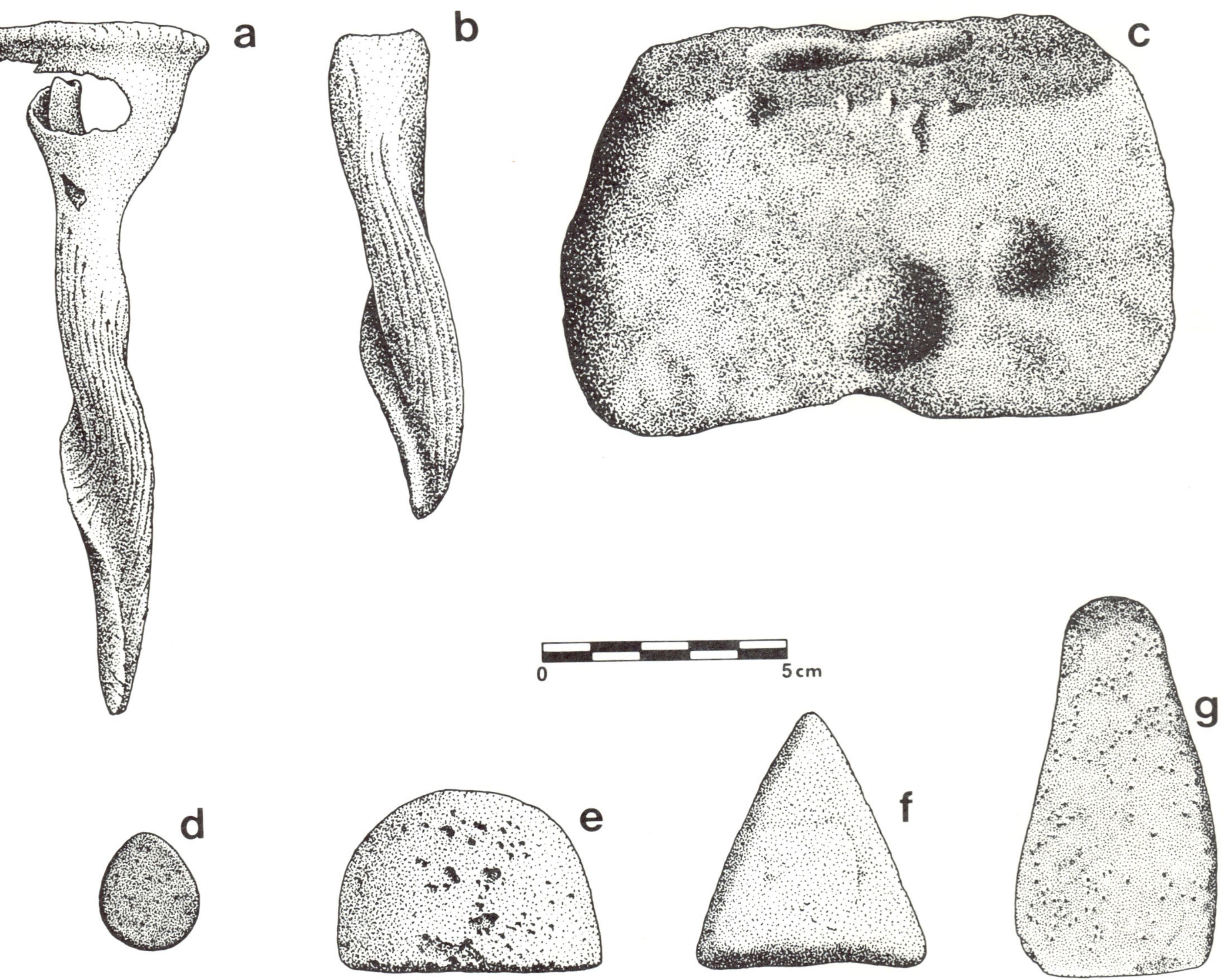

Figure 50. Mississippian Artifacts: a-b, whelk shell columellae; c, nutting stone; d, bauxite pendant; e, Missouri River clinker hemisphere; f, worked limestone triangle; g, worked limestone with red pigment

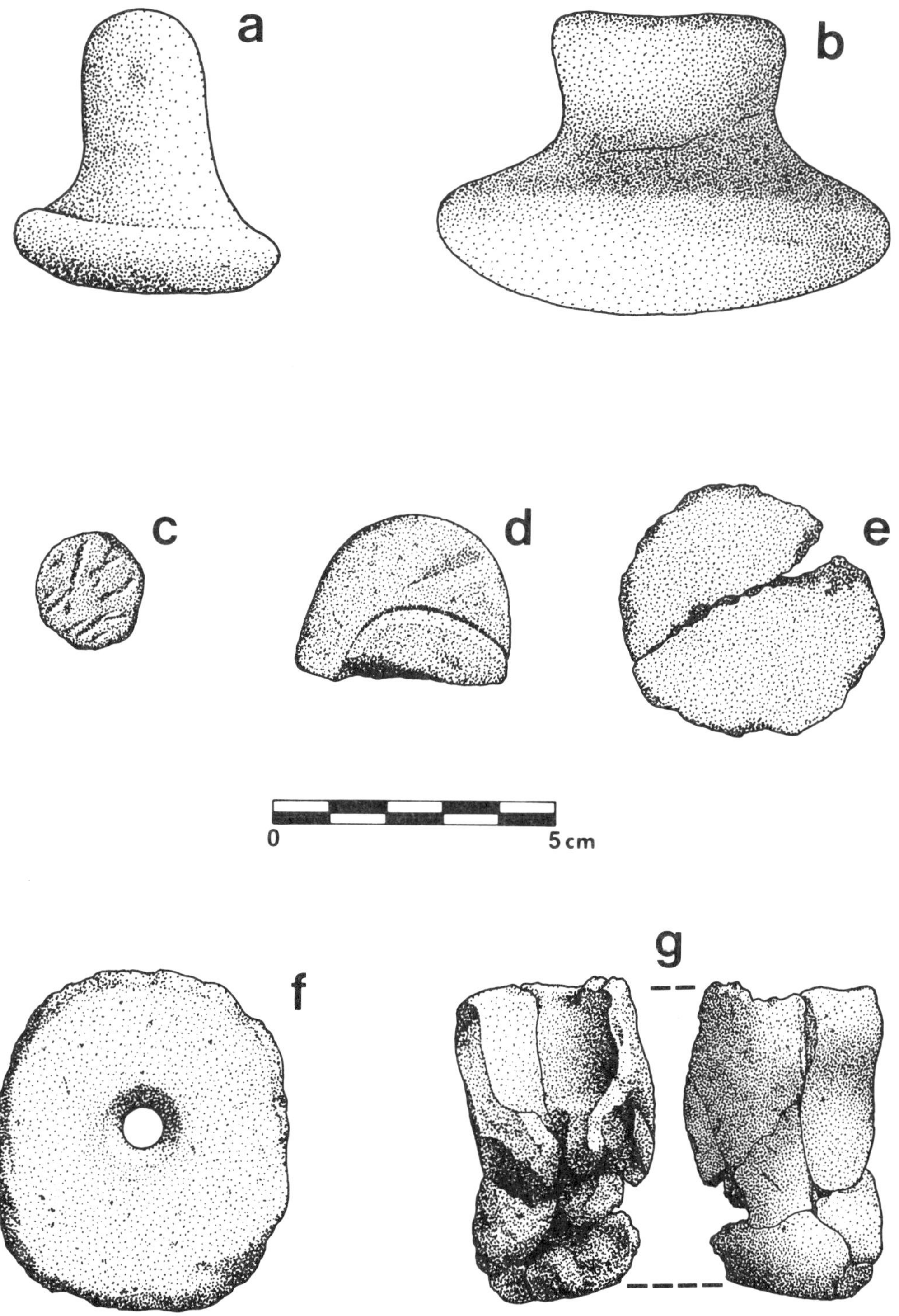

Figure 51. Mississippian Ceramics: a-b, pottery trowels; c, cord-marked disc; d, trailed disc; e, plain disc; f, perforated plain discs; g, pipe

267 (Figure 49). The other object, possibly a pendant blank, weighed 2.0 g. It was found in Feature 88 (Figure 50).

A sandstone nutting stone was recovered from Feature 249 (Figure 50). This 843.2 g artifact had paired indentations on four sides, that ranged from 2.0 cm to 2.5 cm in diameter and were ca. 0.5 cm deep. The depressions on the specimen were uniform and smooth and were much more distinct than the vague, irregularly pecked depressions previously discussed as having been found on several hammerstones.

Four whelk shell columellae, presumably Busycon sp., were recovered from Features 23, 87, 89, and 109 (Figure 50). Their weights ranged from 2.9 g to 35.8 g. Pieces of shell from Feature 293 may also represent fragmentary and highly eroded examples of marine shell. Several of the columellae may have served as pendants. Similar ornaments are often depicted on artifacts from southeastern Mississippian sites (Phillips and Brown 1978).

Ceramic Pipes

Portions of two ceramic pipes were recovered from three Mississippian features. Both pipes were shell-tempered and had plain exteriors. One specimen was from Feature 137, an external pit, and weighed 30.3 g (Figure 51). The other consisted of two fragments and weighed 10.2 g. The two fragments of this specimen were found in separate pits (Features 150 and 303).

Pottery Trowels

Four complete pottery trowels and two fragments were recovered from Mississippian features. The items had been manufactured from a shell-tempered paste and had plain exterior finishes. Two distinctive types of handles were present: one was rounded, and the other was expanded and knob-like (Table 29, Figure 51).

The six specimens were all found in structure contexts. Two were found together in Feature 112, a pit within structure Feature 2. The other pottery trowels were found in Features 5, 17, and 91, all structures.

Ceramic Discs

Seven relatively complete discs and an equal number of fragments were recovered. The discs tended to be circular and ranged from 1.6 cm to 5.9 cm in length, and from 1.3 cm to 5.4 cm in width (Table 30). Perforations occurred in three (23.1%) of the thirteen specimens that were large enough to permit observation as to whether centrally located holes had once been present. At least two classes of discs were

Table 29. Mississippian Pottery Trowels

Dimensions Measured	N	Mean Dimensions (cm)
Maximum Length	4	5.19
Maximum Width	4	6.55
Handle Length	5	2.99
Handle Midshaft Diameter	5	3.15

Table 30. Mississippian Discs

		Length (cm)		Width (cm)		Weight (g)	
	N	Mean	s	Mean	s	Mean	s
Large Discs	5	4.76	0.87	4.65	0.70	13.9	11.6
Small Discs	2	1.84	-	1.66	-	1.0	-
Disc Fragments	7	-	-	-	-	-	-

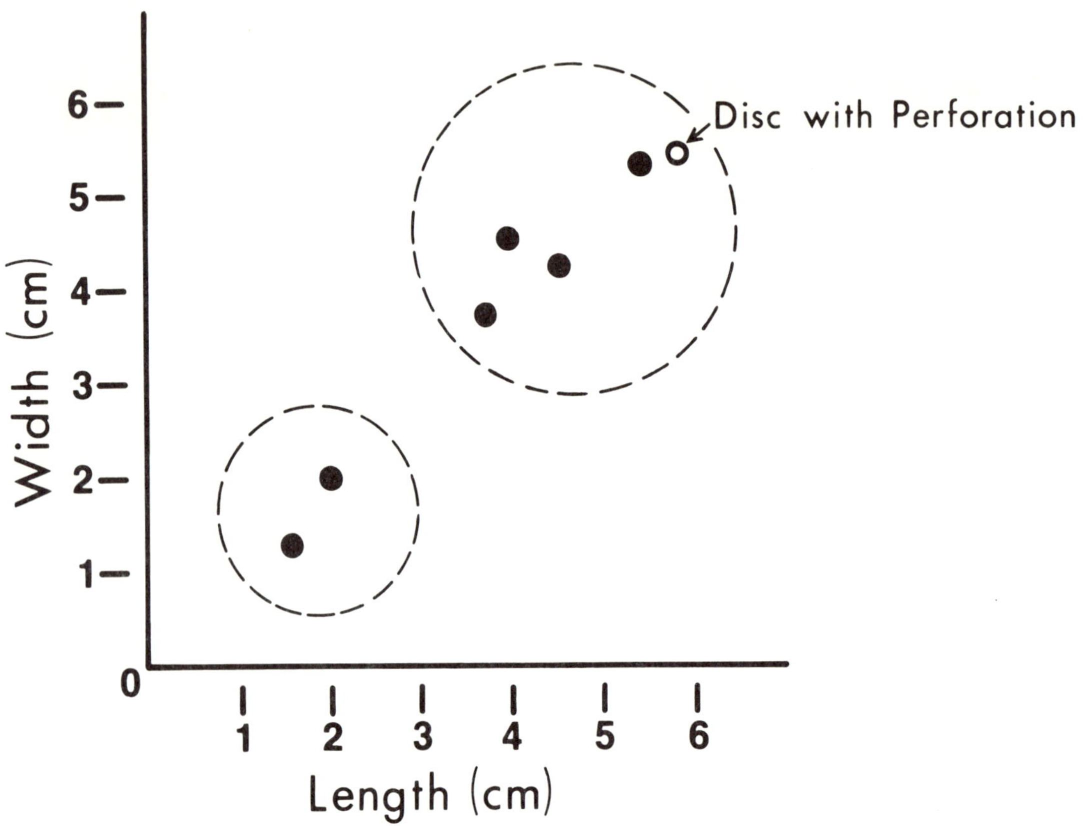

Figure 52. Mississippian Ceramics: Distribution of Discs by Length and Width

distinguished on the basis of size alone (Figures 51 and 52). The function of such small discs is unknown; perhaps they were used as a kind of marker. Larger specimens, several of which were perforated, may have been used for other purposes, such as spindle whorls.

Although the discs had usually been made by grinding the edges of body sherds, one had been made from fired clay. Another large, fired clay object was discussed above, along with the discoidals. Most of the Julien site discs (71.4%) were recovered from structures or their associated features.

Vessels

Rim segments recovered from features formed the basis of the Mississippian vessel descriptions. Occasionally, body sections without rims are also described. These few specimens were included either because of their unusual shapes or because of exterior surface decorations; presumably, some of these vessels were tradewares. One large body segment was included because of its archaeological context; it was found resting on the floor of a burned structure (Feature 91).

Segments of 572 vessels are described on a per feature basis. Each segment was usually composed of sherds from different fill units within a single feature; occasionally, sherds from the same vessel were associated with separate features. At least 553 separate vessels were represented by the 572 vessel segments. Segments of vessels have been assigned two-part reference designations that include feature and rim section numbers (feature number-rim section number).

To ensure consistency, observations of vessel attributes were made by one person and checked by another. Vessel measurements and reference points are described when necessary within the context of the various vessel descriptions. Maximum orifice diameter was one measurement that was taken for all vessels and consistently reported for all vessel forms. That measurement defined the distance between the internal surfaces of the lip, i.e., the points where the vessel would rest if inverted.

Most features contained the fragments of only a few rims (Figure 53). The vessels tended to be represented by relatively short segments of rim relative to their original orifice circumference. The percent of orifice present for the series of 553 different vessels is found in Figure 54. Note that 26 vessels lacking circumference estimates are included within the 0% to 1% interval; most of those rim segments were small, prohibiting accurate measurement.

Vessel shape was the primary criterion used to organize the Julien site collection, consisting as it did of numerous ceramic containers of widely varying shapes and sizes. The most basic distinction among vessels is in the degree of orifice closure. Relatively closed forms

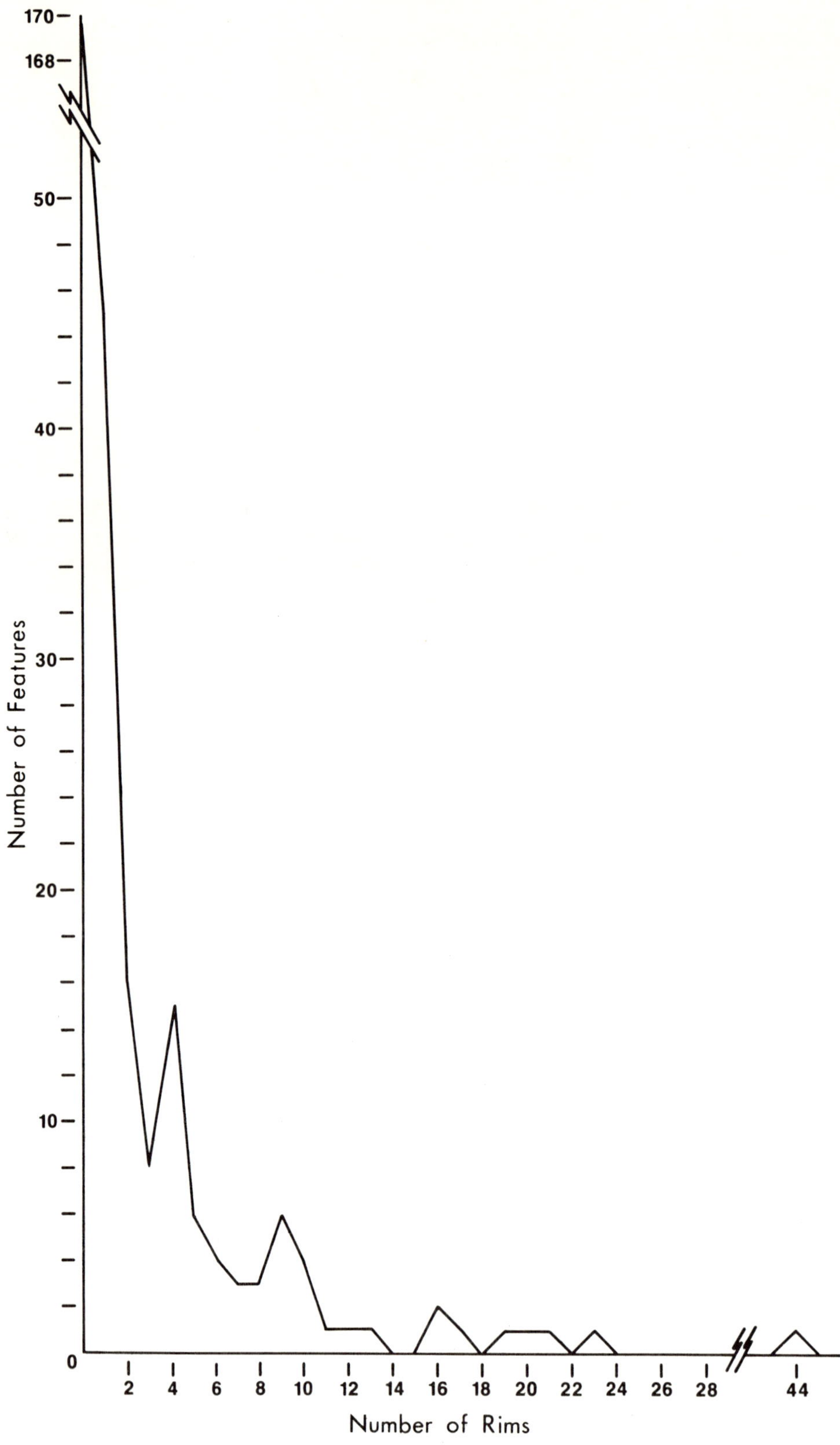

Figure 53. Mississippian Ceramics: Rim Segments per Feature

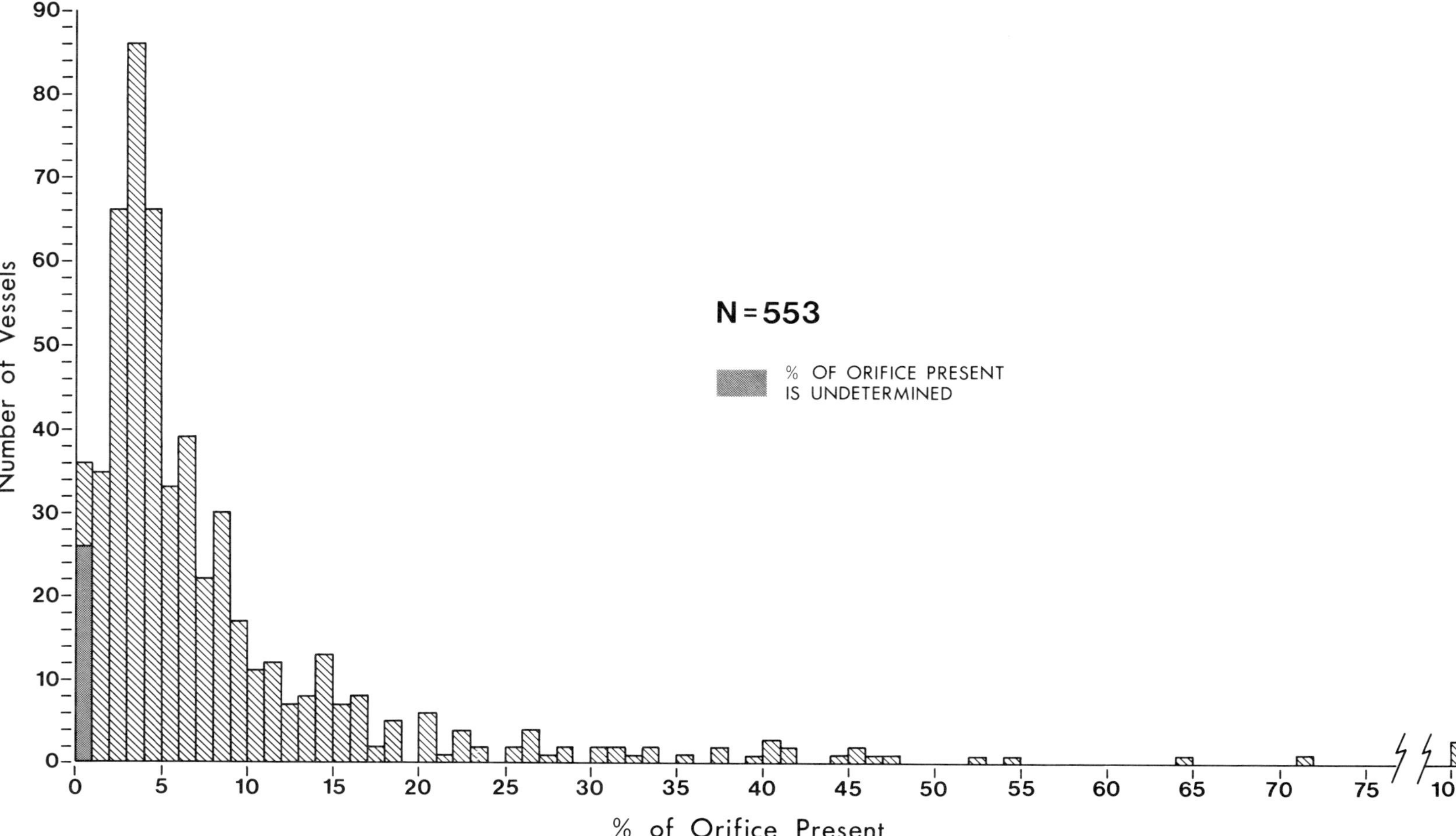

Figure 54. Mississippian Ceramics: Percent of Orfice Present

include jars and water bottles; containers whose orifices permit unrestricted access to their interiors include bowls, pans, and plates. The terms used for vessel forms in this volume are those commonly used in studies of Mississippian ceramics, and they need no further explanation here. They include jars and small, crude pinchpot jars; bowls and pinchpot bowls; water bottles; pans; beakers or bean pots; plates; juice presses; hooded water bottles; stumpware vessels; and a possible seed jar. Thirty-four (6.1%) vessels were unidentifiable as to form.

Jars

Most of the recovered vessels were jars, of which there were 316 (57.1% of all Mississippian vessels). They ranged from small, crude pinchpots, of which there were eight, to large, usually symmetric vessels, which were often finely worked and esthetically pleasing.

Jar morphology was distinctive, permitting the identification of general vessel form even when only small rim segments were present. Therefore, few jars were included with the unidentified vessels. The ability to easily recognize jars may have contributed disproportionately to the assessment of their abundance in the collection, 60.9% when only identifiable vessels are considered. It was initially suspected that jars would be overenumerated since small jar rim segments from separate features could be, in fact, parts of single vessels. Reconstructing the fragmentary ceramics from groups of nearby features helped in the recognition of single vessels that had broken, resulting in sherds having become distributed in different features. Apparently, this effort at reconstruction was successful. Jars constituted 57.9% of the vessels for which there were sherds from two or more different features. That figure closely approximates their total representation in the ceramic series (57.1%).

Jars are discussed in two general sections. First, characteristics of shape and surface treatment are defined as they apply to the entire vessel category (Table 31; Figure 55). The attributes given special consideration were those shared by many of the jars, and they are among those conventionally chosen when this vessel form is described. Second, jars were divided into four groups recognized as distinct types by archaeologists in the American Bottom. The four types by definition share one attribute, that of shell tempering. They were primarily differentiated by their surface treatments, which included plain, filmed, filmed and trailed, and cordmarked vessel exteriors. One aspect of this ceramic discussion is to show how details of shape covary with, or crosscut, the four principal shell-tempered jar types.

The wide variation in exterior surface treatment was one of the more notable aspects of the Julien site jars (Table 31). Exterior finishes included plain, polished, filmed, and cordmarked. Red, brown, and black designations represent a partitioning of a quasicontinuous color range.

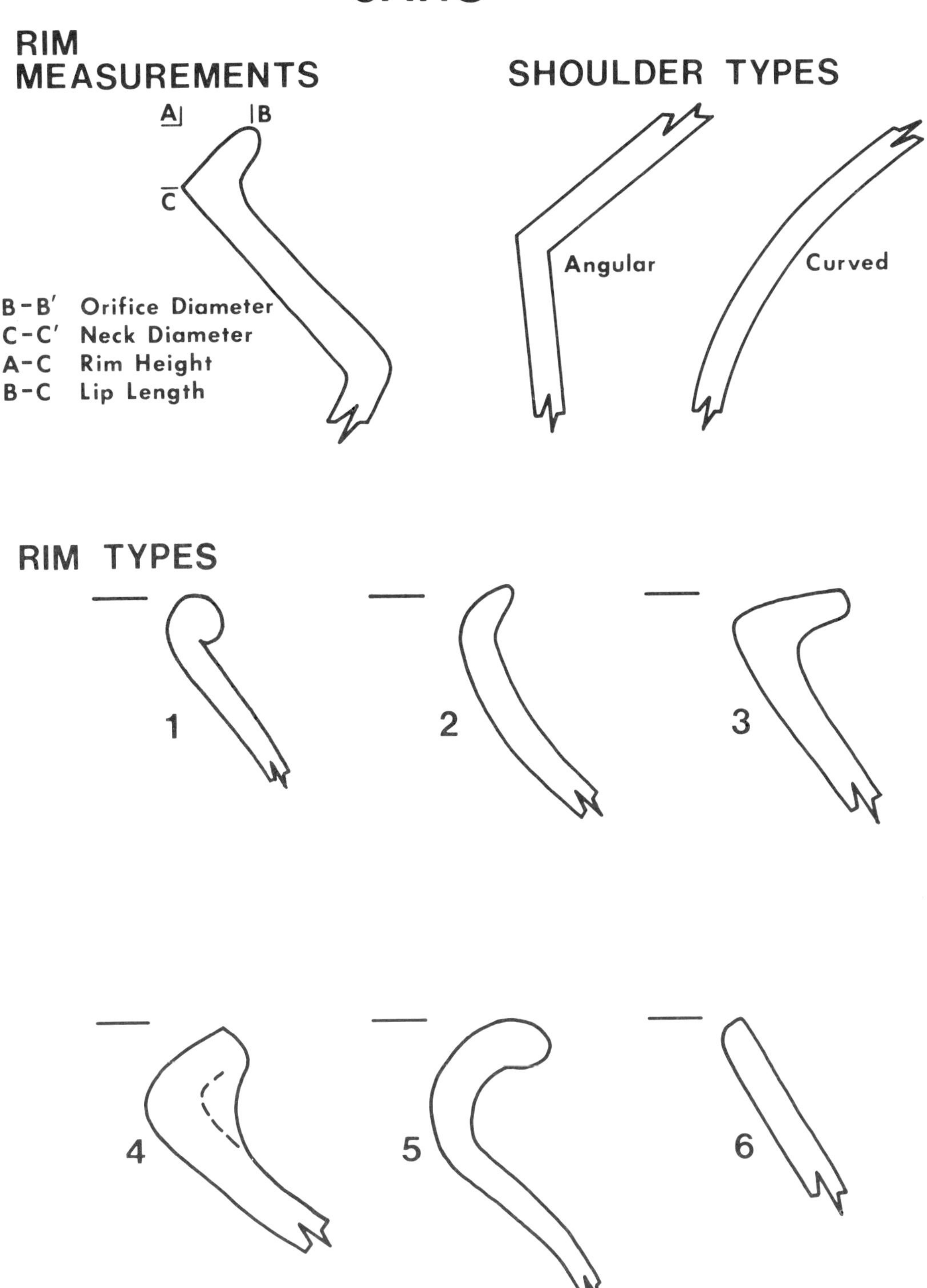

Figure 55. Mississippian Ceramics: Rim Measurements; Shoulder Types; and Rim Types

Table 31. Mississippian Jar Characteristics

Surface Treatment			Temper			Rim			Shoulder			Appendages		
	N	%		N	%		N	%		N	%		N	%
Plain	82	25.9	Shell	301	95.3	Type 1	15	4.7	Angular	29	9.2	Handle	11	3.5
Plain and Decorated	2	0.6	Limestone	9	2.8	Type 2	22	7.0	Curved	44	13.9	Tab/Lug	13	4.1
Polished	39	12.3	Grit	2	0.6	Type 3	256	81.0	Other	3	1.0	Absent	292	92.4
Red Filmed	9	2.8	Grog	3	1.0	Type 4	12	3.8	Indet.	240	75.9			
Red Filmed and Decorated	1	0.3	Shell/Grog	1	0.3	Type 5	7	2.2						
Brown Filmed	16	5.1				Type 6	2	0.6						
Brown Filmed and Decorated	10	3.2				Indet.	2	0.6						
Black Filmed	24	7.6												
Black Filmed and Decorated	14	4.4												
Cordmarked	35	11.1												
Indeterminate	84	26.6												

Color differences presumably resulted from oxidation or reduction during firing of a thin clay wash applied to vessel surfaces. Reds and browns were, on occasion, difficult to separate. The black surface treatment was occasionally better described as a shade of gray. Patches of red or brown were sometimes present on otherwise black filmed vessels; the opposite was also true. Many jar exteriors were also polished, including virtually all (95.9%) of the filmed vessels. Burnishing marks were occasionally visible on surfaces with high sheen. The exteriors of some jars had been intentionally roughened with cordmarks applied with cord-wrapped paddles. Individual cords varied in diameter, and S-twist cords predominated, being present on 62.9% of the cordmarked jars. Finally, many vessels with plain, polished, or filmed exterior finishes were decorated with designs composed of lines or punctates. Decorated vessels represent 8.5% of the jar category.

Crushed shell was employed as the primary tempering medium. Temper was identified macroscopically, so, on occasion, shell may have been identified as a temper when, in fact, a jar was tempered with grog that consisted of crushed shell-tempered pottery. Two factors contributed to problems in identifying temper: some rim segments were quite small, and often shell and limestone had been leached from sherds, leaving behind a very fragile and porous structure. The pinchpot vessel form was disproportionately represented among the temper categories that occurred only infrequently in the jar collection. Two grit-tempered vessels were pinchpots, as were two of the vessels tempered with grog and one of the vessels tempered with limestone.

Six different rim treatments were distinguished (Figures 56 and 57), which were assigned type labels to facilitate recording and description. Not surprisingly, the rim morphology of Julien site jars closely approximates that of jars previously described in ceramic collections from American Bottom sites (O'Brien 1972; Porter 1974; Vogel 1975). Vogel's nomenclature (1975) is frequently used to describe variation in the rims of American Bottom jars.

Type 1 was the "rolled" rim described by Vogel (1975). Type 2 rims had small, somewhat everted lips, a form that has been called "extruded" (Vogel 1975). It appears that the upper portions of these rims were simply pinched to produce this modest decorative detail. Large and more distinctly formed Type 2 rims occasionally resemble those designated as Type 3 rims.

Type 3 rims had distinctly everted lips. This was the most common jar rim form in the Julien site collection. The neck was usually well-defined by a distinct break in the neck surface contour on both the interior and exterior surfaces. Considerable variation was present in lip orientation, ranging from almost vertical rims to rims where the lip and shoulder intersection formed an acute angle. This form would include the everted and angled rims of Vogel (1975). To describe this variation in the Julien site collection, two measurements were taken and designated rim height and lip length (Figure 58). The latter had

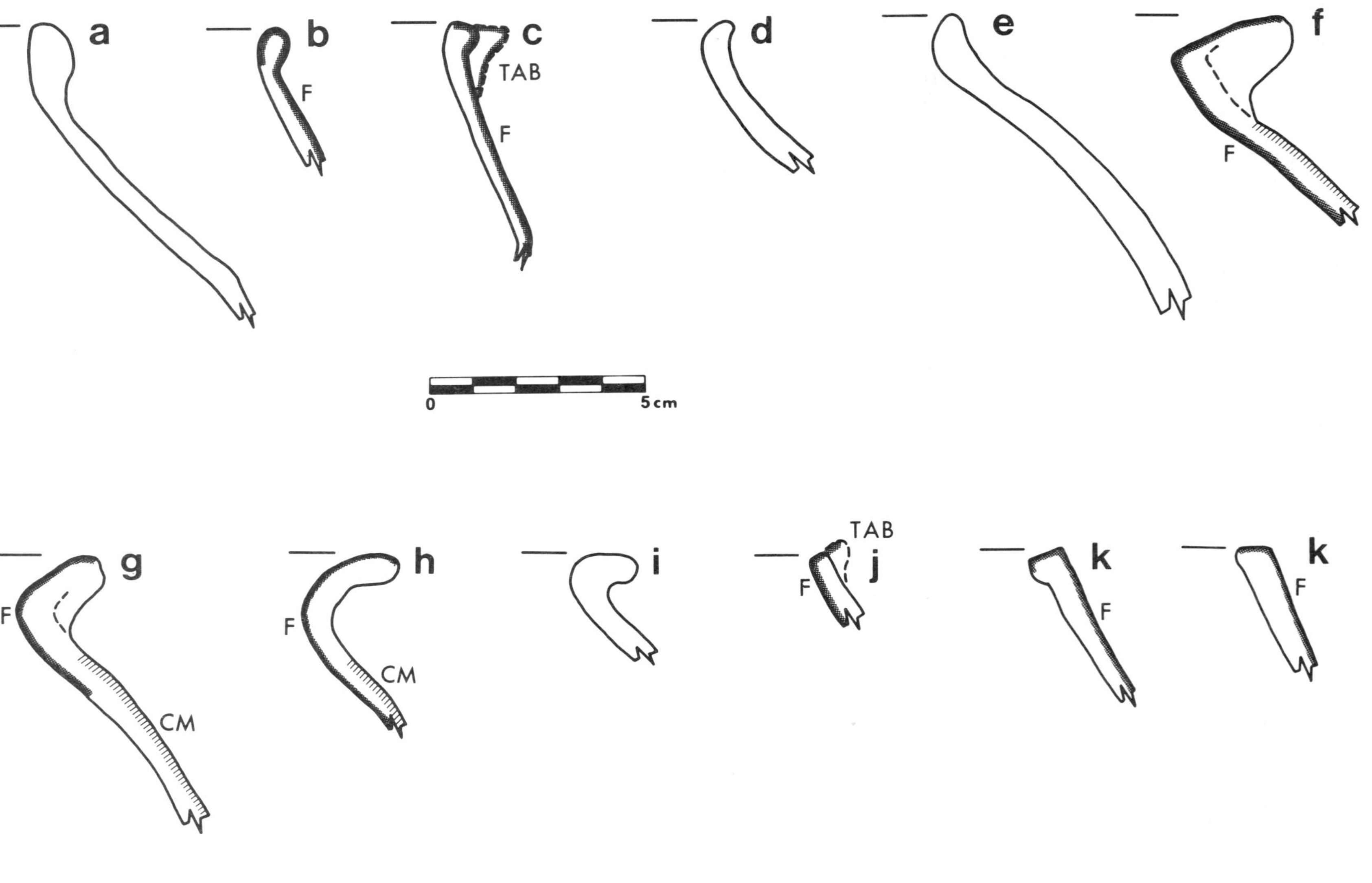

Figure 56. Mississippian Jar Rim Profiles: a, 9-3, Type 1 with angular shoulder; b, 115-5, Type 1; c, 229-5, Type 1 with angular shoulder and tab, d, 177-2, Type 2; e, 64-2, Type 2 with curved shoulder; f, 17-2, Type 4; g, 24-4, Type 4 with curved shoulder; h, 241-3, Type 5; i, 280-3, Type 5; j, 284-1, Type 6 with tab; k, 284-2, Type 6 (two views)

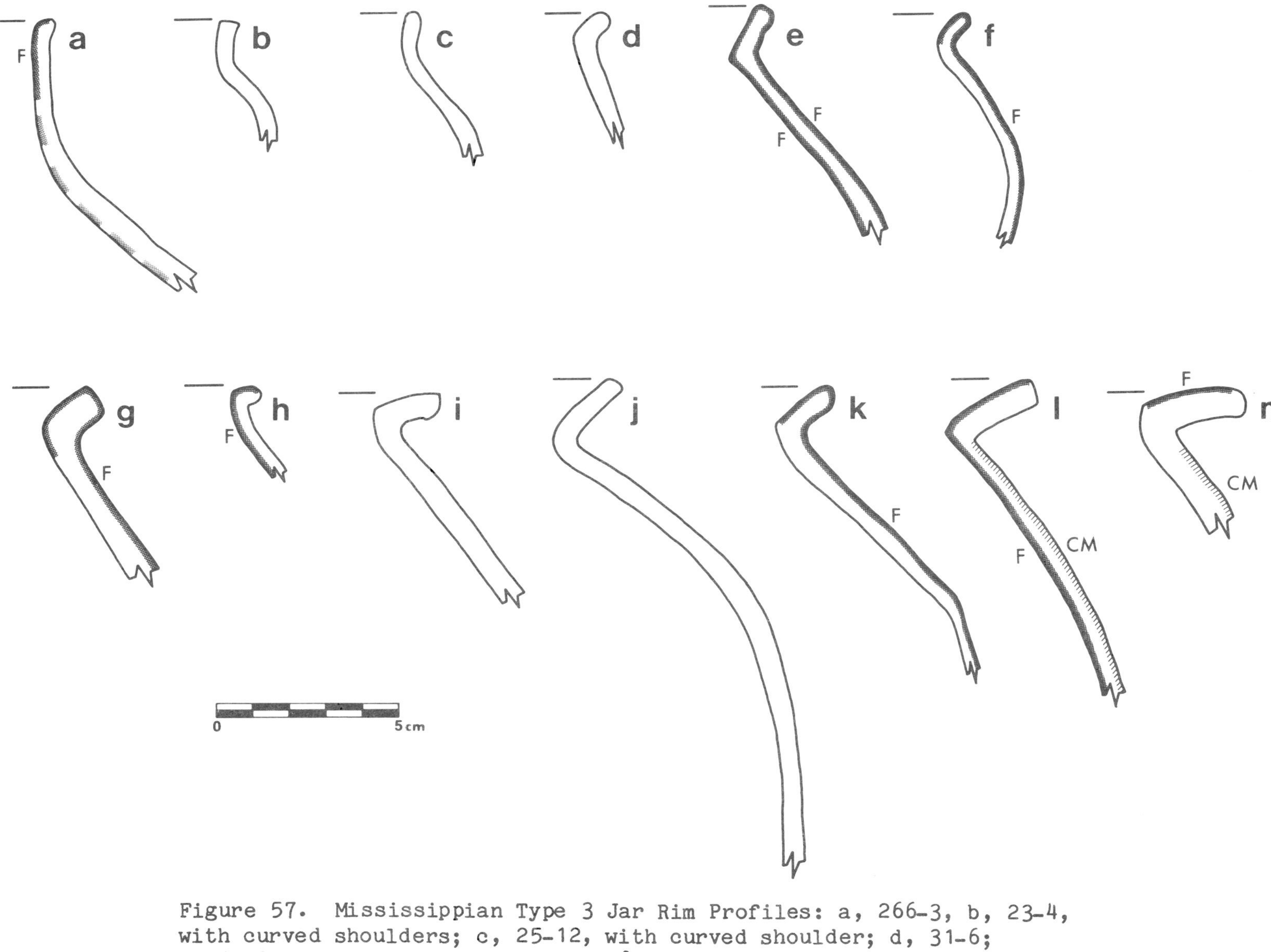

Figure 57. Mississippian Type 3 Jar Rim Profiles: a, 266-3, b, 23-4, with curved shoulders; c, 25-12, with curved shoulder; d, 31-6; e, 19-2, with curved shoulder; f, 89-2, with angular shoulder; g, 16-7; h, 36-6; i, 152-1; j, 295-1, with curved shoulder; k, 295-2, with angular shoulder; l, 303-1, with curved shoulder; m, 14-1

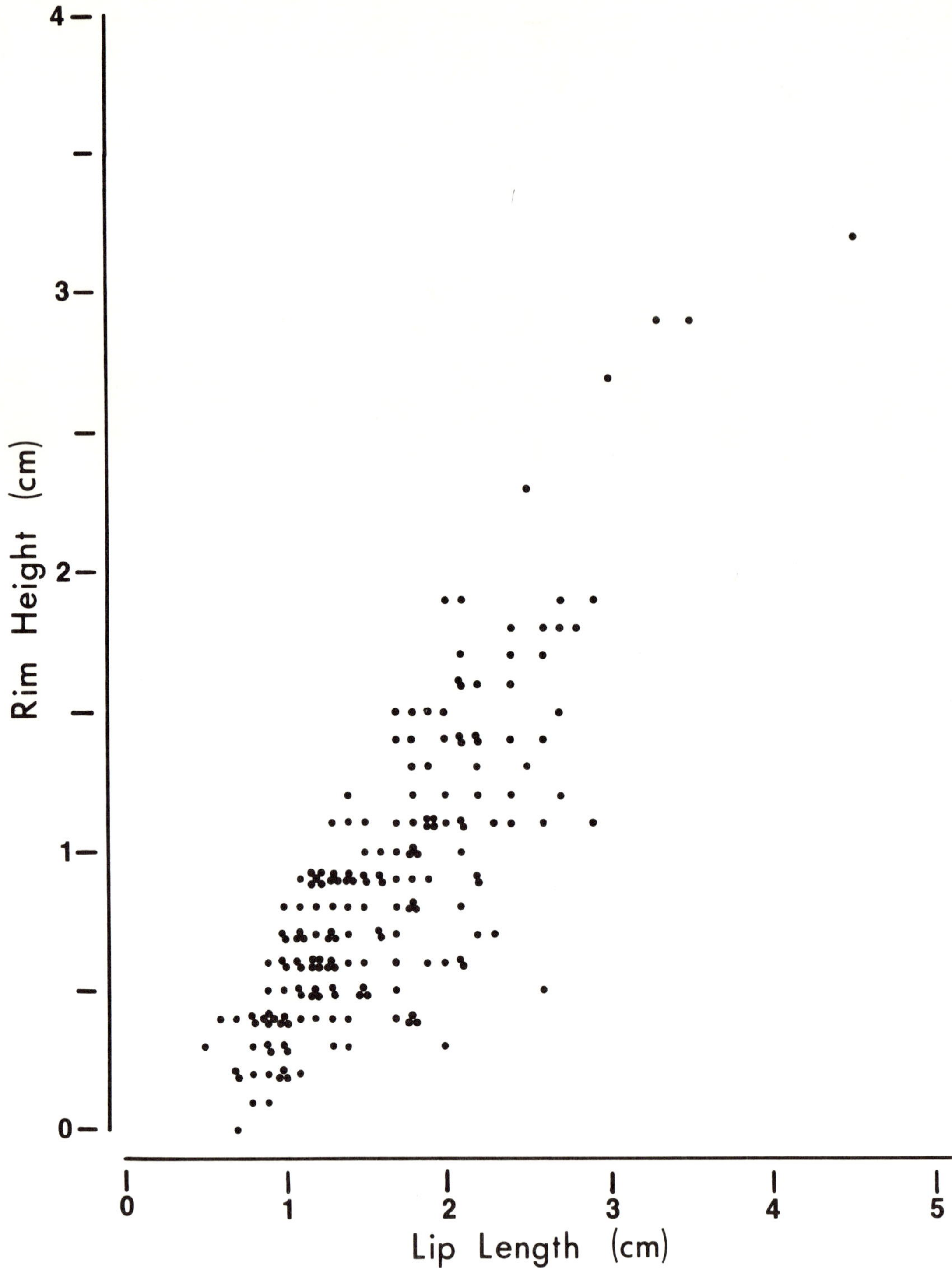

Figure 58. Rim Morphology of Type 3 Mississippian Jars

previously been designated "rim height" by Vogel (1975:38). A rather continuous distribution resulted from a comparison of the two measurements; there did not appear to be any clear, unambiguous separation into distinct rim classes that would have necessitated subdividing the Type 3 category.

The Type 4 rim variant was similar to the Type 3 form, but the neck had been thickened by an addition of clay. This was apparently done by adding a coil of clay to the inferior neck surface or by folding the lip over upon itself. The Type 5 variant was also similar to the Type 3 rim, but instead of being straight, the lip was curved, forming a continuous arc from the neck to the lip edge. The Type 3 and 5 rim variants seemed to form a continuous series; at times they were difficult to separate. The last rim variety, Type 6, was essentially an unmodified rim. No special lip treatment was present on the few rims belonging to this type.

The Julien site jars usually had curved or angular shoulders (Table 31, Figure 55). The former were more common. The sharply angular shoulders that were found on jars from the Turner site (11-S-50), another Mississippian site along the highway alignment, were represented at the Julien site only by one sherd lacking a segment of rim.

There were three unusual shoulders in the Julien site collection (Figures 59 and 63). Two were lobed, representing squash. The other was a Ramey Incised vessel with occasional evaginations that interrupt an otherwise smooth, shoulder circumference.

Several of the first four rim types were represented by vessel segments large enough to have shoulders present. Both curved and angular shoulder configurations occurred on the Types 2, 3, and 4 rim segments. The Type 1 rim was present on three sherds large enough to include a shoulder; each had an angular shoulder.

Fourteen jar handles were present in the collection. Eleven belonged to rim segments, while three were isolated, fragmentary specimens. There seemed to be four different handle varieties (Figure 60). The most common form was represented by six handles that had oval or circular cross sections; these handles originated at vessel lips and inserted at or below vessel necks. A strap handle variety was represented by two small fragments. These curved handles were rectangular in cross section, their widths being much greater than their thicknesses. One particularly fine strap handle displayed a black, polished film on both surfaces. An angular variation of the first handle form mentioned above was also present, being represented by two specimens. Instead of the handle describing an arc, however, these specimens were V-shaped, with the midpoint apices projecting laterally. The cross sections of both specimens were circular. Another common handle, represented by four specimens, was an angular form with a prominent knob of clay applied to the superior handle surface. The knobs projected above the vessel lips and probably were purely

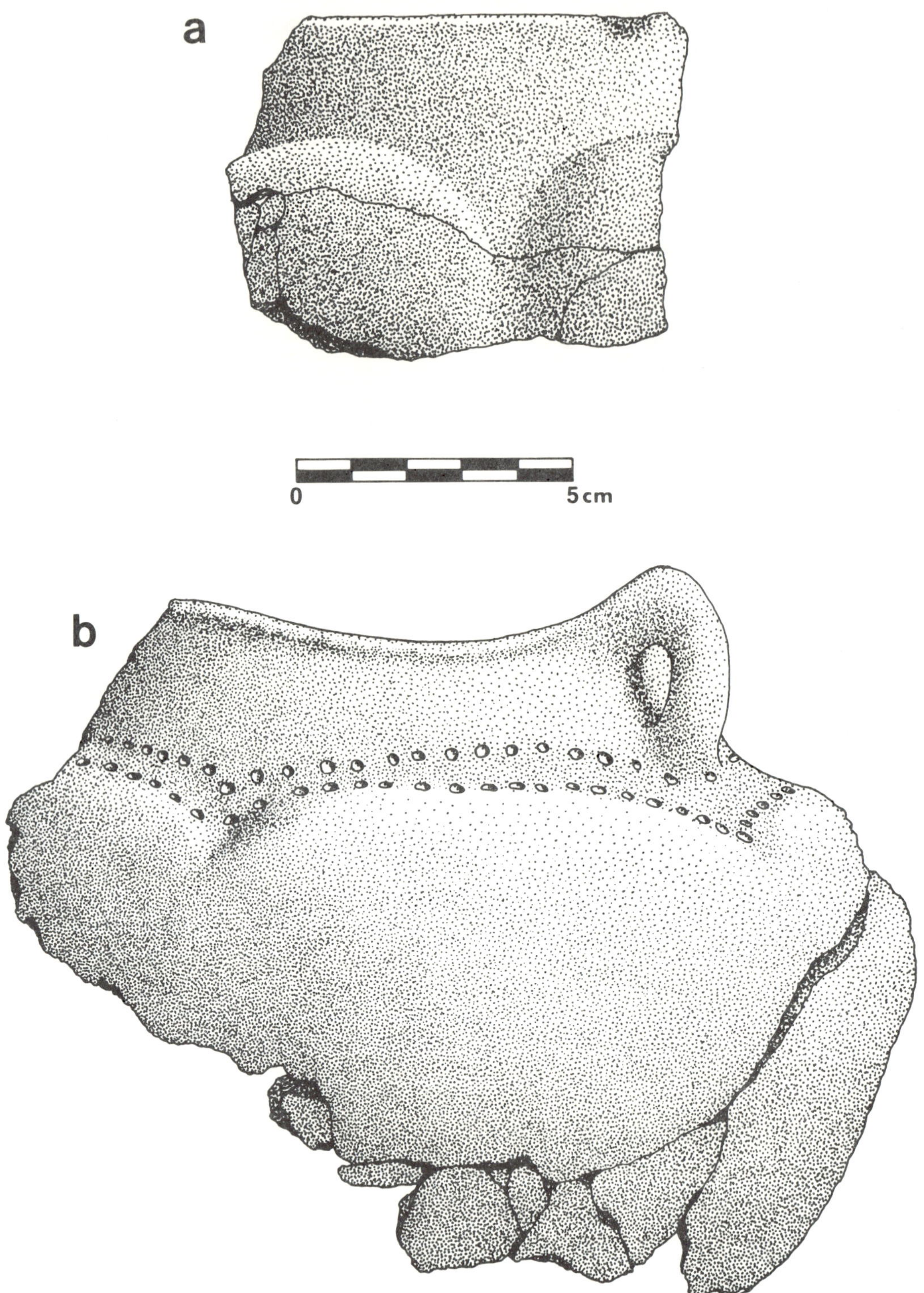

Figure 59. Mississippian Jars with Lobed Shoulders: a, Rim 28-1; b, Rim 9-4

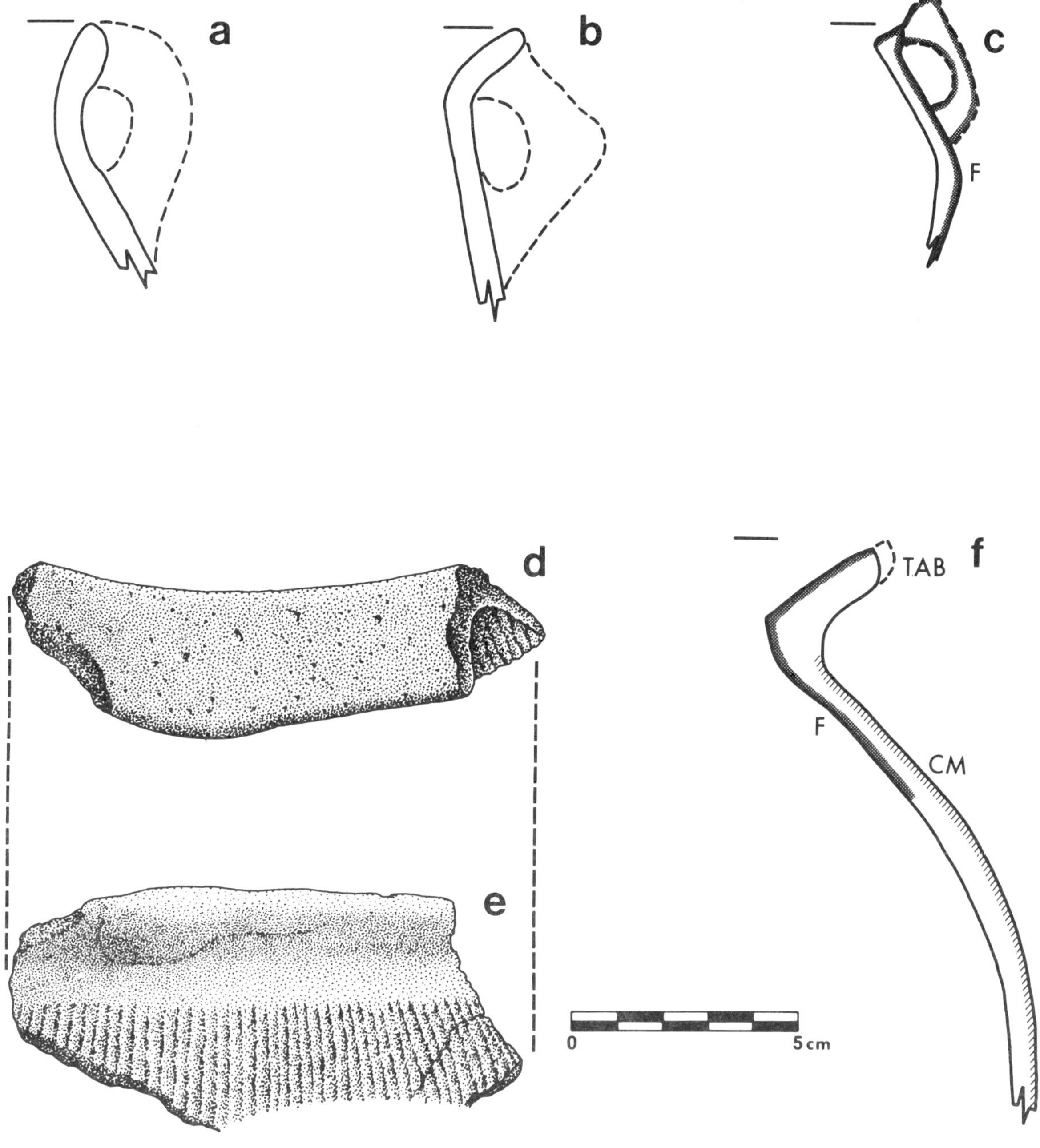

Figure 60. Mississippian Type 3 Jar Rims with Handles and Tabs: a, 1-4, with loop handle; b, 241-9, with v-shaped handle; c, 146-3, with angular shoulder and knob handle; d-f, 88-4, with curved shoulder and tabs

decorative. These four kinds of handles are also found in other American Bottom ceramic series (O'Brien 1972; Porter 1974; Vogel 1975).

Tabs were present on the lips of 13 jars; 8 of these vessels had the Type 3 rim variant. The tabs resembled a very broad "V". In the specimen illustrated in Figure 60, a poorly differentiated tab had been formed by the addition of an extra clay lump, which is still visible on the underside of the lip. Tabs may have been used to suspend vessels.

Shell-tempered jars were further divided into surface treatment categories often employed to describe pottery from American Bottom Mississippian sites. The four surface treatment categories and two aspects of vessel morphology, rim and shoulder shape, are listed for the shell-tempered jars in Table 32. Unfortunately, many shell-tempered jars were represented by only small lip segments; the exterior surface treatments on those sherds could not be distinguished. Julien site jars, particularly those with Type 3 rims, tended to break at the neck.

In the Julien collection there were 109 shell-tempered jars with plain or polished exterior surfaces. Many of the exterior and interior surfaces had been polished, but that attribute was difficult to record systematically, given the eroded nature of many sherds. These vessels conformed to the St. Clair Plain vessel variety.

Many rim types were present on vessels in the St. Clair Plain category, but the Type 3 form predominated. Shoulder morphology was variable; it ranged from the somewhat angular to the curved forms. One example of a scalloped squash pot shoulder was also present (Figure 59). The St. Clair Plain vessels had a mean neck diameter of 22.3 cm, but they varied widely in size (s=7.9). Vogel (1975) has noted previously that shell-tempered, plain jars from Tracts 15A and 15B at Cahokia are a morphologically diverse group, an observation paralleled by the Julien site data.

The Julien site shell-tempered plain or polished jars were not only common, they also were distributed widely throughout the site area. These vessels occurred in 15 of 18 structures, with their associated internal features, that contained shell-tempered jars. That distribution is not unexpected given the probable utilitarian nature of this particular group of vessels.

The exterior surfaces of 46 shell-tempered jars were filmed. A black film was present on 50% of the filmed vessels, brown on 34.8%, and red on 15.2%. All but two red films had been polished. These filmed vessels were usually relatively finely crafted, and, by virtue of their surface treatments, conformed to the Powell Plain jar category.

The Julien site Powell Plain jars displayed diverse morphologies, but like the other jar categories, the Type 3 rim form predominated. Although it does not appear in Table 32, one additional short rim segment with a tab was also included with this jar category. While its

Table 32. Mississippian Shell-tempered Jars

	Rim Types												Shoulder Types					
	1		2		3		4		5		6		Angular		Curved		Other	
Exterior Surface	N	%	N	%	N	%	N	%	N	%	N	%	N	%	N	%	N	%
Plain	2	1.8	14	12.8	83	76.1	4	3.7	5	4.6	1	0.9	12	36.4	20	60.6	1	3.0
Filmed	6	13.3	-	-	37	82.2	1	2.2	1	2.2	-	-	7	63.6	4	36.4	-	-
Filmed and Decorated	1	4.0	-	-	24	96.0	-	-	-	-	-	-	6	60.0	3	30.0	1	10.0
Cordmarked	-	-	-	-	29	82.9	5	14.3	1	2.9	-	-	-	-	12	100.0	-	-

Note: Missing observations are not included.

rim morphology could not be determined, it was probably of the common Type 3 variety. Two Type 3 rims had been modified by decorative details. One had shallow notches impressed on its lip edge; another specimen had radially oriented, short, trailed impressions on its interior lip surface. Angular and curved shoulders were both common, but there were more of the former. The isolated, very angular shoulder section mentioned previously displayed a black, polished exterior film. It should be included in this vessel category, unless a trailed decoration is also missing from this relatively small sherd.

Some of the Powell Plain jars were quite sizeable; the mean neck diameter for these filmed vessels was 21.8 cm (s=8.2). A large vessel capacity was indicated by the size of many of the jar orifices that would be consistent with the use of these vessels as storage containers. A large jar from Feature 252 (Figures 20 and 61; Plate 5) provides direct evidence for this. Its vessel exterior had a black film with occasional brown fire clouds. It had been polished, and burnishing marks were clearly visible. The interior was plain. It was asymmetric in plan view, with an orifice measuring 24 cm by 27 cm. The maximum shoulder diameter measured 34.0 cm by 35.5 cm. This vessel was one of the very few where a measurement of height (24 cm) could be obtained. Note that measurements of orifice diameter, if taken on small rim segments, would provide somewhat different results if the vessel were fragmented. This undoubtedly also applies to other vessels in the collection; therefore, the measurements presented here should be considered as approximations only.

The exterior filmed, shell-tempered jars were relatively well distributed throughout the site area. Of 18 structure contexts with shell-tempered jars, 12 contained this particular vessel type.

Shell-tempered jars with exterior filming and trailed decorations were represented by 25 rim segments. Other decorated sherds were present in the ceramic series, but these were typically small and did not have attached portions of rims. The films were usually black (56% of the total); brown and red films were present on 40% and 4% of the jars, respectively. All films were polished, except for one of the brown films. The decorative lines on the jar shoulders were U-shaped in cross section and filmed. Often, these jars were finely made. They conformed to the Ramey Incised jar formed, which is well represented in the Cahokia area.

Several decorative motifs are illustrated in Figures 62 and 63. Among them are various curvilinear and rectilinear designs, including the curved-ladder and nested scroll-and-line decorations. Each of these Julien motifs can be found in ceramic series from other American Bottom sites (O'Brien 1972; Porter 1974; Vogel 1975). The decorations ranged from esthetically pleasing, symmetric designs to those that were more irregular. Sometimes, the latter had "extra" lines or marks, probably resulting from manufacturing accidents.

Plate 5. Mississippian Jar: Powell plain jar (252-1)

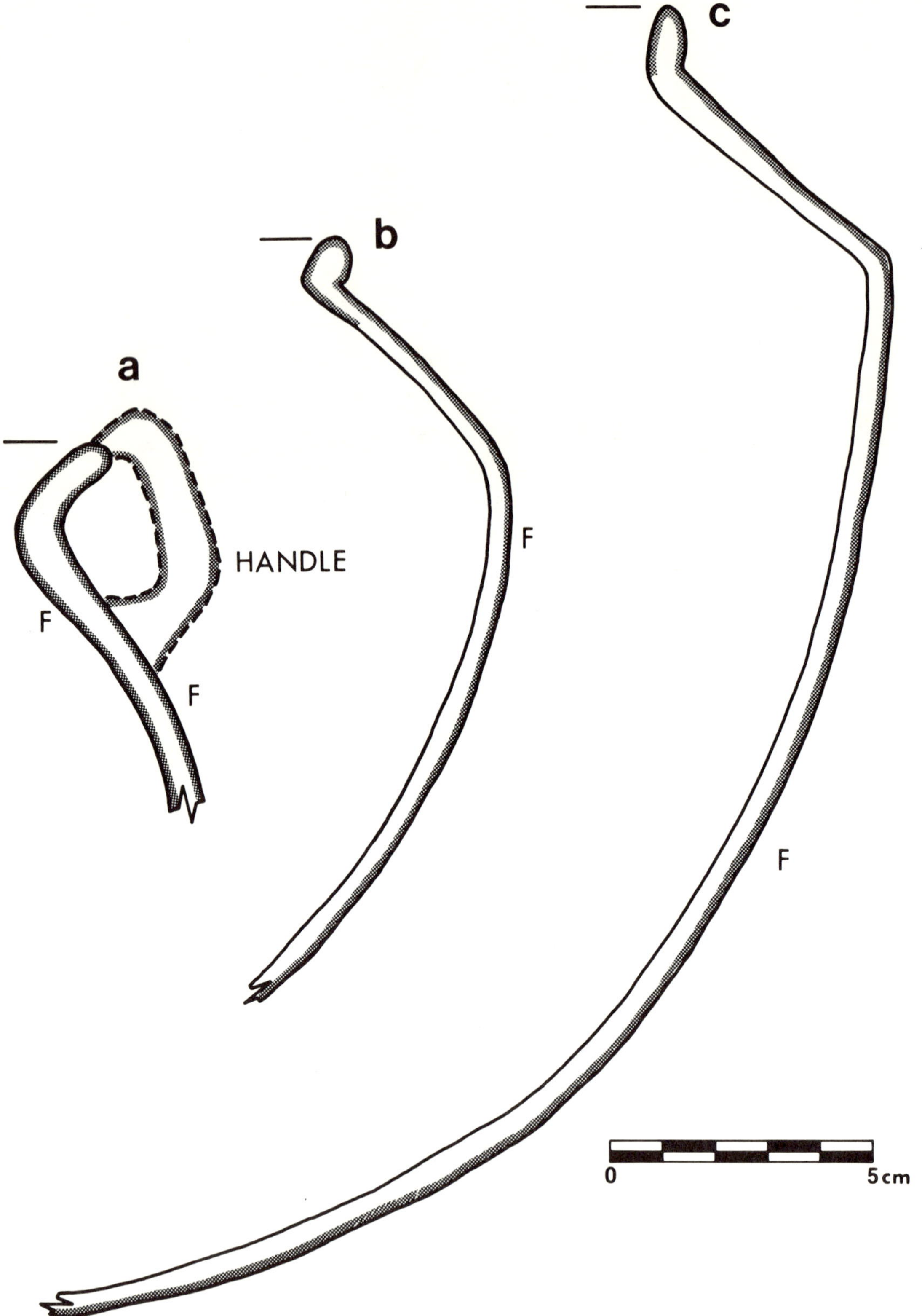

Figure 61. Mississippian Jar Rim Profiles: a, 89-1, Type 3 with curved shoulder; b, 224-1, Type 1 with angular shoulder; c, 252-1, Type 3 with angular shoulder

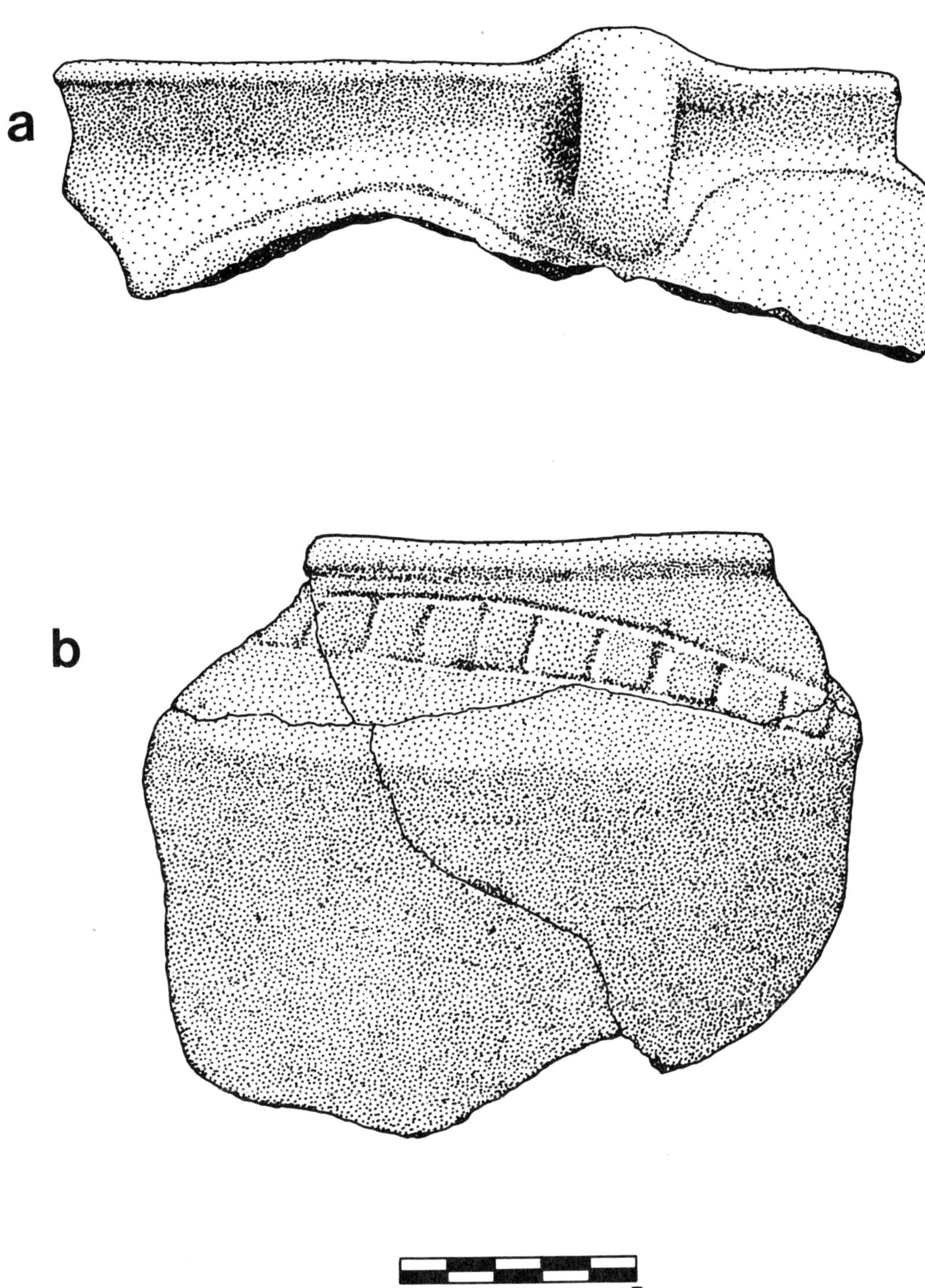

Figure 62. Mississippian Jar Rims: a, 89-1, with wide trailed line; b, 224-1, with ladder motif

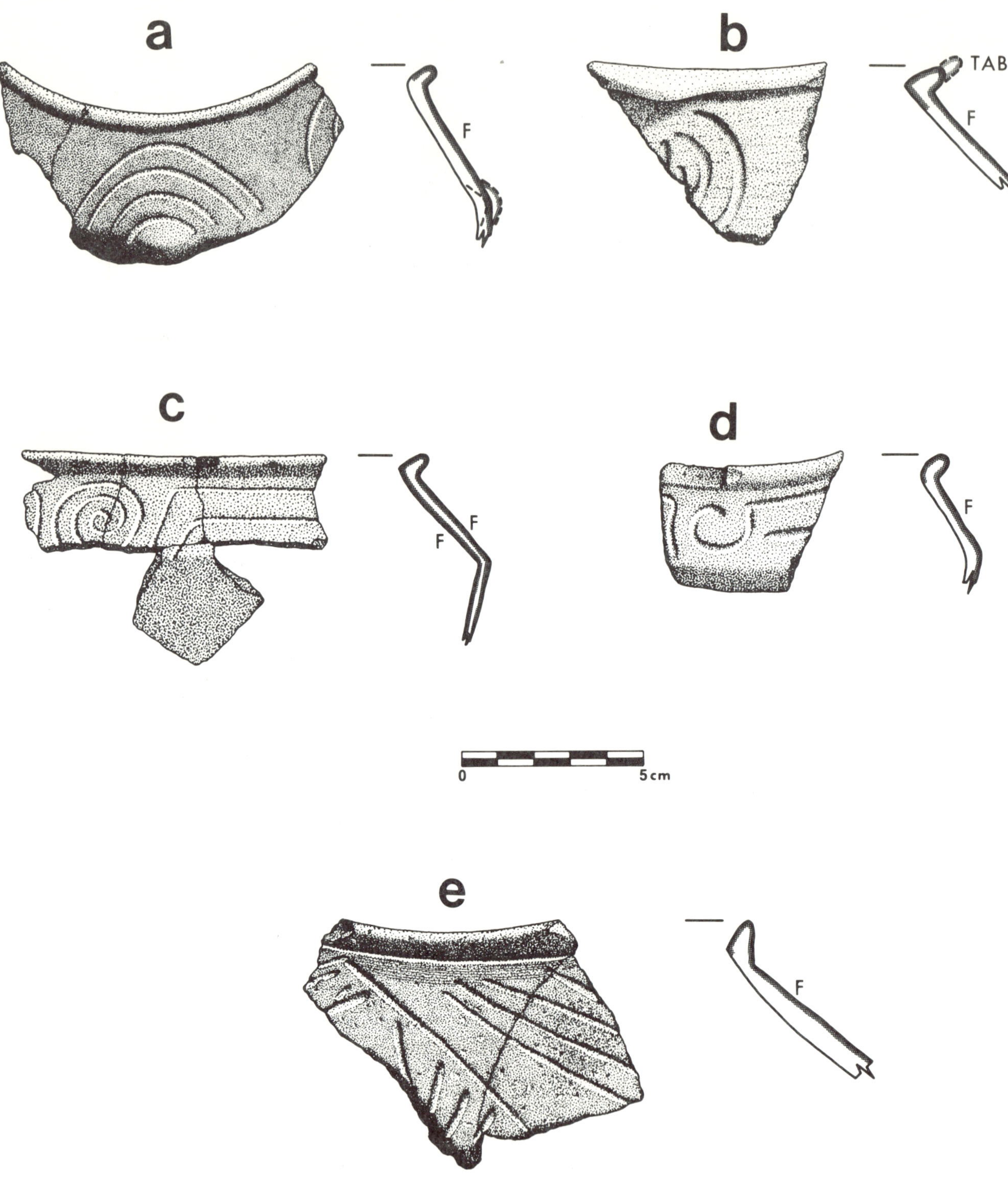

Figure 63. Mississippian Ramey Incised Jar Rim and Shoulders: a, 69-1, Type 3 with angular shoulder; b, 25-4, Type 3; c, 20-1, Type 3 with angular shoulder; d, 25-6, Type 3 with angular shoulder; e, 25-11, Type 3

Most Ramey Incised vessels had Type 3 rims. The rims were not, however, as elongated as those often found on jars of other categories, in particular the St. Clair Plain and Cahokia Cordmarked forms. One of the Type 3 rims had shallow notches impressed on its lip edge; it resembled the Powell Plain segment previously mentioned. Ramey Incised shoulders tended to be angular. Of particular interest was one shoulder, in which the exterior contour had been modified by pushing the shoulder out from the interior when the paste was still moist. Each of the resulting evaginations formed the focus of a nested series of trailed arcs on the vessel shoulder (Figure 63). The Ramey Incised vessels had a mean neck diameter of 21.2 cm (s=6.9).

The Ramey Incised jar segments had a restricted distribution within the excavation area. They occurred in 6 of 18 structures and associated features that contained shell-tempered jars. This is consistent with a suggested restricted temporal range and use in specialized, perhaps nonutilitarian, contexts (Porter 1974, among others).

Thirty-five jars in the Julien site collection were shell-tempered and displayed cordmarked exterior surface treatments. The cordmarking tended to be vertically oriented, at least in the area immediately inferior to the neck. As mentioned previously, S-twist was the most common cord type, occurring on 22 vessels; the Z-twist cord variety was applied to the remaining 13 jars. Often, the interior lip and body surfaces were filmed (77.1% and 70.6% of the vessels, respectively). Twenty vessels had a red film applied to the lip area, six a brown film, and one a black film with small, red fire clouds on the neck. These jars represent the Cahokia Cordmarked type.

These rims were exclusively the Type 3 form or its derived variants, Types 4 and 5. It should be noted that the Type 3 rims were often particularly elongated in this jar form, and all of the shoulders were curved. At times, the jars were relatively large; the mean neck diameter was 24.4 cm (s=7.5).

This particular vessel category was present in 8 of 18 structure contexts that contained shell-tempered jars. Those structures were scattered throughout the entire excavation area. Feature 289 was at the southwesternern end of the feature distribution, and Feature 91 was at the opposite end.

Only a few of the vessels with identifiable exterior finishes and shell tempering did not belong to the above four categories. The five small, crude pinchpots were not included with the plain exterior vessel category. Two of these pinchpots were found in Feature 87, a pit, and are illustrated in Figure 73. In addition, there were portions of three larger, shell-tempered jars that had surface characteristics excluding them from the previously discussed vessel categories. The squash pot illustrated in Figure 59 had a plain exterior and a double row of punctates bordering its lobed shoulder. The punctates were relatively uniform, ca. 2.5 mm in diameter, and their centers were elevated.

Apparently, a grass stalk was used to make these impressions. This vessel was from Feature 9, a pit that also contained portions of two tradeware water bottles discussed below. Two small rim segments with notches on both the interior and exterior surfaces of the neck were recovered from Features 7 and 241, both structures (Figure 73). A horizontal, trailed line was present on one of the two rim segments below the exterior notches. Another unusual shell-tempered segment was thought to be a jar; it lacked a rim, and had a surface decoration of alternating bands of punctates and lines (Figure 73). Sherds of this small body segment were recovered from an internal pit in structure Feature 241 and from a nearby external pit.

As noted previously, only a few jars were tempered with material other than shell. Limestone is the most frequently used of the minor temper media. The exterior surfaces of five limestone-tempered jars were polished, two displayed a red polished film, and one was unidentified. The extèrior surfaces of the two jars tempered with grog and a mixture of shell and grog were unidentified. As mentioned previously, two pinchpots were tempered with grit, two with grog, and one with limestone. One of the two grog-tempered pinchpots had a black filmed and polished exterior.

Bowls and Pans

There were 159 Julien site bowls; 2 of the 159 were pinchpots. They had relatively straight sides that were nearly vertical or insloping. The maximum diameters of these vessels were at, or near, their lips. Most were represented by relatively small vessel fragments, so their base shapes were often unknown. When present, the bases were relatively flat with a distinct, angular shift in the profile contour demarcating the vessel sides from the bases. Also recovered were fragments of seven pans, identified by their comparatively heavy, crude appearance, shallow shapes, and large size. These vessels had large orifice diameters and, like many bowls, insloping sides; basal sections were not present.

The Julien site bowls and pans are discussed together since it was sometimes difficult to separate the two vessel categories according to a consistent set of criteria. The terms, bowl and pan, have been applied to Mississippian ceramics in the region, and there is some justification for using such designations to describe the morphological variability in the Julien site collection. However, the criteria of shape and size employed during the initial sorting and descriptive process did not permit a separation of vessels into wholly coherent morphological vessel categories.

The relationship between orifice diameter and rim orientation illustrates the difficulty in distinguishing bowls from pans in the Julien site collection (Figure 65). [Rim orientation describes the angle of intersection between a vessel´s side and a horizontal plane defined by its lip (Figure 64).]

BOWLS and PANS

A. Rim Orientation

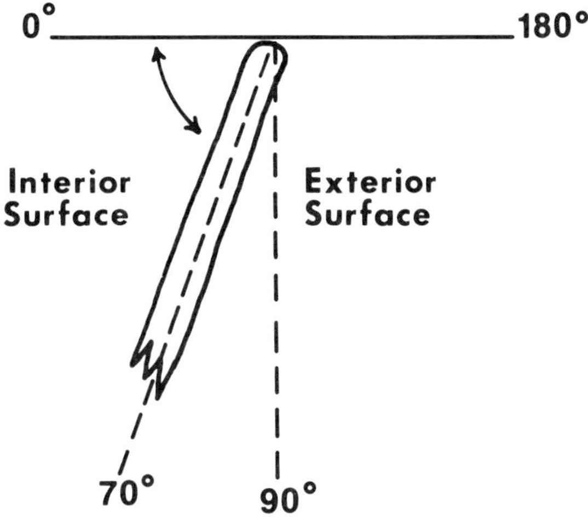

B. Rim Types

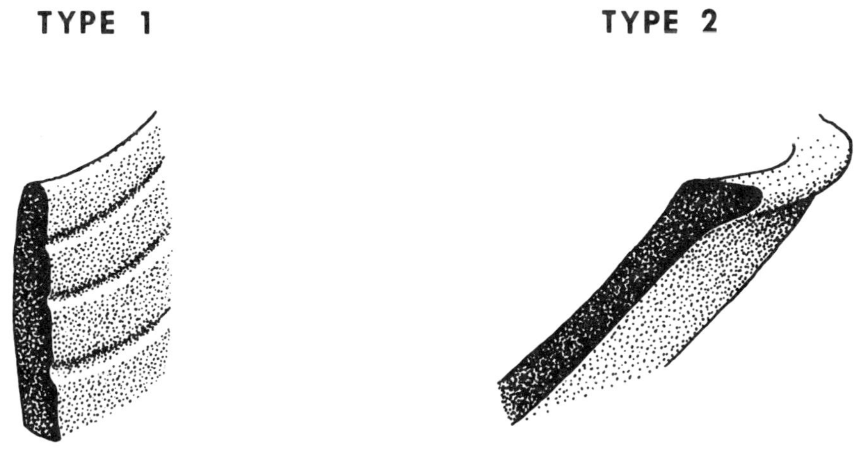

Figure 64. Mississippian Bowl and Pan Rim Orientations and Rim Types

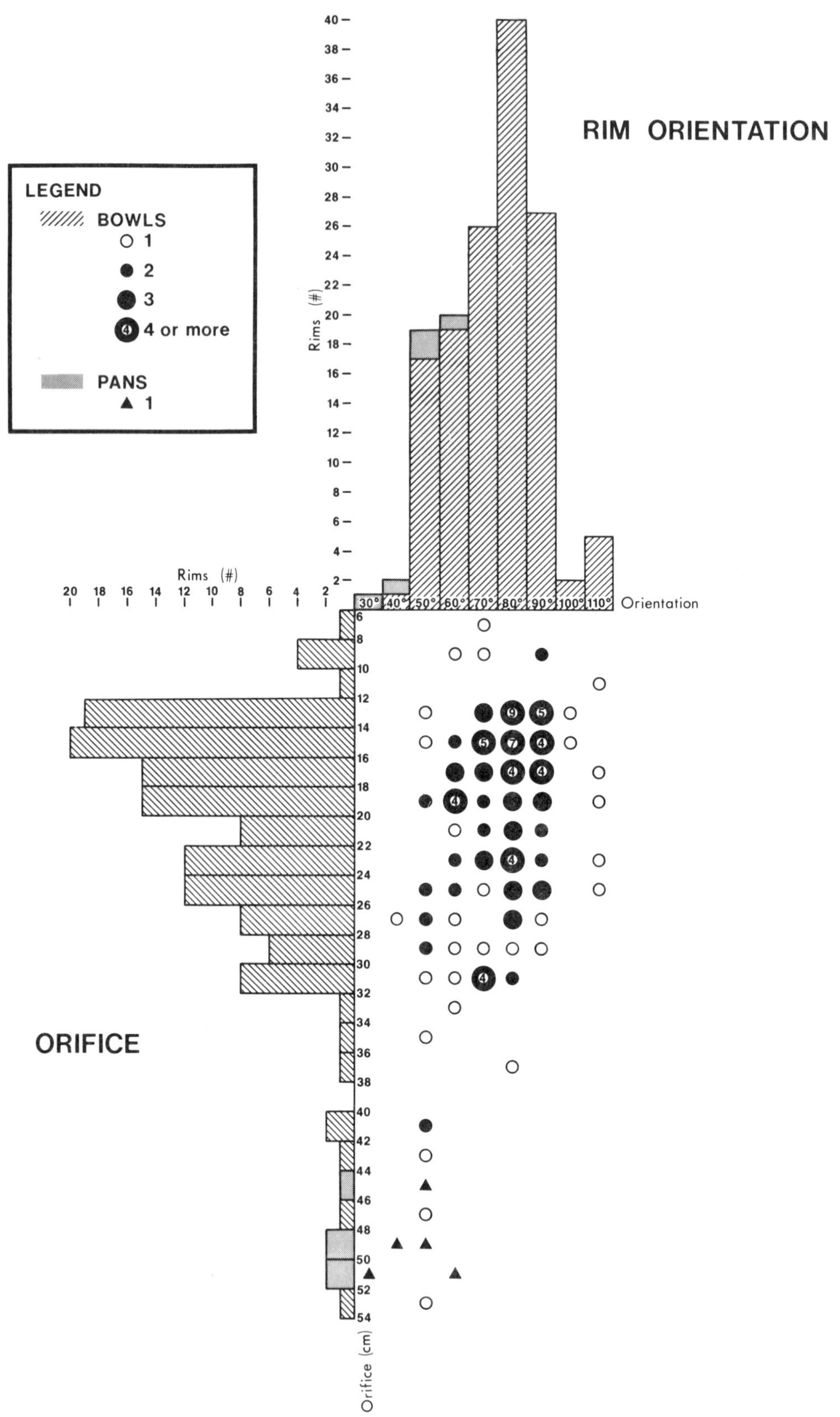

Figure 65. Mississippian Bowl and Pan Rim Orientations and Orifice Diameters

While pan orifices are generally larger and the rim angles less than those of most bowls, these two criteria alone are not sufficient to distinguish the two vessel forms. Vessel wall thickness also helps in differentiating pans from bowls. The vessel wall thickness at ca. 1 cm below the lip was thicker in pans (N=6, range=0.77-0.99 cm, mean=0.91 cm) than in large bowls, those exceeding 30 cm in diameter (N=18, range=0.45-0.81 cm, mean=0.62 cm). The use of those three attributes and others, such as vessel height (usually unknown in this ceramic series), may serve as a more consistent and reliable means to discriminate between such broadly similar morphological groups as bowls and pans.

Instead of distinguishing between bowls and pans, these Julien site containers might be more adequately described as a relatively continuous series ranging from vessels with vertical or somewhat insloping sides and small orifices, to specimens with large orifices and more pronounced insloping sides. However, the vessels were not uniformly distributed throughout the size range. The overwhelming majority shared the characteristics of nearly vertical sides and relatively small orifice diameters. The largest Julien site vessels were ca. 50 cm in diameter, a relatively small orifice diameter considering the diameters of so-called "salt pans," which are so widely distributed throughout much of the Southeast (Brown 1980).

For the purpose of this analysis, further pursuit of the question of appropriate terminology was considered to be of less importance than an examination of inferred container use. Several attributes were examined that were shared by some, but certainly not all, of the bowls and pans. An attempt was made to describe readily recognizable aspects of the vessels as well as to distinguish covarying attributes indicative of vessel use.

As with most vessels at the site, the pastes of the bowls and pans usually were tempered with crushed shell. The majority (88.6%) had only shell as a temper, while two rims, which represent 1.2% of these vessel forms, had both shell and grog as tempers. Grog was found in nine (5.4%) vessels, and eight (4.8%) were tempered with limestone. Seven of the limestone-tempered vessels had both interior and exterior red films. These represent the Monks Mound Red vessel type, which is found in Emergent Mississippian and early Mississippian contexts in the American Bottom. Five Monks Mound Red bowls were from features in a group at the southwestern end of the excavation area, near structure Feature 267, which are thought to have been associated with the Stirling phase.

Most bowls and pans had filmed surfaces. The exteriors were filmed on 59% of the vessels; the remaining vessels were plain or polished. Black, the predominate film color, was found on 27.1% of all vessel exteriors, brown films on 19.3%, and red films on 12.7%. Vessel interiors were also often filmed (50.9%). Again, black predominated, with 21.4% of all vessels displaying a black film. Red and brown films occurred on 16.0% and 13.5% of all vessel interiors, respectively.

With the notable exception of the largest vessels, the frequency of exterior filming was nearly the same throughout the vessel size range (Figure 66). A dramatic decrease in the frequency of exterior filming among the largest vessels may relate to esthetics; the exteriors on those large and relatively shallow vessels would rarely have been seen during normal use. Not only would the rim angle on the large vessels have tended to hide the exterior surface, but it is possible that the vessels were partially supported in shallow depressions. Although there was a gradual, but slight, increase in the frequency of internal filming as the orifice size increased, no pronounced shift similar to that which occurred on the vessel exteriors was evident.

Given the relationship between exterior surface finishes and vessel size, it is perhaps significant that bowls with decorated exteriors tended to have small or moderate orifice diameters and relatively vertical sides (Table 33). Decorations were present on 14 bowls; they consisted of incised or trailed lines. Although most of the vessels were represented only by small, eroded sherds, several are known to have had parallel, trailed lines on their exterior surfaces. Those vessels represent the Mound Place Incised ceramic type, a vessel form widely distributed throughout the central and lower Mississippi River valley (Phillips 1970).

The Julien site bowls had two distinctive rim styles, designated Types 1 and 2 (Figure 64). The Type 1 lips were unmodified. The rims terminated in rounded, flat, or beveled edges. The Type 2 rims were distinctively shaped, and there were only eight in this ceramic series. The lip of the second rim style was flared laterally; there was a distinct angularity at the point of intersection between the insloping vessel sides and the horizontally oriented lip (Figures 67 and 68). The Type 2 lip lengths were relatively consistent, regardless of vessel size (N=8, range=0.95-1.22 cm, mean=1.06 cm, s=0.11). [The lip length measurement refers to the distance between the angle on the vessel′s interior and the end of the lip.] Rims similar to the Julien Type 2 form have been found at the Mitchell site (Porter 1974).

Type 2 rims tended to occur on vessels (all so-called bowls) with moderate or large orifice diameters. Vessels with that rim style usually had relatively thin side walls, regardless of vessel diameter. Perhaps the Type 2 rims reinforced the container edge or served as handles.

Appendages classified as tabs or handles are presumed to have been both functional and decorative. If both the tabs and the Type 2 rims served as handles, it is interesting that they were associated with different shaped vessels. Vessels with the Type 2 rims tended to be larger in diameter than those with appendages, although their distributions overlapped (Table 33). A comparison of rim orientation more clearly separates the two groups. Vessels with tabs tended to have nearly vertical sides. Presumably, some of the vessels with tabs also once had attached animal heads. Animal effigy bowls in the American

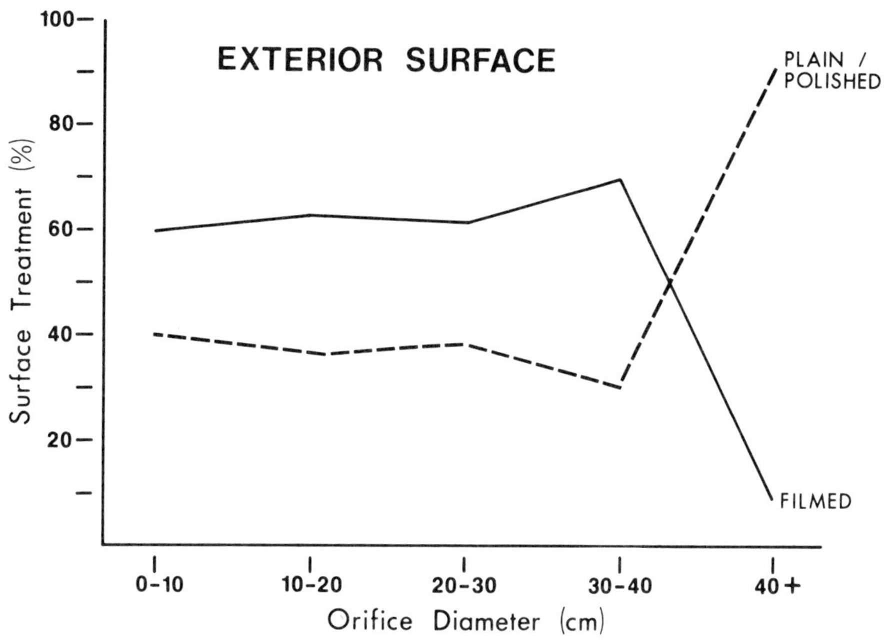

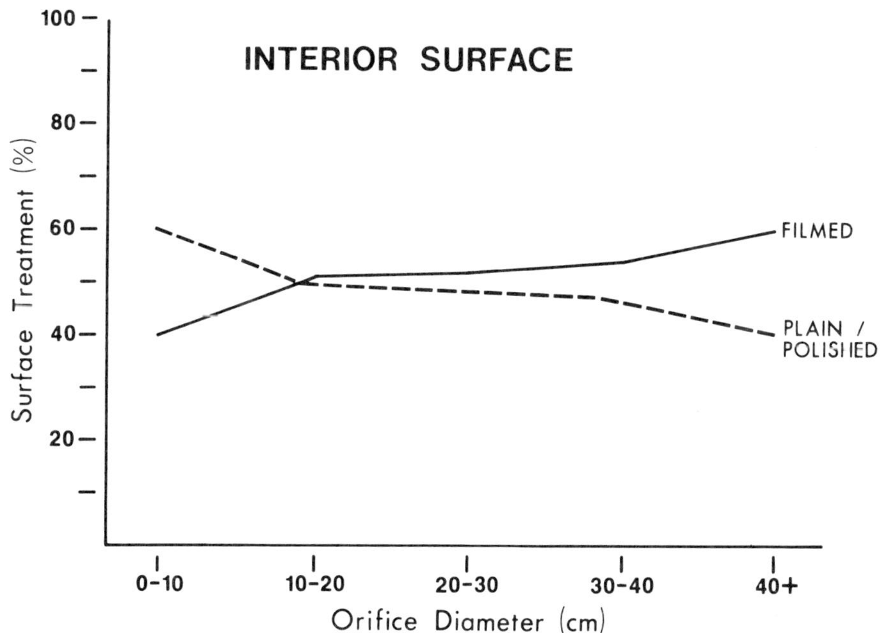

Figure 66. Distribution of Mississippian Bowl and Pan Orifice Diameters by Exterior and Interior Surface Treatments

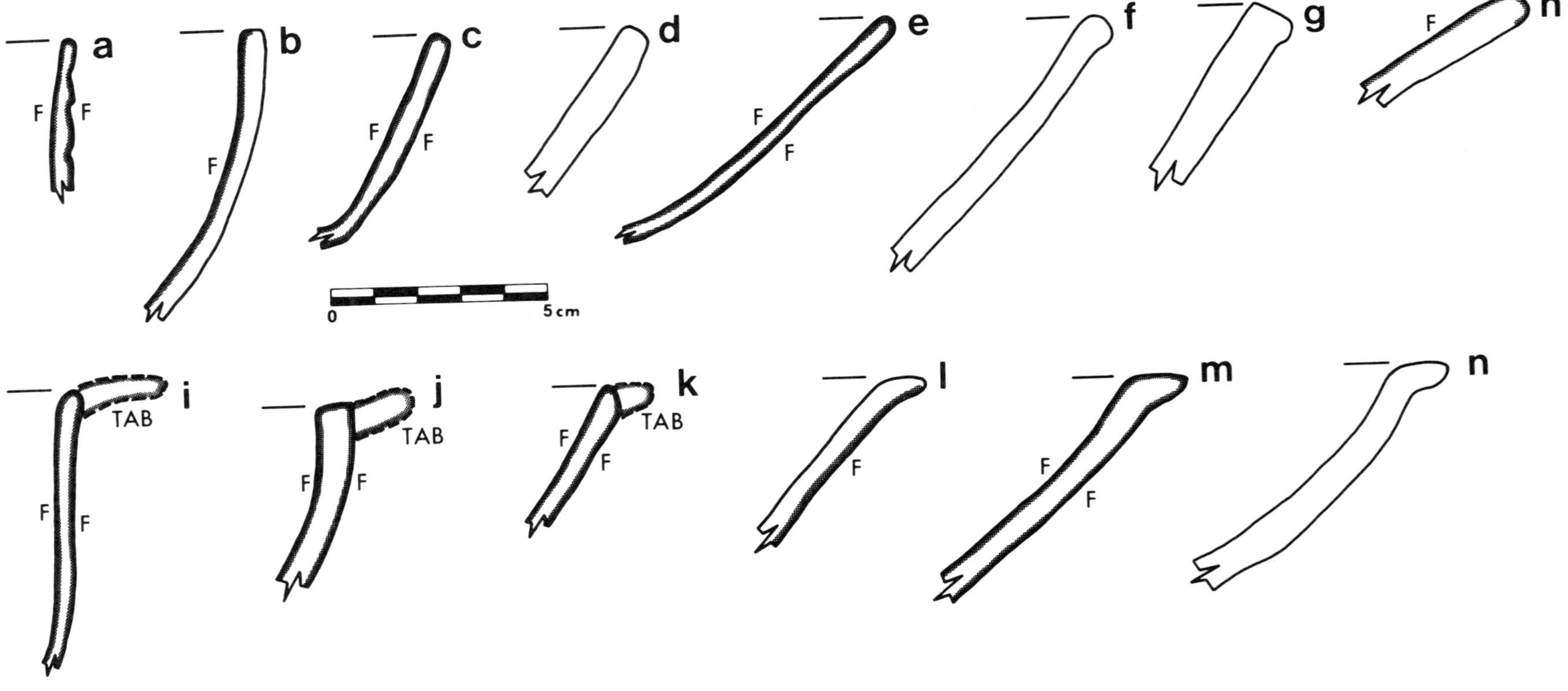

Figure 67. Mississippian Bowl and Pan Rim Profiles: a, 159-1, Bowl, Type 1 rim; b, 293-3, Bowl, Type 1 rim; c, 9-2, Bowl, Type 1 rim; d, 2-6, Bowl, Type 1 rim; e, 295-14, Bowl, Type 1 rim; f, 7-5, Bowl, Type 1 rim; g, 241-40, Pan, Type 1 rim; h, 21-3, Pan, Type 1 rim; i, 115-19, Bowl, Type 1 rim with tab; j, 29-3, Bowl, Type 1 rim with tab; k, 295-9, Bowl, Type 1 rim with tab; l, 7-7, Bowl, Type 2 rim; m, 5-13, Bowl, Type 2 rim; n, 87-4, Bowl, Type 2 rim

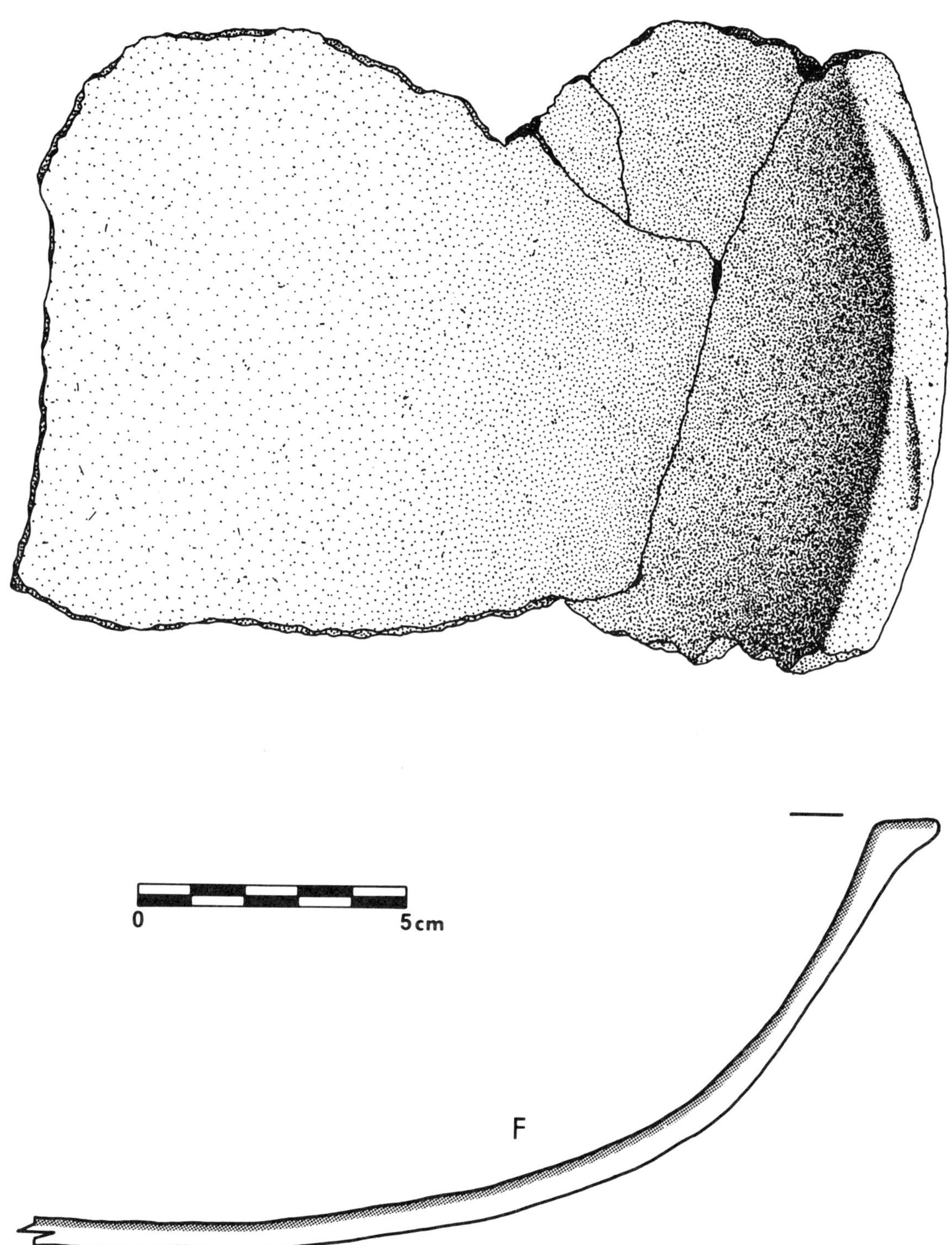

Figure 68. Mississippian Bowl: 57-1, Type 2 rim

Table 33. Bowls and Pans with Type 2 Rims, Appendages, and Exterior Decorations Listed by Orifice Characteristics*

Orifice Diameter (cm)	Type 2 Rims		Tabs		Decoration		Rim Orientation (Degrees)	Type 2 Rims		Tabs		Decoration	
	N	%	N	%	N	%		N	%	N	%	N	%
0-12	-	-	-	-	1	16.7	30, 40, & 50	4	18.2	-	-	-	-
12-18	1	1.7	4	6.8	4	6.8	60	1	5.0	2	10.0	-	-
18-24	2	4.7	4	9.3	4	9.3	70	1	3.8	-	-	1	3.8
24-30	3	10.3	3	10.3	1	3.4	80	1	2.4	3	7.3	2	4.9
30-36	1	7.7	-	-	2	15.4	90	1	3.7	3	11.1	4	14.8
36+	1	8.3	-	-	-	-	100 and 110	-	-	1	14.3	-	-

* Only those vessels with measured orifice orientations are included.

Bottom usually had small or moderate diameters and nearly vertical sides. While animal effigies were not associated with specific rim segments, several isolated bird head ornaments were present in the collection.

Two individual vessels merit special attention: the first because it displayed evidence of use, and the second because it is thought to have been a tradeware. One large (48 cm in diameter) vessel appears to have been used in baking or evaporating liquids, perhaps saline solutions. The vessel had an internal, polished red film that extended to ca. 9 cm below the lip edge. Occasional small patches of red filming were visible for about another centimeter beyond the area of heavy and continuous filming. The remainder of the vessel segment's interior was eroded or scraped away. The exterior was plain, and there was adhering soot that extended 7 cm to 8 cm inferior to the lip. The paste of that portion of the vessel was somewhat darker than the paste of the basal sections. The internal and external surface characteristics indicated that the vessel had been placed on the ground or partially buried and had been surrounded by coals. Perhaps the interior film near the base had been scraped away with an adhering material once the heating process was completed. It is perhaps significant that this relatively large vessel segment (37.2% of the estimated orifice was present) was found in an external pit (Feature 249). Its location in an external feature and its surface characteristics are consistent with its use as a baking or evaporating vessel. Incidentally, it was one of the few vessels classified as a pan during the initial inventory of ceramic materials.

Owing to its unusual appearance and possible tradeware status, fragments of another vessel were included among the numbered vessels even though no rim segment was present. This vessel was from a pit (Feature 272) near structure Feature 267. The vessel's paste was more compact than most of those at the site. The exterior was red filmed and polished, and several fragmentary sherds were incised with fine lines, although the particular decorative motif could not be determined. This vessel is possibly related to vessels more commonly found in the lower Mississippi River valley.

Water Bottles

Fifteen water bottles were present in the Julien site collection. These vessels, portions of which came from 13 separate features, represent 2.7% of the entire Mississippian vessel assemblage. All of the water bottles were shell-tempered, globular vessels with constricted necks and vertical or slightly insloping rims (Figure 69). Rim heights were short relative to total vessel size; the extremely long-necked forms sometimes found in the American Bottom were not represented in this ceramic series.

The Julien site bottles tended to be sizable vessels with large capacities. A notable exception to that pattern was the bottle from

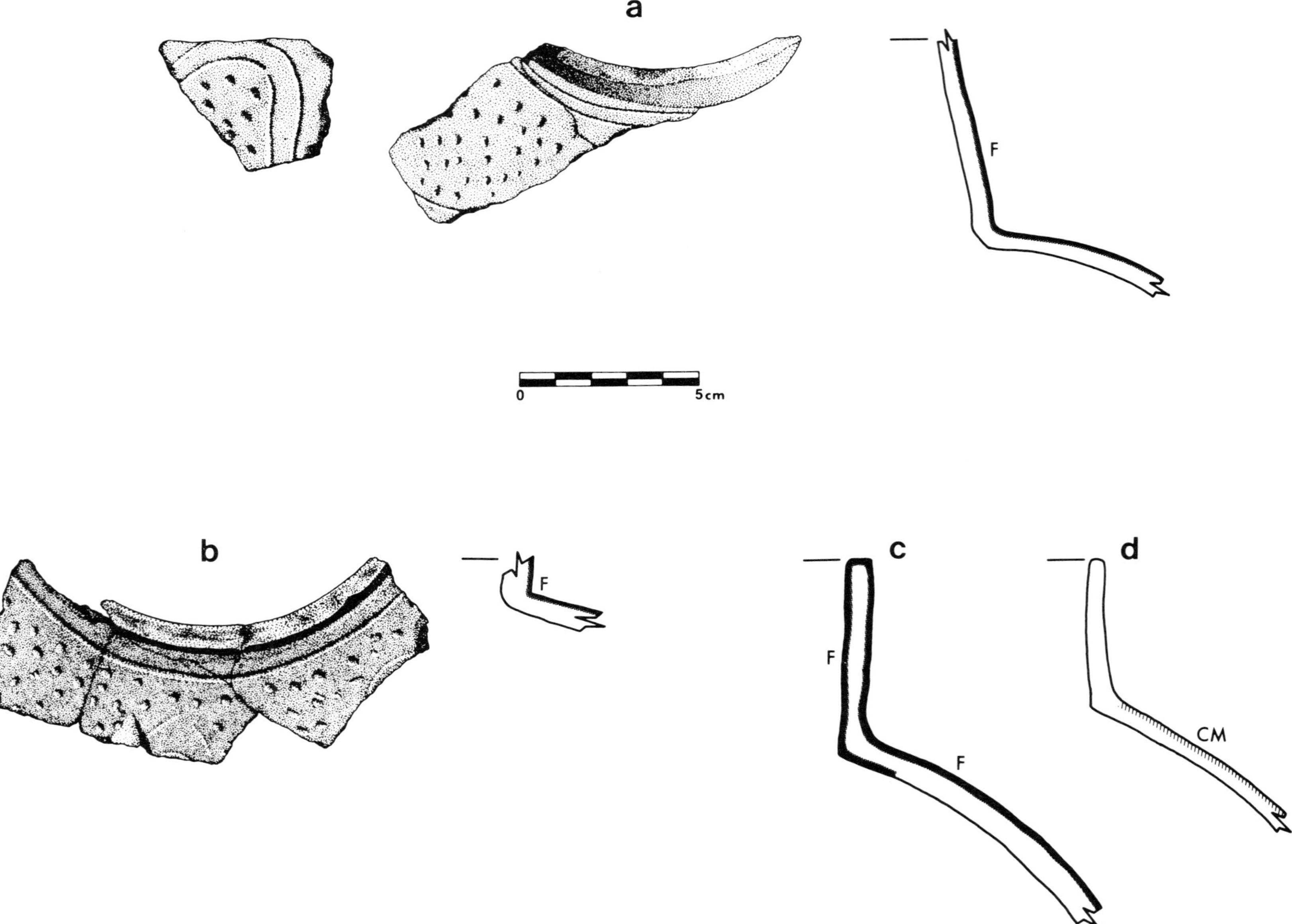

Figure 69. Mississippian Water Bottles: a, 9-8, neck and body; b, 13-1, neck; c, 2-3, rim; d, 295-8, rim

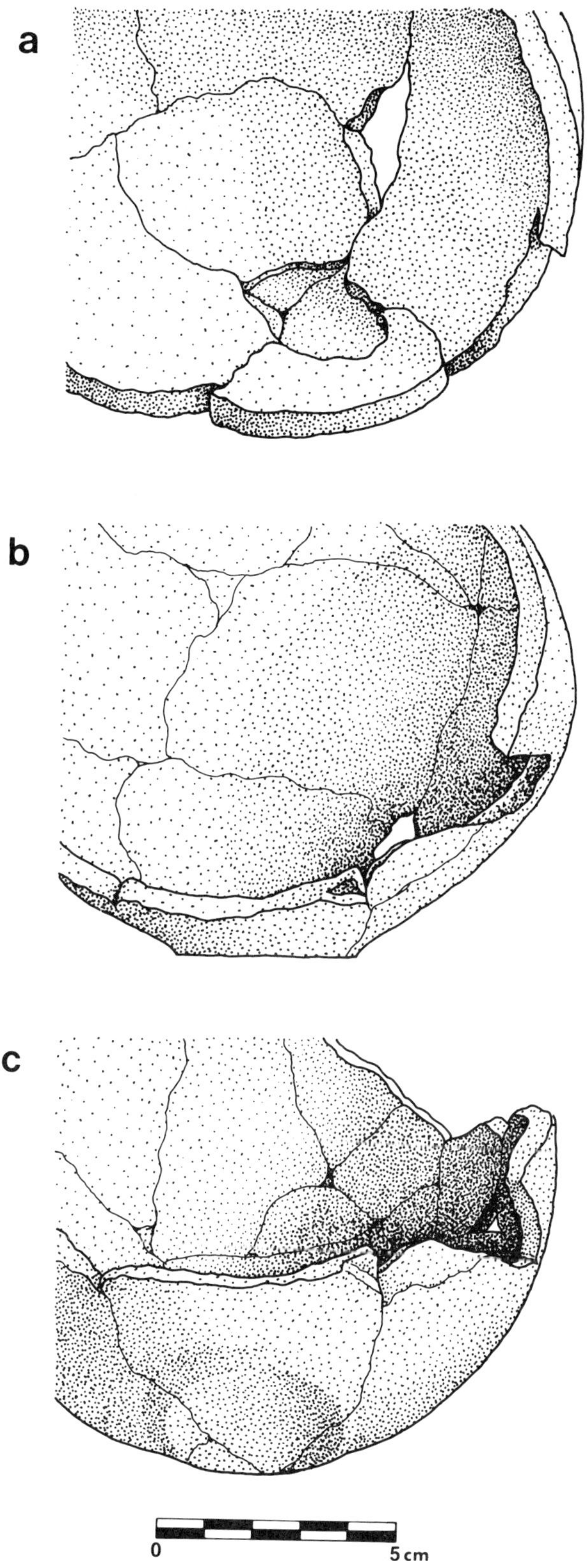

Figure 70. Mississippian Water Bottle 91-1 Construction: a, inside view; b, side view; c, back view

Feature 91, which is discussed below in more detail. Orifice diameters were generally small relative to presumed maximum vessel diameters. Orifice diameters of the 13 measured vessels ranged from 4 cm to 24 cm; one particular vessel was considerably larger than the rest. The mean and median orifice diameters both equaled 10 cm. The vessel exteriors displayed a variety of surface treatments that included eight filmed specimens, on which the film was polished in all but one vessel; three polished and three plain vessels; and one vessel with a cordmarked body and, apparently, a polished neck. Red filming predominated, being present on five vessels. There were also two brown filmed vessels and one black filmed vessel. The interior neck surfaces on nine vessels were plain, four were polished, and two displayed red films. A loop handle was present on the neck of one plain water bottle from Feature 91.

The construction technique of a water bottle from Feature 91 is of special interest (Figure 70). It was the smallest of the water bottles, and was constructed of two hemispheres, each with holes at their apices. The intersection of these two segments was angular, breaking an otherwise smooth exterior surface contour. After having been joined together, one of the holes was plugged and the exterior smoothed to form a small, flat base. The hole at the other end was modified by the addition of clay coils to form a short, insloping neck. The internal surface was roughened with many marks, made during the manufacturing process.

Two vessels from exterior pit Features 9 and 13 were decorated with complex, trailed designs (Figure 69). Both vessels had exterior polished films; one was black, and the other was light brown. The incomplete design motifs on these vessels consisted of broad, trailed lines and relatively large, smooth, and shallow punctations. Presumably, these two vessels were not indigenous to the area, and they probably represent tradewares from the lower Mississippi River valley.

Most water bottles (73.3%) were recovered from structures or from their associated internal features. These structures were numbered Features 2, 7, 17, 36, 91, 231, and 241. Four isolated pits (Features 9, 13, 160, and 290) had portions of water bottles included among their debris. Feature 290 superimposed the feature complex that included structure Features 231 and 241.

Beakers

Six beakers, representing 1.1% of the total Mississippian ceramic assemblage, were present in the collection. These vessels were shell-tempered with polished exterior and interior black films. Their sides were vertical, or nearly so, and relatively thin (Figure 71). The lips were usually somewhat thinner than the vessel walls; the former ranged from about 0.3 cm to 0.5 cm (mean=0.42 cm), and the latter from 0.3 cm to 0.7 cm (mean=0.46 cm). [The wall measurement was taken

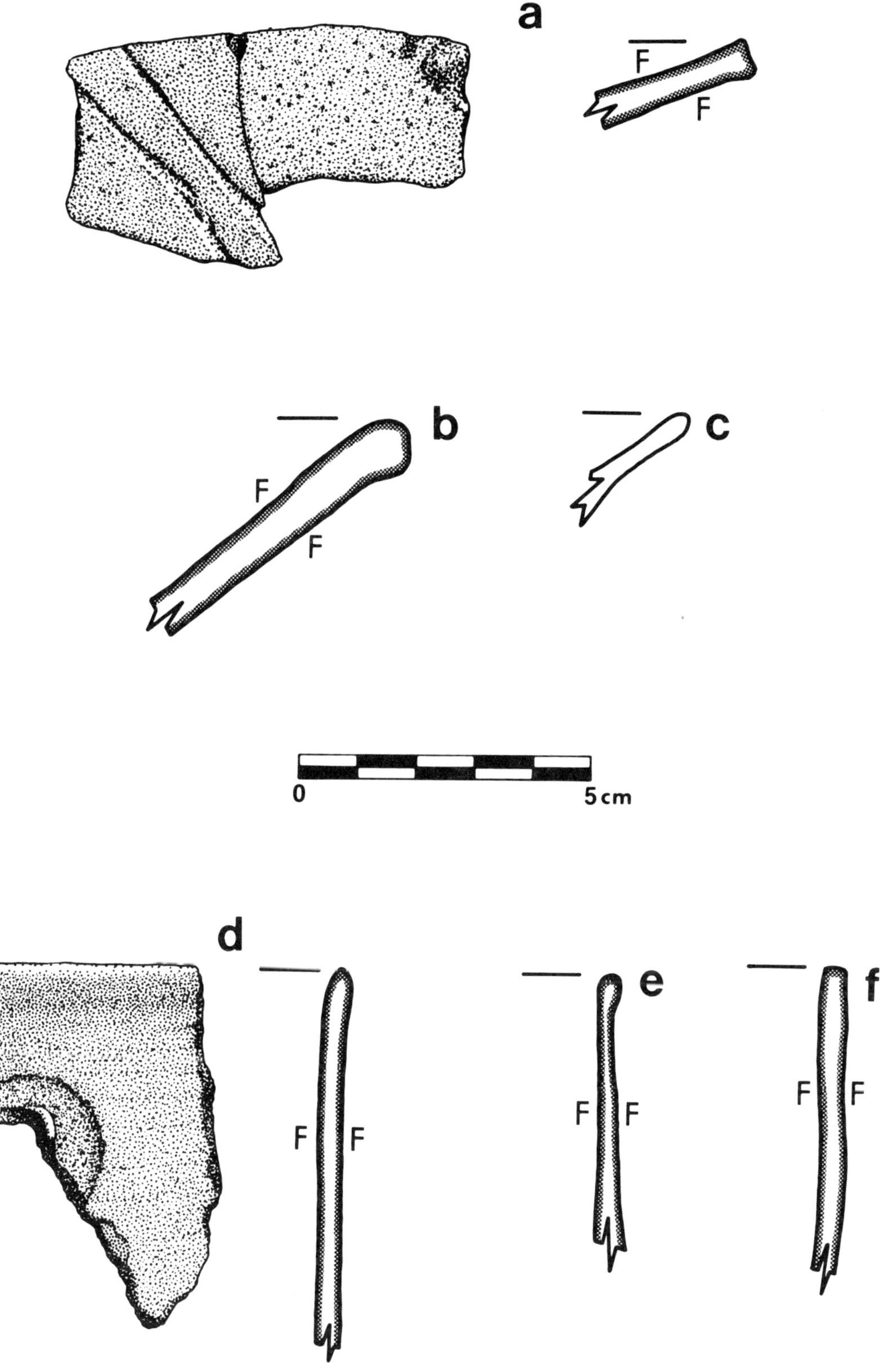

Figure 71. Mississippian Plate and Beaker Rims: a, 2-5, plate; b, 264-1, plate; c, 7-11, plate; d, 162-1, beaker; e, 137-1, beaker; f, 50-1, beaker

ca. 1 cm inferior to the lip.] Estimated orifice diameters ranged from 8 cm to 18 cm (mean=13 cm, s=4.1). Two vessels had areas on their exteriors where handles were once attached. One of the appendages had been riveted to the vessel's body. Handle shapes for these particular vessels are unknown, although there were handle fragments in the collection that, in cross section, ranged from circular to semicircular.

One of the vessels was from an internal pit associated with structure Feature 31, Four were from pits in the cluster near the superimposed feature group including structure Features 208, 215, 231, and 241. The remaining vessel was from an isolated pit near this same feature complex.

Plates

Five rim segments thought to be from plates were recovered. They represent 0.9% of the total Mississippian ceramic assemblage. Although the sherds were relatively small, these plates appeared to be relatively shallow vessels with broad, distinctly out-flaring rims (Figure 71). The Julien site plates were all shell tempered and had moderate orifice diameters (N=4, range=16-31 cm; mean=24.3 cm). On three vessels, the exterior surface finish was a polished black film; the remaining rim segments were only polished. With one exception, which was only polished, the interior surfaces were both filmed and polished. The film was black on three specimens; there was one example of a red-brown film. Trailed designs appeared on the interior surfaces of two rims. One was a rectilinear motif; the other may be curvilinear. The former is illustrated in Figure 71. These two vessels can be classified as Wells Broad Trailed plates as described by Vogel (1975) for Cahokia site Tracts 15A and 15B.

Four of the five rim segments were associated with structures or their internal features. Two were from structure Feature 2, and one each was from from structure Features 7 and 31. The remaining rim segment was associated with an external pit feature.

Juice Presses

Five vessels were assigned to the juice press category. They represent 0.9% of the ceramic assemblage. Two rather obvious juice press forms could be distinguished on the basis of their respective morphologies and paste characteristics. There was a crude form with thick walls, and a thinner-walled variant of finer craftsmanship (Figure 72).

Three vessels of the former variant had walls that ranged from 1.15 cm to 1.35 cm when measured ca. 1 cm below the lip. They were tempered with grog or shell mixed with grog. The orifice diameters ranged from 8 cm to 18 cm (mean=12.7 cm), but their overall shape

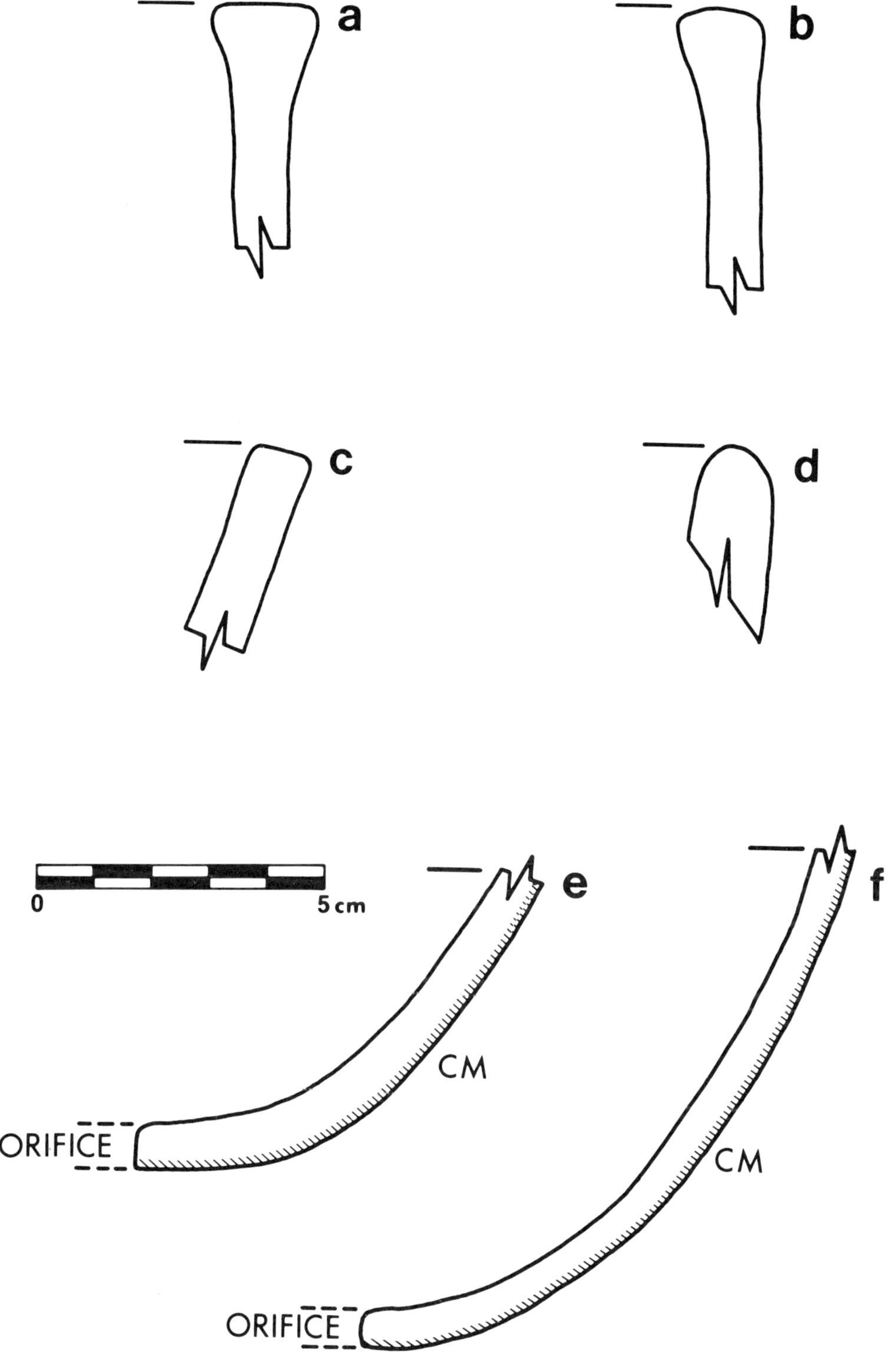

Figure 72. Mississippian Stumpware and Juice Press Rims and Bases: a, 224-2, stumpware rim; b, 229-9, stumpware rim; c, 82-3, juice press rim; d, 16-3, juice press rim; e, 295-12, juice press base; f, 295-13, juice press base

remains unknown, since each was represented by incomplete and fragmentary rim segments. The exterior surface of one vessel displayed a decoration consisting of numerous parallel, incised lines situated about 1 cm apart from one another. The exterior of another vessel was finished with smoothed over cordmarks; the exterior of the third was plain. The rims were associated with structures (Features 82 and 241) or their internal features. Additional body sherds, presumably belonging to this vessel category, were found in several other features at the site.

Two vessels were represented by relatively large, conical base fragments. Neither vessel could be associated with a rim segment. The vessels, which had smooth-sided holes about 2 cm in diameter through their apices, can appropriately be called funnels. These vessels were shell-tempered with cordmarked exterior surfaces. While their sides were not perfectly uniform, they averaged about 0.7 cm in thickness. Small body sherds belonging to these juice presses would be indistinguishable from those of other vessel forms in the ceramic collection, particularly cordmarked jars. Portions of these two vessels were found in a structure (Feature 7) and an internal pit associated with another structure (Feature 241).

Hooded Water Bottles

Fragments of three vessels thought to be hooded water bottles were recovered. The vessels represent 0.5% of the Mississippian ceramic assemblage. The identification of vessel form was based largely on the unusual shape of the sherds and their apparent orientation. Two of the bottles were tempered with shell, one with limestone. The exterior surfaces were covered with black polished films. Orifice diameters ranged from 4 cm to a large oval measuring 8 cm by 12 cm. The latter orifice represents a large vessel reminiscent of the gourd container carried by a Carolina Indian in an often-reproduced sixteenth century engraving (Harriot 1972:51).

The limestone-tempered rim segment was found in the fill of an isolated pit near a pair of wall trench structures (Features 23 and 167). Of the two shell-tempered rim segments, one was found in a pit superimposed by structure Feature 2, and the other was in an internal pit associated with structure Feature 36.

Stumpware

Two stumpware rim segments, representing a minor portion of the entire ceramic assemblage (0.4%), were recovered (Figure 72). Both were grog-tempered, had plain exterior and interior finishes, and had orifice diameters of ca. 16 cm. The lip thicknesses, which ranged from 1.8 cm to 1.9 cm, were relatively uniform. The vessel sides were about 1 cm thick, and tapered immediately below an expanded lip.

The rim segments were from the features inside structure Feature 36. It is possible that they belonged to a single vessel, but the pastes and exterior surfaces suggested that they were segments of entirely different vessels. Stumpware body sherds were also found at the site in the fills of other Julien site features.

Seed Jars

One small rim sherd, which was less than 2 cm long and weighed 1.6 g, may represent a seed jar. Alternatively, this rim segment may be from a bowl. The rim was tempered with limestone and displayed a red film on both the internal and external surfaces. The lip thickness was ca. 0.6 cm. Below a somewhat thickened lip, the vessel walls narrowed to just under 0.5 cm. It is difficult to measure the orifice of such a small sherd, but the vessel had an estimated diameter of ca. 20 cm. The sherd was recovered from a pit associated with a cluster of features around a wall trench structure (Feature 267) at the southwestern end of the site.

Appendages and Effigies

Tabs, handles, and other appendages were present on several vessels, including jars, bowls, beakers, and a water bottle. The tabs and handles on the jars and water bottle have been discussed with those particular vessel forms. Appendages known, or presumed, to have been associated with the remaining two vessel forms are discussed here as a unit, since it is not always possible to distinguish those once attached to bowls from those belonging to beakers.

Several zoomorphic heads, presumably all from bowls, were present in the collection. These specimens were not associated with specific vessels. All were birds, including two owls and two probable ducks (Figure 73). One owl head had a distinct, staring gaze reminiscent of an effigy bowl found at the nearby East St. Louis Stone Quarry cemetery (Milner 1981a). The edges of one duck head had been ground smooth; perhaps once broken, it had continued to be used as an amulet.

Of 16 tabs and handles presumed to have been from bowls or beakers, 10 (62.5%) were associated with specific vessels, all of them bowls. Three (18.8%) of the beaker or bowl appendages had either elevated margins or grooves around their superior surfaces (Figure 73). The items with this unusual decoration were all from isolated pits. Similar specimens have been found at the Cahokia site Powell Tract and illustrated by O'Brien (1972:74, Figure 59). Another, which is from the Fill site, part of the town-and-mound complex of Mitchell, is illustrated by Porter (1974:818, Rim Plate 74; 1074, Plate 42).

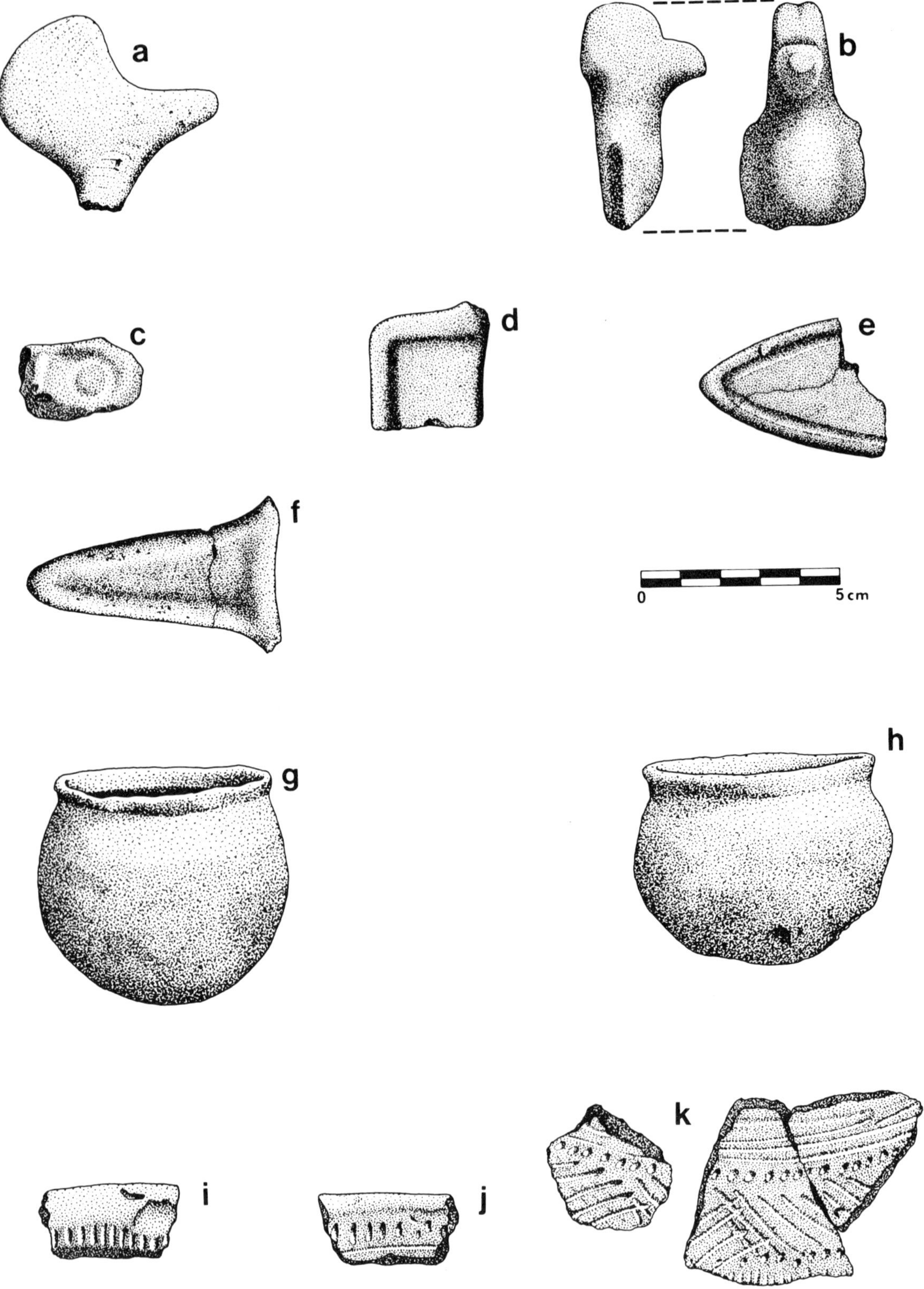

Figure 73. Mississippian Ceramics: a-b, duck head effigies; c, owl effigy; d-f, tabs with modified margins; g, 87-1, pinchpot; h, 87-2, pinchpot; i-j, Rims 7-1 and 241-21, decorated jar (single vessel); k, 295-6 and 154-4, decorated body sherds (single vessel)

Temporal Trends in Ceramics

Early in the excavations it was noticed that the Julien site pottery resembled that from the Cahokia site (Fowler and Hall 1972). Such resemblances were to be expected, of course, given the widespread similarities in Mississippian vessel forms and decorative techniques, and presumed regional integration during this late prehistoric cultural period. Large ceramic assemblages from individual Julien site structures were easily separated into units approximating the Cahokia site Stirling and Sand Prairie phase assemblages. In general, the Stirling phase at the Julien site was typified by a high proportion of filmed jar surfaces, which were often brown. In addition, jar shoulders with trailed designs were well represented. Sand Prairie phase assemblages at the Julien site had a high proportion of cordmarked globular jars with lips that were long relative to overall vessel size. However, much of the Julien site material displayed elements of both the Stirling and Sand Prairie phases, yet fully resembled neither. That material generally conformed to the Cahokia site Moorehead phase, which was temporally intermediate to both the Stirling and Sand Prairie phases.

To arrange the Julien site material in a stylistic sequence, which was assumed to reflect temporally related variation in ceramics, the vessels were grouped into separate lots, each from different structures and their associated internal features. Since features at the site tended to occur in spatially discrete complexes, thus permitting little mixing from unrelated occupations, groupings of this sort were of cultural significance.

The initial sorting of Julien site features into broad temporal units employed 11 structures that contained nine or more rim segments identifiable as to general vessel form. That number represents a compromise between obtaining a sufficiently large sample for comparative purposes and wanting to include in the analysis the in situ material from Feature 91. These structures were then grouped to form more inclusive units according to a suite of data classes that included vessel types; exterior surface finishes of shell-tempered jars; if present, jar film colors; and jar and bowl rim shapes. The ceramic attributes and their relative frequencies within the selected structures are listed in Figure 74. Two of the latest structures (Features 2 and 91) were those with fourteenth century radiocarbon dates. The remainder were assigned to categories on the basis of their ceramic assemblages. The particular order of structures within the three major cultural units in Figure 75 has no necessary temporal significance.

Two aspects of Figure 74 need further explanation. First, a category of missing observations was included in the Feature 7 ceramic attributes. This was because the rim segments in that particular feature were too small to determine exterior surface treatment. Second, the open bars for Feature 2 signify two small rim sections weighing 1.5 g and 6.2 g, respectively. These rims were anomalies in that assemblage, and were probably from the fill of an earlier pit that was superimposed by structure Feature 2. The pit (Feature 89) clearly dates to the Stirling phase.

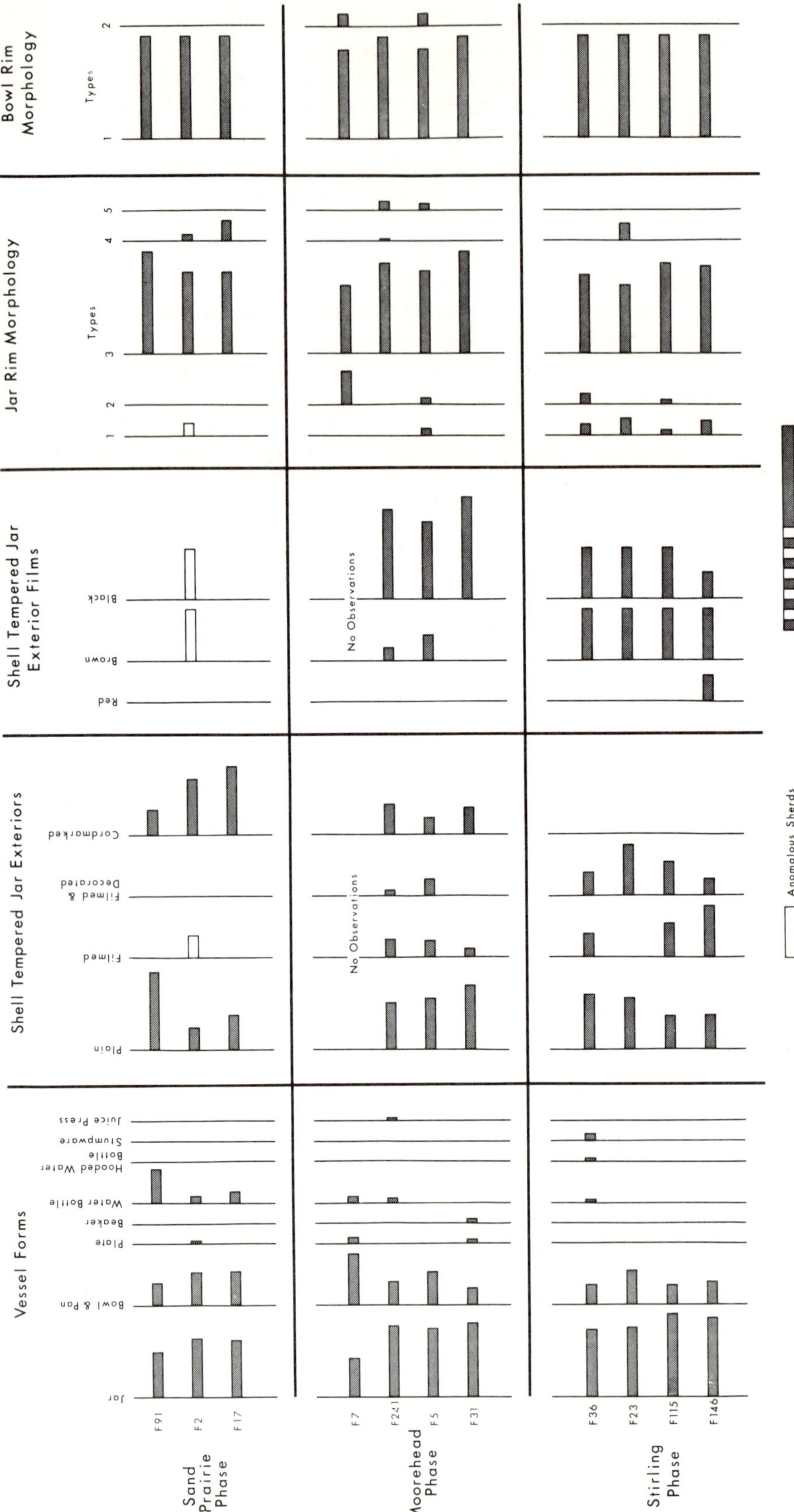

Figure 74. Distribution of Mississippian Vessel Types and Ceramic Attributes

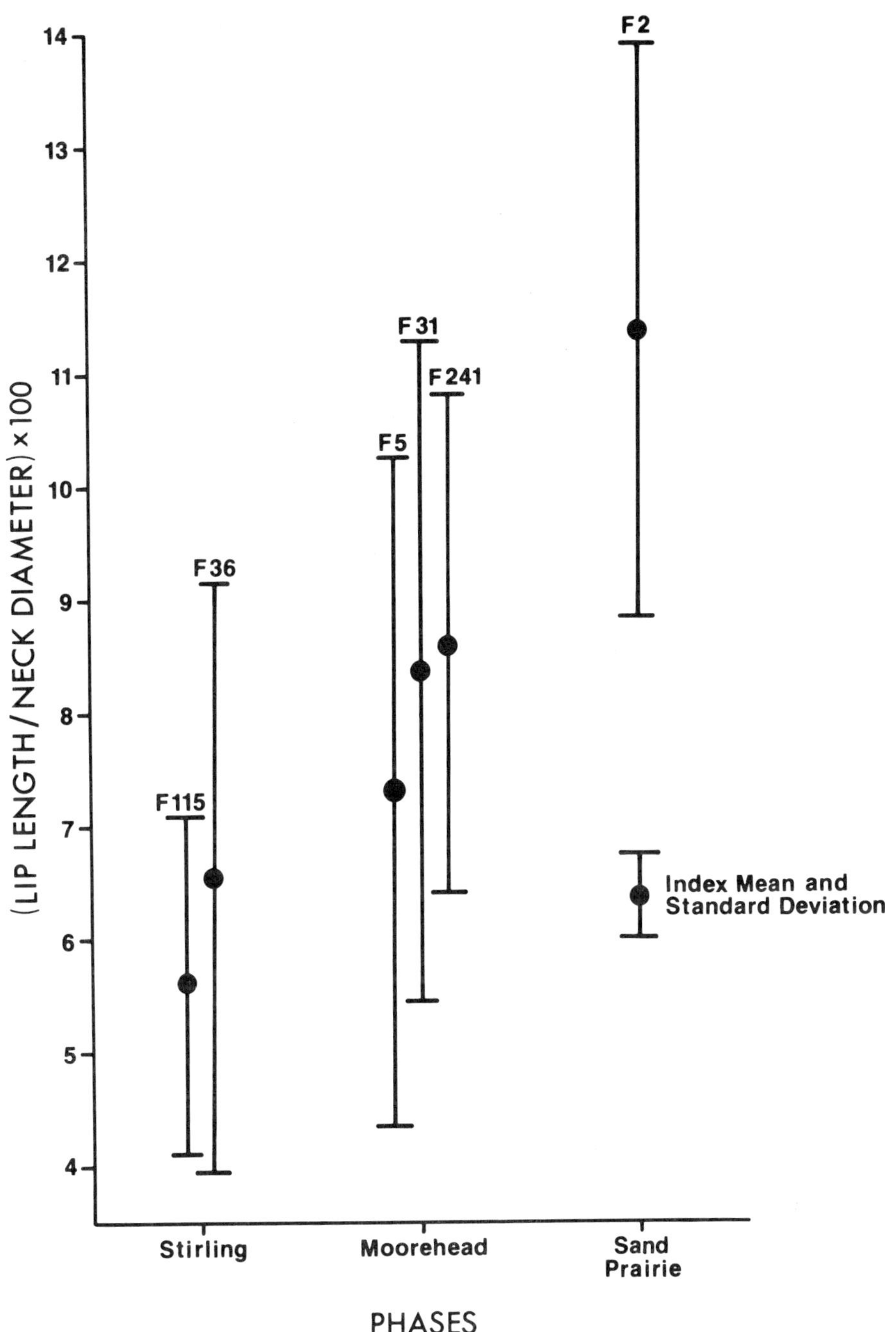

Figure 75. Mississippian Jars with Types 3, 4, or 5 Rims from Selected Structures

Ceramics from the remaining structures were assigned phase designations after a temporal sequence was established for the Julien site using the 11 largest structural assemblages. The relative frequencies of each vessel type and several ceramic attributes are indicated in Table 34 for the three phases represented in the collection. Note the covariation of specific attributes and their close correspondence to the existing Cahokia site sequence (Fowler and Hall 1972). For example, at Cahokia, limestone tempering was replaced by shell during the Stirling phase. At the Julien site, the Stirling phase was well represented, but appreciable quantities of limestone-tempered pottery were only found in one area of the site, in the vicinity of structure Feature 267 (Figure 6).

The frequencies of vessel forms in structure assemblages also seem to change through time at the Julien site. Stumpware and hooded water bottles appeared earlier in the sequence than did plates and juice presses. However, these last two vessel forms occurred infrequently in the Julien collection so their apparent absence in any particular phase is not necessarily significant. Clearly, chronological schemes based on the proportions of specific vessel forms are of limited value for sites like Julien with assemblages dominated by one or two vessel forms; comparing the frequencies of attributes displayed by common vessel forms should represent a more adequate means of establishing temporal relationships. This discussion, therefore, focuses on the characteristics of bowls and jars.

Two distinctive bowl rim shapes were present in the Julien site collection; both were described in a previous section of this volume. The Type 2 rim appeared in several features assigned to the Moorehead phase. On the basis of this small sample, it appears as if the Type 2 bowl rim form serves as a distinguishing characteristic of Moorehead phase ceramic assemblages.

Changes in the exterior surface treatments of the Julien site jars appeared consistent with trends noted for the Cahokia site ceramics (Fowler and Hall 1972). Red and, more important, brown films occurred most often in the Julien site Stirling phase assemblages. This was a period when cordmarking was absent on shell-tempered jars. In the subsequent Moorehead phase, brown films as surface finishes became less frequent. At the same time, black filming and cordmarking became more common. Filmed and decorated jars with trailed lines were also restricted to the Stirling and Moorehead phases. Sand Prairie phase jars in the Julien site collection had plain or cordmarked exterior surfaces.

Jar shoulder morphology was also modified during the Mississippian occupation of the Julien site. Angular shoulders were more common early in the sequence; curved shoulders dominated Sand Prairie phase assemblages.

Changes in the forms of Julien site jar rims were also consistent

Table 34. Ceramic Attributes and Relative Frequencies in Mississippian Phases

Vessel Type	Stirling Phase	Moorehead Phase	Sand Prairie Phase
Jar	+++	+++	+++
Bowl and Pan	++	++	++
Plate	-	+	+
Beaker	-	+	-
Water Bottle	+	+	++
Hooded Water Bottle	+	-	-
Stumpware	+	-	-
Juice Press	-	+	+
Seed Jar	?	-	-
Temper			
Shell	+++	+++	+++
Grog	+	+	+
Limestone	+	-	-
Grit	-	-	-
Shell-tempered Jars			
Plain	+++	+++	+++
Filmed	+++	++	-
Filmed and Decorated	+++	+	-
Cordmarked	-	++	+++
Shell-tempered Jar Film Color			
Red	+	-	-
Brown	+++	+	-
Black	+++	+++	-
Jar Rim Morphology (All Jars)			
Type 1	++	+	-
Type 2	+	+	-
Type 3	+++	+++	+++
Type 4	+	+	+
Type 5	-	+	-
Type 6	+	-	-
Jar Shoulder Morphology			
Angular	+++	++	+
Curved	++	+++	+++
Bowl Rim Morphology			
Type 1	+++	+++	+++
Type 2	-	+	-

Key
- \- Absent or Trace
- \+ Occasional
- ++ Moderate
- +++ Abundant

with those reported for the Cahokia site sequence. An observation that the rolled rim occurred relatively early in the Cahokia sequence helped in the organization of the Julien site assemblages (Fowler and Hall 1972). It should be added that the Julien jar rim designated as Type 2, or extruded, covaried with the rolled Type 1 rim variant. Later Julien site jar rims tended toward the Type 3 form and its derived variants, Types 4 and 5.

Rim size apparently changed throughout the Cahokia site sequence (Fowler and Hall 1972; Vogel 1975); the possibility of there being such a temporal trend in the Julien site data was examined. The term "rim height" as originally used by Vogel (1975) is referred to here as "lip length." Only the Type 3, 4, and 5 rims from structure contexts with 10 or more separate jars were selected to examine the possibility of a temporal trend in rim size at the Julien site. A total of six structures were selected. Small sherds were difficult to orient or accurately measure; therefore, only rim segments representing 5% or more of the estimated orifice circumference were included in metric comparisons of size. This reduction process resulted in sample sizes per structure that ranged from 8 to 26 rim segments. The different-sized vessels were standardized by a proportional index describing lip length in relation to neck diameter: (lip length/neck diameter) X 100. Neck diameter was chosen as representative of overall vessel size. It was one of the few measurements consistently available for the fragmentary Julien vessels. Unlike orifice diameter, it is not affected by the length of the lip.

The mean indices and standard deviations for rims from each of the six structures are plotted in Figure 75. A general trend of increasing size is quite apparent, even though the number of structures examined was small. Given the range of the standard deviations, it was apparent that this index would not be particularly informative when only a few rims were present. The means were then compared with t-tests. [The SPSS t-test subprogram was used for this analysis (Nie et al. 1975).] Note that within-phase comparisons were not significantly different at the .05 level (Table 35). In 8 of 11 between-phase comparisons, however, there were significantly different directional inequalities in means. These results support the trends in overall size that have been reported for Cahokia site ceramics (Fowler and Hall 1972; Vogel 1975).

Since analysis of the Julien site data was primarily based on existing notions of Mississippian ceramic change in the American Bottom, it is circular to suggest that this analysis represents an independent evaluation of the Stirling through Sand Prairie phase chronology. Yet, the Cahokia sequence was found to be a generally useful ordering device. It worked reasonably well when separating the Stirling and Sand Prairie phase vessels in the Julien site collection. Difficulties experienced with the Julien collection pertained to the use of general trends when arranging particular features in a temporal sequence. Such difficulties suggested that an approach focusing on vessel attributes would be of more value in organizing assemblages similar to those of the Julien site

Table 35. Comparisons Employing t-Tests of Indices*
for Jars with Type 3, 4, or 5 Rims Grouped by
Selected Structure Contexts

	Stirling	Moorehead			Sand Prairie
	Fea. 115	Fea. 5	Fea. 31	Fea. 241	Fea. 2
Stirling					
Fea. 36	ns	ns	ns	df=33 p<.05	df=15 p=.001
Fea. 115		ns	df=14 p<.05	df=32 p<.001	df=14 p<.001
Moorehead					
Fea. 5			ns	ns	df=15 p<.01
Fea. 31				ns	df=14 p<.05
Fea. 241					df=32 p<.01

*(Lip Length/Neck Diameter) x 100

than a chronological scheme that focuses on the presence or absence of general vessel forms. The particular activities conducted at a site might be expected to have more effect on the vessel forms present than on their general appearance. The problems involved in arranging in a sequence pottery assemblages from separate structures were not altogether unexpected, since phases represent rather gross divisions of continuous processes of ceramic change. It has yet to be determined if such changes were the result of gradual and continuous processes or stages punctuated by episodic and rapid alterations of technologies and styles.

Artifact Distribution and Recycling

When describing individual artifacts, it was noted that the materials were not distributed uniformly among the Julien site features. Most of the artifacts were recovered from the fills of structures and their associated internal features (Figure 76). Such features comprised 51.4% of all Mississippian features excavated at the site. This distribution was not altogether unexpected, since many activities presumably took place within, or near, structures. Debris scattered around structures could have washed into the large structure basins when those particular features were filled.

Broken materials scattered over the site area also became incorporated in the fills of entirely different features (Table 36). The number of individual ceramic items with pieces found in spatially separated features is indicated in Figure 77. These features were separated by as much as 18 m (distances were calculated using feature midpoints).

In addition to debris distributed throughout feature fills, several apparently intentional artifact caches were found (Table 37). In situ materials in Feature 91 are also listed in Table 37, but they are more properly considered debris scattered on a living floor rather than a cache. The Feature 91 ceramic assemblage is illustrated in Figures 78 to 80, with the exception of the small and fragmentary 91-9 rim segment. In addition, clusters of mussel shells (Feature 91) and hickory nuts (Feature 2) were found on structure floors. The items may have been stored in perishable containers that had been placed on the floor or hung from walls or the roof.

Wall trenches were favored areas for depositing artifacts (Table 37). Artifacts were also cached at or near the bases of five pits. These particular pits were large, and were probably intended primarily for the storage of bulky items, such as foodstuffs. The cache of tools in Feature 187 is shown in Plate 4 as it was encountered in the field. The storage function of the much smaller features that contained a Powell Plain jar (Figure 20; Plate 5) and potter's clay has been discussed.

Table 36. Ceramic Fits Between Mississippian Features

Structures with Associated Pits

Features	2 and 88
	5 and 69
	241 and 295, 297

Pits with Pits within Structures

Features	295 and 303, 297

Pits within Structures with External Pits

Features	46 and 30
	295 and 221, 154
	303 and 150, 155
	69 and 57

Structures with Structures

Features	241 and 5, 7

Structures with Unassociated Pits

Features	7 and 295
	2 and 19
	241 and 150, 290
	5 and 57

External Pits with External Pits

Features	9 and 13
	20 and 21
	148 and 149
	290 and 150

Table 37. Materials in Caches

Feature	Location of Cache	Artifacts in Cache
2	SW corner of structure	4 Ramey knives, 1 adze
2	floor of structure	hickory nuts
3	N wall trench	clinker abrader, chert flakes
7	NW outer wall trench	chert excavating tool and core
9	side wall of pit	celt
30	base of pit	excavating tool
88	near base of pit	excavating tool
91	floor of structure (an internal living floor)	sandstone metate turtle carapace mussel shells celt grinding stone pottery trowel sandstone abrader limestone vessels
187	base of pit	5 excavating tools sandstone slot abrader deer mandible
215	NW wall trench	excavating tool
240	pit fill	potter's clay
252	pit fill	whole vessel
262	pit adjacent to Feature 167 NE wall trench	excavating tool
293	back wall of pit	grinding stone with red pigment

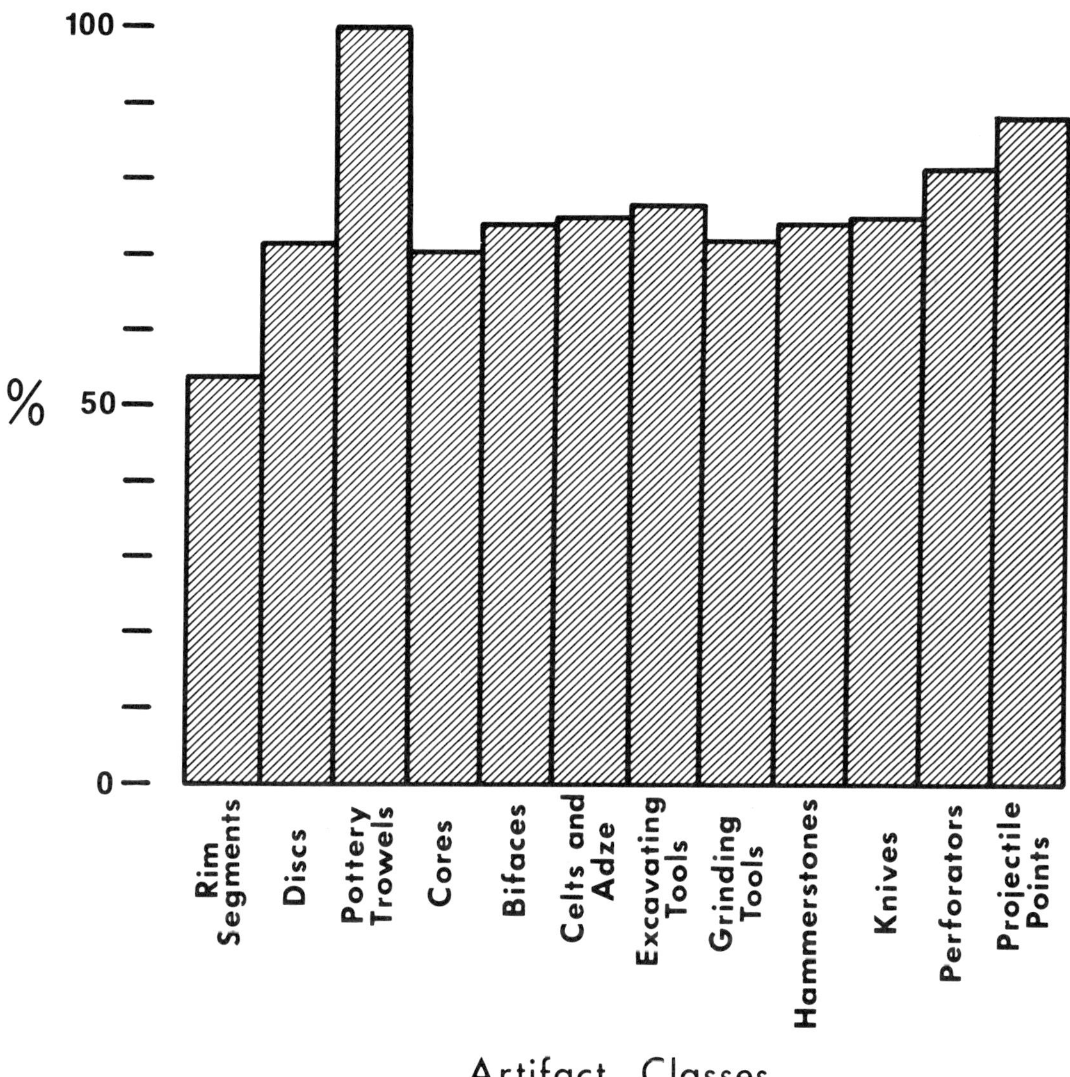

Figure 76. Percent of Artifacts and Artifact Fragments in Structure Fills and Associated Internal Features

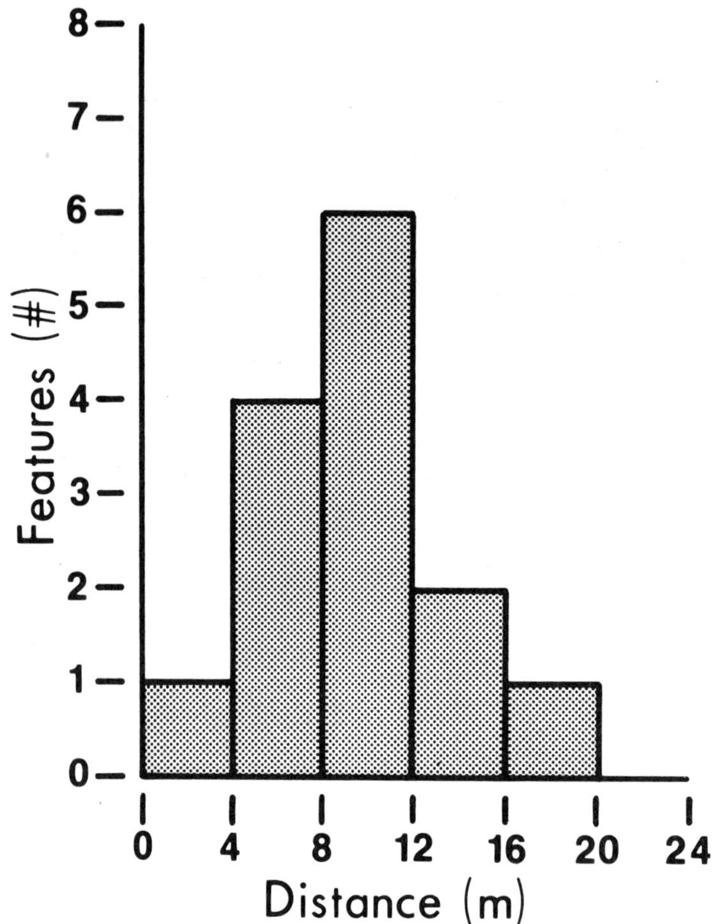

Figure 77. Distance Between Features with Ceramic Fits

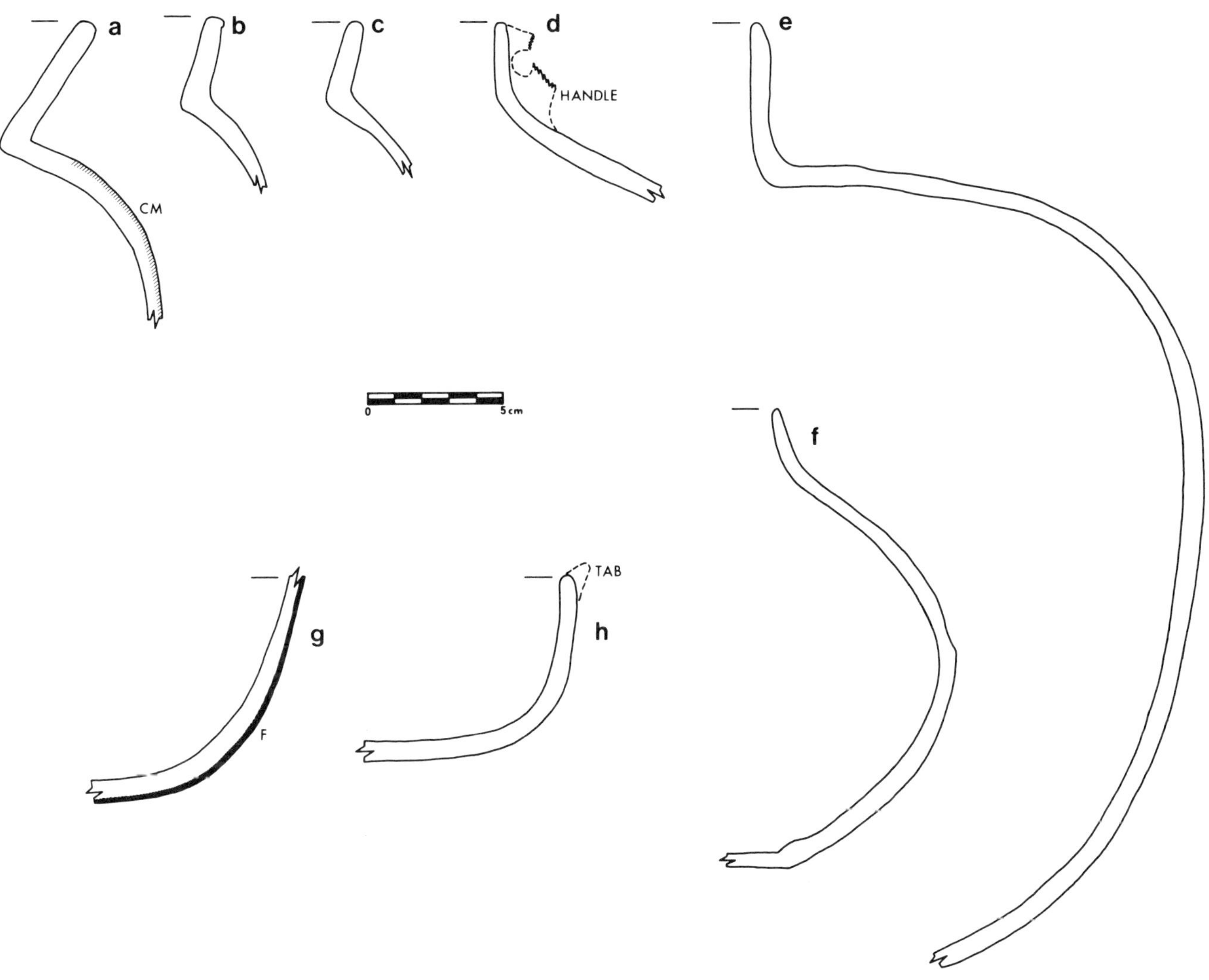

Figure 78. Vessels from Feature 91: a, 91-6, jar with Type 3 rim and curved shoulder; b, 91-7, jar with Type 3 rim; c, 91-8, jar with Type 3 rim; d, 91-5, water bottle with handle; e, 91-2, water bottle; f, 91-1, water bottle; g, 91-3, bowl, rim missing; h, 91-4, bowl with Type 1 rim and tab

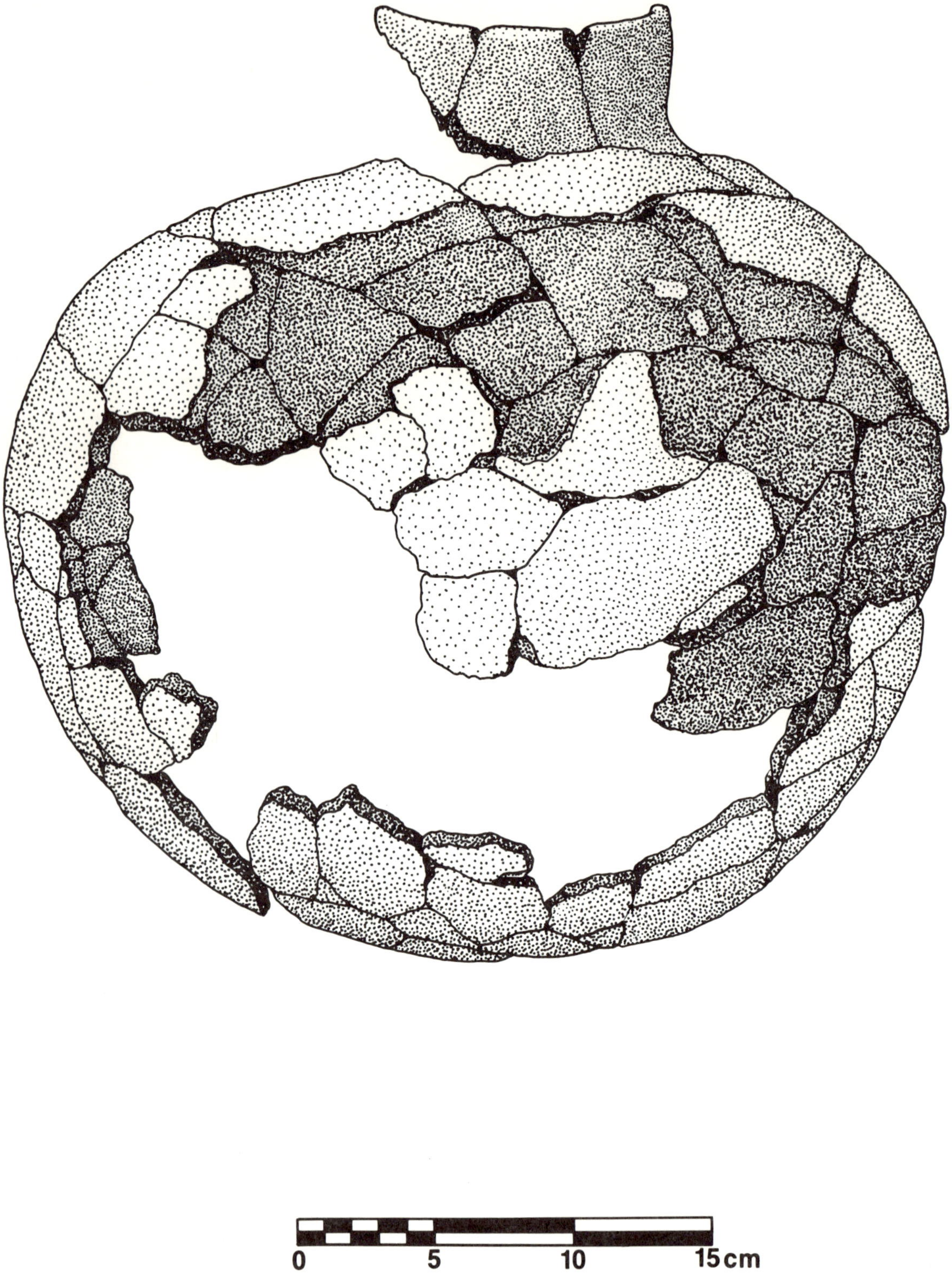

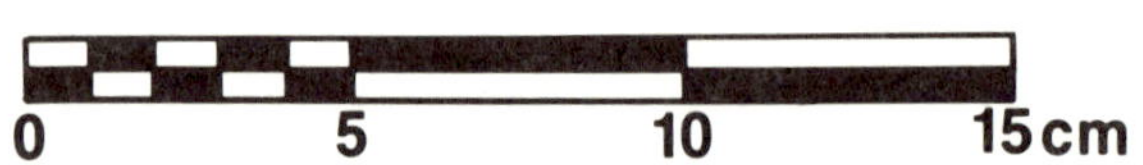

Figure 79. Vessel from Feature 91: Rim 91-2

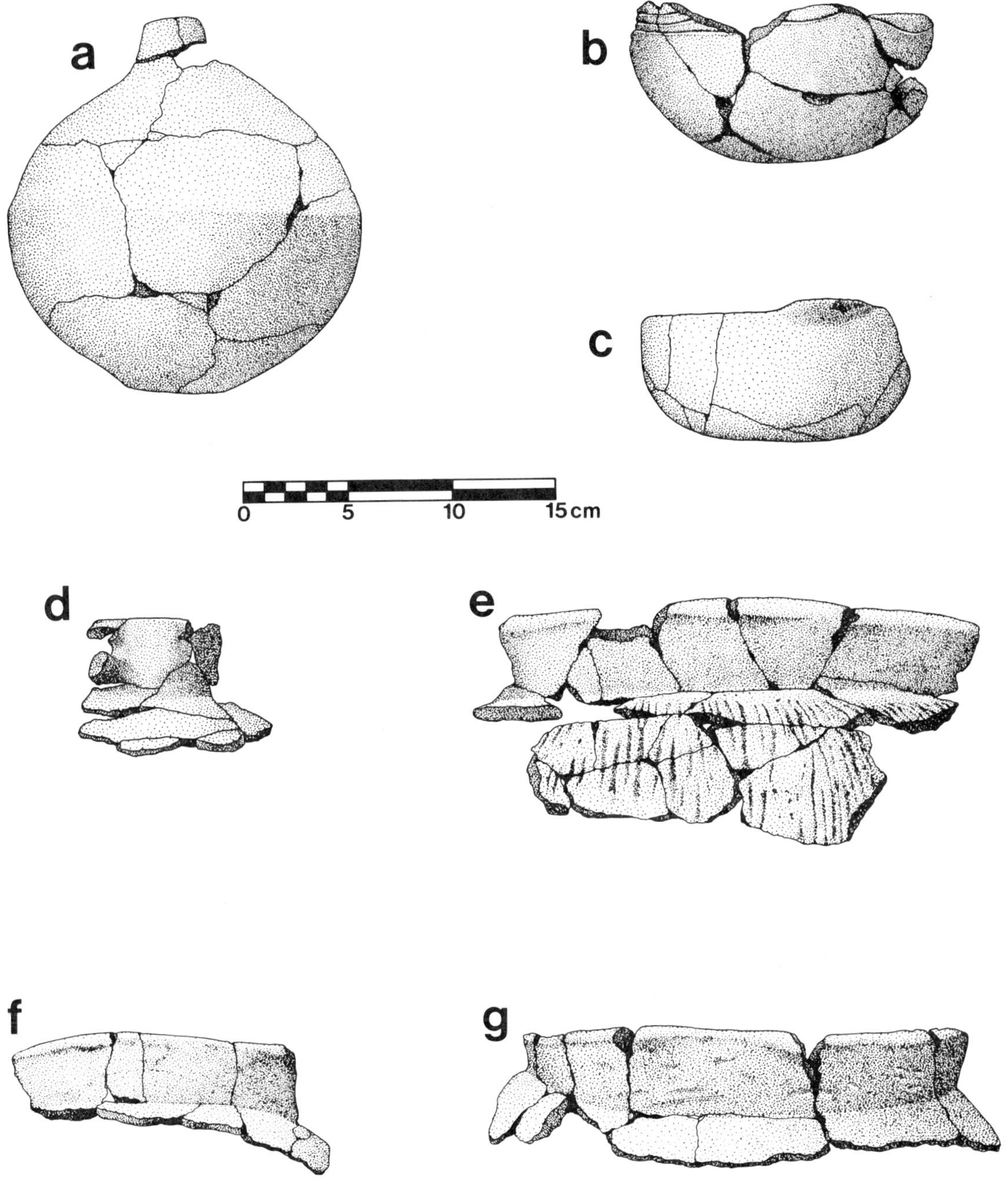

Figure 80. Vessels from Feature 91: a, 91-1; b, 91-3; c, 91-4; d, 91-5; e, 91-6; f, 91-7; g, 91-8

The Mississippian occupants of the site reworked many of their broken artifacts, presumably for use in other tasks. Individual specimens have been described previously. Reworked lithic artifacts or artifact fragments included excavation tools, projectile points, abraders, celts, and biface fragments. Broken vessel fragments had been reworked into discs for use as markers or spindle whorls, and one bird head ornament was perhaps used as a talisman. Broken vessels also continued to serve as containers, and the recycling of these common artifacts is discussed below.

Three partial vessels found on the floor of Feature 91 were apparently in use when the structure burned. These vessels included two bowls and a small water bottle. They were located near debris in the northeastern quadrant of the structure (Figure 23; Vessels 91-1, 91-3, 91-4). Presumably, the broken fragments continued to serve as small containers in what was probably a food-processing area. The water bottle was partially buried in a small depression so that the broken surface was at, or a little above, the floor level.

Also significant in this context were the beaker fragments from an internal pit within structure Feature 36 that exhibited broken edges ground to a smooth lip. Portions of the original lip were found on other sections of the same vessel. Evidently, the section of lip that was broken had been reworked so the beaker could continue to be used.

In addition to these four reworked vessels, 11 sherds with ground surfaces were found in nine different features. These sherds weighed from 0.8 g to 150.5 g, and all had smoothed edges. They are presumed to have once belonged to large sections of containers that had been broken, modified, and reused. One fragmentary piece weighing 76.3 g was found associated with ceramic material on the floor of structure Feature 91. While it could not be established just how this large fragment was used, its size was consistent with use as a platter.

Two observations about the Julien site ceramic material are relevant to this discussion of recycling. Many jars were apparently broken at, or near, the shoulder. That area of the vessel wall is often relatively thin when compared to the rest of the vessel. Secondly, while the ceramics were being reconstructed, it was noticed that the sherds, particularly basal segments, seemed to be underrepresented when considering the number of rim and shoulder segments present. Only a few of the vessels could be reconstructed from their lip to their base; jars, in particular, were rarely pieced together beyond the shoulder. Perhaps once a vessel was damaged, the useless portions were discarded, found their way into abandoned features, and, hence, into the archaeological record. Rims might be considered useless from a functional, if not archaeological, perspective. The edges of the remaining vessel portions could be ground to produce serviceable lips, and these segments would continue to have been used as containers. Since broken pots were presumably of less value than complete vessels, they may have been used primarily as containers outside structures. If that occurred, reworked portions of vessels, primarily sections of bases and sides, should be disproportionately represented in what today is the plowzone. Unfortunately, sherds in the plowzone at American Bottom sites tend to be small, heavily eroded, and very fragmentary, with most probably destroyed by plowing.

A TEMPORAL, SPATIAL, AND FUNCTIONAL PERSPECTIVE

In the previous pages, features and artifacts have been treated as discrete entities belonging to two prehistoric components. The identification of associated groups of features was one goal of the field investigations. In many respects, such clusters serve as primary analytical units when reconstructing aspects of prehistoric life and studying past exploitation of natural resources. Portions of the preceding descriptive sections are integrated in this section to more fully characterize the prehistoric occupations of the Julien site as groups of coherently organized features and artifacts.

Late Woodland

As previously discussed, Late Woodland (Patrick phase) features were clustered together in a small portion of the excavation area (Figure 12). A structure may once have been associated with these pits, but it was not archaeologically visible. The clustered arrangement of pits and a fit between two sherds from separate features indicated that these pits were all used within a relatively short period of time. If the pits were not strictly contemporaneous, and it is unlikely that they were all used simultaneously, they certainly represent continual use of a spatially restricted area. The area was probably worked in some manner; perhaps the area surrounding these features had been cleared of the otherwise lush vegetation that covered bottomland ridges. It was not established, however, why these pits should be the only Late Woodland features located along the excavated portion of this prominent ridge.

The recovered materials indicated rather limited contact with an area beyond the boundaries of the American Bottom. Exotic raw materials included only two Mill Creek chert flakes, and it is possible that these two items were adventitious inclusions in the fills of these features. The presence of a nearby Mississippian structure indicated that this portion of the ridge was occupied during a cultural period when Mill Creek chert was commonly used. Chert from the Mississippian period occupation may have become incorporated in earlier feature fills through extensive rodent burrowing at the site.

Exotic raw materials rarely occurred in Late Woodland feature contexts elsewhere in the American Bottom. For example, only a few nonlocal chert flakes were found with the Late Woodland component at the Schlemmer site (11-S-382) [Szuter 1979], located several kilometers south of the Julien site in present-day Dupo.

Mississippian

The principal prehistoric occupation of the segment of the Goose Lake point bar on which the Julien site was located occurred during the Mississippian period. Mississippian features were found clustered in groups distributed throughout the excavation area (Figures 5 to 10). Although selected aspects of these spatially associated groups have been discussed, it remains to be seen how the features and artifacts at the Julien site were organized into households, also called "homesteads" and "farmsteads" (Smith 1978c). Other aspects of the Mississippian occupation considered here include the longevity of individual households, the distribution of feature clusters, the past occupants' economic pursuits, and the degree to which the households were integrated within a regional Mississippian cultural system.

Households

The small Mississippian households at the Julien site each included one or two structures and associated features. General aspects of the households are discussed before considering these groups of features in a temporal perspective.

The structures at the site varied in size and shape, but most were rectangular, semisubterranean buildings. Relatively substantial walls enclosed numerous pits, posts, and hearths. Rectangular structures could have been used for several purposes: as large storage facilities, enclosed work areas, public facilities, or for other domestic activities. The internal division of structure space, presumably for functional reasons, is well documented in Feature 91. In that structure, three activity areas were defined that included a relatively clean, uncluttered portion of the floor, a place for storage, and a debris-laden area (Figure 23).

Structures of special functional, perhaps ritual, significance included Features 113 and 31 (Figures 14 and 21). Both the sweatlodge (Feature 113) and the large, rectangular structure (Feature 31) were presumably important in the ritual life of the site occupants. Structures thought to have been sweatlodges have also been excavated at the Cahokia site Powell Tract (O'Brien 1972), the Mitchell site (Porter 1974), and the Range site (J. Kelly 1979). Small, circular wall trench structures that were similar in size to the two Julien site circular wall trench structures (Features 227 and 289) have been excavated at the Labras Lake site (Yerkes 1980). At Labras Lake, such structures were interpreted as sweatlodges. The largest rectangular structure at the Julien site (Feature 31) was unusual in a number of respects. Most important, it was large, and it encompassed two internal wall trench partitions, five hearths, and a pit containing 72 projectile points. A large, trinotched point covered with red pigment was found in the structure. Taken together, these characteristics clearly indicate that this structure was used for special activities.

It is unclear how long a Julien site structure may have been maintained in a habitable state. Fire, decay, and infestation by vermin would have reduced the use-life of a pole and thatch structure to only a few years. However, the structures were in use long enough for internal pits to be reexcavated, posts occasionally replaced, and a packed soil zone to be deposited on their floors. Structures were occasionally rebuilt. Three such rebuildings (Features 2, 7, and 245) involved expansions of earlier structures. While there was little direct evidence for the length of time a particular structure at the Julien site was used, a short-term occupancy of three years or less has been suggested for a similar, small occupation in southeastern Missouri (Smith 1978a).

Perhaps small, circular wall trench structures (Features 227 and 289) were storage facilities. Although there was little direct supporting evidence, the small size and substantial wall trenches of these structures suggested they were used for above-ground storage. Perhaps these were granaries that once contained maize.

The frequently occurring pits probably also served as storage facilities. These features were of many sizes; pit volume presumably depended on the nature and amount of stored materials. Pits were often located inside structures. Often the large internally located pits were located along the walls (Figure 18) or in the corners of structures. Externally located pits were often grouped in clusters near the structures. Such feature clusters were situated downslope from the nearest structures. This was also the case in the placement of isolated, external pits. Some temporal duration was indicated by the superpositioning of pits within the externally located feature clusters.

Hearths were rarely found at the Julien site. When present, they were usually shallow and located inside structures. More were probably once scattered outside of structures, perhaps associated with external activity areas. Shallow, externally located hearths would have been destroyed by recent plowing. Considering the plowzone depth, the two hearths found outside structures were once fairly deep relative to those located inside buildings.

Posts were also uncommon outside of structures. Although a number of drying racks, windbreaks, and other constructions were probably once present, today these constructions were represented by only an occasional postmold, post pit, or isolated wall trench.

A major difficulty in interpreting plowed sites is that the original ground surface is now destroyed and surface materials displaced both horizontally and vertically. Therefore, materials with good archaeological context are only recovered from fills that extend below the base of plowzone.

Artifacts in the Julien site features were found in contexts indicating that some had been intentionally cached, presumably for later use, while others had been discarded. Rarely were artifacts intentionally cached in Julien site features (Table 37). Cached items tended to be rather large; often they were of nonlocal materials. Most of the artifacts and debris recovered during the field investigations were dispersed throughout feature fills. Artifacts, or their fragments, were usually recovered from structures or their internal features (Figure 76). That would indicate that many items were used and discarded either within the structures or immediately around them. Of course, many artifacts were to be expected in structure-related fills, because the volume of soil from the structures and their associated internal features was so great.

Materials contained in the fills of features associated with four externally located clusters of features were used to investigate the nature of artifact dispersal in the areas surrounding structures. The four feature clusters consisted primarily of pits. They are clearly visible in various site maps (Figures 6 to 9) near Features 115, 167, 241, and 267. To investigate the disperal of artifacts on a now missing ground surface, a simplifying assumption was made regarding the origin of materials in feature fills. Materials in the Julien site fills were assumed to have been representative of those materials once present on the ground surface near the features. This assumption was consistent with the extent of slumping in many features, which indicated extensive erosion, and fills that generally contained only moderate amounts of well-dispersed debris. The artifacts per feature for the combined four clusters are presented in Figure 81; the features are arranged according to their distance from the closest structures. Distances were calculated using the midpoints of the external features and the nearest edge of the closest structure presumed to have been associated with a particular group of features. Features belonging to these external clusters did not extend beyond the last interval plotted in Figures 81 and 82. The artifact inventory included the categories of items listed in Figure 76. Two of the four feature clusters contained relatively dispersed features; the artifact distributions in these two clusters are also plotted in Figure 81. The other two pit clusters were located immediately adjacent to their respective structures (Features 115 and 167). Little would be gained from plotting these separately.

The number of artifacts increased with distance from a structure (Figure 81). That trend was paralleled when all of the debris found in the features was compared by counts, but not by weights (Figure 82). These patterns are of interest in the context of the previously discussed distribution of artifacts (Figure 76). Apparently, artifacts were discarded primarily in structures or immediately adjacent to them. The distributions in Figures 81 and 82 indicate that relatively clean areas surrounded the structures. Perhaps such areas were periodically swept. Artifacts and debris tended to be more abundant in feature fills located 10 m to 15 m away from the structures. Small items might have been swept or carried farther than large and heavy items, which probably were discarded as close as possible to the original area of use. This would account for the divergent distributions in Figure 82. The debris

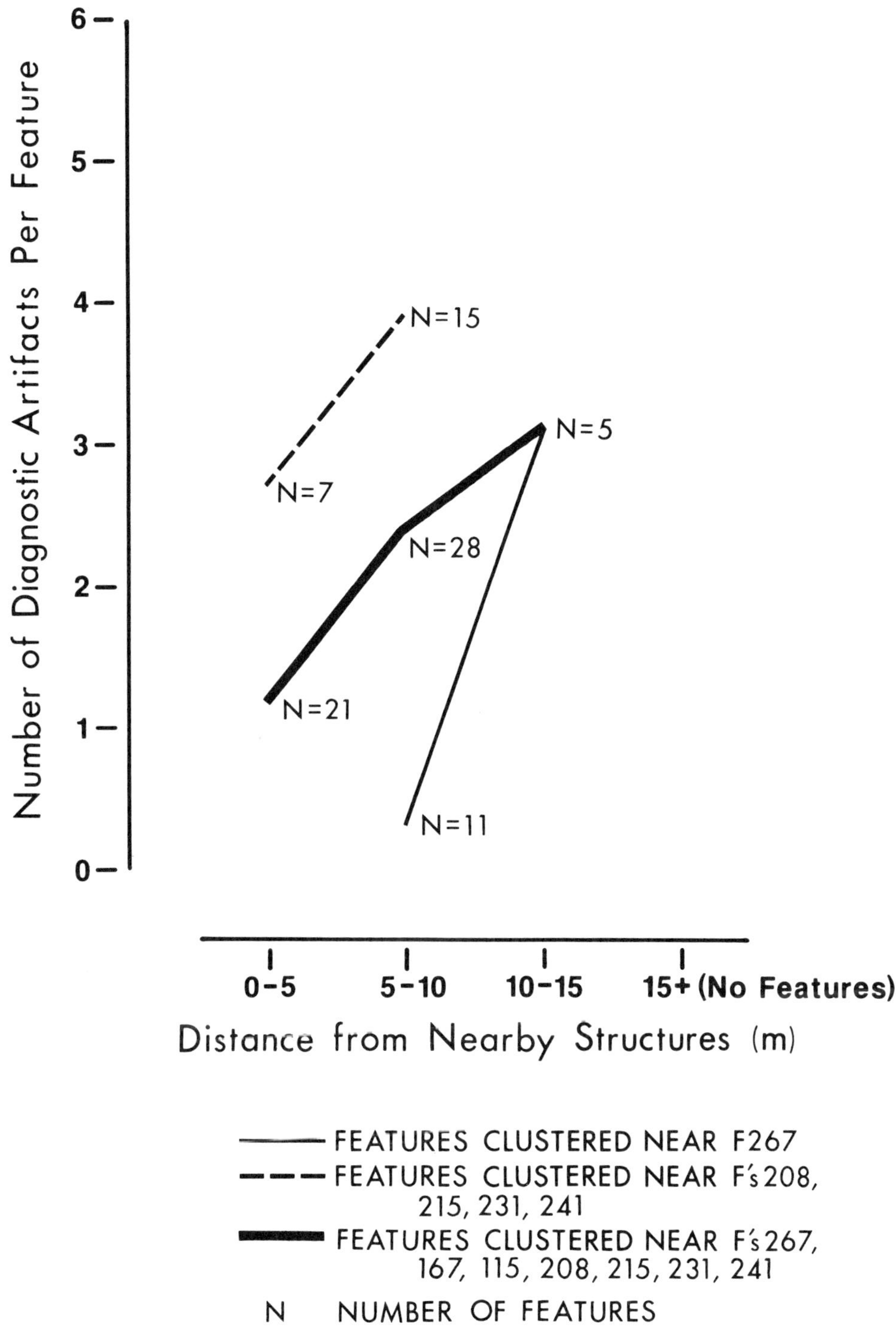

Figure 81. Distribution of Artifacts in External Feature Cluster Fills

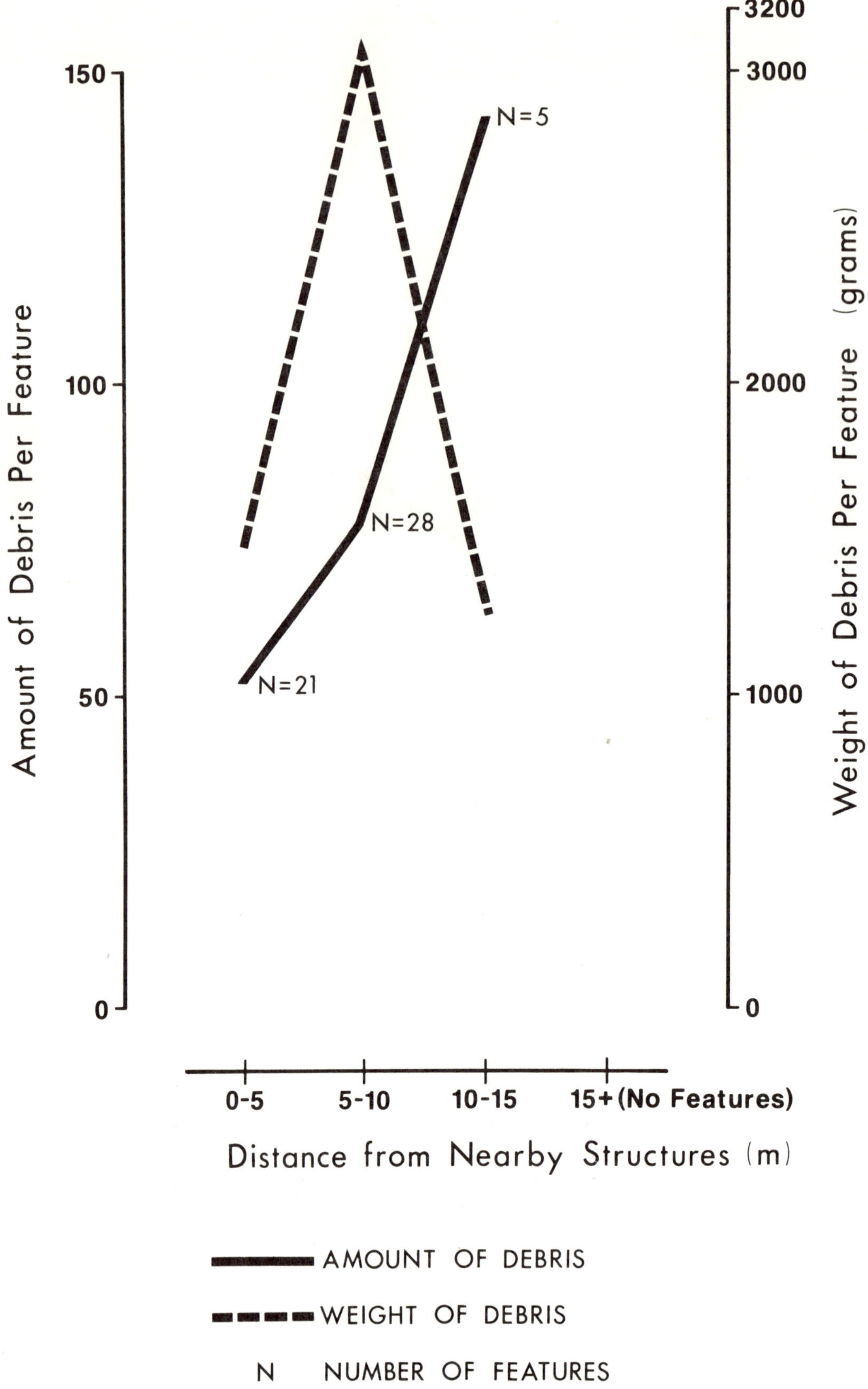

Figure 82. Distribution of Debris in External Feature Clusters by Count and Weight

disposal pattern was supported by the distribution of surface materials in the plowzone around Features 267 and 245 (Figure 11). The heaviest concentrations of surface debris were found near these structures, not immediately over them. Elsewhere at the site there was so much unrelated activity that distributional patterns in surface debris referable to specific structures were obscured.

Temporal Change

In the preceding pages, the Julien site households are described as sets of components organized in space. Differences among the households belonging to different phases are discussed below. Again, the focus is on structures. Phase designations based on existing notions of ceramic change through time were assigned to structures. These phase designations are provided in Table 38.

The rectangular wall trench structures were treated in this analysis as a single feature class, since they shared a number of morphological and constructional similarities. The feature descriptions and maps, however, indicated that no two structures were exactly alike. Size and shape were two rather obvious characteristics that differed markedly. The means and standard deviations of the internal floor areas and the length/width ratios for structures belonging to the three Mississippian phases are plotted in Figure 83. Structures evidently increased in size through time and became more nearly square in shape. The ranges in standard deviations indicated, however, that both dimensions varied within each of the three phases. Differences were attributable to the probable inclusion of structures that originally served entirely different purposes. In the unlikely case that all features were functionally similar, the variation noted in floor area could relate to the sizes of the occupying groups. There is certainly no reason to suspect that the sizes of individual families did not fluctuate in this prehistoric period. Even though the trends in size and shape were clear, the reasons for such changes remain unknown.

Stirling Phase

The Stirling phase was the best represented Mississippian phase at the Julien site. Structures assigned to this phase extended from the central site area to the southwestern group of features that included structure Feature 267. The Stirling phase occupation of this particular ridge continued to the southwest into what is today a subdivision. While testing several yards in this subdivision, a structure and several pits were found and designated the Sandy Ridge site (Jackson 1980).

The Stirling phase occupation of the Julien site was usually represented by isolated structures, but there were exceptions to that rule. As a structure serving a special function, the sweatlodge was probably in use at the same time as one or more nearby rectangular

Table 38. Structure Phase Assignments

Feature	Phase	Feature	Phase
2	Sand Prairie	115	Stirling
3	Moorehead?	143	Stirling?
5	Moorehead	146	Stirling
7	Moorehead	165	Stirling?
17	Sand Prairie	167	Stirling?
23	Stirling	197	Stirling?
31	Moorehead	208	Moorehead?
36	Stirling	215	Moorehead?
37	Stirling?	227	Stirling
45	Stirling/Moorehead	231	Moorehead
82	Sand Prairie	241	Moorehead
85	Moorehead/Sand Prairie	245	Moorehead/Sand Prairie
91	Sand Prairie	267	Stirling
113	Stirling?	289	Moorehead?

domestic structures. Elsewhere at the site, two neighboring, rectangular structures were probably associated with one another. The nature of the rebuilding in structure Features 23 and 167, as well as their orientations relative to one another, suggested simultaneous use. The two structures differed somewhat in size, basin depth, presence of a packed floor in only one building (Feature 167), as well as in the number and types of internal features in each. Such differences indicate that the two structures may have served different functions.

The Stirling phase structures often contained internal pits. On occasion, these pits were substantial storage facilities. Large pits were usually located along one or more walls of a structure (Figure 18). Such a placement of storage facilities is common at Stirling phase sites throughout the American Bottom. Examples of other sites that contain structures which resemble Feature 36 with its large, centrally located storage pit along one wall, include the Range (J. Kelly 1979), Labras Lake (Yerkes 1980), Mitchell (Porter 1974), and Turner (Milner 1981b) sites.

External to the Stirling phase structures were some isolated pits as well as three clearly defined feature clusters, which consisted almost entirely of pits. Structures near these pit clusters included Features 115, 167, and 267. Additional storage space would have been provided by Feature 227, an aboveground storage facility.

Moorehead Phase

The Moorehead phase feature distribution was similar to that of the preceding Stirling phase. Features extended from structure Feature 31, which was at the northeastern edge of the centrally located features, to the southwestern end of the distribution (structure Feature 289 and its associated pits).

Several Moorehead phase structures in the central site area may have been occupied at the same time as the public structure designated Feature 31. As a public structure, it would have been in use while other nearby domestic structures were occupied.

Fits between sherds linked the following Moorehead phase structures or their associated internal features: Feature 7, Feature 5, and the superimposed complex that included Feature 241 (Table 36). In addition, the superimposed complex of features including structure Feature 241 was similarly linked to the neighboring, external feature cluster. These features were all located in the central site area (Figure 8).

A preferential utilization of restricted areas by Moorehead phase peoples for repeated construction episodes is well-documented by the feature complex consisting of structure Features 208, 215, 231, and 241; the rebuilt structure Feature 7, which superimposed structure Feature 45; and the nearby group of pits. It is perhaps significant that there were three structures involved in the Feature 45 and rebuilt Feature 7 sequence and four structures in the Features 208, 215, 231, and 241 complex. This suggests a pattern of building paired structures, followed by their temporary abandonment, and a later rebuilding phase. Features 7 and 45, both structures without associated internal pits, may have been used for domestic purposes. Features 208, 215, 231, 241, and, perhaps, the nearby Feature 5 may have been buildings where other kinds of activities were conducted. Three of the last group (Features 5, 208, and 241) were large, substantial structures and each had only three wall trenches. Two of these structures (Features 5 and 241) contained numerous internal features. Perhaps these three structures were semienclosed storage or work areas.

Pits were present within and outside of the Moorehead phase structures. Some of the Moorehead phase buildings had numerous internal features, others very few. The number of internal features presumably related to differences in structure functions. At least one external pit cluster, which was near structure Feature 241, was affiliated with the Moorehead phase occupation. One of the two circular wall trench structures (Feature 289) was associated with this phase. It is possible that a larger rectangular structure may have been located nearby, but it was not identified. If such a structure was once present, the wall trenches were shallow and destroyed by recent plowing.

Sand Prairie Phase

The Sand Prairie occupation of this ridge extended from the central site area northeast to an isolated structure designated Feature 91. The occupation also extended to the far side of present-day Jerome Lane where it was called the Florence Street site (Emerson 1980a). At that site were found three Sand Prairie phase structures and a small cemetery.

The Sand Prairie structures at the Julien site resembled the Moorehead phase structures in several respects. They were relatively large and tended toward a square shape (Figure 83). Some Sand Prairie phase buildings contained many, and others very few, internal features. For example, although Feature 91 did not contain internal features, Feature 2 had more internal features than any other structure at the site.

Structure Feature 91 was situated by itself, but the other Sand Prairie phase structures may have been arranged in series of pairs like those of the Moorehead phase. Of four nearby structures, two (Features 2 and 82) contained many internal features; two others (Features 17 and 85) had few. Note that the earlier construction of Feature 2 was not associated with any large, internally located storage pits; the later, rebuilt structure had five pits located along its walls (Figure 24). The earlier and later buildings were probably used for different purposes.

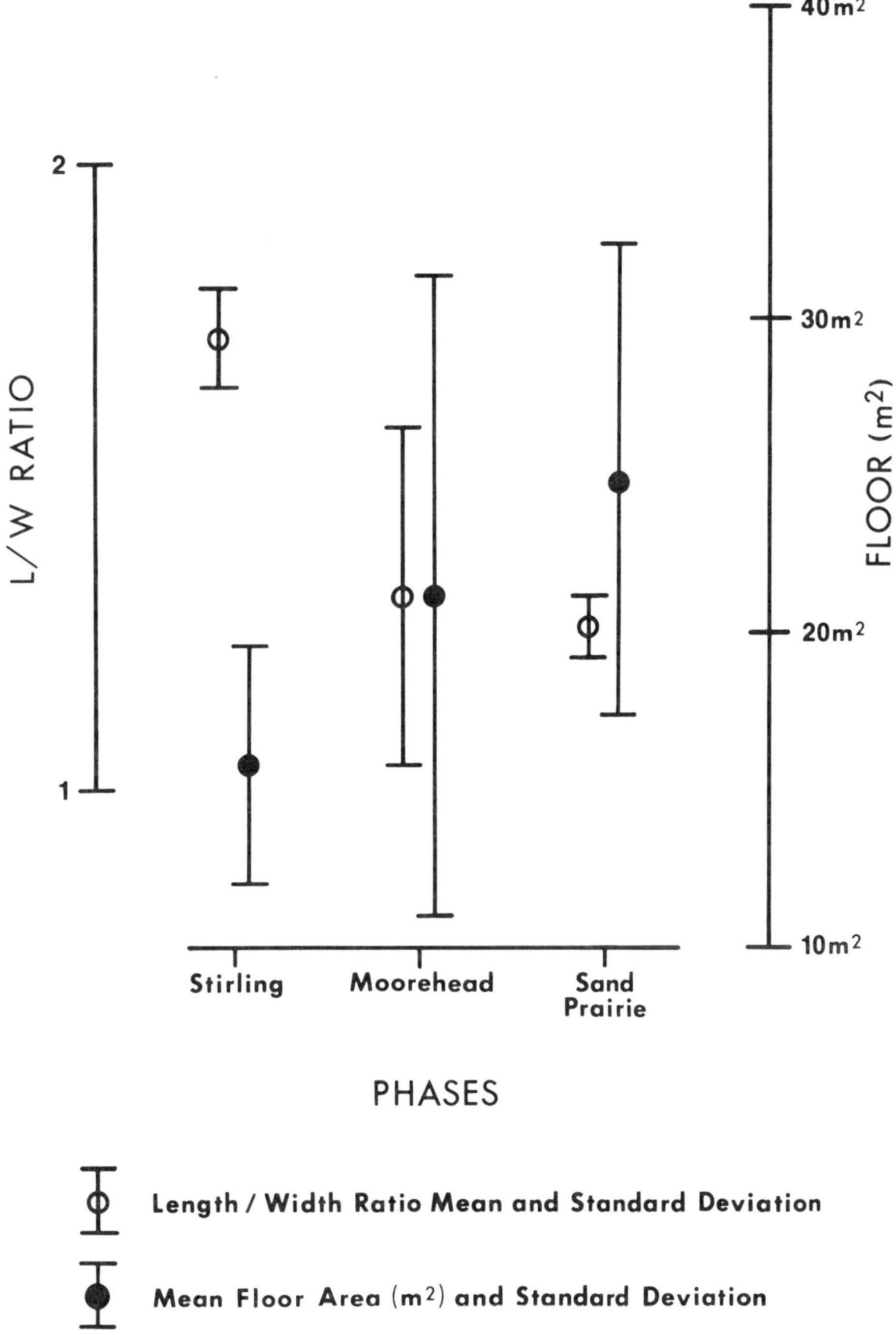

Figure 83. Rectangular Structure Dimensions by Mississippian Phases

While it appears that many Sand Prairie phase structures were paired, this interpretation is supported by little direct archaeological evidence. In addition, Feature 85, one structure of a pair, may have belonged to either the Moorehead phase or the Sand Prairie phase.

Subsistence Strategies

The organization, size, and temporal variation in the small households at the Julien site have been considered in the previous pages. The subsistence strategies as practiced by the Mississippian inhabitants of the Julien site are discussed in this section. More extensive treatments by Cross and Johannessen of the faunal and floral remains are presented below.

Muskrat remains were the most abundant mammal bones in the faunal collection. The relatively large number of muskrat elements indicates their importance to the site inhabitants. They may have been trapped primarily for their pelts. Deer seem to have been infrequently available; this species may have been procured only on a seasonal basis (Smith 1975; L. Kelly 1979). However, the number of deer indicated by bones would have accounted for more available meat than for any other animal. An absence of beaver elements is of interest, given the abundance of muskrat bones, but the reason for the lack of beaver remains unknown.

A wide variety of fish and waterfowl species were apparently included as part of the diet. In addition to migratory waterfowl, which were presumably consumed as food, there were many small passerine-sized bird species. The latter would have provided little meat, but their feathers may have been of some decorative value (L. Kelly 1979).

Many of the fish species represented in the faunal collection tended to dwell in quiet bodies of water, and individual specimens were often small. This suggests that the sloughs near the occupation area were fished, perhaps by seining. Fish may also have been caught when stranded in sloughs, which dry up during the late summer months. Fishing paraphernalia were not present in the Julien site artifact collection.

The only reptile represented in the collection was the snapping turtle, with the exception of a single snake vertebra. The turtle species frequents American Bottom sloughs.

Faunal exploitation was clearly oriented toward the aquatic and semiaquatic habitats near the site. The only relatively well-represented forest or edge dwelling species was deer. Deer might have been attracted to the settlements by nearby garden plots. Other species, including squirrels, which favor forest or edge habitats, were either poorly represented or absent. The faunal inventory was consistent with a focus on a point bar environment. Apparently, most sizeable creatures in the vicinity of Mississippian settlements that could be caught were considered as additions to the diet.

The Julien site faunal remains were consistent with an occupation that would have lasted from the spring through fall months, if not the entire year. A more complete discussion than that presented here on the seasonal availability of species in this region can be found in L. Kelly (1979). The presence of migratory avifauna indicated a spring or fall occupation. However, several of the migratory species represented in the collection are known to occasionally reside for longer than seasonal periods in the American Bottom. Small fish, if obtained from drying sloughs, may have been caught during the summer or early fall. Deer could have been hunted throughout the year, but their presence probably indicates a fall or winter occupation.

The Julien site faunal inventory differed somewhat from that commonly found in small southeastern Mississippian settlements where other species, primarily turkey and raccoon, tend to comprise substantial portions of the recovered skeletal elements (Smith 1978b). At the Julien site, there was almost an exclusive dependence on species that occupied bottomland ridge, swale, and slough habitats close to the relatively isolated site structures. This reflected a primary focus on the point bar environment and, perhaps, localized hunting territories.

Like the faunal elements, the floral remains recovered from Mississippian features indicated a focus on the bottomland point bar environment. Recovered plant remains were charred, with the exception of one partially burned log, a structural support in Feature 91.

Well-represented wood taxa included oak, hickory, and cottonwood/willow. Pecan trees, cottonwoods, and willows probably once grew on the bottomland ridges near the site. Oaks and many hickory species are upland dominants; periodic trips to the bluffs would have been required to obtain large quantities of their wood. Note that the carbonized roof and wall members of one burned structure (Feature 2) consisted primarily of upland species, whereas those of another structure (Feature 91) consisted mostly of bottomland species. Apparently, wood from a variety of sources was obtained for the construction of buildings. Wood for firewood would have been available as driftwood in the numerous tributary creeks and backwater areas scattered throughout the bottoms. Trips to the uplands would have been necessary to collect the amount of nuts present at the site, including the cluster of shells and nutmeats in Feature 2. However, such trips would have been of short duration and undertaken only while nuts were in season.

Maize, squash, and gourds, all tropical American cultigens, indicated the presence of agricultural plots. These plots were presumably located near the structure complexes. Other edible plants in the collection included a suite of three well-represented starchy seed species: goosefoot (*Chenopodium* sp.), maygrass (*Phalaris caroliniana*), and erect knotweed (Polygonum erectum). These three weedy species were presumably tolerated, or even encouraged, in garden plots, and would have been available as dietary supplements. These and other less well-represented weeds probably also grew in abandoned fields and around the household clearings. Additional edible species may have included marsh elder, sunflower, and wild bean (Strophostyles sp.).

It is difficult to assess the relative dietary importance of each plant species represented in the collection, since parts of certain plants are more easily preserved than others. Yet it is quite apparent that a wide spectrum of plant species was included as part of the Mississippian diet. Most of the species would have been available within localized collecting territories that encompassed nearby ridge, swale, and slough habitats. The previously described, large storage facilities may have contained plant products for later use. Note that the species composition of the Julien site collection was consistent with a generalized pattern of floral exploitation that existed throughout the Southeast (Smith 1978b). Temporal trends in the utilization of plant species at the Julien site were difficult to interpret because of possible sampling biases. Most of the remains analyzed were derived from only a few groups of associated features.

Arrangement of Households

The Julien site maps clearly illustrate that features were not uniformly distributed along the ridge (Figures 5-10). Features tended to cluster in the central portion of the excavation area. There were probably two reasons for such a distribution: the local topography and the pattern of prehistoric land use.

The feature distribution undoubtedly was affected by the local point bar topography. The central excavation area was situated opposite a somewhat higher area of the swale that separated the prominent ridge within the highway right-of-way from a neighboring ridge to the northwest. This area formed a convenient avenue between the two ridges, since it was less subject to flooding than portions of the swale located to the southwest. This was very apparent early in the spring of 1979 when standing water filled much of the swale.

The selection of the central area for repeated settlement also may reflect patterns of prehistoric land use. A practice of shifting agriculture would have produced many disturbed habitats, including abandoned and active fields, as well as denuded clearings around the small households. When the occupants relocated their households, abandoned clearings and fields would have been rapidly colonized by weeds. Since the length of occupancy of each structure complex was probably relatively short, the ridges of this point bar were undoubtedly covered by a series of succession plant communities. The rapid rate at which colonization by weeds proceeds was demonstrated at several sites along the highway alignment where archaeological investigations continued for several seasons. In fact, the abandonment of fields may have been due more to their being choked by weeds than to a decrease in soil fertility.

Burning the exuberant weedy growth is an expedient way of clearing new areas for settlement. That practice may account for the several apparently abandoned and burned structures at the site (Features 2, 3, 82, and 85). In addition, the basins of two structures (Features 143 and 146) were partially filled when they burned. Once an area of the ridge was cleared, incompletely filled structure basins would have been readily visible. These depressions seemed to have been purposefully selected for the construction of new semisubterranean buildings. When that occurred, the later building was often oriented at a somewhat oblique angle to the basin of the earlier structure. This was true for Features 197 and 143, Features 7 and 45, and the feature complex including Features 208, 215, 231, and 241.

Most structures were located at, or near, the ridge crest. The relationship between elevation and the location of structures is clearly demonstrated in Figure 84. The line representing the ground surface is an average of six evenly spaced transects that measure elevation relative to the ridge crest. Structures low on the ridge were all affiliated with the Stirling phase. Perhaps hydrologic changes in the floodplain encouraged the occupation of the ridge crest, as opposed to areas nearer the swales, during the Moorehead and Sand Prairie phases.

The Julien and nearby Florence Street sites were the only two sites along the highway alignment with substantial Moorehead or Sand Prairie phase occupations. At the Florence Street site, the Mississippian occupation was restricted to the Sand Prairie phase (Emerson 1980a). A lack of late Mississippian sites may indicate the abandonment of all but the higher bottomland ridges during and after the Stirling phase. Recent fieldwork at the Turner site supports the notion of a movement from lower to higher ridges by Mississippian peoples. The Turner site was occupied during the early Mississippian period, the Lohmann and Stirling phases; it was abandoned at the end of the Stirling phase (Milner 1981b). The prehistoric occupations at the Range (J. Kelly 1979, 1980a), BBB Motor (11-Ms-595) [Emerson 1981], and Labras Lake (Yerkes 1980) sites did not extend beyond the Stirling phase, with the exception of a few isolated Oneota pits at the Range site. There was, however, one excavated Sand Prairie phase occupation, the Schlemmer site, located near the Range site (Szuter 1979). It was located on a ridge that was topographically higher than the Range site ridge. A uniform shift in preferred areas of occupation at widely dispersed sites suggests a common underlying cause, perhaps regional changes in water table levels or the onset of dramatically fluctuating and unpredictable seasonal floods.

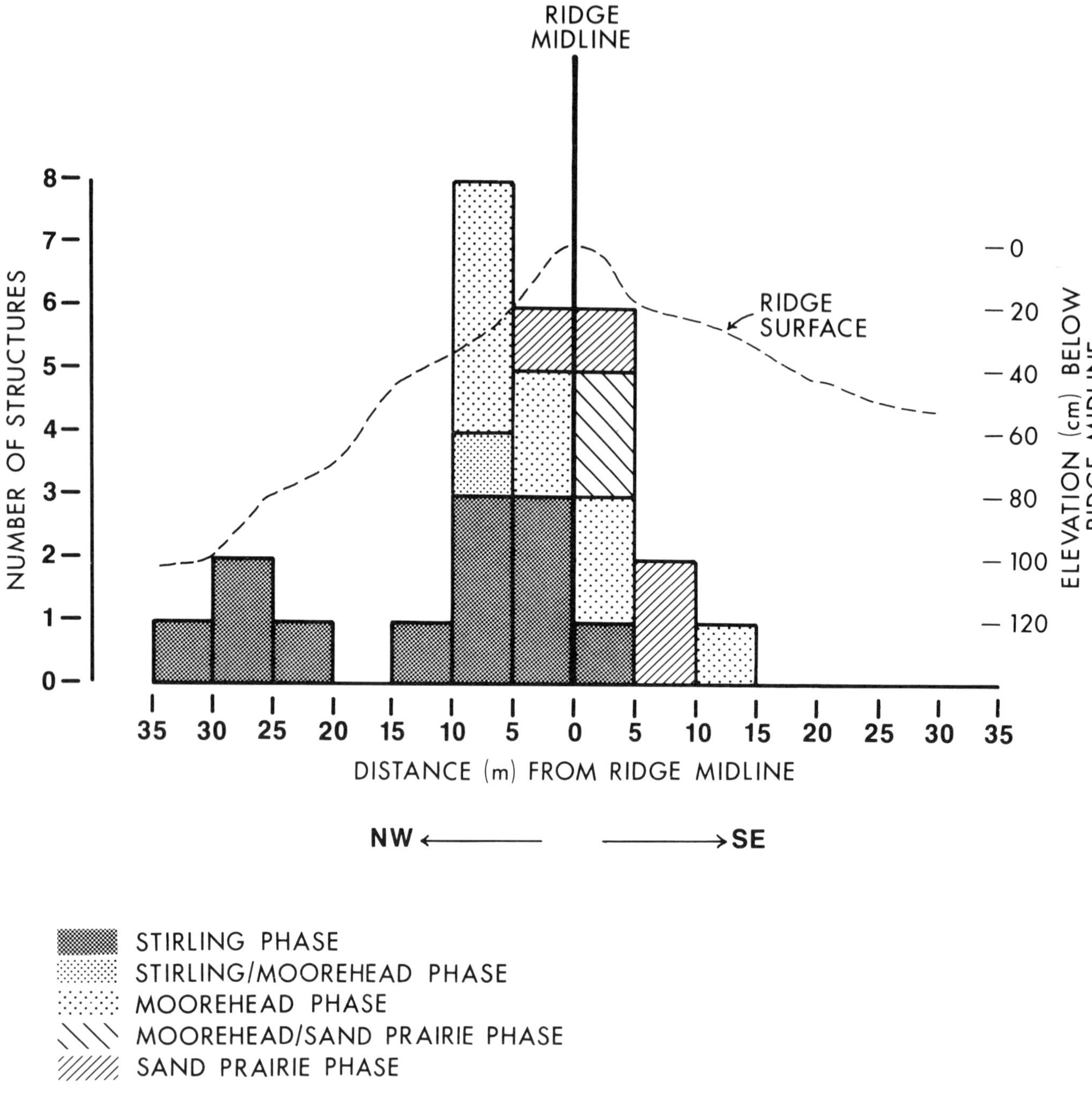

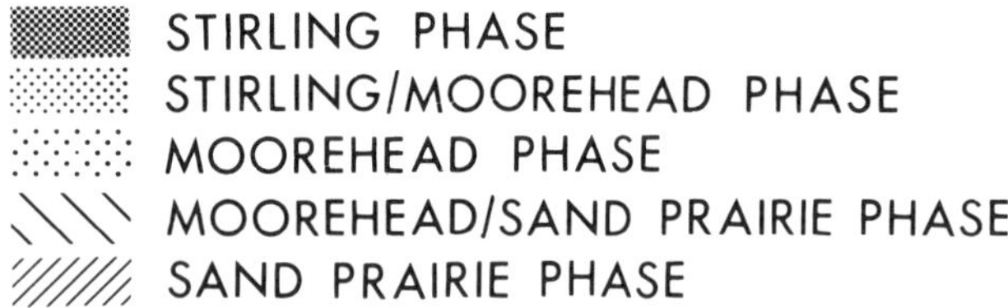

Figure 84. Location of Mississippian Structures Relative to Ridge Slope

Regional Integration

The households at the Julien site would have been part of a regional Mississippian settlement system. The Julien site was one of Fowler's (1974, 1978) fourth-line communities. These were sites that lacked mounds; they have been variously termed "villages", "hamlets", and "farmsteads" (Fowler 1974:32, 1978:471, 473).

It is unlikely that the Julien site was merely an occupation of bottomland ridges by peoples constructing a series of temporally and spatially unrelated groups of features; instead, there was probably a degree of interaction between the occupants of households on several neighboring ridges. Inhabitants of the dispersed households were probably integrated through a variety of kinship mechanisms into more inclusive social and economic groups. This proposed community integration is difficult to demonstrate archaeologically, but collectively, the structures and associated features probably resemble historic southeastern Indian villages (Swanton 1946). The Mississippian occupation of the ridges comprising the Goose Lake point bar may be characterized best as a dispersed community consisting of clusters of one or two structures and nearby storage facilities that were located within clearings surrounded by middens of occupational debris. Between these households there would have been located garden plots, some of which were actively cultivated and others of which were abandoned and choked with weeds. The occupied ridges of the Julien site would have been separated, at least seasonally, by standing water in low marshy areas and sloughs. Such communities would have been organized linearly, with the pattern of settlement corresponding closely to the topographic relief of bottomland alluvial ridges. Individual Mississippian communities in the American Bottom would have corresponded closely to physiographic units, such as point bars, that because of their drainage characteristics, were habitable.

In this context, the presence within the Julien site excavation area of two public or ritually important structures (Features 31 and 113) was significant. Both structures were located within the excavation area where there was reasonably good access across a swale separating two adjacent ridges. Such a "centralized" location might be expected of a sweatlodge and, especially, a community structure like Feature 31, which was possibly a men's house. People might gather from a number of separate households to take part in activities conducted at such public structures. The location of the nearby Florence Street site Sand Prairie phase cemetery is also important in this respect (Emerson 1980a). This burial area was isolated near the end of the ridge, but it was large enough to have served as a cemetery for the occupants of a number of structures that were scattered across several neighboring ridges. The recently excavated East St. Louis Stone Quarry site cemetery was also separated from the nearest habitation area (Milner 1981a). Like the Florence Street site cemetery, it was a Sand Prairie phase mortuary area.

Communities, such as the Julien site, undoubtedly participated in a wider hierarchical network of Mississippian period sites, the largest of which would have been Cahokia. Presumably, that interaction involved the exchange of goods produced at small sites for materials with distributions controlled by individuals occupying the large sites.

Sites like Julien may have contributed foods and other locally obtainable materials needed to maintain nearby, large, town-and-mound centers. The number of large storage pits and two possible granaries at the Julien site could indicate that foodstuffs were produced or collected for trading purposes in excess of that needed for immediate consumption. In addition, there is some evidence that muskrats were trapped for their pelts.

Certain artifacts and exotic raw materials clearly indicate that the Julien site inhabitants interacted with those of Cahokia and other large centers. Individual vessels, or their contents, may have been traded throughout the area. The often finely-made Ramey Incised pottery has been suggested as having been produced by specialists in large centers (Porter 1974). Specialists might also have made some of the more finely worked projectile points found at the Julien site. The two points covered with red pigment were examples of well-made, symmetric points (Figure 45). Presumably, the pigments on these two specimens were of some ritual significance, and the points were considered to be special objects. The poorly crafted flake points found at the site may have been locally produced equivalents of more finely worked bifacial points that were obtained through trade.

Several of the raw materials recovered from Julien site features indicated contact with wide-ranging trading networks, although the mechanisms through which the raw materials were obtained by the small, peripheral communities have yet to be determined. Nonlocal cherts were used as tools during each of the Mississippian phases represented at the Julien site. Seven other nonlocal raw materials were present that included hematite, galena, quartz crystals, bauxite, mica, whelk shell, and copper. The sources of the last four materials were located far from the American Bottom. Assemblages from structure complexes have been compared to establish the relative importance of these nonlocal materials during the three Julien site Mississippian phases. The assemblages were derived from structure basin fills and their associated internal features. Of the Stirling phase structure-related assemblages, 25.0% contained one or more of the seven exotic raw materials. Figures of 66.7% and 75.0% were obtained for the Moorehead and Sand Prairie phase structure assemblages, respectively. These totals were largely made up of hematite, and, to a lesser extent, pieces of galena and fragmented quartz crystals. The numbers of these three items per structure context increased from 0.67 to 4.67 and 6.00 for the Stirling to Moorehead and Sand Prairie phases. In part, these differences reflected the disproportionate distribution of hematite. That material was not present in Stirling phase features, although a piece of rubbed galena had an adhering red pigment, which was probably hematite. The number of bauxite, mica, marine shell, and copper pieces per structure complex were 0.25, 1.00, and 0.25 for the three phases. Such variation presumably reflected the nature of regional raw material distribution at various times during the Mississippian period.

SUMMARY

This volume is a descriptive summary of the field and laboratory investigations of that portion of the Julien site occurring within the FAI-270 highway right-of-way. Such summaries are an integral aspect of archaeological investigations, since they provide a firm basis upon which future research can build.

The Julien site was excavated according to a strategy that emphasized the delineation of prehistoric occupations in their entirety. The excavation area conformed closely to the topographically high portions of one ridge of the Goose Lake point bar. During the course of field work, 310 features were identified and completely excavated. Late Woodland and Mississippian occupations were represented by diagnostic materials recovered from these features.

The Late Woodland (Patrick phase) occupation was restricted to a group of 13 pits. These features were clustered at one end of the excavation area.

Two hundred ninety Mississippian features were excavated, and that occupation was the focus of this volume. The Mississippian occupation consisted of a series of Stirling, Moorehead, and Sand Prairie phase feature clusters. These clusters were composed of structures and associated internal and external features, mostly pits and posts. The subsurface features in the vicinity of structure Feature 267 are illustrated in Plate 6, as they were first recognized at the base of plowzone.

The Julien site features, their organization, and the recovered artifacts have been described in this volume. The results of field and laboratory investigations were then used in interpreting the late prehistoric occupation of the Julien site locality. A reconstruction of one small settlement unit, that of structure Feature 267, is included in Plate 6. Of particular importance to this volume was the definition of the spatial organization and areal distribution of Mississippian households in the American Bottom, and the nature of their integration into more inclusive communities of residential, economic, and social significance.

Plate 6. Mississippian Household: upper, structure Feature 267 and nearby pits; lower, reconstruction of household, including a structure, pits, a clearing, and a garden

APPENDIX 1. FEATURE DESCRIPTIONS

Metric and nonmetric data on feature size and shape are listed in the following series of tables. The Mississippian structures can be found separately in Table 39. The remainder of the Mississippian features are listed in Table 40. The Late Woodland and unidentified features are listed in Tables 41 and 42, respectively. The codes used are explained below.

Feature Class

fill - fill or midden area
hrth - hearth
pm - postmold
pp - post pit
smp - smudge pit
wt - wall trench
td - tree disturbance

Plan Shape

cir - circular
irr - irregular
oval - oval
rec - rectangular
unkn - unknown

Profile Shape

basin - basin
bell - bell
conic - conical
insfb - inslanting sides with flat bottom
insib - inslanting sides with irregular bottom
insrb - inslanting sides with round bottom
inssb - inslanting sides with slanting bottom
irreg - irregular
irsfb - irregular sides with flat bottom
irsrb - irregular sides with round bottom
irssb - irregular sides with slanting bottom
osfb - outslanting sides with flat bottom
osib - outslanting sides with irregular bottom
osrb - outslanting sides with round bottom
ossb - outslanting sides with slanting bottom
ppor - post pit with one ramp
pptr - post pit with two ramps
unkn - unknown
usfb - unknown sides with flat bottom
usib - unknown sides with irregular bottom
usrb - unknown sides with round bottom
ussb - unknown sides with slanting bottom
vsfb - vertical sides with flat bottom
vsib - vertical sides with irregular bottom
vsrb - vertical sides with round bottom
vssb - vertical sides with slanting bottom

Table 39. Mississippian Structures

Feature	General Feature Shape	Construction Type: Wall Trenches (N)	Posts (Field Designation): Posts in Wall Trenches	Posts (Field Designation): Isolated Wall Posts	Basin Characteristics: Maximum Basin Dimensions Length (m)	Maximum Basin Dimensions Width (m)	Floor Dimensions Length (m)	Floor Dimensions Width (m)	Internal Floor Area (m2)	Basin Depth (m)	Associated Interior Features: Pit Features	Hearth Features	Posts: Features	Posts: PM	Other
2	Rectangular	8	PM 1-11	-	7.10+	5.50+	A) 6.28 B) 4.87	4.94 3.77	31.02 18.36	0.33	110, 111 112, 282 187, 186 88, 263	-	185, 209 210, 211 212, 244 258, 260 261, 264	12-16	-
3	Rectangular	4	-	-	5.47	5.00	4.52	4.28	19.35	0.48	132, 133	-	-	1	-
5	Rectangular	3	F 77	PM 9	6.28	4.50	5.60	3.00	16.80	0.23	64, 67 69, 70	-	65, 66 68, 71 72, 73 74, 75 76, 79 78, 80	1-8	-
7	Rectangular	8	PM 1-9	-	5.98	4.94+	A) 5.67 B) 5.07	4.60 3.86	26.08 19.57	0.25	-	-	-	-	-
17	Rectangular	4	-	-	7.25+	5.90+	5.88	4.85	28.52	0.33	55, 62 63	-	60, 61	-	-
23	Rectangular	4	-	-	6.76	4.68	5.81	3.58	20.80	0.23	196, 206 213, 216 217	235	202, 203 207	1-7	-
31	Rectangular	4	-	-	8.42	6.24+	7.50	5.60	42.00	0.27	46, 52 47, 58 50, 48 53	39, 40 41, 42 49	54, 56 51, 59	-	Interior wall trenches 1, 2
36	Rectangular	4	-	-	6.52	4.07	5.63	3.19	17.96	0.31	224, 229 252	-	242	1-6	-
37	Square	0	-	PM 1-4	2.60	2.45	2.60	2.45	6.37	0.32	-	-	-	-	-
45	Rectangular	2	-	-	5.25+	2.75+	5.00+	2.50+	12.50	0	-	-	-	-	-
82	Rectangular	3	-	PM 1-8	4.54+	4.08+	4.18	3.53	14.76	0.18	84, 134 141, 142	90	-	9	-
85	Rectangular	4	-	-	6.07+	5.42+	5.62	5.24	29.45	0.08	-	-	-	1-5	-
91	Rectangular	4	-	-	-	-	6.35	5.00	31.75	0.32	-	-	-	1-3	-
113	Circular	0	-	PM 1-11	Dia.	3.62	Dia.	2.85	6.38	0.13	140	139, 147	-	-	-
115	Rectangular	4	-	-	6.39	4.12	5.46	3.22	17.58	0.40	145, 174 183, 184	-	-	1-3	-

Table 39. Continued

		Construction Type			Basin Characteristics						Associated Interior Features				
			Posts (Field Designation)										Posts		
Feature	General Feature Shape	Wall Trenches (N)	Posts in Wall Trenches	Isolated Wall Posts	Maximum Basin Dimensions l (m)	Maximum Basin Dimensions w (m)	Floor Dimensions l (m)	Floor Dimensions w (m)	Internal Floor Area (m2)	Basin Depth (m)	Pit Features	Hearth Features	Features	PM	Other
143	Rectangular	4	-	-	5.36	3.56+	4.90	3.16	15.48	0.27	237	236	-	1 (?)	-
146	Rectangular	4	-	-	6.40	4.26	5.67	3.40	19.28	0.35	219, 223 228, 230	225	220, 222 226	1-2	-
165	Rectangular	3	-	F. 194 F. 195 PM 1-6	4.83	3.00	4.32	2.44	10.54	0.14	193	-	192	-	-
167	Rectangular	4	-	-	6.22	4.28	5.32	3.08	16.39	0.15	232, 233 238, 239 262	-	234	1-3	-
197	Rectangular	4	PM 1	-	4.46	2.76+	4.06	2.29	9.30	0.14	-	-	-	1 (?)	-
208	Rectangular	3	-	-	4.90+	-	4.30	3.85	16.56	0.35	293, 307 (?)	-	308 (?)	1	Wall Trench F. 309
215	Square	4	-	-	3.40	3.12	2.66	2.44	6.49	0.37	-	-	-	-	-
227	Circular	1 (circular)	-	-	-	-	Dia.	1.75	3.06	-	-	-	-	-	-
231	Rectangular	0	-	-	2.48	2.22	-	-	(Max.) 5.37	0.20	240	-	-	-	-
241	Rectangular	3	-	-	7.20	4.44+	5.60	3.80	21.28	0.54	295, 297 298, 303 305, 310 311 307 (?)	302	308 (?)	1	-
245	Rectangular	8	-	-	-	-	A) 5.97 B) 5.18	4.30 3.76	25.67 19.48	-	250, 251 254	-	-	-	-
267	Rectangular	4	-	-	-	-	5.42	3.02	16.37	-	286, 291	-	-	-	-
289	Circular	1 (circular)	-	-	-	-	Dia.	1.04	0.85	0.20	-	-	-	-	-

Key
A = outer wall trench
B = inner wall trench
(?) Features and postmolds whose structure associations are questionable.

Table 40. Mississippian Features

Feature	Feature Class	Plan Shape	Length (cm)	Width (cm)	Profile Shape	Depth (cm)	N of Zones
1	pit	cir	111	110	insfb	70	4
4	pit	rec	122	77	unkn	15	1
6	pit	oval	160	128	vsfb	28	1
8	pit	oval	243	206	basin	31	2
9	pit	cir	114	114	insfb	53	1
10	pit	cir	94	88	vsib	64	1
12	pit	cir	110	109	insib	53	1
13	pit	cir	137	132	usfb	16	1
14	pit	oval	126	112	insfb	30	3
15	pit	oval	152	138	bell	74	6
16	pit	oval	205	189	insfb	36	4
18	pit	cir	109	103	insfb	76	1
19	pit	oval	110	79	insfb	34	3
20	pit	rec	178	155	vsfb	27	2
21	pit	oval	242	180	usfb	30	1
22	pit	oval	145	60	basin	19	2
24	pit	rec	174	132	vsib	49	8
25	pit	oval	324	205	basin	30	3
26	pit	cir	47	40	unkn	-	-
27	pit	oval	135	132	basin	15	2
28	pit	oval	105	78	vsfb	22	3
29	pit	cir	135	133	vsfb	55	3
30	pit	cir	130	119	bell	52	3
32	pit	oval	99	80	vsrb	59	5
33	pm	cir	40	34	insrb	27	3
34	pit	oval	77	48	insfb	11	2
35	pit	oval	40	25	basin	11	2
38	pit	oval	108	90	insib	60	7
39	hrth	rec	70	67	none	-	3
40	hrth	cir	30	30	none	-	1
41	hrth	oval	42	34	none	-	2
42	hrth	cir	24	22	none	-	1
43	pp	oval	105	77	ppor	57	7
44	hrth	cir	45	45	basin	12	5
46	pit	oval	118	104	vsfb	77	5
47	pit	oval	38	18	irreg	9	2
48	pit	cir	51	50	basin	9	1
49	hrth	cir	84	82	basin	15	3
50	pit	cir	160	150	insfb	90	7
51	pm	cir	38	32	insfb	35	2
52	pit	oval	64	58	vsfb	57	3
53	pit	oval	106	74	vsrb	41	3

Table 40. Continued

Feature	Feature Class	Plan Shape	Length (cm)	Width (cm)	Profile Shape	Depth (cm)	N of Zones
54	pp	oval	55	30	ppor	33	2
55	pit	oval	52	36	insfb	47	2
56	pp	oval	48	43	ppor	30	2
57	pit	oval	140	121	insfb	72	4
58	pit	oval	40	30	insfb	8	1
59	pm	oval	28	30	vsrb	35	2
60	pp	oval	36	32	ppor	21	1
61	pp	oval	60	30	ppor	42	1
62	pit	oval	64	50	basin	24	2
63	pit	oval	54	42	conic	35	2
64	pit	rec	70	68	vsrb	50	5
65	pm	cir	22	22	conic	20	3
66	pm	oval	28	19	insfb	21	2
67	pit	oval	60	41	insfb	39	4
68	pp	oval	98	43	pptr	57	4
69	pit	oval	76	66	insfb	33	2
70	pit	oval	34	28	insfb	21	1
71	pm	cir	22	18	conic	31	2
72	pm	cir	22	20	vsfb	11	1
73	pp	oval	35	30	ppor	21	2
74	pp	oval	79	32	ppor	35	3
75	pp	oval	76	28	ppor	20	3
76	pm	oval	38	36	conic	30	3
77	pm	oval	27	24	conic	19	1
78	pp	oval	39	23	ppor	23	3
79	pm	oval	23	20	basin	10	1
80	pm	oval	21	20	conic	19	2
81	pit	oval	153	135	vsfb	50	3
83	pit	oval	48	37	usib	6	1
84	pit	oval	82	77	vsfb	53	5
86	pit	oval	68	50	insfb	8	1
87	pit	rec	116	94	vsfb	41	3
88	pit	oval	146	83	insfb	63	11
89	pit	rec	147	120	vsfb	67	7
90	hrth	oval	97	88	insib	21	4
105	pit	rec	90	68	insfb	13	2
106	pit	oval	100	87	basin	15	2
107	pit	oval	50	43	usfb	5	1
108	pit	oval	91	76	vsfb	17	2
109	pit	cir	149	140	vsfb	38	5
110	pit	cir	119	113	vsfb	64	8
111	pit	rec	138	98	vssb	60	6

Table 40. Continued

Feature	Feature Class	Plan Shape	Length (cm)	Width (cm)	Profile Shape	Depth (cm)	N of Zones
112	pit	oval	88	80	vsfb	80	5
114	pit	oval	80	70	vsfb	37	3
116	pit	oval	188	130	insib	19	2
117	pit	oval	203	124	insfb	21	3
118	pit	oval	163	153	insib	24	2
119	pit	oval	143	110	vsib	40	4
120	pit	oval	110	91	vsfb	31	1
121	pit	oval	80	50	vsfb	25	3
122	pit	oval	98	85	irsfb	24	3
123	pit	oval	187	180	vsfb	17	1
124	pit	rec	137	135	insfb	27	2
125	pit	cir	98	97	vsib	63	5
126	wt	rec	196	32	irreg	16	2
127	pit	oval	103	98	insfb	13	2
128	pit	oval	118	108	insfb	41	4
129	pit	oval	135	113	irreg	16	1
130	pit	oval	87	64	insfb	17	2
131	pit	cir	94	90	vsfb	36	1
132	pit	cir	51	44	insfb	10	2
133	pit	oval	49	43	conic	27	2
134	pit	oval	36	24	conic	22	1
137	pit	cir	104	96	insfb	26	2
138	pit	oval	65	61	basin	12	1
139	hrth	oval	42	30	conic	18	4
140	smp	cir	23	21	irreg	23	2
141	pit	cir	45	42	vsrb	33	3
142	pit	oval	47	30	vsfb	16	2
144	wt	oval	135	29	inssb	17	2
145	pit	rec	64	52	vsrb	57	6
147	hrth	oval	71	66	conic	30	2
148	pit	oval	169	100	insib	36	2
149	pit	oval	170	154	vsfb	52	4
150	pit	oval	157	141	insfb	82	9
151	pit	oval	158	115	insfb	15	3
152	pit	oval	190	132	vsrb	29	2
153	pit	oval	124	95	insib	21	1
154	pit	oval	98	91	vsfb	48	1
155	pit	oval	145	124	vsfb	39	4
156	pit	oval	92	71	insfb	10	1
157	pit	rec	86	80	vsib	30	1
158	pit	oval	106	46	insfb	46	4
159	pit	cir	98	94	usfb	7	1

Table 40. Continued

Feature	Feature Class	Plan Shape	Length (cm)	Width (cm)	Profile Shape	Depth (cm)	N of Zones
160	pit	oval	109	100	vsfb	38	1
161	pit	oval	100	67	insfb	20	2
162	pit	oval	237	159	vsib	20	1
166	pit	oval	137	123	vsfb	27	4
168	pit	oval	150	102	insfb	25	1
169	pit	oval	156	108	insfb	48	2
170	pit	oval	150	120	vsrb	24	1
171	pit	oval	114	112	vsfb	21	2
172	pit	oval	103	82	vsrb	31	1
173	pit	oval	124	108	vsfb	58	5
174	pit	oval	34	30	irreg	21	3
175	pit	oval	98	64	inssb	30	3
176	pit	oval	87	70	insfb	14	1
177	pit	oval	177	154	insfb	59	3
178	hrth	oval	60	58	insrb	20	1
179	pit	cir	118	111	vsfb	49	3
181	pit	oval	57	45	basin	19	1
182	pit	oval	183	170	vsfb	69	2
183	pit	oval	39	31	insrb	24	2
184	pit	oval	52	39	vsfb	36	3
185	pp	oval	48	41	ppor	46	2
186	pit	oval	59	45	insib	18	1
187	pit	rec	116	91	bell	69	4
188	pit	oval	189	175	insfb	21	2
189	pit	cir	109	94	insfb	16	2
190	pit	oval	101	65	inssb	29	3
191	pit	unkn	50	20	vsfb	17	1
192	pp	oval	70	55	pptr	26	3
193	pit	oval	108	78	insfb	22	1
194	pm	cir	24	24	vsfb	26	2
195	pm	oval	24	19	conic	20	2
196	pit	oval	103	78	vsrb	52	3
198	pit	oval	90	62	vsfb	15	1
199	pit	oval	161	185	insib	25	2
200	pm	oval	49	41	inssb	50	3
201	pit	oval	82	66	insrb	20	2
202	pp	oval	34	27	ppor	20	1
203	pm	oval	25	19	conic	33	2
204	pit	oval	116	104	osfb	42	1
205	pit	oval	73	36	insfb	11	1
206	pit	cir	45	45	basin	14	2
207	pp	oval	34	27	ppor	18	2

Table 40. Continued

Feature	Feature Class	Plan Shape	Length (cm)	Width (cm)	Profile Shape	Depth (cm)	N of Zones
209	pm	oval	28	18	vssb	30	2
210	pm	cir	24	24	vsrb	22	2
211	pm	cir	26	25	vsrb	36	3
212	pm	oval	26	22	vssb	42	1
213	pit	oval	53	36	vsfb	22	1
214	pit	oval	156	88	vsib	25	2
216	pit	cir	30	29	vsfb	18	2
217	pit	oval	85	74	insib	51	4
218	pit	cir	98	95	vsfb	38	4
219	pit	cir	110	101	insib	26	2
220	pm	cir	35	34	insrb	45	3
221	pit	rec	141	127	vsfb	55	4
222	pm	cir	26	25	vsfb	33	3
223	pit	oval	48	42	vsfb	33	3
224	pit	oval	99	88	vssb	85	8
225	hrth	cir	40	39	vsrb	26	4
226	pm	oval	24	17	insfb	39	2
228	pit	oval	50	45	conic	25	1
229	pit	cir	161	158	vsib	89	3
230	pit	oval	58	29	irsrb	25	2
232	pit	oval	36	26	basin	11	1
233	pit	oval	60	47	insfb	15	1
234	pm	cir	24	21	vsrb	28	2
235	hrth	cir	32	32	none	-	2
236	hrth	cir	45	41	basin	11	4
237	pit	oval	127	92	inssb	26	2
238	pit	oval	89	66	usfb	9	1
239	pit	cir	60	56	basin	20	1
240	pit	oval	42	34	irreg	15	3
242	pm	oval	41	32	insrb	40	2
243	pit	rec	139	128	inssb	75	5
244	pm	cir	30	27	conic	20	1
246	pit	cir	50	46	insfb	19	1
247	pit	oval	152	138	insfb	26	3
248	pit	oval	90	70	insfb	12	2
249	pit	oval	130	108	vsfb	51	4
250	pit	rec	65	55	insib	29	2
251	pit	cir	80	74	inssb	16	2
252	pit	oval	47	44	vsrb	33	1
253	pit	rec	124	118	vsfb	27	3
254	pit	oval	50	37	insfb	23	2
255	pit	oval	92	80	vsfb	57	4

Table 40. Continued

Feature	Feature Class	Plan Shape	Length (cm)	Width (cm)	Profile Shape	Depth (cm)	N of Zones
256	pit	oval	124	107	insfb	36	3
258	pm	oval	30	25	vsrb	32	1
260	pm	cir	27	27	vsrb	26	1
261	pm	cir	30	30	insrb	12	2
262	pit	oval	54	40	usfb	11	2
263	pit	cir	40	37	irreg	11	1
264	pm	cir	34	31	vsrb	36	2
265	pit	oval	80	47	vsrb	20	1
266	pit	cir	102	100	insrb	33	4
268	pit	oval	37	33	vsfb	9	1
269	pit	oval	76	62	insfb	38	4
270	pit	oval	131	118	insfb	41	3
271	pit	oval	64	56	osib	14	1
272	pit	oval	152	109	insfb	38	2
273	pit	oval	109	94	vsfb	36	2
274	pit	oval	69	54	inssb	29	1
275	pit	oval	58	38	vsfb	8	1
276	pp	oval	79	45	ppor	44	3
277	pit	cir	71	67	vsfb	16	1
278	pit	oval	108	86	usfb	17	1
279	pit	oval	156	112	insfb	19	3
280	pit	oval	130	103	vsfb	40	4
281	pit	oval	109	99	vsfb	33	2
282	pit	cir	37	36	insfb	21	3
283	pit	oval	220	196	insfb	14	1
284	pit	cir	105	104	vsib	29	2
285	pit	rec	117	96	vsib	26	2
286	pit	oval	37	26	basin	17	1
287	pit	oval	117	102	insfb	19	1
288	pit	oval	109	78	inssb	16	1
290	pit	oval	182	140	vsfb	61	1
291	pit	oval	139	128	insrb	107	4
292	pit	rec	176	147	osrb	38	3
293	pit	oval	140	128	insfb	96	1
294	pit	oval	37	32	basin	12	1
295	pit	rec	122	118	irsfb	74	8
296	fill	irre	247	83	insfb	12	1
297	pit	rec	160	118	insfb	100	9
298	pit	oval	50	42	conic	33	1
299	pit	oval	131	110	irreg	52	9
300	pit	cir	101	92	vsfb	22	2
301	fill	irre	234	208	irreg	13	1

Table 40. Continued

Feature	Feature Class	Plan Shape	Length (cm)	Width (cm)	Profile Shape	Depth (cm)	N of Zones
302	hrth	oval	92	79	unkn	-	4
303	pit	oval	133	124	vsfb	78	7
304	pit	oval	64	32	insrb	32	1
305	pit	oval	86	52	irreg	30	1
306	pit	rec	140	137	inssb	95	7
307	pit	oval	48	34	irsfb	30	2
308	pm	cir	24	22	conic	21	2
309	wt	rec	235	22	insfb	28	1
310	pit	oval	26	19	vsib	12	1
311	pit	cir	40	37	conic	22	2

Table 41. Late Woodland Features

Feature	Feature Class	Plan Shape	Length (cm)	Width (cm)	Profile Shape	Depth (cm)	N of Zones
92	pit	cir	66	63	insfb	16	2
93	pit	rec	107	86	bell	54	5
94	pit	oval	167	140	insfb	53	2
95	pit	oval	99	70	vsfb	20	1
96	pit	cir	100	92	vsib	48	4
97	pit	cir	168	168	vsfb	76	7
98	pit	rec	86	61	vssb	22	2
99	pit	rec	160	123	vsfb	73	7
100	pit	oval	75	64	vsfb	28	2
101	pit	oval	135	119	vsfb	37	4
102	pit	oval	169	139	vsfb	64	8
103	pit	oval	120	103	vsfb	51	5
104	pit	cir	99	99	insfb	19	1

Table 42. Unidentified Features

Feature	Feature Class	Plan Shape	Length (cm)	Width (cm)	Profile Shape	Depth (cm)	N of Zones
135	td	oval	196	102	irreg	36	1
136	pit	oval	38	26	inssb	16	1
163	pit	oval	115	74	insib	17	3
164	pit	oval	45	42	vsib	26	1
180	pit	oval	64	44	basin	22	1
257	pit	rec	97	87	inssb	18	1
259	pit	cir	99	97	vsfb	23	3

APPENDIX 2. MATERIAL RECOVERED FROM FEATURE CONTEXTS

The materials recovered from feature contexts are listed in Tables 43 and 44. The first table is a tabulation of artifacts discussed in the preceding text. The second table lists the materials recovered by counts and weights for the various features according to seven general categories. The types of items included within each category are listed below.

Ceramics

vessel fragments
pottery trowels
pottery discs
ceramic beads

Burned Clay

burned clay and daub
fired clay discoidal
fired clay coils
unfired potter's clay
mud dauber's nests

Chert

worked chert
unworked chert

Limestone

worked limestone
unworked limestone

Sandstone

worked sandstone
unworked sandstone

Miscellaneous Rock, etc.

ground stone tools
igneous rock
quartzite
silicified sediments
rough rock
gravel
waterworn pebbles
fossils
Missouri River clinker
shale
coal (historic?)
cinder (historic?)

Various Minerals and Exotic Rocks

hematite
limonite
red ochre
calcite
bauxite
galena
mica
quartz crystal
copper

Table 43. Artifacts from Feature Contexts

Feature	Rims	Discs	Pottery Trowels	Cores	Bifaces	Celts and Adze	Excavating Tools	Grinding Tools	Hammer-stones	Knives	Perfor-ators	Projectile Points	Other
1	7	-	-	4	2	-	-	-	1	1	-	3	-
2	19	-	-	-	-	1	3	5	2	6	2	4	microdrill, core
3	2	-	-	-	-	-	3	4	2	-	-	14	-
4	1	-	-	-	-	-	-	-	-	-	-	-	-
5	23	-	1	3	2	-	-	8	1	-	-	3	-
6	1	-	-	-	-	-	-	-	-	-	-	-	-
7	20	1	-	7	4	3	8	5	8	1	3	4	graver
8	4	-	-	-	-	-	-	-	-	-	-	-	-
9	9	-	-	-	1	1	1	1	1	-	1	-	-
10	8	-	-	1	-	-	-	1	-	1	-	-	-
12	2	-	-	-	-	-	-	-	-	-	-	-	-
13	1	-	-	-	-	-	-	1	-	-	-	-	-
14	1	-	-	-	-	-	-	-	-	-	-	-	-
15	4	-	-	1	-	-	-	-	-	-	-	-	-
16	10	-	-	-	-	-	-	-	-	-	1	-	-
17	9	-	2	1	-	2	3	8	3	-	3	9	limestone triangle
18	4	-	-	-	-	-	-	1	-	-	-	-	-
19	4	-	-	-	-	-	-	1	-	-	-	-	-
20	3	-	-	-	-	-	-	1	-	-	-	-	-
21	5	-	-	-	1	1	-	-	-	-	-	-	-
23	6	1	-	1	-	-	-	-	-	-	-	-	whelk shell
24	13	-	-	-	1	-	1	1	1	-	-	1	-
25	17	-	-	-	-	-	-	1	-	-	-	1	-
26	1	-	-	-	-	-	-	-	-	-	-	-	-
27	1	-	-	-	-	-	-	-	-	-	-	-	-
28	3	-	-	-	-	-	-	-	-	-	-	-	-
29	3	-	-	-	-	-	-	-	-	-	-	-	-
30	3	-	-	-	-	-	1	-	-	-	-	1	-
31	10	-	-	-	1	-	-	6	1	-	2	4	limestone with red pigment
32	1	-	-	-	-	-	-	1	-	-	-	-	-
36	12	1	-	-	-	-	-	3	1	-	-	2	microdrill, graver
37	4	-	-	-	-	-	-	-	-	-	-	-	-
43	1	-	-	-	-	-	-	2	-	-	-	-	-
45	1	-	-	-	-	-	-	-	-	-	1	-	-
46	3	-	-	1	-	-	-	3	-	-	-	1	-
47	1	-	-	-	-	-	-	-	-	-	-	1	-
50	9	-	-	2	3	-	2	6	2	-	6	72	gravers (2)
53	1	-	-	-	-	-	-	-	-	-	-	-	-
54	-	-	-	-	-	-	-	-	-	-	-	1	-
57	5	-	-	1	-	-	-	1	1	-	-	-	-
59	-	-	-	-	-	-	-	-	-	-	-	1	-
60	1	-	-	-	-	-	-	-	-	-	-	-	-
63	1	-	-	-	-	-	-	-	-	-	-	-	-
64	2	-	-	-	-	-	-	2	1	-	-	-	-
69	1	-	-	-	-	-	-	1	-	-	-	-	
80	-	-	-	1	-	-	-	-	-	-	-	-	-
81	-	-	-	1	-	-	-	1	-	-	-	-	-
82	4	-	-	-	-	-	2	1	-	-	-	4	-
84	1	-	-	-	-	1	-	-	2	-	-	-	-
85	-	-	-	-	-	-	-	-	-	-	-	1	-
87	9	-	-	-	-	-	2	6	1	-	1	1	whelk shell
88	5	-	-		-	-	2	2	2	-	1	1	galena bead bauxite pendant
89	4	-	-	1	-	-	2	3	-	-	1	1	whelk shell deer mandible tool
90	1	-	-	-	-	-	-	-	-	-	-	-	-
91	9	-	1	-	2	1	-	4	-	-	-	-	-
93	1	-	-	-	-	-	-	-	-	-	-	-	-
94	2	-	-	-	-	-	-	1	-	-	-	-	-
96	1	-	-	-	-	-	-	-	-	-	-	-	-
97	4	-	-	-	-	-	-	-	-	-	-	-	-
99	3	-	-	1	-	-	-	2	1	-	1	-	-
101	5	-	-	-	-	-	-	-	-	-	-	-	-
102	-	-	-	-	1	-	-	-	-	-	-	-	-
103	2	-	-	-	-	-	-	-	-	-	-	1	-
105	1	-	-	-	-	-	-	-	-	-	-	-	-
108	-	-	-	-	-	1	-	-	-	-	-	-	-
109	4	-	-	-	-	-	-	1	-	-	-	-	whelk shell
110	2	-	-	1	-	-	-	-	-	-	-	1	-
111	2	-	-	-	2	-	2	-	-	1	-	1	-
112	2	-	2	1	-	-	-	1	2	-	2	-	-
115	21	-	-	3	1	-	4	4	1	-	-	-	-
118	1	-	-	-	-	-	-	-	-	-	-	-	-
119	-	-	-	-	-	-	-	-	-	-	-	1	-
120	1	-	-	-	-	-	-	-	-	-	-	-	-
123	1	-	-	-	-	-	-	-	-	-	-	-	-
124	1	-	-	-	-	-	-	-	-	-	-	-	-
125	-	-	-	-	-	-	-	1	-	-	-	-	-
127	-	-	-	1	-	-	-	-	-	-	-	-	-
131	-	-	-	3	-	-	-	-	-	-	-	-	-

Table 43. Continued

Feature	Rims	Discs	Pottery Trowels	Cores	Bifaces	Celts and Adze	Excavating Tools	Grinding Tools	Hammer-stones	Knives	Perfor-ators	Projectile Points	Other
137	4	-	-	1	-	-	-	3	2	-	-	-	graver
143	1	-	-	1	-	-	-	-	-	1	-	-	-
146	8	2	-	1	-	-	-	2	2	-	2	1	graver
148	2	-	-	-	-	-	-	-	-	-	-	-	-
149	4	-	-	-	-	-	-	-	1	-	-	-	-
150	16	1	-	-	-	-	-	-	1	-	-	1	ceramic bead
151	2	-	-	-	-	-	-	-	-	-	-	-	-
152	1	-	-	-	-	-	-	-	-	-	-	-	-
154	4	-	-	-	-	-	-	-	-	-	-	-	-
155	6	-	-	-	-	-	-	-	-	-	-	-	-
157	-	-	-	1	-	-	1	1	2	-	-	2	-
158	2	-	-	-	-	-	-	-	-	-	-	-	-
159	1	-	-	-	-	-	-	-	-	-	-	-	-
160	2	-	-	-	-	-	-	-	-	-	-	-	-
162	6	-	-	-	-	-	-	-	-	-	-	-	-
165	1	-	-	-	1	-	-	-	-	-	-	-	-
166	1	-	-	-	-	-	-	-	-	-	-	-	-
167	1	-	-	-	-	-	-	2	-	-	-	-	-
170	2	-	-	-	-	-	-	-	-	-	-	-	-
173	1	-	-	-	-	-	-	-	-	-	-	-	-
175	1	-	-	-	-	-	-	-	-	-	-	-	-
177	6	-	-	-	-	-	-	-	-	-	-	-	discoidal
179	-	-	-	-	-	-	-	1	-	-	-	-	-
180	-	-	-	-	-	-	-	-	-	1	-	-	-
182	1	-	-	-	-	-	-	-	-	-	-	-	-
187	-	-	-	-	-	-	5	3	1	-	-	-	deer mandible tool
188	7	-	-	-	-	-	-	-	-	-	-	-	-
196	2	-	-	-	-	-	-	-	-	-	-	-	-
199	1	-	-	-	-	-	1	1	-	-	-	-	-
204	4	-	-	-	-	-	-	-	-	-	-	-	-
206	1	-	-	-	-	-	-	-	-	-	-	-	-
208	-	-	-	-	-	1	-	-	1	-	-	1	-
215	5	-	-	-	-	-	1	-	-	-	1	-	microdrill
217	-	-	-	1	-	-	-	-	-	-	-	-	-
218	1	-	-	-	-	-	-	-	-	-	-	-	-
219	1	-	-	-	-	-	-	-	-	-	-	-	-
221	10	-	-	-	-	-	-	-	-	-	1	-	-
224	4	-	-	-	-	-	1	1	-	-	-	-	-
229	10	-	-	1	-	-	1	2	-	-	-	1	-
230	-	-	-	-	-	-	-	-	-	-	-	-	hemisphere
231	4	-	-	-	-	-	-	1	-	-	-	-	-
241	44	2	-	3	2	-	-	10	3	-	5	8	crinoid bead discoidal (2) graver
243	11	-	-	-	1	-	1	1	1	-	2	1	-
246	-	-	-	-	-	-	1	-	-	-	-	-	-
249	3	-	-	-	-	-	-	2	-	-	-	-	-
250	-	-	-	-	-	-	-	1	-	-	-	-	-
252	1	-	-	-	-	-	-	-	-	-	-	-	-
262	-	-	-	-	-	-	1	-	-	-	-	-	
264	2	-	-	-	-	-	-	-	-	-	-	-	-
265	1	-	-	-	-	-	-	-	-	-	-	-	-
266	5	1	-	-	-	-	1	1	-	-	-	-	-
267	1	-	-	-	-	-	-	-	-	-	-	-	earspool
272	4	-	-	-	-	-	-	1	-	-	-	1	-
279	1	-	-	-	-	-	-	-	-	-	-	-	ceramic beads (3)
280	3	1	-	-	-	-	-	1	-	-	-	-	-
282	1	-	-	-	-	-	-	-	-	-	-	-	-
283	1	-	-	-	-	-	-	-	-	-	-	-	-
284	2	-	-	-	-	-	-	-	-	-	-	-	-
286	1	-	-	-	-	-	-	-	-	-	-	-	-
289	1	-	-	1	-	-	1	-	-	-	-	-	-
290	7	1	-	-	-	-	-	2	-	-	-	4	-
291	3	-	-	1	-	-	-	-	-	-	-	-	crinoid bead
292	1	-	-	-	-	-	-	-	-	-	-	-	-
293	5	-	-	1	-	-	1	6	1	-	2	1	whelk shell, gravers (3)
294	-	-	-	-	-	-	-	1	-	-	-	-	-
295	16	1	-	-	-	-	-	7	2	-	-	2	-
296	-	-	-	-	-	-	-	1	1	-	-	-	-
297	9	-	-	2	1	-	1	5	1	-	1	5	-
299	2	-	-	-	-	-	-	-	-	-	-	1	-
300	2	-	-	1	-	-	-	1	1	-	-	-	-
303	8	1	-	3	-	-	-	1	-	-	-	1	crinoid bead
304	-	-	-	-	1	-	-	-	-	-	-	-	-
305	1	-	-	-	-	-	-	-	-	-	-	-	-
306	1	-	-	-	-	-	-	-	-	-	-	-	-
Mixed Miss. Feature Contexts	6	1	-	2	1	-	1	1	1	-	-	-	-

Table 44. Material from Feature Contexts by Counts and Weights

Feature	Ceramics		Burned Clay		Chert		Limestone		Sandstone		Miscellaneous Rock, etc.		Various Minerals and Exotic Rocks	
	N	Wt(g)	N	Wt(g)	N	Wt(g)	N	Wt(g)	N	Wt(g)	N	Wt(g)	N	Wt(g)
1	342	985.4	115	226.8	209	663.4	59	3165.2	18	54.6	6	247.2	-	-
2	794	1475.8	428	868.5	606	1953.5	104	1106.8	78	1332.0	23	1017.6	12	280.5
3	79	269.2	101	134.5	122	701.7	16	61344.4	8	397.7	7	1358.4	3	2.7
4	9	20.2	5	30.6	13	30.9	-	-	-	-	-	-	-	-
5	785	1719.9	170	258.1	325	854.8	92	7041.3	22	759.6	18	1325.4	8	62.8
6	6	17.2	-	-	8	47.8	6	105.7	2	112.1	-	-	-	-
7	1184	1286.0	40	26.2	894	3361.3	23	2228.5	74	636.4	35	1922.4	15	72.1
8	129	297.4	6	9.2	16	41.4	2	9.9	2	39.0	2	0.2	-	-
9	334	1049.2	108	96.2	54	288.0	10	944.8	3	122.5	2	377.5	1	9.8
10	104	281.1	3	2.1	67	236.0	3	69.4	4	91.0	1	0.8	-	-
12	116	89.9	17	8.5	22	82.7	2	14501.7	1	4.5	3	153.1	1	0.7
13	32	43.1	4	4.4	7	3.8	2	76.1	1	282.4	2	1.2	-	-
14	12	76.6	-	-	5	4.8	-	-	2	9.7	-	-	-	-
15	101	352.8	8	20.6	20	64.7	-	-	7	240.9	-	-	1	21.2
16	181	840.3	5	9.1	58	120.6	24	1841.3	-	-	7	164.3	-	-
17	566	900.0	38	46.4	290	1606.1	39	848.5	29	728.2	53	1153.1	8	376.5
18	169	309.9	20	30.3	100	126.1	19	118.6	14	373.6	3	3.3	-	-
19	42	219.8	3	1.8	27	51.6	13	175.1	5	120.5	3	9.6	-	-
20	91	132.3	50	16.7	25	33.0	2	334.1	1	64.0	-	-	-	-
21	334	513.0	13	216.1	33	63.1	17	255.1	3	9.1	1	20.9	-	-
23	119	241.8	-	-	64	223.0	5	942.1	1	10.6	-	-	1	12.5
24	477	1786.2	24	55.0	151	559.1	43	1852.3	9	88.3	21	512.2	1	0.3
25	450	892.2	14	24.8	80	182.5	12	358.2	3	77.5	2	130.8	1	0.7
26	25	33.6	-	-	4	8.0	2	4.5	2	39.4	-	-	-	-
27	11	33.1	1	2.4	4	20.8	-	-	1	13.3	-	-	-	-
28	33	130.6	4	53.5	5	5.9	1	12.5	-	-	-	-	-	-
29	63	251.2	3	12.6	12	21.5	5	121.3	2	17.8	-	-	-	-
30	53	132.9	-	-	14	326.9	-	-	-	-	-	-	-	-
31	127	520.9	2	2.2	140	625.0	16	1544.4	21	1187.8	5	180.6	3	35.6
32	90	66.8	4	2.0	58	82.1	1	12.9	4	109.7	5	3.3	-	-
33	1	0.9	-	-	6	6.3	-	-	-	-	-	-	-	-
34	-	-	-	-	2	0.7	-	-	-	-	-	-	-	-
36	254	885.5	3	2.9	93	341.3	6	562.3	7	265.3	8	1080.7	-	-
37	47	179.7	-	-	7	32.6	1	2.1	-	-	-	-	-	-
38	11	11.3	-	-	1	0.6	1	3.1	-	-	-	-	-	-
43	8	19.5	-	-	9	42.9	1	61.0	1	86.1	-	-	1	312.3
45	1	4.9	-	-	11	29.0	-	-	-	-	-	-	-	-
46	39	294.4	2	15.1	51	310.4	6	124.4	8	176.4	-	-	-	-
47	1	70.1	-	-	4	2.9	-	-	-	-	-	-	-	-
48	1	0.9	-	-	2	2.7	-	-	-	-	-	-	-	-
49	20	40.4	2	1.8	14	25.7	1	107.2	2	20.8	-	-	-	-
50	229	519.2	43	197.7	600	1249.4	16	1862.0	21	718.9	5	1063.9	5	15.6
51	8	19.2	1	5.2	11	25.5	-	-	-	-	-	-	-	-
52	79	115.4	1	38.0	6	7.6	-	-	-	-	2	128.7	-	-
53	11	32.7	-	-	8	15.2	3	301.1	-	-	-	-	-	-
54	4	2.8	-	-	13	62.8	-	-	-	-	1	334.4	-	-
55	2	14.7	-	-	2	2.9	-	-	-	-	-	-	-	-
57	161	692.1	5	17.7	82	476.8	3	169.9	4	71.4	7	131.2	1	1.5
59	-	-	-	-	1	0.6	-	-	-	-	-	-	-	-
60	4	7.7	-	-	-	-	-	-	-	-	-	-	-	-
61	-	-	-	-	1	0.2	-	-	-	-	-	-	-	-
62	1	2.9	-	-	2	7.5	-	-	-	-	-	-	-	-
63	22	248.0	-	-	6	13.9	-	-	-	-	-	-	-	-
64	43	571.3	-	-	16	95.5	3	417.5	5	458.5	-	-	-	-
65	2	6.8	-	-	1	0.9	-	-	-	-	1	181.6	-	-

Table 44. Continued

Feature	Ceramics		Burned Clay		Chert		Limestone		Sandstone		Miscellaneous Rock, etc.		Various Minerals and Exotic Rocks	
	N	Wt(g)	N	Wt(g)	N	Wt(g)	N	Wt(g)	N	Wt(g)	N	Wt(g)	N	Wt(g)
66	-	-	-	-	1	3.5	-	-	-	-	-	-	-	-
67	5	13.1	-	-	-	-	-	-	2	181.4	-	-	-	-
68	2	2.7	-	-	1	1.4	-	-	-	-	-	-	-	-
69	2	20.7	1	3.9	2	1.3	-	-	1	85.1	-	-	-	-
70	-	-	-	-	1	4.0	-	-	-	-	-	-	-	-
71	1	1.3	-	-	1	1.8	-	-	-	-	-	-	-	-
73	7	10.1	1	1.8	2	0.9	-	-	-	-	-	-	-	-
74	-	-	-	-	1	0.4	-	-	-	-	-	-	-	-
75	-	-	-	-	-	-	4	359.4	-	-	-	-	-	-
76	2	2.5	-	-	-	-	-	-	-	-	-	-	-	-
78	-	-	-	-	1	4.9	-	-	-	-	-	-	-	-
80	2	2.2	-	-	1	66.9	-	-	-	-	-	-	-	-
81	60	69.9	1	1.0	49	104.1	17	1343.7	13	282.5	-	-	-	-
82	100	421.1	24	111.1	60	210.1	9	100.3	6	23.8	8	19.9	-	-
83	4	15.5	-	-	-	-	-	-	-	-	-	-	-	-
84	44	511.5	23	82.7	21	98.4	3	336.5	1	18.8	2	174.5	1	32.3
85	7	56.4	-	-	6	6.7	7	1120.7	2	16.1	-	-	-	-
86	2	3.7	-	-	-	-	-	-	-	-	-	-	-	-
87	135	678.4	82	445.9	120	356.0	7	398.9	9	413.9	4	127.2	1	19.2
88	151	1194.6	9	43.0	108	1373.3	5	1021.3	3	78.6	2	650.5	3	10.2
89	93	360.9	2	1.3	217	476.1	7	1049.1	13	777.0	2	32.6	1	7.4
90	8	118.7	2	3.0	7	12.3	-	-	-	-	-	-	-	-
91	1164	5003.6	6	29.3	43	369.9	34	5270.8	25	1938.3	5	535.4	-	-
92	1	6.7	-	-	-	-	-	-	-	-	-	-	-	-
93	25	190.3	1	0.3	15	40.6	7	85.9	2	22.3	-	-	-	-
94	83	697.1	3	2.2	27	25.5	26	184.6	1	44.1	-	-	-	-
95	5	14.8	-	-	4	1.4	1	20.5	-	-	-	-	-	-
96	31	133.1	-	-	16	82.7	11	141.2	1	18.3	3	12.8	-	-
97	67	332.8	3	9.0	42	124.3	38	433.9	1	215.4	1	48.9	-	-
98	16	51.8	1	1.0	2	2.9	8	179.9	-	-	-	-	-	-
99	49	504.0	10	33.9	37	112.0	136	3019.1	5	88.1	3	545.9	2	11.1
100	12	1.3	-	-	-	-	2	159.4	-	-	-	-	-	-
101	86	390.2	5	6.0	6	2.3	54	761.2	1	34.3	-	-	-	-
102	38	166.9	5	7.0	20	42.4	66	2006.9	-	-	1	0.1	-	-
103	57	553.1	5	7.9	10	19.3	58	1244.4	2	23.7	1	1.9	-	-
104	72	66.7	-	-	-	-	8	23.9	-	-	-	-	-	-
105	10	37.3	2	3.6	-	-	-	-	-	-	-	-	-	-
107	2	1.3	-	-	1	0.7	-	-	-	-	-	-	-	-
108	-	-	-	-	-	-	1	15.6	-	-	-	-	-	-
109	108	171.7	34	68.1	35	49.7	4	721.9	6	101.3	4	220.7	-	-
110	14	159.7	4	53.3	45	80.8	2	172.5	3	10.0	-	-	-	-
111	36	144.2	6	41.9	97	363.8	1	114.6	2	16.8	-	-	3	55.9
112	60	175.7	1	2.4	99	228.5	6	556.6	4	58.5	2	515.9	-	-
113	12	17.0	-	-	3	18.3	-	-	-	-	-	-	-	-
114	30	57.4	-	-	9	23.9	3	87.4	-	-	-	-	1	5.3
115	869	1909.4	4	45.0	381	1568.6	10	702.7	23	1459.3	5	607.6	36	187.0
116	93	231.3	1	1.5	7	24.3	-	-	1	3.0	1	0.5	1	0.5
117	31	58.4	-	-	12	24.2	-	-	-	-	2	0.6	2	0.1
118	11	27.6	-	-	2	30.4	-	-	-	-	1	1.1	-	-
119	22	33.3	-	-	9	7.6	1	10.8	-	-	-	-	-	-
120	30	50.5	-	-	1	2.6	9	18.6	-	-	-	-	-	-
121	5	0.5	-	-	-	-	1	806.8	-	-	-	-	-	-
122	-	-	-	-	1	3.4	-	-	-	-	1	0.1	-	-
123	26	58.5	-	-	3	42.5	-	-	-	-	-	-	-	-
124	33	167.8	-	-	10	21.5	-	-	-	-	-	-	-	-

Table 44. Continued

Feature	Ceramics		Burned Clay		Chert		Limestone		Sandstone		Miscellaneous Rock, etc.		Various Minerals and Exotic Rocks	
	N	Wt(g)	N	Wt(g)	N	Wt(g)	N	Wt(g)	N	Wt(g)	N	Wt(g)	N	Wt(g)
125	85	192.9	-	-	7	7.6	1	92.0	1	16.9	-	-	-	-
127	-	-	-	-	2	128.1	4	382.1	-	-	-	-	-	-
128	7	19.5	-	-	-	-	-	-	-	-	-	-	-	-
129	-	-	4	7.1	-	-	-	-	-	-	-	-	-	-
130	2	0.8	-	-	-	-	-	-	-	-	-	-	-	-
131	8	9.9	-	-	17	78.5	-	-	-	-	-	-	-	-
133	2	6.4	-	-	-	-	-	-	-	-	-	-	-	-
134	-	-	-	-	1	1.5	-	-	-	-	-	-	-	-
137	78	196.8	13	35.0	52	279.3	10	1756.9	3	284.7	4	1149.3	-	-
141	-	-	-	-	4	4.6	-	-	-	-	-	-	-	-
142	12	124.6	-	-	-	-	3	6.6	-	-	-	-	-	-
143	105	101.2	1	10.4	26	97.0	-	-	-	-	-	-	-	-
144	1	4.0	-	-	-	-	-	-	-	-	-	-	-	-
145	13	18.2	-	-	9	4.6	1	175.6	-	-	-	-	-	-
146	415	914.8	8	25.9	238	601.4	14	36.1	7	965.8	5	642.4	9	79.7
148	8	9.4	-	-	4	8.6	3	114.5	-	-	3	68.9	-	-
149	127	390.3	-	-	72	221.6	46	1821.5	1	1.8	4	118.6	1	1.1
150	430	1336.0	136	280.1	240	295.6	36	1108.9	39	120.5	5	141.3	-	-
151	24	80.2	-	-	8	7.8	4	829.3	-	-	-	-	3	1.6
152	36	115.8	-	-	24	58.3	3	236.8	6	142.6	-	-	1	8.6
153	5	12.5	-	-	8	17.7	-	-	1	20.6	-	-	-	-
154	98	161.7	1	1.6	61	66.1	7	18.8	1	1.8	1	0.1	-	-
155	66	282.9	-	-	20	47.2	14	973.4	6	92.9	-	-	1	9.5
156	4	5.1	-	-	3	5.7	-	-	-	-	-	-	-	-
157	37	63055.7	1	19.5	37	260.5	15	2717.1	24	503.3	2	839.4	1	0.1
158	7	10.2	-	-	2	10.0	1	194.1	1	1.5	-	-	-	-
159	25	30.7	-	-	2	3.0	5	34.1	-	-	1	0.3	1	2.1
160	12	30.6	-	-	8	17.0	1	117.2	-	-	-	-	-	-
161	4	9.3	-	-	1	0.9	-	-	-	-	-	-	-	-
162	162	312.1	-	-	18	38.0	33	458.6	1	47.3	-	-	-	-
163	2	7.0	-	-	-	-	-	-	-	-	-	-	-	-
165	131	649.5	-	-	21	91.3	-	-	1	4.7	-	-	-	-
166	60	306.2	-	-	36	28.0	7	112.3	-	-	-	-	-	-
167	20	43.2	-	-	9	20.1	2	378.2	4	213.6	4	0.7	-	-
168	13	31.2	-	-	1	3.0	1	50.3	-	-	-	-	-	-
169	10	10.3	-	-	5	5.7	-	-	-	-	-	-	-	-
170	33	131.4	-	-	5	7.2	3	304.3	1	269.1	-	-	-	-
171	9	15.8	1	9.8	-	-	-	-	-	-	-	-	-	-
172	39	88.1	-	-	4	19.5	1	20.3	1	135.1	-	-	-	-
173	64	284.7	2	28.4	4	13.8	-	-	-	-	-	-	-	-
174	-	-	-	-	1	3.4	-	-	-	-	-	-	-	-
175	2	13.9	-	-	16	48.7	21	6932.8	-	-	-	-	-	-
176	32	127.0	-	-	7	17.5	4	3500.0	-	-	-	-	-	-
177	131	457.8	10	19.0	21	64.6	8	258.3	2	14.0	1	43.3	-	-
178	-	-	-	-	5	6.1	-	-	1	2.7	-	-	-	-
179	13	55.9	1	0.7	10	38.1	5	7.5	1	37.0	-	-	-	-
181	5	8.0	57	80.2	5	1.6	-	-	-	-	-	-	-	-
182	5	21.8	-	-	-	-	-	-	1	41.5	1	6.2	-	-
183	9	45.3	-	-	10	8.8	-	-	-	-	-	-	-	-
184	3	6.4	-	-	7	3.9	-	-	-	-	-	-	-	-
185	13	18.7	-	-	4	4.8	-	-	-	-	-	-	2	10.2
186	4	5.2	1	7.1	6	11.9	-	-	-	-	-	-	-	-
187	46	189.7	7	30.8	81	3158.3	8	323.0	8	350.4	1	169.6	-	-
188	128	368.3	-	-	15	99.3	-	-	2	8.3	-	-	1	37.5
189	-	-	-	-	1	1.2	-	-	-	-	-	-	-	-

Table 44. Continued

Feature	Ceramics		Burned Clay		Chert		Limestone		Sandstone		Miscellaneous Rock, etc.		Various Minerals and Exotic Rocks	
	N	Wt(g)	N	Wt(g)	N	Wt(g)	N	Wt(g)	N	Wt(g)	N	Wt(g)	N	Wt(g)
190	4	1.8	-	-	4	4.2	1	84.5	-	-	-	-	-	-
191	-	-	-	-	-	-	-	-	-	-	1	0.5	-	-
192	-	-	-	-	3	11.2	-	-	-	-	-	-	-	-
195	-	-	-	-	1	1.0	-	-	-	-	-	-	-	-
196	18	49.6	1	10.9	14	54.0	-	-	1	3.5	1	0.5	-	-
197	13	29.9	1	2.8	3	8.1	-	-	-	-	-	-	1	0.1
198	6	13.7	-	-	1	0.6	-	-	-	-	1	47.6	-	-
199	19	44.2	1	0.2	10	12.5	1	227.8	2	464.4	1	1.6	-	-
200	13	2.4	-	-	-	-	-	-	-	-	-	-	-	-
201	8	14.4	-	-	1	0.2	-	-	-	-	-	-	-	-
203	-	-	-	-	-	-	1	559.1	-	-	-	-	-	-
204	45	120.2	2	1.5	4	19.5	7	57.0	1	5.1	1	7.3	-	-
206	9	30.3	-	-	-	-	-	-	-	-	-	-	-	-
208	19	31.6	-	-	25	81.4	1	183.5	-	-	2	325.7	-	-
209	-	-	-	-	1	11.5	-	-	-	-	-	-	-	-
211	-	-	-	-	2	3.8	-	-	-	-	-	-	-	-
213	1	5.8	-	-	1	0.5	-	-	-	-	-	-	-	-
214	8	10.5	2	2.0	6	8.7	6	3.8	1	0.9	1	0.3	-	-
215	170	618.6	9	12.3	43	422.1	13	297.3	-	-	1	0.2	-	-
216	4	5.5	-	-	4	17.6	-	-	-	-	-	-	-	-
217	2	1.3	-	-	9	66.1	-	-	-	-	-	-	-	-
218	22	36.1	-	-	7	12.2	1	5.3	1	0.4	2	12.6	-	-
219	6	12.5	-	-	15	64.6	-	-	-	-	-	-	-	-
220	7	19.2	1	1.5	10	13.6	-	-	-	-	-	-	2	1.8
221	213	515.0	4	3.7	80	87.1	64	27621.7	6	16.5	1	0.1	1	0.4
222	3	13.2	-	-	1	0.1	-	-	-	-	-	-	-	-
223	2	7.7	-	-	7	14.3	-	-	1	3.5	-	-	-	-
224	103	583.3	3	6.2	46	142.2	3	12.2	4	79.4	-	-	-	-
225	4	10.3	-	-	-	-	-	-	-	-	-	-	-	-
226	-	-	-	-	2	1.4	-	-	-	-	-	-	-	-
227	-	-	-	-	1	2.0	-	-	-	-	-	-	-	-
228	-	-	-	-	1	2.7	-	-	-	-	-	-	-	-
229	247	1306.4	17	93.6	65	180.5	10	394.2	14	274.3	3	341.0	-	-
230	-	-	-	-	6	3.1	-	-	-	-	1	41.5	-	-
231	127	184.8	8	308.9	32	107.1	2	178.4	3	128.5	2	20.5	-	-
236	1	0.2	-	-	2	2.5	-	-	-	-	-	-	-	-
237	2	6.8	1	1.0	3	29.2	-	-	-	-	-	-	-	-
239	-	-	-	-	1	0.8	-	-	-	-	-	-	-	-
240	-	-	-	-	3	4.3	-	-	-	-	-	-	-	-
241	972	2251.5	134	507.9	505	2434.9	98	5739.0	81	3526.1	13	2011.4	12	18.7
242	3	3.7	-	-	-	-	-	-	-	-	-	-	-	-
243	312	504.2	37	38.2	134	489.2	15	281.4	16	60.7	3	446.9	1	4.4
244	1	0.4	-	-	1	4.6	-	-	-	-	-	-	-	-
245	4	6.3	-	-	1	5.5	-	-	-	-	-	-	-	-
246	2	13.3	-	-	3	1427.0	1	0.8	-	-	-	-	-	-
247	10	10.9	-	-	7	15.5	1	15.9	-	-	1	0.6	-	-
248	3	7.6	-	-	-	-	-	-	-	-	-	-	-	-
249	95	933.4	1	0.2	40	204.8	2	95.7	8	1622.1	3	182.8	3	2.3
250	4	31.5	-	-	4	5.1	1	148.7	1	76.4	-	-	-	-
251	2	2.8	-	-	-	-	-	-	-	-	-	-	-	-
253	-	-	-	-	2	25.8	-	-	-	-	-	-	-	-
254	2	1.2	-	-	2	0.7	-	-	1	7.5	-	-	-	-
255	20	134.7	-	-	2	3.4	-	-	-	-	-	-	1	0.5
256	1	6.0	-	-	1	5.7	-	-	-	-	-	-	-	-
258	-	-	-	-	1	3.3	-	-	-	-	-	-	-	-

Table 44. Continued

Feature	Ceramics		Burned Clay		Chert		Limestone		Sandstone		Miscellaneous Rock, etc.		Various Minerals and Exotic Rocks	
	N	Wt(g)	N	Wt(g)	N	Wt(g)	N	Wt(g)	N	Wt(g)	N	Wt(g)	N	Wt(g)
259	-	-	-	-	2	3.6	-	-	-	-	-	-	-	-
260	-	-	-	-	2	3.0	-	-	-	-	-	-	-	-
262	7	5.1	-	-	1	324.9	-	-	-	-	-	-	-	-
263	1	0.3	-	-	3	0.4	-	-	-	-	-	-	-	-
264	5	17.6	-	-	1	0.4	-	-	-	-	-	-	-	-
265	62	84.3	1	1.5	6	41.5	7	1269.3	-	-	-	-	-	-
266	313	1470.7	18	20.4	52	131.5	67	1373.8	9	119.6	1	0.1	-	-
267	17	25.0	-	-	41	174.8	1	63.9	-	-	-	-	1	1.3
268	1	0.4	-	-	-	-	1	227.9	-	-	-	-	-	-
269	2	2.4	-	-	-	-	-	-	-	-	-	-	-	-
270	43	160.6	9	25.1	19	28.8	31	616.8	-	-	1	3.7	-	-
271	5	10.5	1	0.2	2	3.7	7	49.8	-	-	-	-	-	-
272	52	164.7	6	21.3	12	27.0	28	1123.8	1	6.4	-	-	-	-
273	14	14.2	2	1.4	5	2.4	6	302.5	-	-	-	-	-	-
274	2	3.3	-	-	2	4.9	-	-	-	-	-	-	-	-
276	15	46.5	1	0.7	9	18.1	-	-	-	-	-	-	-	-
277	-	-	-	-	1	0.7	-	-	-	-	-	-	-	-
278	4	13.1	-	-	3	5.6	1	2.4	-	-	-	-	-	-
279	14	60.4	-	-	14	33.3	1	290.0	-	-	1	4.8	-	-
280	63	162.2	3	4.6	28	203.9	37	580.9	2	182.3	-	-	-	-
281	10	24.1	-	-	3	25.7	7	232.1	-	-	-	-	-	-
282	1	1.7	-	-	1	0.9	-	-	-	-	-	-	-	-
283	13	18.8	-	-	1	0.4	56	17000.0	-	-	-	-	-	-
284	91	231.8	3	3.9	15	37.4	8	317.3	1	2.5	-	-	-	-
285	6	13.5	2	4.1	3	13.0	-	-	-	-	-	-	-	-
286	1	5.1	-	-	-	-	-	-	-	-	-	-	-	-
287	-	-	-	-	2	8.7	-	-	-	-	-	-	-	-
288	1	1.3	-	-	2	8.1	1	53.1	-	-	-	-	-	-
289	5	30.6	-	-	7	32.1	67	20442.2	-	-	-	-	-	-
290	232	635.2	189	406.3	157	215.4	35	2197.2	29	442.5	7	16.2	-	-
291	83	282.7	4	11.4	46	183.2	4	460.1	3	773.6	1	7.5	-	-
292	11	38.1	3	2.9	6	6.7	59	6698.9	-	-	-	-	-	-
293	124	350.0	9	18.2	218	990.0	9	1517.4	28	745.2	4	5747.4	7	49.3
294	2	1.5	-	-	2	2.1	-	-	1	12.6	-	-	-	-
295	314	1848.0	44	48.1	197	662.9	8	1356.9	18	378.8	4	751.0	1	12.6
296	2	1.2	-	-	1	1.5	1	155.1	1	117.0	1	804.2	-	-
297	233	1243.9	2	4.9	190	1081.4	12	601.9	12	734.1	4	285.4	-	-
298	13	14.2	-	-	16	42.7	-	-	1	98.0	-	-	1	4.7
299	73	392.4	12	52.2	46	148.2	6	573.7	6	350.8	-	-	3	15.4
300	84	179.5	4	7.4	19	58.9	10	493.4	3	60.2	1	116.5	1	1.9
301	2	2.9	-	-	1	0.5	-	-	-	-	1	0.7	-	-
303	503	1317.9	198	449.6	294	408.9	103	6364.5	78	6179.7	9	240.8	2	5.9
304	-	-	-	-	2	3.5	-	-	-	-	-	-	-	-
305	30	71.4	-	-	6	20.2	-	-	-	-	-	-	-	-
306	14	48.2	1	8.3	18	42.2	10	102.6	4	33.7	1	5.7	-	-
307	22	45.0	-	-	1	0.9	-	-	-	-	-	-	-	-
308	2	5.7	-	-	-	-	-	-	-	-	-	-	-	-
309	-	-	-	-	1	2.5	-	-	-	-	-	-	-	-
310	-	-	-	-	2	2.4	-	-	-	-	-	-	-	-
311	1	0.9	-	-	1	10.9	1	83.2	-	-	-	-	-	-

Section 2: Ancillary Research

HUMAN REMAINS FROM THE JULIEN SITE

by

George R. Milner

The human remains from the Julien site consisted of 10 teeth that collectively weighed 4.0 g (Table 45). All but one were obtained from Mississippian feature contexts; the exception was a single specimen recovered from backdirt. The teeth were recovered from Mississippian period Stirling and Moorehead phase features. Had additional skeletal material once been present at the Julien site, it probably would not have been preserved. Bone preservation at the site was generally poor.

Adults and one immature individual were represented by the teeth. The degree of attrition displayed by these specimens was slight to moderate. Several of the permanent teeth displayed macroscopically visible enamel hypoplasia; the degree of expression was slight, with minute linear defects being transversely oriented.

It is difficult to evaluate the significance of scattered remains in Mississippian habitation contexts, but disarticulated skeletal elements are a conspicuous feature of Mississippian cemeteries in the American Bottom (Milner 1980,1981a; Melbye 1963). Perhaps bodies in the Stirling and Moorehead phases were skeletonized within the confines of settlements before the bones were cleaned and transported to cemeteries for final interment. Isolated human remains have been found previously in other Mississippian habitation sites in the American Bottom area, such as the Lab Woofie site (Prentice and Mehrer 1981).

Table 45. Human Remains from the Julien Site

Tooth*	Feature	Phase
upper right central incisor	5	Moorehead
upper right second premolar	5	Moorehead
lower right canine	5	Moorehead
upper right canine	16	Moorehead?
upper right first premolar	114	Stirling?
upper left first premolar	114	Stirling?
upper right first molar	115	Stirling
enamel fragment	249	Stirling or Moorehead?
deciduous upper left second molar	295	Moorehead
lower right first premolar	Backdirt Block 4	-

* Permanent dentition unless otherwise noted.

VERTEBRATE FAUNAL REMAINS FROM THE JULIEN SITE

by

Paula G. Cross

Introduction

Located on sandy ridges which form part of the Goose Lake point bar, the multicomponent Julien site was surrounded during prehistoric times by marshy lowlands. Aquatic resources typical of floodplain topographies, such as sloughs and backwater lakes, were abundant and within the immediate vicinity of this Mississippi River valley site. The closest upland forested areas would have been about 2 km to the south-southwest. The faunal assemblage recovered from the Julien site reflects this very aquatic environment.

Since both Late Woodland and Mississippian features were identified, this would have been an excellent chance for comparison of differential faunal exploitation through time. Unfortunately, the small number of Late Woodland features, which contained only scant faunal remains; the overall poor preservation of bone at the site; and the fragmentary nature of most of the bone, made comparisons between components infeasible. A diversity of fauna was exploited during both time periods, but the Mississippian faunal remains were 25 times greater in number and contained a wider variety of species within each of the faunal classes.

Methods

Faunal material was recovered by two methods. Large fragments (>0.5 cm) were collected by the excavator in the field, put in general material bags, and later sorted for analysis. The bones of large mammals and birds were primarily recovered by this method. The second method of recovery was by flotation samples. Random 10 l samples were taken from Julien site features by fill zones or by arbitrary 10 cm levels. Sampling methods were gradually modified, so all features were not sampled consistently. Occcasionally, larger numbers of samples were taken when an abundance of faunal or botanical remains were observed by the excavator. This differential method of sampling precluded one-to-one comparisons of weights and amounts of faunal material from different features. The samples were processed using a modified form of the IDOT flotation system (Wagner 1976). All bones larger than 1 mm were sorted from the processed flotation samples once they had dried.

The recovery technique of flotation was particularly important for achieving an overall view of the fauna utilized by the Julien site inhabitants. The majority of bones from the fish, reptile, amphibian, and small bird species were recovered by this method. Table 46 lists

Table 46. Flotation Recovery of Faunal Materials

Occupation	Class	Total N of Elements/ Fragments	Total N from Flotation Samples	Percentage of Total Recovered by Flotation
Late Woodland	Mammal	23	8	34.78
	Bird	11	7	63.64
	Fish	90	90	100.00
	Amphibian	3	3	100.00
	Unidentifiable	853	825	96.72
	Total	980	933	95.20
Mississippian	Mammal	1798	332	18.46
	Bird	755	384	50.86
	Fish	3534	3272	92.59
	Turtle	190	119	62.63
	Amphibian	22	20	90.91
	Snake	1	1	100.00
	Unidentifiable	18218	15194	83.40
	Total	24518	19322	78.81

the major classes of fauna, the total number of elements/fragments recovered, and the number and percentage of elements/fragments recovered through flotation. Without flotation samples, large fauna, especially deer, may be assigned undue importance in a prehistoric diet.

After all the bone was received and inventoried by faunal laboratory personnel, selected features were chosen for analysis. The small number of Late Woodland features (13) and their relatively scant faunal material made it possible to do a complete analysis of all bone from that component. The larger number of Mississippian features and the relative abundance of faunal material in those features precluded a complete analysis. Eight structures and their associated internal features as well as four external features that contained much faunal material but had no known structure associations were chosen for analysis. All faunal materials from these Mississippian features, except freshwater mussels and fish scales, were analyzed. Identification of fish, bird, and large mammals was made by Lucretia Kelly and Paula Cross. Jennifer Bardwell assisted with the small mammal identification.

Elements were identified to the most specific level possible. A complete listing by component is given in Table 47. Listed are the specific identification, the minimum number of individuals (MNI), and the number of elements used to calculate the MNI. The MNI was calculated by counting the most frequently occurring element within a species after dividing the bones into lefts and rights and taking into account differences in bone size and the portions of bone present for analysis. Care should be taken when calculating the MNI of large game such as deer. Communal sharing between households may have taken place, thus distributing an animal's remains among several features. Since it cannot be determined whether this occurred, an MNI of one is given for every nonassociated feature in which a species was recovered; houses and their associated pits are treated as single units. Some overenumeration of individuals may have occurred due to this method.

Any bone or bone fragment which could not be identified to class level (e.g., fish, bird, mammal) was termed "unidentifiable." Most of this bone was less than 0.5 cm in size and was recovered through flotation. Burned and unburned bone were separated, then counted and weighed by feature. Tablulation of unidentifiable bone is given in Table 48.

Results

Late Woodland

Thirteen features clustered at the northeastern end of the excavation area were identified as Late Woodland. All of them were pits, with no associated structures. In 11 of these features, there

Table 47. Minimum Number of Individuals Calculated for Faunal Remains from Prehistoric Occupations

Occupation	Class	Taxa	Feature	MNI	N of Elements
Late Woodland	Fish	Ictaluridae (catfish family)	93, 97, 99, 102	4	6
	Bird	Tetraonidae (grouse family)	102	1	1
		passerine (perching bird)	102	1	1
	Mammal	*Geomys bursarius* (plains pocket gopher)	94	1	1
Mississippian					
Stirling Phase	Fish	*Amia calva* (bowfin)	89, 229	6	286
		Lepisosteus sp. (gar)	89	1	5
		Esox sp. (pike)	89	1	5
		Ictiobus sp. (buffalo)	89	1	1
		Ictalurus natalis (yellow bullhead)	89	1	2
		Ictalurus nebulosus (brown bullhead)	89	1	1
		Ictalurus melas (black bullhead)	89	1	2
		bullhead sp.	89	-	4
		Ictaluridae (catfish family)	89, 229	2	19
		Micropterus sp. (smallmouth and/or largemouth bass)	89	1	3
		Lepomis sp. (sunfish)	89	5	11
		Ambloplites rupestris (rock bass)	89	1	2
		Centrarchidae (sunfish family)	89	-	9
	Bird	*Anas discors/carolinensis* (blue-winged and/or green-winged teal)	89	1	4
		Anas sp.	89	1	1
		Aix sponsa (wood duck)	89	1	3
		Indeterminate duck	89, 229	3	15

Table 47. Continued

Occupation	Class	Taxa	Feature	MNI	N of Elements
Mississippian Stirling Phase (cont.)	Bird (cont.)	Colymbidae (grebe family)	89	1	1
		Gruidae (crane family)	89	1	1
		passerine (perching bird)	229	1	3
	Mammal	*Scalopus aquaticus* (eastern mole)	252	1	2
		Geomys bursarius (plains pocket gopher)	229, 291	2	5
		Mustela vison (mink)	229	1	1
		Ondatra zibethicus (muskrat)	89, 291	4	30
		Odocoileus virginianus (white-tailed deer)	89	1	3
Moorehead Phase	Fish	*Amia calva* (bowfin)	150	2	49
		Lepisosteus sp. (gar)	150	1	3
		Esox sp. (pike)	150	1	1
		Catostomidae (sucker family)	150	1	1
		Ictaluras nebulosus (brown bullhead)	150	1	1
		bullhead sp.	150	1	3
		Ictaluridae (catfish family)	150	3	12
		Micropterus sp. (smallmouth and/or largemouth bass)	150	2	2
		Lepomis sp. (sunfish)	150	1	2
		Centrarchidae (sunfish family)	150	-	7
		Aplodinotus grunniens (freshwater drum)	150	1	2
	Bird	*Anas discors/carolinensis* (blue-winged and/or green-winged teal)	150	5	18
		Anas platyrhynchos (mallard)	150	1	2

Table 47. Continued

Occupation	Class	Taxa	Feature	MNI	N of Elements
Mississippian					
Moorehead Phase (cont.)	Bird (cont.)	*Anas acuta* (pintail)	150	1	1
		Anatinae (surface feeding duck)	150	-	9
		Indeterminate duck	150	-	41
		Anserinae (geese)	150	2	4
		Gruidae (crane family)	150	1	1
		passerine (perching bird)	150	3	11
		Colinus virginianus (bobwhite)	150	1	1
	Mammal	*Sciurus carolinensis* (eastern gray squirrel)	150	1	1
		Odocoileus virginianus (white-tailed deer)	150	1	2
	Turtle	*Chelydra serpentina* (snapping turtle)	46, 150, 289	3	17
Sand Prairie Phase	Fish	*Amia calva* (bowfin)	2, 24, 84, 87, 88, 91, 110, 112, 185, 187, 211, 244, 261	16	317
		Lepisosteus sp. (gar)	84, 87, 88, 112	4	19
		Esox sp. (pike)	88, 110	2	3
		Ictiobus bubalus/niger (smallmouth and/or black buffalo)	24, 87	2	2
		Ictiobus sp. (buffalo)	24, 87, 88	2	8
		Catostomidae (sucker family)	24, 84, 87, 88, 91	2	16
		Ictalurus natalis (yellow bullhead)	84, 87	2	6

Table 47. Continued

Occupation	Class	Taxa	Feature	MNI	N of Elements
Mississippian					
Sand Prairie Phase (cont.)	Fish (cont.)	*Ictaluras nebulosus* (brown bullhead)	84, 87	4	6
		Ictalurus melas (black bullhead	84	2	6
		bullhead sp.	84, 87, 88, 112, 187	2	36
		Pylodictis olivaris (flathead catfish)	24	1	1
		Ictaluridae (catfish family)	2, 84, 87, 88, 110 112	5	36
		Lepomis sp. (sunfish)	24, 88, 187	3	3
		Centrarchidae (sunfish family)	88, 187	-	6
		Aplodinotus grunniens (freshwater drum)	88	1	1
	Bird	*Anas discors/carolinensis* (blue-winged and/or green-winged teal)	84, 88, 111, 187	5	9
		Anas sp.	84	2	4
		Aix sponsa (wood duck)	88	1	2
		Aythyinae (diving duck)	88	1	1
		Indeterminate duck	2, 24, 84, 87, 88, 110, 187, 212,	12	36
		Colymbidae (grebe family)	88	1	1
		Gruidae (crane family)	84, 87, 110	5	18
		Olor sp. (swan)	187	1	1
		passerine (perching bird)	88, 111	2	3
	Mammal	*Geomys bursarius* (plains pocket gopher)	24, 88	2	3

Table 47. Continued

Occupation	Class	Taxa	Feature	MNI	N of Elements
Mississippian					
Sand Prairie Phase (cont.)	Mammal (cont.)	Ondatra zibethicus (muskrat)	2, 24, 84, 87, 88, 112, 187, 211	17	126
		Tamias striatus (eastern chipmunk)	87	1	1
		Oryzomys palustris (rice rat)	24	1	4
		Canis sp. (dog/coyote)	2, 90, 142	2	4
		Odocoileus virginianus (white-tailed deer)	2, 24, 82, 87, 88, 91, 111, 112, 142, 187	7	46
		Cervidae (elk and/or deer)	24	-	1
		Procyon lotor (raccoon)	84	1	1
	Turtle	Chelydra serpentina (snapping turtle)	88	1	2

Table 48. Unidentifiable Bone

Occupation	Feature	Burned N	Burned Wt(g)	Unburned N	Unburned Wt(g)
Late Woodland	93	35	0.30	-	-
	94	12	0.25	-	-
	96	52	0.70	3	0.10
	97	104	2.30	10	0.40
	99	183	3.70	50	0.95
	100	1	0.10	-	-
	101	40	2.25	1	0.20
	102	195	2.95	38	1.00
	103	89	1.80	31	1.20
	104	9	0.35	-	-
Total		720 (84.41%)	17.40 (81.88%)	133 (15.59%)	3.85 (18.12%)
Mississippian	2	289	8.90	112	2.80
	3	18	0.30	1	0.10
	24	156	5.00	658	11.80
	46	66	1.30	-	-
	48	2	0.20	-	-
	49	3	0.20	3	0.10
	50	14	0.40	21	0.50
	52	2	0.10	-	-
	82	1489	26.20	1029	23.00
	84	274	2.75	1293	17.50
	87	512	8.05	453	6.87
	88	2474	42.70	124	1.70
	89	343	6.00	869	12.95
	90	144	3.55	19	0.40
	91	33	1.40	8	0.20
	110	923	14.45	7	0.30
	111	159	2.85	32	2.90
	112	585	5.50	155	1.40
	132	2	0.10	-	-
	134	2	0.10	-	-
	141	11	0.30	-	-
	142	7	0.15	-	-
	150	2167	44.70	1649	30.30
	185	48	0.90	10	0.30
	186	17	0.70	-	-
	187	286	2.90	420	5.20
	210	30	0.30	-	-
	211	40	0.70	-	-
	212	63	0.50	-	-
	229	1085	11.70	17	0.10
	244	5	0.10	4	0.10
	261	8	0.10	9	0.10
	263	1	0.20	-	-
	264	32	0.50	-	-
	267	4	0.10	-	-
	291	31	0.20	-	-
Total		11325 (62.16%)	194.10 (62.07%)	6893 (37.84%)	118.60 (37.93%)

were scant, but diverse, faunal remains, including mammal, bird, fish, and amphibian elements. These remains indicate that a diverse faunal exploitation strategy was utilized. Table 49 lists the number of elements recovered and the weights of bone for each faunal class. Unfortunately, only a small amount of the faunal material could be identified beyond the class level (Table 47), thus limiting information regarding specific environments exploited.

Mammalian remains were widely dispersed, being recovered from seven features (Features 93, 94, 96, 100, 101, 102, and 103). This may be due to the better chance for preservation and recovery of large mammalian fragments, rather than indicating a prehistoric preference for mammals in the diet. The only element identified to species level was an unburned plains pocket gopher (Geomys bursarius) incisor found in Feature 94. Gophers are common throughout this area (Hoffmeister and Mohr 1957:153) and the tooth may have been intrusive in the feature fill. Two teeth fragments, too partial to identify, were recovered from Feature 93. A burned caudal vertebra from a small rodent-sized mammal was recovered from Feature 103. The burning indicates that it was not a later intrusion. The remaining elements and fragments were too fragmentary to identify beyond a general range of medium to large mammal (i.e., raccoon to deer).

Fish remains occurred in six features (Features 93, 97, 98, 99, 102, and 103) and represent the major faunal class recovered in terms of the number of fragments. Catfish (Ictaluridae) was the only family of fish identified, with elements recovered from four different features. None of the elements could be identified to species level due to their fragmentary nature. Fish scales were also recovered, indicating that a variety of other fish were caught in addition to catfish.

Only two features yielded bird remains. Feature 102 contained a grouse (Tetraonidae) partial radius and a passerine tibiotarsus. It has been suggested that passerine-sized birds may have been captured for feathers to be used for decoration (L. Kelly 1979:15) or for fletching, since birds of this size would have added little to the diet. Feature 99 contained only unidentifiable diaphysis fragments and a claw.

Three burned amphibian elements were recovered from Feature 101. No species identification was possible due to the fragmentary nature of the bones.

Ten features contained bone that was unidentifiable to class. Most of this bone was recovered through flotation (Table 46) and was less than 0.5 cm in size. Counts and weights are given in Table 48.

This small faunal inventory, totaling 980 pieces of bone, provides only limited information on Late Woodland subsistence patterns. Even so, the animal remains found in this assemblage portray an exploitation strategy utilizing both aquatic and terrestrial habitats and a diversity of fauna. This diversity of the Late Woodland diet is well documented

Table 49. Total Number and Weight of Faunal Classes by Occupation

	Late Woodland				Mississippian												Total	
					Stirling Phase				Moorehead Phase				Sand Prairie Phase					
	Burned		Unburned		Burned		Unburned		Burned		Unburned		Burned		Unburned			
Class	N	Wt(g)	N	Wt(g)	N	Wt(g)	N	Wt(g)	N	Wt(g)	N	Wt(g)	N	Wt(g)	N	Wt(g)	N	Wt(g)
Fish	18	0.90	72	3.10	844	32.20	634	21.95	82	3.30	326	17.20	368	14.50	1280	64.90	3624	158.05
Bird	3	0.20	8	0.85	86	16.20	13	5.15	80	14.00	286	65.55	169	55.95	121	93.75	766	251.65
Mammal	13	4.45	10	2.80	29	25.55	32	61.35	17	10.80	61	22.95	404	90.15	1255	633.50	1821	851.55
Turtle	-	-	-	-	19	8.35	-	-	11	1.35	61	64.60	97	13.20	2	0.30	190	87.80
Amphibian	3	0.10	-	-	-	-	-	-	-	-	6	0.40	-	-	16	0.50	25	1.00
Snake	-	-	-	-	-	-	-	-	-	-	1	0.20	-	-	-	-	1	0.20
Unidentifiable	720	14.60	133	3.85	1463	18.00	886	13.05	2274	47.30	1674	31.00	7588	128.80	4333	74.55	19071	331.15
Total	757	20.25	223	10.60	2441	100.30	1565	101.50	2464	76.75	2415	201.90	8626	302.60	7007	867.50	25498	1681.40

by larger faunal assemblages from other American Bottom sites such as the Mund site (Cross 1982).

Mississippian

Three Mississippian phases were represented at the Julien site: Stirling, Moorehead, and Sand Prairie. Features were assigned to phases on the basis of ceramics and, in the case of Sand Prairie phase features, were corroborated by radiocarbon dating. Features of each phase were analyzed separately and then the assemblages were compared to determine if there were any changes in faunal exploitation. All three phases exhibited a very generalized pattern of faunal utilization with no observable evidence for the dominance of any one faunal class.

Stirling Phase

Stirling phase features included two structures (Features 36 and 267), their associated internal pits, and Feature 89, a nonassociated external pit. Overall, moderate amounts of faunal material were recovered from the pits and very scant amounts from the structure fills.

Feature 36, a structure with four internal pits, yielded no faunal material even though over 325 l of fill was floated. Neither did either of two internal pits (Features 224 and 242) yield any faunal material. However, Feature 252 contained a whole vessel which nearly filled the feature, and two unburned eastern mole (*Scalopus aquaticus*) humeri were found in the fill inside the vessel; they were almost certainly intrusive. Feature 229, therefore, was the only feature of the four to contain prehistoric faunal remains. Turtle remains were recovered that included shell fragments and a partial burned humerus from an unidentified species. Identified fish elements were recovered that included bowfin (*Amia calva*) and catfish. Recovered mammalian remains were slightly more varied, including an unburned mink (*Mustela vison*) ulna, a burned plains pocket gopher humerus and femur, along with several unidentified small mammal elements. The bird remains included three passerine-sized elements and a duck coracoid.

Structure 267 was defined by its wall trenches; it had no basin. Four unidentifiable bone fragments were recovered from the small amount of wall trench fill that was floated. The structure had two associated internal pits: Feature 286, which yielded no faunal remains; and Feature 291, which contained a plains pocket gopher mandible, molar, and incisor, and three muskrat (*Ondatra zibethicus*) teeth fragments. All of these elements were unburned.

Feature 89 was the only Stirling phase feature analyzed that contained an abundance of faunal material. It was a nonassociated feature that was superimposed by a Sand Prairie phase structure (Feature 2). Mammalian remains included a white-tailed deer (*Odocoileus virginianus*) mandible, axis, and antler. Twenty-six muskrat elements, representing at least three individuals, were identified. Fish elements were by far the most numerous, totaling 1188; 306 of these were identified to family or species level. Bowfin accounted for 252 of these elements; 221 of these were the distinctive bowfin vertebrae. Other fish species identified are listed in Table 47. Identifiable bird elements were all aquatic or semiaquatic species. A crane (Gruidae) tarsometatarsus and a grebe (Colymbidae) coracoid were identified, along with several wood duck (*Aix sponsa*) and blue-winged or green-winged teal (*Anas discors* or *A. carolinensis*) elements. Four burned turtle shell fragments and two turtle phalanges were recovered. One of the shell fragments was a partial plastron with cut marks and smoothed edges (Figure 85). It is discussed in more detail in the worked bone section of this volume.

Moorehead Phase

Three structures with associated internal pits and one nonassociated external pit were identified as belonging to the Moorehead phase. As with the Stirling phase features, scant faunal material was recovered from the Moorehead phase structures and their internal pits. Abundant faunal material, however, was recovered from an external feature (Feature 150).

Feature 3, a large structure with two internal pits, yielded slightly more remains. Recovered were a partial turtle carapace in very poor condition and several teeth fragments from an unidentified mammal. Of the two internal pits, Feature 133 had no recovered faunal remains and Feature 132 yielded only two unidentifiable fragments.

Structure Feature 31 had 16 internal pits and hearths, only 6 of which yielded faunal remains. As Milner noted above, Feature 31 may have been a public structure and, therefore, an anomalous faunal assemblage would be expected since routine food preparation and other daily activities would not be carried on here. This appears to be the case. No faunal material was recovered from the structure fill, although extensive flotation samples were taken. One internal hearth (Feature 49) yielded six unidentifiable fragments, both burned and unburned. The other five internal features were pits with few remains. Feature 46 contained a snapping turtle vertebra and 66 unidentifiable fragments. Feature 52 yielded a bird diaphysis fragment and two unidentifiable fragments. Feature 53 contained an unidentified mammal tooth fragment and a rodent incisor fragment. Features 48 and 50 contained only unidentifiable fragments (Table 48).

Feature 289, a small structure with no internal features, yielded five snapping turtle (*Chelydra serpentina*) elements and two indeterminate fish fragments.

Feature 150, an external pit with good preservation, contained an abundance of faunal remains, particularly fish and bird. Four hundred four fish elements were recovered; 83 of these were identifiable to a species or family level (Table 47). Bird remains were also recovered in quantity, with a total of 365 elements or fragments identified. As with the Stirling phase, waterfowl and semiaquatic birds, such as blue-winged or green-winged teal, mallard (*Anas platyrhynchos*), pintail (*A. acuta*), goose (Anserinae), and crane were identified. Forty-one indeterminate duck elements were also recovered. Nonaquatic bird bones included 11 passerine-sized elements and a bobwhite (*Colinus virginianus*) carpometacarpus. Mammal remains were only a small part of the faunal inventory. Seventy-five mammal elements or fragments were recovered, of which only two white-tailed deer elements, consisting of a mandible, and an auditory bulla, as well as an eastern gray squirrel (*Sciurus carolinensis*) mandible were identified to species. Eleven snapping turtle elements, possibly all from a single turtle, were also identified. Miscellaneous frog and toad (Salientia) elements and one snake vertebra were also recovered.

Sand Prairie Phase

The Sand Prairie phase was represented by three structures (Features 2, 82, and 91), their associated internal pits, and two nonassociated external features (Features 24 and 87). This phase differed from the earlier Stirling and Moorehead phases by having more faunal materials in the structures and their internal pits.

Structure Feature 2 had 18 internal features. Nine were designated as postmolds, one as a postpit, and eight as pits. All but two postmolds and one pit contained some faunal material.

The faunal assemblage from the structure included catfish family and bowfin elements and one duck tarsometatarsus. Mammalian remains were slightly more varied, including six white-tailed deer elements, a dog/coyote molar, and a muskrat tibia and upper incisor. Additionally, 54 fragments representing medium-to-large unidentifiable mammals were recovered.

Faunal materials from the internal features were distributed among 15 of the 18 postmolds and pits. Most contained scant unidentifiable fragments from several faunal classes. The material recovered is presented in Table 50 based on presence/absence of each major faunal class by feature. Table 47 lists the species identified.

Feature 82, a structure with four internal pits and one internal hearth, contained one of two concentrations of deer remains found in Mississippian features. One of its internal pits (Feature 142) contained the other concentration. Feature 82 yielded 12 elements, and 19 elements were recovered from Feature 142. Taken as a single unit, an MNI of three was determined. All body parts were represented, indicating that deer were processed at the site. Also recovered from

Table 50. Faunal Materials in Featurs Internal to Structure Feature 2

Feature	Mammal	Bird	Fish	Turtle	Amphibian	Unidentifiable
88	X	X	X	X	-	X
110	X	X	X	-	X	X
111	X	X	X	-	-	X
112	X	-	X	-	-	X
185	X	-	X	-	-	X
186	X	-	-	-	-	X
187	X	X	X	-	-	X
209	X	-	X	-	-	-
210	X	-	-	-	-	X
211	X	-	X	-	-	X
212	X	X	X	-	-	X
244	-	-	-	-	-	-
261	-	-	X	-	-	X
263	-	-	-	-	-	X
264	-	-	X	-	-	X

Key
X = presence
- = absence

Feature 82 were two fish vertebrae and two bird fragments. Feature 142 yielded exclusively white-tailed deer remains, except for a dog/coyote (Canis sp.) tibia.

Other internal features included Features 134 and 141, which contained only unidentifiable fragments, and Feature 90, an internal hearth, which yielded a dog/coyote molar and maxilla fragment, a bird carpometacarpus, and several other unidentifiable bone fragments. Feature 84, the deepest internal feature, contained a wide variety of fauna. Fish elements included bowfin, gar (Lepisosteus sp.), sucker, and several species of the catfish/bullhead family. Muskrat comprised the most numerous mammalian elements, with an MNI of three represented by 29 elements and several fragmentary teeth. A raccoon (Procyon lotor) was also identified by an unburned ulna. Bird remains included crane, blue-winged or green-winged teal, and indeterminate duck elements.

Feature 91, a burned structure, unlike the other two Sand Prairie phase structures, had little faunal material. When it burned, the structure roof collapsed, filling the basin and preserving living and work areas intact. Although there was much in situ debris, faunal remains, except for freshwater mussel, were scant. The recovered material included 95 turtle shell fragments and 6 frog or toad elements. Fish remains were slightly more numerous, with bowfin and sucker (Catostomidae) elements identified. Two white-tailed deer molar fragments were also recovered.

Feature 24, an external pit, had a diverse faunal assemblage. Fish species identified were bowfin, flathead catfish (Pylodictis olivaris), smallmouth or black buffalo, and sunfish (Lepomis sp.). Mammal remains included a white-tailed deer scapula and metatarsal, a Cervidae sesamoid, a rice rat (Oryzomys palustris) mandible, a plains pocket gopher incisor fragment, and several Rodentia incisor fragments. Muskrat elements numbered 16, with an MNI of three. The bird remains included five duck elements and many unidentifiable bird fragments.

Feature 87, another external pit, superimposed Feature 2. The faunal material in Feature 87 was diverse, including fish species such as bowfin, gar, yellow bullhead (Ictalurus natalis), brown bullhead (Ictalurus nebulosus), and smallmouth or black buffalo (Ictiobus bubalus or I. niger). Mammalian remains included a white-tailed deer metatarsal, a chipmunk (Tamias striatus) pelvis and several Rodentia elements. Muskrat was the most frequently occurring mammal, with 15 elements recovered, representing an MNI of two. Three indeterminate duck and two crane elements constituted the identifiable bird.

Discussion

Species Composition

A total of 24518 fragments were recovered from the Mississippian component features. Of this total, 6300 were identifiable to at least the class level (Table 49). Due to poor preservation and the fragmentary nature of most of the bone, only a small percentage could be identified to a generic or species level.

Consistently, fish was the major class represented by the number of recovered elements. Fish bones were widely dispersed among features and within features, indicating their importance to the diet. Fish remains were abundant, even though only small amounts of fill per feature were floated. The species identified were consistent between phases, indicating utilization of similar aquatic habitats. The majority of the species identified can be found in backwaters, sloughs, and lakes, all of which are found near the site. Based on the MNI, the catish/bullhead family and bowfin appeared to be the most utilized fish, with sunfish and suckers having a lesser role. The size of fish was not individually determined, but on the whole, fish were estimated to have weighed less than 250 g apiece. No fishing equipment was recovered, so procurement methods are unknown.

The American Bottom is located along one of the major migration flyways, so the abundance of migratory waterfowl and semiaquatic birds at the site is not surprising. Ducks, geese, cranes, grebes, and swans were all represented. Ducks, in particular, were recovered in large amounts, accounting for 76.44% of all bird remains. Nonaquatic birds represented a very small percentage (9.42%) of the avian elements. Only 1 bobwhite and 17 passerine elements were identified. As stated before, passerines may have been used for nonfood purposes.

Mammals appeared to play a lesser role in this prehistoric diet than at other sites in the American Bottom. Parmalee (1975:154) has noted that: "If any one species could be designated as <u>the</u> most valued animal used by prehistoric Indian peoples of Illinois, it would be the white-tailed deer" (original emphasis). This may not hold true for sites such as Julien that were located in the floodplain with easy access to aquatic and semiaquatic environments. Fish and waterfowl were very important as indicated by Table 47. These groups tend to be underestimated at sites where flotation is not used as a recovery method (Table 46). The large number of mammalian fragments in Table 49 may be due to their easier identification and better chance for preservation because of their density and size and does not necessarily represent large numbers of individuals.

The only differences in exploitation patterns occurred in the mammalian class. Muskrat, a small, aquatic mammal weighing 1 kg to 2 kg and historically valued for its pelt (Burt and Grossenheider 1976:194), consitituted most of the identifiable mammalian remains. Muskrat, so prevalent in the Stirling and Sand Prairie phases, was absent in the Moorehead phase. Deer, very scant in the Stirling and Moorehead phases (only 1 feature each), was more prevalent in the Sand Prairie phase. Ten features of the Sand Prairie phase contained deer remains. There were two concentrations, one in structure Feature 82 and the other in one of its internal pits (Feature 142). These two concentrations accounted for 31 of the 46 elements recovered from this phase. The remaining elements were dispersed throughout the other eight analyzed features. Even though a single deer would have provided large amounts of meat, the scant remains in the Stirling and Moorehead phases would indicate that it may not have been a primary food resource. Day-to-day subsistence may have depended more on fish and waterfowl resources (L. Kelly 1979:20). The large amount of deer from the Sand Prairie phase features appears to indicate an intense utilization of this species and a shift in exploitation patterns. These apparent shifts may be the result of sampling and if all features from every phase were included in the analysis these shifts might disappear.

Turtle, amphibian, and snake were all represented by only scant remains. It is difficult to determine if these fauna were used as food or, in the case of the amphibian and turtle, were incidental catches during fishing. Their small numbers suggest that they were not considered a major food resource.

Seasons of occupation are difficult to determine given this diversity of fauna. The migratory birds would have been in this area during spring and fall, and possibly would have wintered in the area during mild years. Fauna exploited during the winter, such as deer and wild turkey, were either scarce or absent in the faunal inventories of the Stirling and Moorehead phases; however, this does not provide any conclusive evidence for a nonwinter habitation of the Julien site. The Sand Prairie phase features yielded a large amount of deer remains. The wide variety of fauna indicates more than single season occupation and, possibly, indicates a year-round habitation.

The spatial arrangements and depths of internal features were compared to determine if there were any patterns between these characteristics and the amounts of faunal remains recovered. No patterns could be distinguished. Internal features with abundant faunal remains were not restricted to any particular areas of structure floors. Shallow and deep features both contained faunal materials. There was a slight tendency for faunal remains to be clustered in only one or two features per structure, but no conclusions can be drawn since some structures had many internal features while others had none. The limestone content of features was also checked to see if differential preservation might have contributed to the distribution of faunal remains. Limestone has some positive effect on preservation; however, there seemed to be no correspondence between the amount of limestone in a feature and the amount of recovered faunal material.

Worked Bone and Shell

Several pieces of worked bone and shell were recovered from the Mississippian component of the Julien site. Among these were two modified deer mandibles. A mandible from Feature 89 (Stirling phase) was partial and in poor condition, while a mandible from Feature 187 (Sand Prairie phase) was almost complete (Figure 85). Both had very worn premolars and a smoothed finish on their buccal and lingual medial areas. The second and third molars of the Feature 187 mandible were complete and did not appear to have been utilized or modified. Most of the anterior end was present in both specimens, and a few striations appeared on the buccal surface of the Feature 187 mandible. These last two characteristics, along with the wear patterns, do not correspond to Brown's (1964) definition of deer mandible sickles. Although obviously modified, the use to which these mandibles were put was not determined.

A possible awl, fashioned from an unidentifiable mammal long bone, was recovered from the Sand Prairie phase Feature 87. The bone was worked to dull points on both ends and all the cut edges had been smoothed.

The Moorehead phase Feature 150 contained a small long bone fragment, ca. 1.8 cm in length and burned to a gray finish. It had abundant cut marks on its highly polished surface. One end had a smoothed edge while the other had been freshly broken. The function of this piece is unknown.

The distal epiphysis of a swan humerus was recovered from the Sand Prairie phase Feature 187 (Figure 85). It appeared to have been what Parmalee (1975:152) calls "ringed and snapped". A cut had been made completely around the bone and then the end had been snapped off.

Stirling phase Feature 89 contained a burned partial turtle plastron. No species identification could be made. The edges had been worked smooth. Cut marks were on both sides of the shell at approximately the same location, perhaps indicating an attempt to cut off the end. The plastron was found in two pieces, having broken along a suture between plastron fragments. The pieces fit together but displayed differential burning, indicating that the burning occurred after the plastron was broken. The initial working of the edges had been done before breakage. Perhaps the breaking resulted in a discontinuation of further modification of the shell.

Definite whelk shell columellae were recovered from Features 23, 87, 89, 109, and a possible one from Feature 293. The Feature 89 whelk shell had been fashioned into a pendant. The others were too fragmentary to determine if they had been worked.

Summary

The Julien site Late Woodland and Mississippian faunal assemblages were comprised almost exclusively of fauna found within the marshy lowland environment surrounding the site. A few species, such as bobwhite, raccoon, and eastern gray squirrel, all edge environment

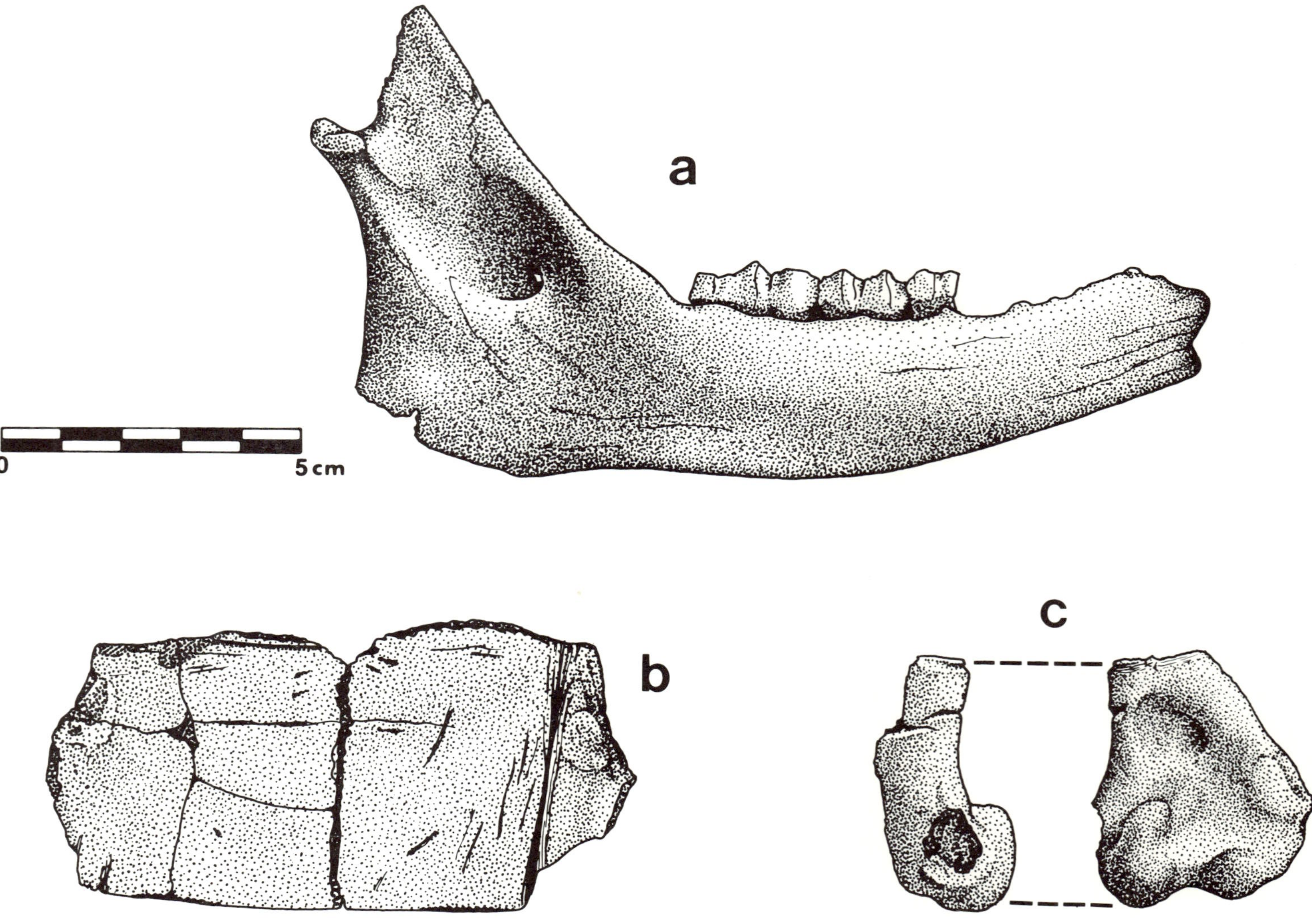

Figure 85. Cut and Worked Bone and Turtle Shell: a, modified deer mandible; b, modified turtle shell; c, "ringed and snapped" swan humerus

fauna, were represented by only a few elements scattered among the features. They may have been serendipitous catches rather than representing intentional efforts to exploit fauna not found within the immediate vicinity. The upland forested areas, several kilometers from the site, appeared not to have been utilized for food resources.

Late Woodland faunal remains were scant, and little information on exploitation patterns could be ascertained. The Mississippian faunal inventory was much more varied and extensive. The utilization of local fauna appeared to continue throughout the three Mississippian phases analyzed with no major changes in exploitation patterns.

PLANT REMAINS FROM THE JULIEN SITE

by

Sissel Johannessen

The presence of Late Woodland and several well-defined Mississippian cultural components makes the analysis of plant remains from the Julien site especially interesting. The full range of plant taxa used prehistorically is not represented in the carbonized remains recovered through flotation; only a small and biased sample is created by differential conditions of deposition, preservation, and recovery. In examining the plant remains from a single component, these factors make it difficult to assess the relative importance of the various classes of plant remains present. However, as Asch and Asch (1978:329) have argued, "...variation in the percentages of different plants between archaeological assemblages can indicate changes in utilization". Since the Julien site represents several temporally distinct occupations of the same ridge, it is possible to look for relative differences in the plant record which could indicate trends in plant use through time.

Methods

Flotation samples of known volume (usually 10 l) were taken from each natural stratum of each feature at the Julien site. Charcoal samples were collected when excavators observed concentrations of charcoal. Flotation samples were water-floated according to the IDOT system (Wagner 1976).

At that point, features and individual samples were selected for analysis of their botanical contents. Features were selected from each component and from each feature category within that component in order to obtain a sample representative of the site as a whole. Only features with firm component associations were selected. From each natural stratum of the selected features, 10 l samples were chosen for analysis.

A total of 220 samples, representing 2217 l of feature fill from 62 features at the Julien site, were selected for analysis. One hundred fifty-five charcoal samples were also identified.

Selected flotation samples were sieved through a 2 mm screen, and the carbonized botanical material was sorted by hand under low magnification (10X-30X). All material >2 mm in size was sorted into categories (e.g., wood and nuts), and the fragments in each category were counted and weighed. The <2 mm fraction was scanned carefully, and all seeds and remains of cultivated plants were removed. The sample weights and the counts of nutshell and wood fragments were based on only the >2 mm material. An attempt was made to identify all seeds, nut fragments, and the first 20 randomly selected wood fragments from each sample. Identifications were made with the aid of standard texts

(Martin and Barkley 1961; Montgomery 1977; Panshin and de Zeeuw 1970) and ultimately by a one-to-one comparison with a modern reference collection. Identifications were made to the genus level where possible. Specific identifications were made only when a genus is represented by only one species in the area (e.g., *Diospyros virginiana*), or all other species of the genus could be ruled out on the basis of comparative morphology (e.g., *Polygonum erectum*). Thanks are extended to Nancy and David Asch of the Northwestern University Archaeobotanical Laboratory for their identification of *Polygonum erectum* and *Phalaris caroliniana*.

Results

As noted above, 62 of the Julien site features were selected for analysis of their botanical contents. Thirteen of these features were associated with the Late Woodland component, and the remaining 49 with the Mississippian component (17 with the Stirling phase, 17 with the Moorehead phase, and 15 with the Sand Prairie phase). These selected features represent 100% of the Late Woodland component and 17% of the Mississippian component. The plant remains are discussed in three sections: 1) material from the Late Woodland features, 2) material from the Mississippian features as a whole, and 3) a comparison of complexes of features representing each of the Stirling, Moorehead, and Sand Prairie phases.

Late Woodland

One cluster of 13 pit features at the Julien site was assigned a Late Woodland cultural affiliation. Samples were selected from all 13 features for analysis, entailing the processing of 455 l of feature fill. The results are presented in Table 51.

Carbonized botanical material in the samples was neither abundant nor diverse. The average 10 l sample contained 0.3 g of material, consisting of 14 wood charcoal fragments, 9 fragments of nutshell, and 3 seeds. The botanical material from all features was very similar in composition.

Most (81.1%) of the identifiable wood charcoal fragments were oak, with red oaks especially well represented. Represented by low counts were hickory (5.1% of identifiable wood fragments), mulberry (4.9%), honey locust or Kentucky coffee-tree (3.1%), walnut (2.2%), sycamore (1.1%), pecan hickory (1.1%), ash (0.6%), dogwood (0.6%), and maple (0.3%).

Nutshell was almost completely thick-shelled hickory, although a few fragments of hazelnut and acorn were recovered.

Only 138 seeds were recovered from the 455 l of analyzed fill. Of

Table 51. Flotation-recovered Plant Remains from the Late Woodland Component

	Features												
	92	93	94	95	96	97	98	99	100	101	102	103	104
Total wt. charcoal (g)	0.2	2.4	1.0	0.1	0.3	3.1	0.3	0.7	0.2	1.3	2.7	1.2	1.2
Total vol. flot. (l)	20	42	40	20	30	40	20	60	20	40	53	50	20
NUT (total fragments)	1	77	5	2	1	36	6	8	12	68	132	31	22
Carya sp. (hickory)	-	61	4	2	1	20	6	5	9	43	85	22	18
Corylus americana (hazel)	-	1	-	-	-	-	-	-	-	3	-	-	-
Juglandaceae (walnut or hickory)	-	12	1	-	-	15	-	3	3	22	47	8	4
Quercus sp. (acorn)	1	3	-	-	-	1	-	-	-	-	-	1	-
WOOD (total fragments)	20	82	47	10	24	179	3	18	3	37	89	50	40
Acer sp. (maple)	-	-	-	-	-	-	-	-	-	-	1?	-	-
Carya sp. (hickory)	-	6	10	-	-	-	-	-	-	-	1	-	1
C. illinoensis/cordiformis (pecan hickory)	-	-	4	-	-	-	-	-	-	-	-	-	-
Cornus sp. (dogwood)	-	-	-	-	-	-	-	-	-	-	-	2?	-
Fraxinus sp. (ash)	1?	-	-	-	-	-	-	1	-	-	-	-	-
Gymnocladus/Gleditsia (coffee-tree/honey locust)	2	4?	-	-	-	-	-	-	-	2	2	1	-
Juglans sp. (walnut)	-	-	-	-	-	-	-	4	1	-	1	2	-
Morus sp. (mulberry)	-	-	13	-	-	4	-	-	-	-	-	-	-
Platanus occidentalis (sycamore)	-	-	2	-	-	1	-	-	-	-	-	1	-
Quercus sp. (oak)	1	20	1	3	7	60	-	10	-	2	8	21	4
Quercus, red group (red oaks)	1	14	3	2	5	60	2	4	1	10	24	2	12
Quercus, white group (white oaks)	-	-	-	-	1	9	-	-	-	-	-	-	1
Diffuse-porous	-	2	-	-	-	-	-	-	-	-	1	-	3
Ring-porous	6	19	7	1	4	15	1	18	1	11	26	12	12
Unidentifiable	6	16	3	4	7	29	-	10	-	12	24	8	6
Bark	3	-	4	-	-	-	-	-	-	-	1	-	1
SEEDS (total)	7	20	-	-	2	8	6	26	6	11	34	16	1
Chenopodium sp. (goosefoot)	-	-	-	-	-	-	-	2	-	-	1	-	-
Iva sp. (marsh elder)	-	-	-	-	-	-	-	1?	-	-	-	-	-
Phalaris caroliniana (maygrass)	3	10	-	-	1	2	3	8	2	8	10	11	-
Polygonum erectum (erect knotweed)	-	-	-	-	-	-	-	-	-	1	3	1	-
P. cf. *pensylvanicum* (pinkweed)	-	1	-	-	-	-	-	-	-	-	-	-	-
Solanum cf. *americanum* (black nightshade)	-	-	-	-	-	-	1?	-	-	-	-	-	-
Unknowns	-	-	-	-	1	-	-	4	1	-	2	-	-
Unidentifiable	4	9	-	-	-	6	3	11	3	2	18	4	1

the 79 identifiable seeds, 60 (76%) were maygrass (*Phalaris caroliniana*). The remaining 19 seeds included erect knotweed (*Polygonum erectum*), goosefoot (*Chenopodium* sp.), one possible marsh elder achene (*Iva* sp.), and one black nightshade seed (*Solanum* cf. *americanum*).

All seeds identified from the Late Woodland features are common constituents of archaeological seed spectra from archaeological deposits dating from Middle Woodland through Mississippian times.

The seed type most often recovered from the Late Woodland features at the Julien site, maygrass, is one of a triad of species (*Phalaris caroliniana*, *Chenopodium bushianum*, and *Polygonum erectum*) that consistently makes up the majority of seeds recovered from assemblages dating from Middle Woodland times onwards (Asch et al. 1979:83). Cowan (1978) has established that maygrass was used throughout the northeast, and its archaeological occurrence north of its present natural range may indicate that it was cultivated.

Fifty-eight *Phalaris* caryopses from the Late Woodland samples at the Julien site were measured and compared to measurements from an earlier assemblage (Truck #7 site, Middle Woodland period) and from a later assemblage (Julien site, Mississippian period Sand Prairie phase) [Figure 86 and Table 52]. The Late Woodland and Mississippian measurements did not seem to vary significantly, but the mean lengths of the Middle Woodland *Phalaris* were 0.4 mm less than those associated with later assemblages.

These indications of an increase in the size of *Phalaris* caryopses through time are only very tentative, and must be tested further. However, a size increase would be further evidence for prehistoric *Phalaris* cultivation.

In general, the undifferentiated nature of the botanical contents of the Late Woodland features at the Julien site, both qualitatively and quantitatively, suggests that the plant remains were associated with general site refuse rather than with the original functions of the individual features.

Mississippian

From the Mississippian component at the Julien site (including Stirling, Moorehead, and Sand Prairie phases), 49 features were selected for analysis. From the 1762 l of feature fill examined, 606.9 g of carbonized botanical material was recovered, not including the weight of small seeds (Table 53).

Wood

Wood charcoal recovered through flotation was distributed fairly

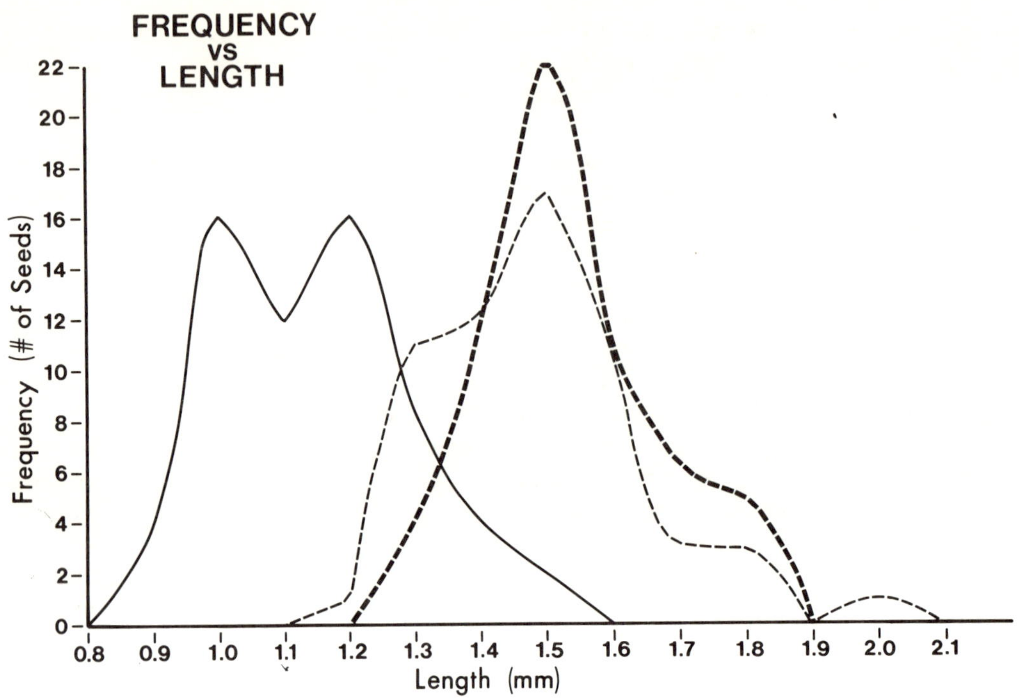

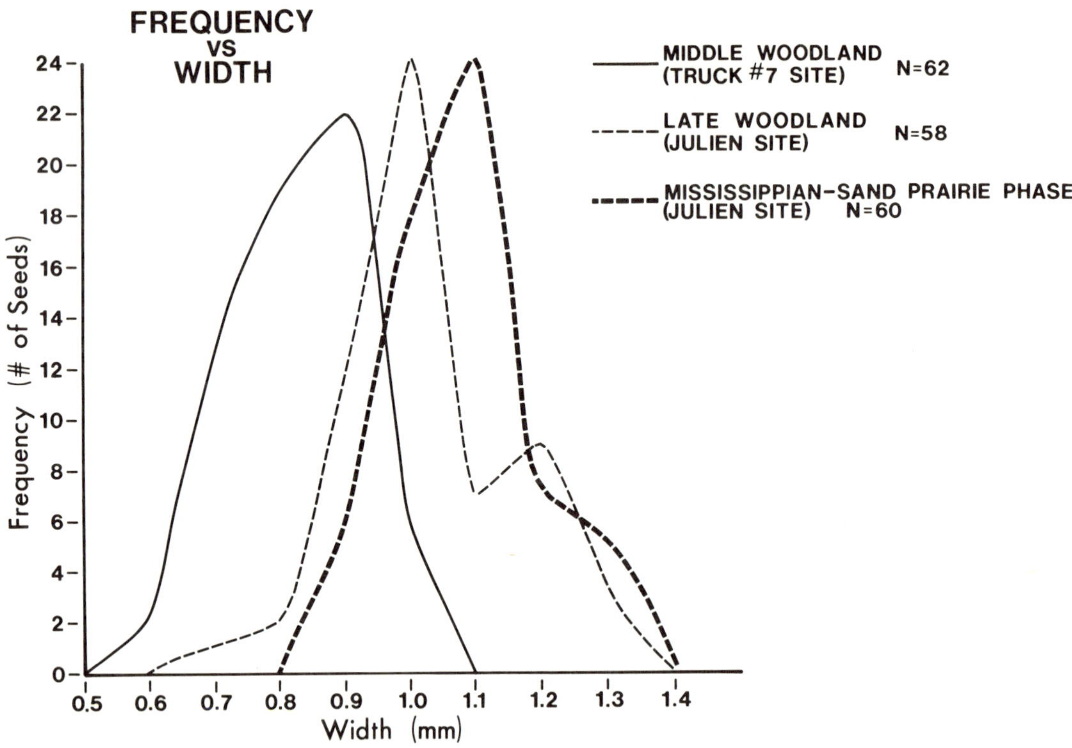

Figure 86. Comparison of Phalaris caroliniana Measurements from Middle Woodland, Late Woodland, and Mississippian Assemblages

Table 52. Phalaris caroliniana (Maygrass) Size from Assemblages in the American Bottom

Assemblage	Number of Seeds	Mean Length x Width (mm)	Standard Deviation	Range Length x Width (mm)
Middle Woodland (Truck #7)	62	1.1 x 0.8	0.15 x 0.10	0.9-1.5 x 0.6-1.0
Late Woodland (Julien)	58	1.5 x 1.0	0.16 x 0.13	1.2-2.0 x 0.7-1.3
Mississippian, Sand Prairie Phase (Julien)	60	1.5 x 1.1	0.13 x 0.11	1.3-1.8 x 0.9-1.3

Table 53. Flotation-recovered Plant Remains

	Features																									
	2	3	24	31	36	40	41	46	47	48	49	50	52	53	54	56	58	82	84	85	88	89	90	91	110	111
Total wt. charcoal (g)	79.0	4.2	3.9	1.2	0.1	0.2	0.1	4.2	<0.1	1.7	2.1	1.8	1.2	2.2	0.6	0.2	<0.1	3.9	2.8	1.4	11.9	2.0	1.9	12.0	137.8	2.1
Total vol. flot. (l)	70	110	85	46	34	8	13	70	2	20	15	63	40	26	28	20	14	30	82	15	111	73	20	40	70	30
NUT (total fragments)	893	8	62	30	1	8	3	115	2	65	133	47	37	116	27	3	1	15	74	1	596	13	15	4	4500	33
Carya sp. (hickory)	341	7	44	19	-	1	1	61	1	43	88	24	19	68	16	2	1	6	33	1	152	7	7	2	3134	17
C. illinoensis (pecan hickory)	1	1	-	-	-	3	-	42	-	3	19	-	-	-	-	-	-	1	-	-	-	-	4	-	118	2
Juglandaceae (walnut family)	534	-	17	11	-	3	1	12	1	18	2	20	18	47	11	1	-	5	40	-	442	6	3	2	963	14
Nut-meat	17	-	-	-	-	-	-	-	-	1	11	-	-	-	-	-	-	-	-	-	2	-	-	-	278	-
Nut-husk	-	-	-	-	-	-	-	-	-	-	-	-	-	-	-	-	-	-	-	-	-	-	-	-	-	-
Juglans nigra (black walnut)	-	-	1	-	-	-	-	-	-	-	-	1	-	1	-	-	-	-	1	-	-	-	-	-	1	-
Quercus sp. (acorn)	-	-	-	-	1	1	1	-	-	-	1	1	-	-	-	-	-	-	-	-	-	-	1	-	-	-
Unidentifiable	-	-	-	-	-	-	-	-	-	-	12	1	-	-	-	-	-	3	-	-	-	-	-	-	6	-
WOOD (total fragments)	2174	253	140	12	-	2	2	14	-	4	3	46	31	3	3	3	-	276	148	159	319	56	128	912	2002	56
Acer sp. (maple)	-	-	2	-	-	-	-	2	-	-	-	4	-	-	-	-	-	-	32	-	-	-	-	-	-	-
Betula sp. (birch)	-	-	2	-	-	-	-	-	-	-	-	8	-	-	-	-	-	-	-	-	9	-	-	-	-	-
Carya sp. (hickory)	346	-	4	-	-	-	-	-	-	-	-	-	-	-	-	-	-	231	33	-	39	2	7	-	194	-
C. illinoensis (pecan hickory)	706	-	-	-	-	-	-	-	-	-	-	-	-	-	-	-	-	-	-	-	5	-	-	-	-	-
Cornus sp. (dogwood)	-	-	1	-	-	-	-	-	-	-	-	-	-	-	-	-	-	-	-	-	-	-	-	-	-	-
Diospyros virginiana (persimmon)	-	-	9	-	-	-	-	-	-	-	-	2	1	-	-	-	-	-	-	-	-	-	-	-	89	-
Fraxinus sp. (ash)	-	1	-	1	-	-	-	-	-	-	-	-	-	-	-	-	-	-	-	-	5	-	-	40	-	-
Gleditsia sp. (locust)	-	-	-	-	-	-	-	-	-	-	-	-	-	-	-	-	-	-	-	-	-	-	-	-	-	-
Gymnocladus dioica (Kentucky coffee-tree)	-	-	-	-	-	-	-	-	-	-	-	-	-	-	-	-	-	-	-	-	-	-	-	-	-	-
Gleditsia/Gymnocladus spp. (locust/coffee-tree)	-	-	-	-	-	-	-	-	-	-	-	2	-	-	-	-	-	-	-	-	-	-	-	-	-	-
Juniperus virginiana (red cedar)	-	92	-	-	-	-	-	-	-	-	-	-	-	-	-	-	-	-	-	-	-	-	-	42	-	-
Morus rubra (mulberry)	-	-	-	-	-	-	-	-	-	-	-	-	-	-	-	-	-	-	-	-	-	-	-	100	-	-
Ostrya virginiana (hop-bornbeam, ironwood)	-	-	-	-	-	-	-	-	-	-	-	-	-	-	-	-	-	-	-	-	-	-	-	-	-	-
Platanus sp. (sycamore)	-	-	1	-	-	-	-	-	-	-	-	-	2	-	-	-	-	-	-	-	-	-	-	-	-	-
Prunus sp. (cherry)	27	-	-	-	-	-	-	-	-	-	-	-	-	-	-	-	-	-	-	-	4	-	-	-	-	-
Quercus sp. (oak)	52	-	7	-	-	-	-	-	-	-	-	2	-	-	-	-	-	-	9	-	5	2	-	-	3	-
Quercus, red group (red oak)	1034	88	17	1	-	-	-	-	-	-	-	2	-	1	-	-	-	14	7	-	16	7	6	50	1625	38
Quercus, white group (white oak)	-	-	-	-	-	-	-	-	-	-	-	-	-	-	-	-	-	-	-	-	1	-	-	-	6	-
Salicaceae (cottonwood/willow)	-	56	-	-	-	-	-	-	-	-	-	-	11	-	-	-	-	-	-	158	-	1	17	660	-	-
Ulmaceae (elm family)	-	-	1	-	-	-	-	2	-	-	-	-	-	-	-	-	-	27	8	-	-	-	92	-	-	-
Ulmus sp. (elm)	-	-	-	-	-	-	-	-	-	-	-	-	-	-	-	-	-	-	-	-	-	-	-	20	-	-
Unknown Type Q (diffuse-porous)	-	-	-	-	-	-	-	-	-	-	-	-	-	-	-	-	-	-	7	-	1	-	-	-	-	-
Diffuse-porous	1	-	4	1	-	-	1	3	-	3	3	-	15	1	1	2	-	-	1	1	3	6	-	-	8	5
Ring-porous	5	12	45	5	-	2	-	3	-	1	-	5	-	-	-	-	-	4	25	-	28	8	5	-	14	4
Unidentifiable	3	2	42	4	-	-	1	4	-	-	-	17	2	1	2	1	-	-	24	-	28	18	1	-	56	-
Unknown	-	-	-	-	-	-	-	-	-	-	-	4	-	-	-	-	-	-	-	-	-	-	-	-	-	-
Bark	-	2	5	-	-	-	-	-	-	-	-	-	-	-	-	-	-	-	2	-	175	12	-	-	7	9
Monocot stem	10	29	1	-	-	-	-	1	-	-	-	-	-	-	-	-	-	-	4	30	15	2	13	89	51	-

Table 53. Continued

	Features																						
	112	113	132	133	139	140	147	155	186	187	224	229	242	252	263	267	270	272	280	282	283	289	291
Total wt. charcoal (g)	2.6	0.1	0.5	0.0	0.5	152.0	0.0	150.0	0.5	1.0	1.3	16.2	0.0	0.1	0.3	0.1	0.1	1.9	0.4	0.2	<0.1	0.2	0.4
Total vol. flot. (l)	30	20	10	4	30	40	10	50	20	40	60	60	20	20	5	20	30	30	50	8	10	20	40
NUT (total fragments)	17	1	-	-	1	-	-	4894	14	23	5	65	-	1	1	-	-	1	1	4	-	8	6
Carya sp. (hickory)	5	-	-	-	-	-	-	2526	7	12	4	33	-	-	1	-	-	1	-	4	-	3	4
C. illinoensis (pecan hickory)	-	-	-	-	-	-	-	348	-	-	-	7	-	-	-	-	-	-	-	-	-	-	-
Juglandaceae (walnut family)	12	1	-	-	1	-	-	1866	7	11	1	25	-	-	-	-	-	-	1	-	-	5	2
Nut-meat	-	-	-	-	-	-	-	94	-	-	-	-	-	-	-	-	-	-	-	-	-	-	-
Nut-husk	-	-	-	-	-	-	-	27	-	-	-	-	-	-	-	-	-	-	-	-	-	-	-
Juglans nigra (black walnut)	-	-	-	-	-	-	-	-	-	-	-	-	-	-	-	-	-	-	-	-	-	-	-
Quercus sp. (acorn)	-	-	-	-	-	-	-	30	-	-	-	-	-	-	-	-	-	-	-	-	-	-	-
Unidentifiable	-	-	-	-	-	-	-	3	-	-	-	-	-	1	-	-	-	-	-	-	-	-	-
WOOD (total fragments)	176	-	28	-	2	190	-	315	17	35	46	621	-	1	16	1	6	35	27	8	3	-	20
Acer sp. (maple)	2	-	-	-	-	-	-	-	-	-	-	7	-	-	-	-	-	-	-	-	-	-	-
Betula sp. (birch)	-	-	-	-	-	-	-	-	-	-	-	-	-	-	-	-	-	-	-	-	-	-	-
Carya sp. (hickory)	-	-	-	-	-	39	-	-	4	2	6	25	-	-	3	-	-	2	1	-	-	-	-
C. illinoensis (pecan hickory)	-	-	-	-	-	-	-	-	-	-	-	5	-	-	-	-	-	-	-	-	-	-	-
Cornus sp. (dogwood)	-	-	-	-	-	-	-	-	-	-	-	-	-	-	-	-	-	-	-	-	-	-	-
Diospyros virginiana (persimmon)	-	-	-	-	-	-	-	-	-	-	-	-	-	-	-	-	-	-	-	-	-	-	-
Fraxinus sp. (ash)	-	-	-	-	-	-	-	-	-	-	-	-	-	-	-	-	-	-	-	-	-	-	-
Gleditsia sp. (locust)	-	-	-	-	-	-	-	35	-	-	-	180	-	-	-	-	-	-	-	-	-	-	-
Gymnocladus dioica (Kentucky coffee-tree)	-	-	-	-	-	-	-	-	-	2	-	-	-	-	-	-	-	-	-	-	-	-	-
Gleditsia/Gymnocladus spp. (locust/coffee-tree)	-	-	-	-	-	-	-	-	-	-	-	-	-	-	-	-	-	-	-	-	-	-	-
Juniperus virginiana (red cedar)	-	-	-	-	-	-	-	-	-	-	-	-	-	-	-	-	-	-	-	-	1	-	-
Morus rubra (mulberry)	-	-	-	-	-	-	-	-	-	-	-	-	-	-	-	-	-	-	-	-	-	-	-
Ostrya virginiana (hop-hornbeam, ironwood)	1	-	-	-	-	-	-	-	-	-	-	-	-	-	-	-	-	-	-	3	-	-	-
Platanus sp. (sycamore)	2	-	-	-	-	-	-	-	-	2	-	-	-	-	-	-	-	-	-	-	-	-	-
Prunus sp. (cherry)	-	-	-	-	-	-	-	38	-	-	-	-	-	-	-	-	1	-	-	-	-	-	-
Quercus sp. (oak)	2	-	-	-	2	-	-	-	3	-	-	17	-	-	-	-	1	2	2	-	-	-	5
Quercus, red group (red oak)	159	-	-	-	-	64	-	-	1	-	15	287	-	-	-	-	-	2	3	1	-	-	2
Quercus, white group (white oak)	8	-	-	-	-	-	-	-	-	-	7	9	-	-	-	-	-	-	-	-		-	-
Salicaceae (cottonwood/willow)	-	-	25	-	-	-	-	4	-	1	-	4	-	-	-	-	-	-	-	-	-	-	-
Ulmaceae (elm family)	-	-	-	-	-	-	-	-	-	-	-	4	-	-	-	-	-	-	-	-	-	-	-
Ulmus sp. (elm)	-	-	-	-	-	-	-	-	-	-	-	-	-	-	-	-	-	-	-	-	-	-	-
Unknown Type Q (diffuse-porous)	-	-	-	-	-	-	-	123	1	1	-	40	-	-	-	1	-	2	1	-	-	-	3
Diffuse-porous	-	-	2	-	-	-	-	20	2	2	-	3	-	-	-	-	-	1	1	-	-	-	-
Ring-porous	-	-	-	-	-	13	-	32	4	10	13	40	-	-	13	-	3	7	8	3	-	-	10
Unidentifiable	2	-	1	-	-	2	-	63	2	6	5	-	-	1	-	-	1	17	11	1	2	-	-
Unknown	-	-	-	-	-	72	-	-	-	-	-	-	-	-	-	-	-	-	-	-	-	-	-
Bark	-	-	-	-	-	-	-	-	-	9	-	-	-	-	-	-	-	2	-	-	-	-	-
Monocot stem	15	-	-	-	-	-	-	99	-	1	1	3	-	-	-	-	-	-	-	-	-	-	-

Table 53. Continued

	Features																								
	2	3	24	31	36	40	41	46	47	48	49	50	52	53	54	56	58	82	84	85	88	89	90	91	110
SEED Totals	215	115	32	9	18	10	2	11	1	-	24	35	11	5	10	-	-	7	9	3	544	24	7	51	542
Amaranthus sp. (amaranth)	3	-	-	-	-	-	-	-	-	-	-	-	-	-	-	-	-	-	-	-	4	-	-	-	-
Brasenia Schreberi (watershield)	-	-	-	-	-	-	-	-	-	-	-	-	-	-	-	-	-	-	-	-	-	-	-	-	2
Chenopodium sp. (goosefoot)	9	16	2	2	6	1	1	1	-	-	-	-	-	-	-	-	-	2	-	-	15	3	1	7	211
Compositae (composite family)	-	-	-	-	-	-	-	-	-	-	-	-	-	-	-	-	-	-	-	-	-	-	-	-	-
Croton sp. (croton)	-	-	-	-	-	-	-	-	-	-	-	-	1	-	-	1	-	-	-	-	-	-	-	-	-
Diospyros virginiana (persimmon, frags.)	-	-	-	-	-	-	-	-	-	-	-	-	-	3	3	-	-	1	-	-	1	-	-	-	-
Euphorbia sp. (spurge)	-	-	-	-	-	-	-	-	-	-	-	-	-	-	-	-	-	-	-	-	1	-	-	-	-
Gramineae (grass family)	3	1	-	-	1	2	-	-	-	-	-	-	-	-	-	-	-	-	-	-	4	1	-	2	13
Gramineae Type 6 L & F (grass)	29	14	-	-	-	-	-	-	-	-	-	-	-	-	-	-	-	-	-	-	38	2	-	1	20
Gramineae Type 20/21 (grass)	-	-	-	-	-	-	-	-	-	-	-	-	-	-	-	-	-	-	-	-	2	-	-	-	-
Helianthus sp. (sunflower)	-	-	-	-	-	1	-	-	-	-	2	-	-	-	-	-	-	-	-	-	12	-	-	-	-
Ipomoea sp. (morning-glory)	2	-	-	-	-	-	-	-	-	-	-	-	-	-	-	-	-	-	-	-	-	-	-	-	4
Ipomoea/Convolvulus spp. (morning-glory/bindweed)	-	-	-	-	-	-	-	-	-	-	-	-	-	-	-	-	-	-	-	-	2	-	-	-	-
Iva annua (marsh elder)	1	-	-	-	-	-	-	-	-	-	9	-	-	-	-	-	-	-	-	-	3	-	-	-	1
Iva/Helianthus spp. (marsh elder/sunflower)	-	-	-	-	-	-	-	-	-	-	-	-	-	-	-	-	-	-	-	-	1	-	-	-	-
Labiatae (mint family)	-	1	-	-	-	-	-	-	-	-	-	-	-	-	-	-	-	-	-	-	-	-	-	-	1
Leguminosae (small legumes)	-	1	-	-	-	-	-	-	-	-	-	-	-	-	-	-	-	-	-	-	4	-	-	1	16
cf. *Lespedeza* sp. (bush clover)	3	-	-	-	-	-	-	-	-	-	-	-	-	-	-	-	-	-	-	-	-	-	-	-	-
Nelumbo lutea (American lotus, frags.)	3	-	-	-	-	-	-	-	-	-	-	1	-	-	-	-	-	-	-	-	-	-	-	-	-
Phalaris caroliniana (maygrass)	14	1	1	-	3	-	-	2	-	-	2	3	2	1	1	-	-	-	2	-	269	9	-	1	124
Phytolacca americana (pokeweed)	-	-	1	-	-	-	-	-	-	-	-	-	-	-	-	-	-	-	-	-	16	-	-	-	6
Polygonum spp. (knotweeds, smartweeds)	1	-	-	1	-	-	-	-	-	-	-	-	-	-	-	-	-	-	-	-	-	-	-	6	2
Polygonum erectum (erect knotweed)	-	-	-	-	-	-	-	2	1	-	2	1	-	-	-	-	-	-	-	-	1	-	-	-	1
cf. *Portulaca* sp. (purselane)	-	-	-	-	-	-	-	-	-	-	-	-	-	-	-	-	-	-	-	-	8	-	-	-	-
Prunus sp. (cherry)	-	-	-	-	-	-	-	-	-	-	-	-	-	-	-	-	-	-	-	-	-	-	-	-	1
Rhus sp. (sumac)	1	-	-	-	-	-	-	-	-	-	-	-	-	-	-	-	-	-	-	-	-	-	-	-	-
Rumex sp. (dock)	-	-	-	-	-	-	-	-	-	-	-	-	1	-	-	-	-	-	-	-	-	-	-	-	-
Sida cf. *spinosa* (prickly mallow)	1	1	-	-	-	-	-	-	-	-	-	-	-	-	-	-	-	-	-	-	2	-	-	-	2
Solanum cf. *americanum* (black nightshade)	16	-	8	-	1	-	-	-	-	-	-	-	1	-	-	-	-	-	-	-	9	1	-	-	46
Solanum/Physalis spp. (nightshade/ground cherry)	10	-	-	-	-	-	-	-	-	-	-	-	-	-	-	-	-	-	1	-	-	-	-	-	-
Strophostyles sp. (wild bean)	1	-	5	-	-	-	-	-	-	-	-	-	2	-	1	-	-	-	-	-	24	-	-	1	-
Vitis sp. (grape)	1	-	-	-	-	-	-	-	-	-	-	-	-	-	-	-	-	-	-	-	-	-	-	-	-
Unknown	11	12	2	-	-	4	-	1	-	-	-	-	-	-	1	-	-	1	-	-	-	-	-	7	4
Unidentifiable	106	68	13	6	7	2	1	5	-	-	9	30	4	1	4	-	-	3	6	3	128	8	6	25	88
TROPICAL CULTIGENS																									
Cucurbita sp. (squash rind frags.)	-	-	-	-	-	-	-	-	-	-	-	-	-	-	-	-	-	-	-	-	-	1	-	-	-
Lagenaria siceraria (bottle gourd rind frags.)	-	-	-	-	-	-	-	-	-	-	-	-	-	-	-	-	-	-	-	-	-	-	-	-	-
Zea mays (maize)																									
cob fragments	174	1	18	29	4	-	1	8	-	2	4	5	1	-	-	-	-	1	5	-	14	9	2	2	355
kernel fragments	4	-	7	5	2	-	-	15	-	1	3	8	-	-	-	-	-	2	18	-	1	12	-	-	4

Table 53. Continued

	Features																							
	111	112	113	132	133	139	140	147	155	186	187	224	229	242	252	263	267	270	272	280	282	283	289	291
SEEDS (total)	18	15	2	23	3	31	3	5	468	2	8	12	637	4	11	2	1	9	56	109	-	2	1	3
Amaranthus sp. (amaranth)	-	-	-	-	-	-	-	-	-	-	-	1	-	-	-	-	-	-	-	-	-	-	-	-
Brasenia Schreberi (watershield)	-	-	-	-	-	-	-	-	-	-	-	-	-	-	-	-	-	-	-	-	-	-	-	-
Chenopodium sp. (goosefoot)	5	1	-	10	1	9	-	-	4	-	1	5	13	-	1	-	-	-	-	6	-	-	-	-
Compositae (composite family)	-	-	-	-	-	-	-	-	1	-	-	-	-	-	-	-	-	-	-	-	-	-	-	-
Croton sp. (croton)	-	-	-	-	-	-	-	-	1	-	-	-	-	-	-	-	-	-	-	-	-	-	-	-
Diospyros virginiana (persimmon, frags.)	1	-	-	-	-	-	-	-	11	-	-	-	-	-	-	-	-	-	-	-	-	-	-	-
Euphorbia sp. (spurge)	-	-	-	-	-	-	-	-	-	-	-	-	-	-	-	-	-	-	-	-	-	-	-	-
Gramineae (grass family)	-	-	-	2	-	-	-	-	-	-	-	-	1	-	-	-	-	-	-	-	-	-	-	-
Gramineae Type 6L & F (grass)	2	-	-	-	-	2	-	-	1/1	-	1	1	3	-	-	-	-	-	-	-	-	-	-	-
Gramineae Type 20/21 (grass)	-	-	-	4	1	-	-	-	-	-	-	-	-	-	-	-	-	-	-	2	-	-	-	-
Helianthus sp. (sunflower)	-	-	-	-	-	-	-	-	5	1	1	-	-	-	-	-	-	-	-	-	-	-	-	-
Ipomoea sp. (morning-glory)	-	-	-	-	-	-	-	-	-	-	-	-	-	-	-	-	-	-	-	-	-	-	-	-
Ipomoea/Convolvulus spp. (morning/glory/bindweed)	-	-	-	-	-	-	-	1	1	-	-	-	-	-	-	-	-	-	-	-	-	-	-	-
Iva annua (marsh elder)	-	-	-	-	-	-	-	-	87	-	-	-	-	-	-	-	-	-	-	-	-	-	-	-
Iva/Helianthus spp. (marsh elder/sunflower)	-	1	-	-	-	-	-	-	-	-	-	-	-	-	-	-	-	-	-	-	-	-	-	-
Labiatae (mint family)	-	-	-	-	-	-	-	-	-	-	-	-	-	-	-	-	-	-	-	-	-	-	-	-
Leguminosae (small legumes)	-	-	-	-	-	-	-	3	1	-	-	-	-	-	-	-	-	-	-	-	-	-	-	-
cf. Lespedeza sp. (bush clover)	-	-	-	-	-	-	-	-	-	-	-	-	-	-	-	-	-	-	-	-	-	-	-	-
Nelumbo lutea (American lotus, frags.)	-	-	-	-	-	-	-	-	-	-	-	-	2	-	-	-	-	-	-	-	-	-	-	-
Phalaris caroliniana (maygrass)	-	5	1	-	-	-	-	1	11	-	1	1	295	-	-	-	1	6	37	25	-	-	1	1
Phytolacca americana (pokeweed)	-	-	-	-	-	-	-	-	2	-	-	-	-	-	-	-	-	-	-	-	-	-	-	-
Polygonum spp. (knotweeds, smartweeds)	-	-	-	-	-	3	-	-	-	-	-	-	1	-	-	-	-	-	-	2	-	-	-	-
Polygonum erectum (erect knotweed)	-	-	-	1	-	1	-	-	164	-	-	-	20	-	-	-	-	-	1	-	-	-	-	-
cf. Portulaca sp. (purslane)	-	-	-	-	-	-	-	-	-	-	-	-	-	-	-	-	-	-	-	-	-	-	-	-
Prunus sp. (cherry)	-				-	-	-	-	-	-	-	-	-	-	-	-	-	-	-	-	-	-	-	-
Rhus sp. (sumac)	-	-	-	-	-	4	-	-	-	-	-	-	1	-	-	-	-	-	-	-	-	-	-	-
Rumex sp. (dock)	-	-	-	-	-	-	-	-	-	-	-	-	-	-	-	-	-	-	-	-	-	-	-	-
Sida cf. spinosa (prickly mallow)	-	-	-	-	-	3	-	-	-	-	-	-	-	-	-	-	-	-	-	1	-	-	-	-
Solanum cf. americanum (black nightshade)	-	-	-	-	-	-	-	-	-	-	-	-	1	-	-	-	-	-	1	-	-	-	-	-
Solanum/Physalis spp. (nightshade/ground cherry)	-	-	-	-	-	-	-	-	-	-	-	-	-	-	-	-	-	-	-	-	-	-	-	-
Strophostyles sp. (wild bean)	-	1	-	-	-	-	-	-	6	-	-	-	-	-	2	-	-	-	-	1	-	-	-	1
Vitis sp. (grape)	-	-	-	-	-	-	-	-	1	-	1	-	-	-	-	-	-	-	-	-	-	-	-	-
Unknown	1	-	-	-	-	1	-	-	5	-	-	-	-	-	-	2	-	-	-	2	-	-	-	-
Unidentifiable	9	7	1	6	1	8	3	-	166	1	3	4	300	4	8	-	-	3	17	70	-	2	-	1
TROPICAL CULTIGENS																								
Cucurbita sp. (squash rind frags.)	-	-	-	-	-	-	-	-	-	-	-	-	-	-	-	-	-	-	-	-	-	-	-	-
Lagenaria siceraria (bottle gourd rind frags.)	-	-	-	-	-	1	-	-	-	-	-	1	-	-	-	-	-	-	-	-	-	-	-	-
Zea mays (maize) cob fragments	3	5	3	-	-	15	5110	2	454	4	6	28	80	-	-	-	2	1	79	10	-	-	8	4
kernel fragments	6	14	-	-	-	1	-	-	137	-	6	3	241	-	-	-	2	6	42	12	-	-	-	3

evenly throughout feature fills, although 8 of the 49 features analyzed yielded no >2 mm charcoal. A total of 8656 fragments were recovered, for an average frequency of 49 fragments per 10 l sample. Table 54 shows the percentage composition of the flotation-recovered wood charcoal.

At least 20 wood taxa were represented, but 85% of all identifiable wood fragments belonged to only 3 taxa: oak, hickory, and cottonwood/willow (Salicaceae). These 3 taxa are typically dominant in other Late Woodland and Mississippian assemblages in the American Bottom. For example, at the Range site, an analysis of 21 Stirling phase features showed that oak, hickory, and cottonwood/willow were the three most commonly occurring taxa, together making up 84.2% of the identifiable wood charcoal (45.2%, 33.0%, and 6.0%, respectively).

This pattern is distinctive of the Late Woodland and Mississippian components. Earlier assemblages in the American Bottom show a different pattern of wood use. For example, in the Late Archaic Missouri Pacific #2 and Dyroff site assemblages, the most common wood types were ash, elm, and honey locust. Oak occurred less frequently and hickory hardly at all. Ash, elm, and honey locust are dominants of the bottomland forests, while oak and hickory are dominant upland forest taxa.

At the Julien site, oak and hickory were found in several types of features, but most of the cottonwood/willow (94.2% of flotation-recovered charcoal) was recovered from structures. Also, of 84 charcoal samples identified from a burned structure (Feature 91), 72 contained cottonwood/willow. Evidently, it was a favored building material.

In addition to flotation-recovered wood charcoal, wood was identified from 155 charcoal samples from 12 Julien site Mississippian features (Table 55).

An interesting contrast was evident when comparing Features 2 and 91. Both were Sand Prairie phase structures, but they evinced completely different uses of building materials. Of 25 samples identified from Feature 2, 15 were oak and 5 were hickory. Of the 85 samples identified from Feature 91, 72 were cottonwood/willow, only 3 contained oak or hickory, and a wide variety of other taxa (at least 8) were also present. The wider spectrum of wood taxa from Feature 91 could be due to the fact that more samples were identified from this structure, but the contrast between the primary building materials (oak and hickory vs. cottonwood/willow) was marked. Feature 91 also contained a large (minimum diameter=13 cm) red cedar log, which was incompletely carbonized.

Nut

Nut remains were the most abundant class of charcoal recovered from

Table 54. Percentage Frequencies of Flotation-recovered Wood Charcoal from the Mississippian Component

Taxa	% of Identifiable Fragments
oak (*Quercus* sp.)	1.6
red oaks (*Quercus*, red group)	47.4
white oaks (*Quercus*, white group)	0.4
hickory (*Carya* sp.)	12.9
cottonwood/willow (Salicaceae)	12.9
pecan hickory (*Carya illinoensis/cordiformis*)	9.9
honey locust (*Gleditsia* sp.)	3.0
unknown Type Q (diffuse-porous)	2.5
red cedar (*Juniperus virginiana*)	1.9
elm family (Ulmaceae)	1.8
persimmon (*Diospyros virginiana*)	1.4
mulberry (*Morus rubra*)	1.4
cherry (*Prunus* sp.)	1.0
maple (*Acer* sp.)	0.7
ash (*Fraxinus* sp.)	0.6
elm (*Ulmus* sp.)	0.3
birch (*Betula* sp.)	0.2
sycamore (*Platanus occidentalis*)	0.1
hop hornbeam, ironwood (*Ostrya virginiana*)	0.1
Kentucky coffee-tree (*Gymnocladus dioica*)	0.1
locust/coffee-tree (*Gleditsia/Gymnocladus*)	0.1
dogwood (?) (cf. *Cornus* sp.)	0.1
	100.2

Sample Size 7263

Table 55. Charcoal Samples Identified from Mississippian Features

	Features											
	2	3	5	17	82	85	87	91	143	146	236	252
No. of Samples Id'ed	25	9	1	5	1	2	1	85	18	5	1	2
NUT												
Carya sp. (hickory)	1	-	-	-	-	-	-	-	-	-	-	-
WOOD												
Acer or *Betula* (maple or birch)	-	-	-	-	-	-	-	1	-	-	-	-
Carya sp. (hickory)	5	-	-	-	1	-	-	-	-	-	1	1
C. illinoensis/cordiformis (pecan hickory)	-	-	-	-	-	-	-	-	3	-	-	-
Celtis sp. (hackberry)	-	-	-	-	-	-	-	1	-	-	-	-
cf. *Cercis* sp. (redbud?)	-	-	-	-	-	-	-	-	1?	-	-	-
Fraxinus sp. (ash)	-	-	-	-	-	-	-	2	-	-	-	-
F. americana (white ash)	-	1	-	-	-	-	-	-	-	-	-	-
Juglans sp. (walnut)	-	-	-	-	-	-	-	1	-	-	-	-
J. cinerea (butternut)	-	-	-	-	-	-	-	2	-	-	-	-
J. nigra (black walnut)	-	-	-	-	-	-	-	4	-	-	-	-
Juniperus virginiana (red cedar)	-	-	-	-	-	-	-	6	-	-	-	-
Morus sp. (mulberry)	-	1	-	-	-	-	-	-	-	-	-	-
Pinus sp. (pine)	-	-	1	-	-	-	-	-	-	-	-	-
Platanus occidentalis (sycamore)	-	-	-	2	-	-	-	3	-	-	-	-
Quercus sp. (oak)	1	-	-	-	-	-	-	1	-	-	-	-
Q., red group (red oaks)	13	-	-	2	-	-	-	2	-	-	-	-
Q., white group (white oaks)	1	-	-	-	-	-	-	-	-	-	-	-
Salicaceae (cottonwood/willow)	-	7	-	1?	-	-	-	72	4	-	-	-
Ulmaceae (elm/hackberry)	-	-	-	-	-	-	-	1	-	-	-	-
Conifer	-	-	-	-	-	1?	-	-	-	-	-	-
Diffuse-porous	-	-	-	-	-	-	-	2	-	-	-	-
Unidentifiable	4	-	-	-	-	1	-	1	-	-	-	1
OTHER												
Monocotyledonous stem (thatch?)	-	-	-	-	-	-	-	2	8	5	-	-
Bark twine	-	-	-	-	-	-	-	1	-	-	-	-
Zea mays (maize) fragments	-	-	-	-	-	-	1	-	2	-	-	-

Note: Counts represent number of samples in which taxon was present.

Table 56. Percentage Frequencies of Flotation-recovered Nut Fragments from the Mississippian Component

Nut Taxa	% of Identifiable Nut Fragments
thick-shelled hickory (*Carya* sp.)	56.7
walnut or hickory (Juglandaceae)	34.7
nut-meat (Juglandaceae)	3.4
nut-husk (Juglandaceae)	0.2
pecan hickory (*Carya illinoensis/cordiformis*)	4.6
acorn (*Quercus* sp.)	0.3
black walnut (*Juglans nigra*)	<0.1
	99.9

Sample Size 11,818

(Total Fragments 11,844)

the Mississippian component at the Julien site. Almost 12,000 fragments were recovered. The distribution of nutshell was uneven. Two features (Features 110 and 155) of the 49 features analyzed yielded 79% of the total nutshell fragments, while 4 features (Features 2, 88, 110, and 155) yielded 92% of the total nut fragments.

Table 56 presents the percentage composition of identifiable nut fragments from the Mississippian component at the Julien site. The table shows that the nut remains were overwhelmingly thick-shelled hickory. The category "Juglandaceae" includes fragments that do not show diagnostic characteristics of either walnut or hickory. However, since only 5 recognizable fragments of black walnut were found overall, while hickory fragments totaled 6695, it seems likely that most, if not all, of the fragments assigned to the category "Juglandaceae" were hickories rather than walnuts. Of interest were a number of whole and broken hickory or walnut nutmeats, many of which were found in a pit (Feature 110) within structure Feature 2, as well as on the floor of structure Feature 2. Feature 155, a basin-shaped pit, also contained a number of nutmeats as well as nuthusks. The presence of nuthusk and nutmeat was unusual and may reflect a particular nut processing or storage technique.

Asch and Asch (1980) have suggested the use of a nut:wood ratio as an index when comparing the relative importance of nuts between assemblages. In most Late Archaic assemblages, for example, the quantity of nutshell generally equals or exceeds the quantity of wood charcoal (Asch et al. 1979:81). In later assemblages, the proportion of nutshell relative to wood charcoal decreases. Asch et al. (1979:84) have suggested that this decrease reflects the declining role of nuts in the diet as small seeds and maize are on the increase. In the Mississippian component at the Julien site, however, although seeds and maize are common, the quantity of nutshell exceeds the quantity of wood charcoal (nut:wood ratio 1.4:1). This apparent abundance of nutshell at the Julien site may be due in part to sampling bias, but it nevertheless demonstrates that even though agriculture was practiced, the role of nuts in subsistence was not negligible.

Seeds

A total of 3110 seeds (not including maize) were recovered from the 49 analyzed Mississippian features, for an average frequency of 18 seeds per 10 l sample. At least 32 taxa of seed plants were represented. Table 57 lists the percentage composition of the seed taxa.

The three taxa composing the starchy seed complex (*Chenopodium* sp., *Phalaris caroliniana*, and *Polygonum erectum*) made up 68.4% of all identifiable seeds. The high proportion of starchy seeds in the floral assemblage parallels their frequent occurrence in most Late Woodland and Mississippian assemblages in the American Bottom. For example, at the Range site (Stirling phase), the Lohmann site (Late Woodland period),

Table 57. Percentage Frequencies of Flotation-recovered Seeds from the Mississippian Component

Seed Taxa	% of Identifiable Seeds
maygrass (*Phalaris caroliniana*)	41.6
goosefoot (*Chenopodium* sp.)	16.9
erect knotweed (*Polygonum erectum*)	9.9
grass (Gramineae Types 6L and F)	5.8
marsh elder (*Iva annua*)	5.1
black nightshade (*Solanum* cf. *americanum*)	4.3
wild bean (*Strophostyles* sp.)	2.3
grasses (Gramineae)	1.5
pokeweed (*Phytolacca* sp.)	1.3
small legumes (Leguminosae)	1.3
sunflower (*Helianthus annuus*)	1.1
persimmon (*Diospyros virginiana*)	1.0
knotweeds, smartweeds (*Polygonum* spp.)	0.8
*nightshade/ground cherry (*Solanum/Physalis*)	0.6
grass (Gramineae Type 20)	0.5
prickly mallow (*Sida* cf. *spinosa*)	0.5
amaranth (*Amaranthus* sp.)	0.4
purslane (?) [cf. *Portulaca* sp.]	0.4
morning glory (*Ipomoea* sp.)	0.3
American lotus (no. pcs.) [*Nelumbo lutea*]	0.3
sumac (*Rhus* sp.)	0.3
*bindweed/morning glory (*Convolvulus/Ipomoea*)	0.2
bush clover (?) [cf. *Lespedeza* sp.]	0.2
grape (*Vitis* sp.)	0.2
croton (*Croton* sp.)	0.1
*marsh elder/sunflower (*Iva/Helianthus*)	0.1
mint family (Labiatae)	0.1
watershield (*Brasenia Schreberi*)	<0.1
composite (Compositae)	<0.1
spurge (*Euphorbia* sp.)	<0.1
grass (Gramineae Type 6F)	<0.1
cherry (*Prunus* sp.)	<0.1
dock (*Rumex* sp)	<0.1
UNKNOWNS	2.7
	100.2

Sample Size 1973

(Total Seeds 3110)

*Lacking diagnostics necessary to distinguish genera.

and the Range site (Late Woodland period), the starchy seeds made up 81%, 92%, and 94% of identifiable seeds, respectively.

Asch and Asch (1978, 1980) have argued convincingly that the taxa of the starchy seed complex were cultivated. Their argument is based on field studies of the three species, which show that none of the plants occur naturally in sufficient quantities to account for their consistently high numbers and dominance in archaeological seed spectra. The conclusion is that they must have been encouraged (i.e., cultivated), although they show no morphological signs of domestication (i.e., genetic response to cultivation).

The seed types that occurred most frequently after the starchy seeds at the Julien site were grasses (Gramineae Types 6 and 20), marsh elder (Iva annua), black nightshade (Solanum cf. americanum), wild bean (Strophostyles sp.), and sunflower (Helianthus annuus). These form a suite of seeds that occur commonly, though in low numbers, in most Late Woodland and Mississippian assemblages that have been analyzed from American Bottom sites.

Marsh elder and sunflower were almost certainly domesticated prehistorically, since the sizes of the archaeological achenes show an increase over time. This, presumably, was a response to human selection for large-achened plants (Asch and Asch 1978; Yarnell 1972, 1978).

The grass types recovered (Gramineae Types 6 and 20) are as yet unidentified to genus. Gramineae Type 6L was a small (ca. 1 mm) caryopsis, that was ovoid with a basal ventral embryo area. Gramineae Type 20 can be seen in Figure 88.

Wild bean (Figure 87) grows in "rich rocky woods and thickets, moist alluvial ground, sand and gravel bars" (Steyermark 1963:951). Steyermark's further remarks on the species are interesting: "[The plant] does well on poor acid soils and is able to enrich the soils upon which it grows with the nitrogen-fixing bacteria contained in the enlarged nodules of its roots. It is, therefore, a good wild plant for fallow and wornout fields." The taxon was certainly of some economic importance to the people of the Late Woodland and Mississippian periods, as evinced by its frequent appearance in features. At the Julien site, wild bean was present in 22.4% of the analyzed features; at the Range site (Stirling phase) and the Lohmann site (Late Woodland period), it was present in 28.6% and 43%, respectively, of the analyzed features.

The small reticulate seeds identified as black nightshade (Solanum cf. americanum) also occurred frequently in features of this time period. At the Julien site, they were present in 18% of the features, while at the Range (Stirling phase) and Lohmann (Late Woodland period) sites, black nightshade was present in 19% and 29%, respectively, of analyzed features. Although the green and unripe berries of this species are poisonous, the ripe black berries may be eaten. Boiling apparently destroys their toxicity (Muenscher 1975:208).

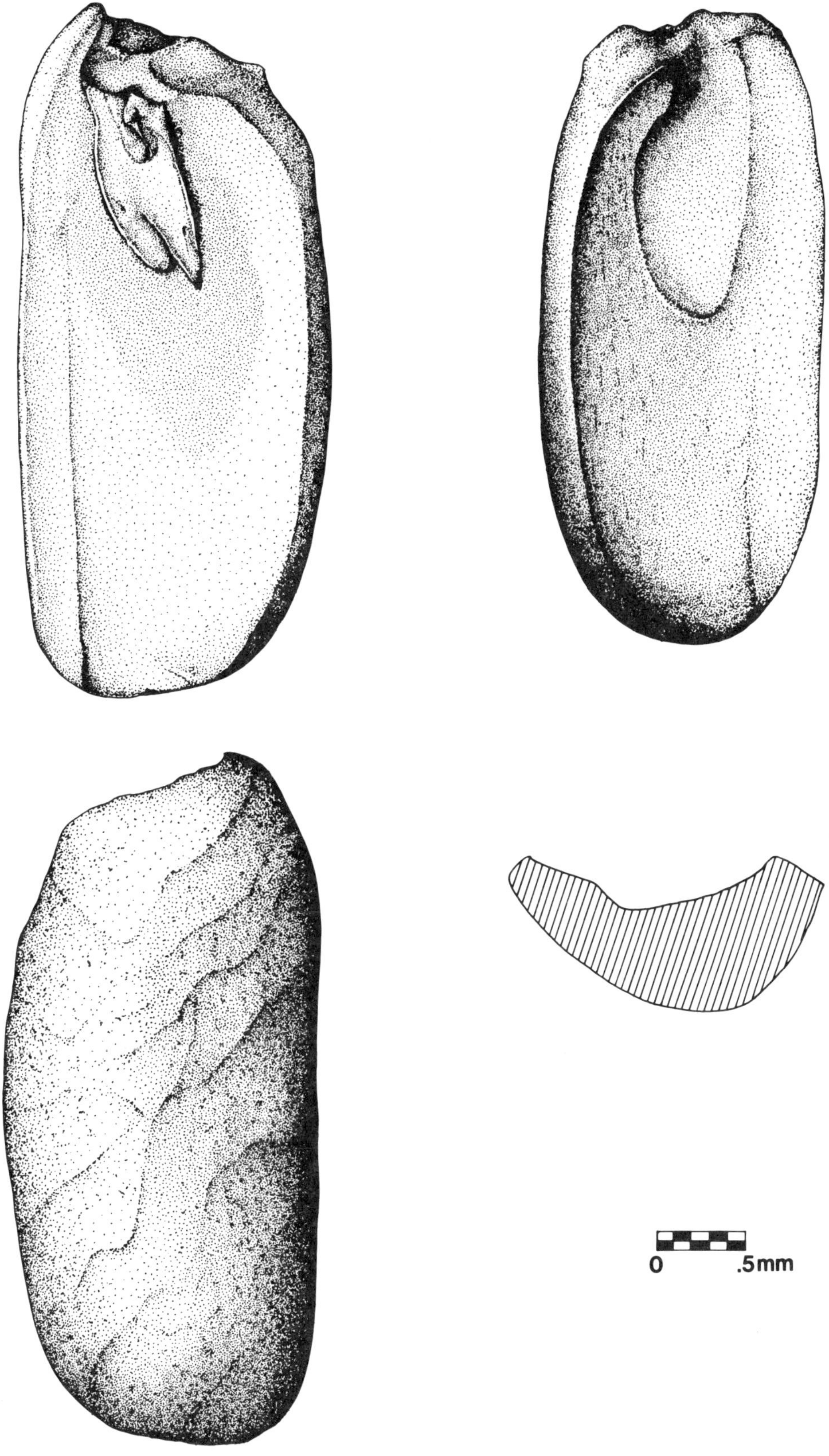

Figure 87. Wild Bean (Strophostyles sp.)

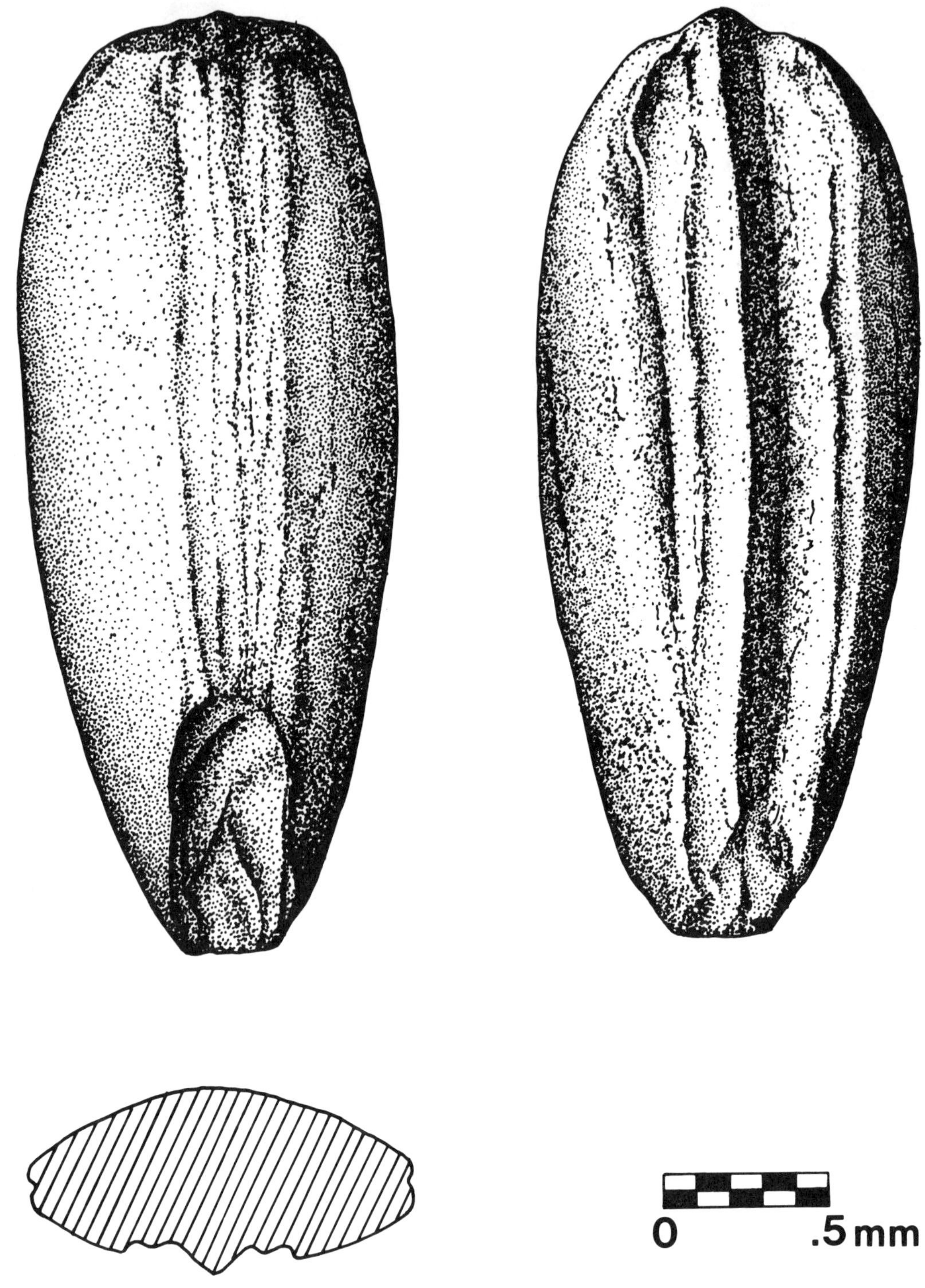

Figure 88. Gramineae Type 20

In addition to the seed types mentioned above, low counts of other seed taxa were also present. Two hydrophytic plants were represented: watershield (*Brasenia Schreberi*) and American lotus (*Nelumbo lutea*). Species of morning glory (*Ipomoea* spp.) generally grow on low, alluvial ground. One species of the genus, *I. pandurata*, produces large, edible, tuber-like roots. Many *Rumex* species also grow on low, alluvial ground.

The other seeds represented in low quantities at the Julien site include persimmon, pokeweed, cherry, sumac, grape, and ground cherry. All occur occasionally in archaeological deposits and probably were used by the prehistoric inhabitants of the Julien site.

Prickly mallow (*Sida* cf. *spinosa*) is not indigenous to North America, but a native of the tropics (Steyermark 1963:1052). The presence of 10 carbonized seeds of this species in six features at the Julien site makes it probable that these seeds were of archaeological origin and not modern intrusions. Edgar Anderson (1969) has discussed "camp-followers", or alien weeds, that can be brought unintentionally by man to new areas, for example when a few major crop plants are introduced. The tropical crops squash and maize were well established in North America by the Mississippian period, and it may be that the *Sida* recovered from the Julien site was an instance of one such weedy camp-follower from the tropics.

Tropical Cultigens

Three tropical cultigens were represented in samples identified from the Mississippian component of the Julien site: maize (*Zea mays*), squash (*Cucurbita* sp.) and gourd (*Lagenaria siceraria*).

The last two taxa were represented by only three tiny rind fragments: one squash rind fragment from Feature 89, and one gourd rind fragment each from Features 139 and 224. Paleoethnobotanical research in the lower Illinois River valley indicates that the quantity of squash and gourd rind declines in Late Woodland and Mississippian assemblages from Middle Woodland assemblages (Asch et al. 1979). However, the minute amount of squash and gourd rind at the Julien site did not necessarily reflect its lack of importance. At the historical Zimmerman site, only two tiny squash rind fragments were recovered through flotation from the site, in spite of the fact that early observers had noted that there were abundant pumpkins grown and dried for storage (Asch and Asch 1975).

Maize remains were recovered from 35 of the 49 analyzed features at the Julien site. Quantities were generally low (0.7 g per 10 l sample), with one exception. Feature 140, a pit within a circular Stirling phase structure (Feature 113), contained a great quantity of maize (37 g per 10 l). All recovered fragments were cob fragments; no kernel fragments were recovered. In addition to maize, Feature 140 contained a small amount of red oak and hickory wood and an unusual number of small twigs. No nutshell was recovered.

The maize remains have not been analyzed further; however, some maize cupules from the Sand Prairie phase features only exhibited the wide, shallow, crescent shape characteristic of the 8-row Northern Flint race of maize.

Comparison of the Three Mississippian Phases

In order to see if any major trends in plant use could be discerned, plant material from the three consecutive Mississippian phases (Stirling, Moorehead, and Sand Prairie) were compared. Features selected by the site director as having unmixed temporal association were grouped for comparison. The selected features were:

Stirling phase:	Structure Feature 113 and associated pit Features 139, 140, and 147. Structure Feature 267 and associated pit Feature 291. Structure Feature 36 and associated pit Features 224, 229, 242, and 252. Pit Features 270, 272, 280, and 283.
Moorehead phase:	Structure Feature 31 and associated Features 40, 41, 46, 47, 48, 49, 50, 52, 53, 54, 56, and 58. Pit Feature 155.
Sand Prairie phase:	Structure Feature 2 and associated Features 110, 111, 112, 186, 187, 263, and 282. Structure Feature 82 and associated Features 84 and 90. Structure Feature 91.

Tabulated data on plant remains from these three groups are provided in Tables 58, 59, and 60.

Table 61 compares the material from the three phases. Carbonized plant material was analyzed from 474 l of fill from the Stirling phase features, 415 l from the Moorehead phase features, and 445 l from the Sand Prairie phase features. For comparative purposes, the overall quantities of material have been converted into average frequencies per liter of fill.

The nut taxa represented were similar in composition and proportions in all three phases, but the relative quantities varied considerably. The average frequencies of nut fragments for both the Moorehead and Sand Prairie phases were similar (13.21 and 12.56 fragments per liter, respectively). The Stirling phase frequency, however, was strikingly lower, averaging only 0.17 fragments per liter, or about 75 times lower than that of the two subsequent phases.

Perhaps a better index to the relative quantity of nutshell can be achieved by using a nut:wood ratio. If the frequency of wood charcoal can be seen as a general index to the intensity of occupation at a particular site locus, then the quantity of nut relative to the amount of wood charcoal may better indicate fluctuations in intensity of use of nuts than would a simple average frequency. When the quantity of nuts in the three phases is viewed relative to the amount of wood charcoal (i.e., nut:wood ratio), one can see that the frequency of nut fragments in the Stirling phase features was 128 times lower than in the Moorehead phase (nut:wood ratios of 0.08:1 and 10.24:1, respectively). The very high nut:wood ratio in the Moorehead phase features (10.24:1) was aberrant; most Mississippian assemblages analyzed yielded less nutshell than wood charcoal.

Since the Sand Prairie phase features averaged a higher frequency of wood charcoal (13.52 fragments per liter), the nut:wood ratio here was 0.93:1. This was 12 times higher than in the Stirling phase features and about 11 times lower than in the Moorehead features. However, since the samples of all three phases were relatively small, these differences in the nut:wood ratio may reflect idiosyncrasies of the features rather than actual changes in nut utilization.

To compare the composition of the wood charcoal from the three phases, the six dominant taxa from each phase are listed in Table 61 in order of frequency. The pattern from the Moorehead phase features appeared anomalous. Generally, the two most frequently appearing taxa in Mississippian assemblages analyzed were oak and hickory, both dominants of the upland forest. These two taxa appeared frequently in the Stirling and Sand Prairie phase features at the Julien site, but not in the Moorehead phase features. Besides Type Q (an unknown diffuse-porous wood) and cherry, the four most common woods in the Moorehead phase features were honey locust, cottonwood/willow, birch, and maple. These four taxa are generally characteristic of low, wet, alluvial habitats.

The seeds recovered from the three phases were not dissimilar in frequency or composition. The average frequency of seeds was about two seeds per liter of fill in all three phases. Although the number of taxa represented in each phase varied somewhat, in each phase, over three-quarters of all identifiable seeds belonged to only three taxa. The following taxa were present in all three phases: goosefoot (*Chenopodium* sp.), maygrass (*Phalaris caroliniana*), erect knotweed (*Polygonum erectum*), grasses (Gramineae Types 6 and 20/21), wild bean (*Strophostyles* sp.), black nightshade (*Solanum* cf. *americanum*), American lotus (*Nelumbo lutea*), and morning glory (*Ipomoea* sp.).

The only striking dissimilarities in the plant remains from the three phases, then, appear to be widely disparate nut:wood ratios, which were exceptionally high in the Moorehead phase features and low in the Stirling phase, and a dominance of lowland taxa in the wood spectrum of the Moorehead phase features. The lowland wood taxa in the Moorehead

Table 58. Flotation-recovered Plant Remains from the Stirling Phase

	Features															
	113*	139	140	147	267*	291	36*	224	229	242	252	270	272	280	283	Totals
Total liters analyzed	20	30	40	10	20	40	34	60	60	20	20	30	30	50	10	474
NUT (total fragments)	1	1	-	-	-	6	1	5	65	-	1	-	1	1	-	82
Carya sp. (hickory)	-	-	-	-	-	4	-	4	33	-	-	-	1	-	-	42
C. illinoensis/C. cordiformis (pecan hickory)	-	-	-	-	-	-	-	-	7	-	-	-	-	-	-	7
Juglandaceae (walnut or hickory)	1	1	-	-	-	2	-	1	25	-	-	-	-	1	-	31
Quercus sp. (acorn)	-	-	-	-	-	-	1	-	-	-	-	-	-	-	-	1
Unidentifiable	-	-	-	-	-	-	-	-	-	-	1	-	-	-	-	1
WOOD (total fragments)	-	2	189	-	1	20	-	47	621	-	1	6	35	27	3	952
Acer sp. (maple)	-	-	-	-	-	-	-	-	4?	-	-	-	-	-	-	4?
Carya sp. (hickory)	-	-	39	-	-	-	-	6	25	-	-	-	2	1	-	73
C. illinoensis/C. cordiformis (pecan hickory)	-	-	-	-	-	-	-	-	5	-	-	-	-	-	-	5
Gleditsia sp. (honey locust)	-	-	-	-	-	-	-	-	180	-	-	-	-	-	-	180
Juniperus virginiana (red cedar)	-	-	-	-	-	-	-	-	-	-	-	-	-	-	1	1
Prunus sp. (cherry)	-	-	-	-	-	-	-	-	-	-	-	1?	-	-	-	1?
Quercus sp. (oak)	-	2	-	-	-	5	-	-	17	-	-	1	2	2	-	29
Quercus, red group (red oaks)	-	-	64	-	-	2	-	15	287	-	-	-	2	3	-	373
Quercus, white group (white oaks)	-	-	-	-	-	-	-	7	9	-	-	-	-	-	-	16
Salicaceae (cottonwood/willow)	-	-	-	-	-	-	-	-	4	-	-	-	-	-	-	4
Ulmaceae (elm/hackberry)	-	-	-	-	-	-	-	-	4	-	-	-	-	-	-	4
Unknown Type Q	-	-	-	-	1	3	-	-	40	-	-	-	2	2	-	48
Diffuse-porous	-	-	-	-	-	-	-	-	3	-	-	-	1	1	-	5
Ring-porous	-	-	13	-	-	10	-	13	40	-	-	3	7	8	-	94
Unidentifiable	-	-	74	-	-	-	-	5	-	-	-	1	17	10	2	109
Bark	-	-	-	-	-	-	-	-	-	-	-	-	2	-	-	2
Monocotyledonous stem	-	-	-	-	-	-	-	1	3	-	-	-	-	-	-	4

Table 58. Continued

	Features															
	113*	139	140	147	267*	291	36*	224	229	242	252	270	272	280	283	Totals
SEEDS (total)	2	29	3	5	1	3	18	12	637	4	11	9	56	109	2	901
cf. *Amaranthus* sp. (amaranth)	-	-	-	-	-	-	-	1?	-	-	-	-	-	-	-	1?
Chenopodium sp. (goosefoot)	-	9	-	-	-	-	6	5	13	-	1	-	-	6	-	40
Gramineae (grasses)	-	-	-	-	-	-	-	-	1	-	-	-	-	-	-	1
Gramineae Type 6L (grass)	-	2	-	-	-	-	1	1	3	-	-	-	-	-	-	7
Gramineae Type 20/21 (grass)	-	-	-	-	-	-	-	-	-	-	-	-	-	2	-	2
Ipomoea sp. (morning glory)	-	-	-	1	-	-	-	-	-	-	-	-	-	-	-	1
Leguminosae (small legume)	-	-	-	3	-	-	-	-	-	-	-	-	-	-	-	3
Nelumbo lutea (American lotus)	-	-	-	-	-	-	-	-	2	-	-	-	-	-	-	2
Phalaris caroliniana (maygrass)	1	-	-	1	1	1	3	1	295	-	-	6	37	25	-	371
Polygonum spp. (knotweeds)	-	1	-	-	-	-	-	-	1	-	-	-	-	2	-	4
Polygonum erectum (erect knotweed)	-	1	-	-	-	-	-	-	20	-	-	-	1	-	-	22
Rhus sp. (sumac)	-	4	-	-	-	-	-	-	1	-	-	-	-	-	-	5
Sida cf. *spinosa* (prickley mallow)	-	3	-	-	-	-	-	-	-	-	-	-	-	1	-	4
Solanum cf. *americanum* (black nightshade)	-	-	-	-	-	-	1	-	1	-	-	-	1	-	-	3
Strophostyles sp. (wild bean)	-	-	-	-	-	1	-	-	-	-	2	-	-	1	-	4
Unknown	-	1	-	-	-	-	-	-	-	-	-	-	-	2	-	3
Unidentifiable	1	8	3	-	-	1	7	4	300	4	8	3	17	70	2	428
TROPICAL CULTIGENS																
Zea mays (maize) kernel fragments	-	1?	-	-	2	4	4	28	80	-	-	1	72	10	-	202
cob fragments	3	15	ca.5110	2	2	1	2	3	241	-	-	6	42	12	-	5439
weight (g)	0.1	0.4	147.9	<0.1	<0.1	-	0.1	0.2	2.3	-	-	<0.1	1.6	0.1	-	152.8
Lagenaria sp. (gourd rind frags.)	-	1	-	-	-	-	-	1	-	-	-	-	-	-	-	2

*These features are structures; all others are pits.

Table 59. Flotation-recovered Plant Remains from the Moorehead Phase

	Features														
	31*	40	41	46	47	48	49	50	52	53	54	56	58	155	Total
Total liters analyzed	46	8	13	70	2	20	15	63	40	26	28	20	14	50	415
NUT (total fragments)	30	8	3	115	2	65	133	47	37	116	27	3	1	4894	5481
Carya sp. (hickory)	19	1	1	61	1	43	88	24	19	68	16	2	1	2526	2870
C. illinoensis/c. cordiformis (pecan hickory)	-	3	-	42	-	3	19	-	-	-	-	-	-	348	415
Juglandaceae (walnut or hickory)	11	3	1	12	1	18	2	20	18	47	11	1	-	1866	2011
nut-meat/nut-husk	-	-	-	-	-	1/-	11/-	-	-	-	-	-	-	94/27	106/27
Juglans nigra (black walnut)	-	-	-	-	-	-	-	1	-	1	-	-	-	-	2
Quercus sp. (acorn)	-	1	1?	-	-	-	1	1	-	-	-	-	-	30	33,1?
Unidentifiable	-	-	-	-	-	-	12	1	-	-	-	-	-	-	13
WOOD (total fragments)	12	2	2	14	-	4	3	46	31	3	3	3	-	414	534
Acer sp. (maple)	-	-	-	2	-	-	-	4	-	-	-	-	-	-	6
Betula sp. (birch)	-	-	-	-	-	-	-	8	-	-	-	-	-	-	8
Diospyros (persimmon)	-	-	-	-	-	-	-	2	1	-	-	-	-	-	3
Gleditsia sp. (honey locust)	-	-	-	-	-	-	-	-	-	-	-	-	-	35	35
Gymnocladus/Gleditsia (coffee-tree/honey locust)	-	-	-	-	-	-	-	2	-	-	-	-	-	-	2
Fraxinus sp. (ash)	1?	-	-	-	-	-	-	-	-	-	-	-	-	-	1?
Platanus occidentalis (sycamore)	-	-	-	-	-	-	-	-	2	-	-	-	-	-	2
Prunus sp. (cherry)	-	-	-	-	-	-	-	-	-	-	-	-	-	38	38
Quercus sp. (oak)	-	-	-	-	-	-	-	2	-	-	-	-	-	-	2
Quercus, red group (red oaks)	1	-	-	-	-	-	-	2	-	1	-	-	-	-	4
Salicaceae (cottonwood/ willow)	-	-	-	-	-	-	-	-	11	-	-	-	-	4	15
Ulmaceae (elm/hackberry)	-	-	-	2	-	-	-	-	-	-	-	-	-	-	2
Unknown Type Q	-	-	-	-	-	-	-	4	-	-	-	-	-	123	127
Diffuse-porous	1	-	1	3	-	3	3	-	15	1	1	2	-	20	50
Ring-porous	5	2	-	3	-	1	-	5	-	-	-	-	-	32	48
Unidentifiable	4	-	1	4	-	-	-	17	2	1	2	1	-	63	95
Monocotyledonous stem	-	-	-	-	-	-	-	-	-	-	-	-	-	99	99

Table 59. Continued

	Features														
	31*	40	41	46	47	48	49	50	52	53	54	56	58	155	Total
SEEDS (total)	9	10	2	11	1	-	24	35	11	5	10	-	-	468	586
Chenopodium sp. (goosefoot)	2	1	1	1?	-	-	-	-	1?	-	-	-	-	4	8,2?
Compositae (composite)	-	-	-	-	-	-	-	-	-	-	-	-	-	1	1
Croton sp. (croton)	-	-	-	-	-	-	-	-	-	3	-	-	-	1	4
Diospyros (persimmon)	-	-	-	-	-	-	-	-	-	-	3	-	-	11	14
Gramineae (grasses)	-	2	-	-	-	-	-	-	-	-	-	-	-	-	2
Gramineae Type 6L (grass)	-	-	-	-	-	-	-	-	-	-	-	-	-	1	1
Gramineae Type 6F (grass)	-	-	-	-	-	-	-	-	-	-	-	-	-	1	1
Gramineae Type 20 (grass)	-	-	-	-	-	-	-	-	-	-	-	-	-	1	1
Helianthus sp. (sunflower)	-	1	-	-	-	-	2	-	-	-	-	-	-	5	8
Ipomoea sp. (morning glory)	-	-	-	-	-	-	-	-	-	-	-	-	-	1	1
Iva sp. (marsh elder)	-	-	-	-	-	-	9	-	-	-	-	-	-	87	96
Nelumbo lutea (American lotus)	-	-	-	-	-	-	-	1	-	-	-	-	-	-	1
Phalaris caroliniana (maygrass)	-	-	-	2	-	-	2	3	2	1	1	-	-	11	22
Phytolacca sp. (pokeweed)	-	-	-	-	-	-	-	-	-	-	-	-	-	2	2
Polygonum spp. (knotweeds)	1	-	-	-	-	-	2	-	-	-	-	-	-	-	3
Polygonum erectum (erect knotweed)	-	-	-	2	1	-	-	1	-	-	-	-	-	164	168
Rumex sp. (dock)	-	-	-	-	-	-	-	-	1	-	-	-	-	-	1
Solanum cf. *americanum* (black nightshade)	-	-	-	-	-	-	-	-	1	-	-	-	-	-	1
Strophostyles sp. (wild bean)	-	-	-	-	-	-	-	-	2	-	1	-	-	6	9
Vitis sp. (grape)	-	-	-	-	-	-	-	-	-	-	-	-	-	1	1
Unknown	-	4	1	1	-	-	-	-	-	-	1	-	-	5	12
Unidentifiable	6	2	-	5	-	-	9	30	4	1	4	-	-	166	227
TROPICAL CULTIGENS															
Zea mays (maize)															
kernel fragments	5	-	1	15	-	1	4	8	1?	-	-	-	-	137	171,1?
cob fragments	29	-	-	8	-	2	4	5	-	-	-	-	-	454	502
OTHER															
Coal	-	-	3	-	-	-	-	3	-	1	-	-	-	-	7

*These features are structures; all others are pits.

Table 60. Flotation-recovered Plant Remains from the Sand Prairie Phase

	Features												
	2*	110	111	112	186	187	263	282	82*	84	90	91*	Total
Total liters analyzed	70	70	30	30	20	40	5	8	30	82	20	40	445
<u>NUT (total fragments)</u>	893	4494	33	17	14	23	1	4	15	74	15	4	5587
<u>Carya</u> sp. (true hickory)	341	3134	17	5	7	12	1	4	6	33	7	2	3569
<u>C. illinoensis</u> (pecan hickory)	1	118	2	-	-	-	-	-	1	-	4	-	126
Juglandaceae (walnut or hickory)	534	963	14	12	7	11	-	-	5	40	3	2	1591
nut-meat	17	278	-	-	-	-	-	-	-	-	-	-	295
<u>Juglans nigra</u> (black walnut)	-	1	-	-	-	-	-	-	-	1	-	-	2
<u>Quercus</u> (acorn)	-	-	-	-	-	-	-	-	-	-	1	-	1
<u>WOOD (total fragments)</u>	2174	2053	56	176	17	36	16	8	276	148	128	932	6020
<u>Acer</u> sp. (maple)	-	-	-	2	-	-	-	-	32	-	-	-	34
<u>Carya</u> sp. (true hickory)	346	194	-	-	4	2	3	-	231	33	7	-	820
<u>C. illinoensis</u> (pecan hickory)	706	-	-	-	-	-	-	-	-	-	-	-	706
<u>Diospyros</u> sp. (persimmon)	-	89	-	-	-	-	-	-	-	-	-	-	89
<u>Fraxinus</u> sp. (ash)	-	-	-	-	-	-	-	-	-	-	-	40	40
<u>Gymnocladus dioca</u> (Kentucky coffee-tree)	-	-	-	-	-	2	-	-	-	-	-	-	2
<u>Juniperus virginiana</u> (red cedar)	-	-	-	-	-	-	-	-	-	-	-	42	42
<u>Morus</u> sp. (mulberry)	-	-	-	-	-	-	-	-	-	-	-	100	100
<u>Ostrya</u> sp. (ironwood)	-	-	-	1	-	-	-	3	-	-	-	-	4
<u>Quercus</u> sp. (oak)	52	3	-	2	3	-	-	-	-	9	-	-	69
<u>Quercus</u>, red group (red oaks)	1034	1626	38	159	1	-	-	1	14	7	6	50	2936
<u>Quercus</u>, white group (white oaks)	-	6	-	8	-	-	-	-	-	-	-	-	14
<u>Flatanus occidentalis</u> (sycamore)	-	-	-	2	-	2	-	-	-	-	-	-	4
<u>Prunus</u> sp. (cherry)	27	-	9?	-	-	-	-	-	-	-	-	-	27,9?
Salicaceae (cottonwood/willow)	-	-	-	-	-	1	-	-	-	-	17	660	678
Ulmaceae (elm/hackberry)	-	-	-	-	-	-	-	-	27	8	92	40	167
Unknown Type Q	-	-	-	-	1	1	-	-	-	7	-	-	9
Diffuse-porous	1	8	-	-	2	2	-	-	-	1	-	-	14
Ring-porous	5	14	5	-	4	10	13	3	4	25	5	-	88
Unidentifiable	3	56	4	2	2	6	-	1	-	24	1	-	99
Bark	-	7	-	-	-	9	-	-	-	2	-	-	18
Monocotylendonous stem	10	52	-	15	-	1	-	-	-	4	13	89	184

Table 60. Continued

	Features												
	2*	110	111	112	186	187	263	282	82*	84	90	91*	Total
SEEDS (total)	215	540	18	15	2	8	2	-	7	9	7	51	874
Amaranthus sp. (amaranth)	3?	-	-	-	-	-	-	-	-	-	-	-	3?
Chenopodium/Amaranthus	-	55	2	-	-	-	-	-	-	-	-	-	57
Chenopodium sp. (chenopod)	9	156	3	1	-	1?	-	-	2	-	1	7	179,1?
Gramineae (grass)	3	13	-	-	-	-	-	-	-	-	-	-	16
Gramineae Type 6 (grass)	29	20	2	-	-	1	-	-	-	-	-	1	53
Iva sp. (marsh elder)	1	1	-	-	-	-	-	-	-	-	-	-	2
cf. *Lespedeza* (bush clover?)	3	-	-	-	-	-	-	-	-	-	-	-	3
Nelumbo lutea (American lotus)	3	-	-	-	-	-	-	-	-	-	-	-	3
Phalaris caroliniana (maygrass)	14	124	-	5	-	1	-	-	-	2	-	1	147
Phytolacca sp. (pokeweed)	-	6	-	-	-	-	-	-	-	-	-	-	6
Polygonum spp. (knotweed)	1	2	-	-	-	-	-	-	-	-	-	6	9
Polygonum erectum (erect knotweed)	-	1	-	-	-	-	-	-	-	-	-	-	1
Rhus sp. (sumac)	1	-	-	-	-	-	-	-	-	-	-	-	1
Sida cf. *spinosa* (prickly mallow)	1	-	-	-	-	-	-	-	-	-	-	-	1
Solanum cf. *americanum* (black nightshade)	16	46	-	-	-	-	-	-	-	1	-	-	63
Solanum/Physalis (nightshade/ ground cherry)	10	-	-	-	-	-	-	-	-	-	-	-	10
Strophostyles sp. (wild bean)	1	-	-	-	-	-	-	-	-	-	-	1	2
Vitis sp. (grape)	1	-	-	-	-	1?	-	-	-	-	-	-	1,1?
Ipomoea sp. (morning glory)	2	4	-	-	-	-	-	-	-	-	-	-	6
Diospyros virginiana (persimmon)	-	-	1?	-	-	-	-	-	1	-	-	-	1,1?
Iva/Helianthus (marsh elder/ sunflower)	-	-	-	1	-	-	-	-	-	-	-	-	1
Helianthus sp. (sunflower)	-	-	-	-	1	1?	-	-	-	-	-	-	1,1?
Leguminosae (small legume)	-	16	-	-	-	-	-	-	-	-	-	1	17
Brasenia Schreberi (watershield)	-	2	-	-	-	-	-	-	-	-	-	-	2
Labiatae (mint family)	-	1	-	-	-	-	-	-	-	-	-	-	1
Prunus sp. (cherry)	-	1?	-	-	-	-	-	-	-	-	-	-	1?
Unknown	11	4	1	-	-	-	2	-	1	-	-	7	26
Unidentifiable	106	88	9	7	1	3	-	-	3	6	6	25	254
TROPICAL CULTIGENS													
Zea mays (maize) cob fragments	174	355	3	5	4	6	-	-	1	5	2	-	555
kernel fragments	4	4	6	14	-	6	-	-	2	18	-	-	54
weight (g)	2.9	3.6	0.2	0.3	-	-	-	-	-	-	-	-	7.0

*These features are structures; all others are pits.

Table 61. Comparison of Plant Remains from Three Mississippian Phases

	Stirling	Moorehead	Sand Prairie
Total liters of fill analyzed	474	415	44
Mean nut fragments per liter	0.17	13.21	12.56
Number of nut taxa	3	4	4
	Carya *C. illinoensis* *Quercus*	*Carya* *C. illinoensis* *Quercus*	*Carya* *C. illinoensis* *Juglans nigra* *Quercus*
Mean wood fragments per liter	2.01	1.29	13.52
Number of wood taxa	11	12	16
Nut-to-wood ratio	0.08:1	10.24:1	0.93:1
6 dominant taxa	*Quercus*, red *Gleditsia* *Carya* Type Q *Quercus* *Quercus*, white	Type Q *Prunus* *Gleditsia* Salicaceae *Betula* *Acer*	*Quercus* *Carya* *C. illinoensis* Salicaceae Ulmaceae *Morus*
Mean seeds per liter	1.90	1.41	1.96
Number of seed taxa	15	20	24
	Phalaris 92% *Chenopodium* *Polygonum erectum* Gramineae Type 6L *Rhus* *Polygonum* *Sida* *Strophostyles* *Solanum americanum* Leguminosae Gramineae Type 20/21 *Nelumbo lutea* *Ipomoea* Gramineae *Amaranthus*	*Polygonum erectum* 82% *Iva* *Phalaris* *Diospyros* *Chenopodium* *Strophostyles* *Helianthus* *Croton* *Polygonum* Gramineae *Phytolacca* Compositae Gramineae Type 6L Gramineae Type 6F Gramineae Type 20 *Ipomoea* *Nelumbo lutea* *Rumex* *Solanum americanum* *Vitis*	*Chenopodium* 75% *Phalaris* *Solanum americanum* Gramineae Type 6L Leguminosae Gramineae *Solanum/Physalis* *Polygonum* *Phytolacca* *Ipomoea* *Nelumbo lutea* cf. *Lespedeza* *Amaranthus* *Iva* *Strophostyles* *Vitis* *Diospyros* *Helianthus* *Brasenia* *Polygonum erectum* *Rhus* *Sida spinosa* Labiatae *Prunus*

phase replaced the usually dominant oak and hickory that characterized the two other phases.

Summary

Carbonized plant remains from the Julien site were analyzed from assemblages associated with several cultural components. These components were represented by Late Woodland period features and features of three successive Mississippian phases.

The Late Woodland material was relatively sparse. The nut:wood ratio was 0.6:1 and few seeds were recovered. Most of the seeds were maygrass, a seed plant that was probably cultivated. The mean size of these seeds was greater than that of a number of specimens from a Middle Woodland assemblage. Further testing is necessary to confirm that there was indeed a size increase through time.

The plant remains from the Mississippian features, in contrast, showed a relatively greater contribution from food plants (i.e., nuts, wild seeds, and cultigens). The nut:wood ratio characterizing the Mississippian features analyzed was 1.4:1. The average frequency of seeds was six times higher than in the Late Woodland samples, and the seed spectrum was dominated by seeds from plants that were probably cultivated. The greatest contrast between the Late Woodland and Mississippian samples was the presence of maize in 71% of the Mississippian features analyzed, whereas no maize was recovered from the Late Woodland features.

Although maize agriculture evidently achieved importance sometime between Late Woodland and Mississippian times at the Julien site, there was no evidence that maize replaced other food sources. Wild resources (nuts, fruits such as grape and persimmon, and possibly tubers such as American lotus and wild sweet potato) and cultivated plants (squash, gourd, marsh elder, sunflower, and the starchy seed complex) were well-represented in the Mississippian features. Together they demonstrate the existence of a wide floral subsistence base. A comparison of the three successive Mississippian phases revealed no evidence for great fluctuations in this subsistence base through the Mississippian period at the Julien site.

REFERENCES CITED

Anderson, Edgar
1969 *Plants, man and life*. University of California Press, Berkeley.

Asch, David L. and Nancy B. Asch
1978 The economic potential of *Iva annua* and its prehistoric importance in the lower Illinois valley. In The nature and status of ethnobotany, edited by Richard I. Ford, pp. 301-341. *Museum of Anthropology, University of Michigan, Anthropological Papers* 67.

Asch, Nancy B. and David L. Asch
1975 Plant remains from the Zimmerman site - grid A: a quantitative perspective. In The Zimmerman site: further excavations at the Grand Village of Kaskaskia, by Margaret K. Brown. *Illinois State Museum, Reports of Investigations* 35.

1980 The Dickson Camp and Pond sites: Middle Woodland archaeobotany in Illinois. In Dickson Camp and Pond: two early Havana tradition sites in the central Illinois valley, by Anne-Marie Cantwell, Appendix B, pp. 152-160. *Illinois State Museum, Reports of Investigations* 36.

Asch, David L., Kenneth B. Farnsworth, and Nancy B. Asch
1979 Woodland subsistence and settlement in west central Illinois. In *Hopewell archaeology: the Chillicothe Conference*, edited by David S. Brose and N′omi Greber, pp. 80-85. Kent State University Press, Kent, Ohio.

Binford, Lewis R.
1967 Smudge pits and hide smoking: the use of analogy in archaeological reasoning. *American Antiquity* 32:1-12.

Brown, Ian W.
1980 Salt and the eastern North American Indian: an archaeological study. *Peabody Museum, Harvard University, Lower Mississippi Survey Bulletin* 6.

Brown, James A.
1964 The identification of a prehistoric bone tool from the Midwest: the deer-jaw sickle. _American Antiquity_ 29:381-386.

Burt, William H., and Richard P. Grossenheider
1976 _A field guide to the mammals_ (Third edition). Houghton Mifflin Co., Boston.

Cowan, C. Wesley
1978 The prehistoric use and distribution of maygrass in eastern North America: cultural and phytogeographic implications. In The nature and status of ethnobotany, edited by Richard I. Ford, pp. 263-288. _Museum of Anthropology, University of Michigan, Anthropological Papers_ 67.

Cross, Paula
1982 Faunal remains from the Mund site. In The Mund site (11-S-435): a stratified, multi-component occupation in the American Bottom, by Andrew C. Fortier, Fred A. Finney, and Richard B. Lacampagne, pp. 339-366. _Department of Anthropology, University of Illinois at Urbana-Champaign, FAI-270 Archaeological Mitigation Project Report_ 41.

Denny, Sidney G.
1974 Archaeological resources of the Blue Waters Area. In _Environmental inventory report, East St. Louis and vicinity, Illinois, Blue Waters area, St. Clair County, Illinois._ United States Army Corp of Engineers, St. Louis District.

Emerson, Thomas E.
1980a Annual report of 1979 investigations conducted by the University of Illinois in Urbana at various sites in the Southern Illinois University-Edwardsville package. In Annual report of 1979 investigations, pp. 75-103. _Department of Anthropology, University of Illinois at Urbana-Champaign, FAI-270 Archaeological Mitigation Project Annual Report._

1980b The Dyroff (11-S-463) and Levin (11-S-462) sites: a Late Archaic occupation in the American Bottom. _Department of Anthropology, University of Illinois at Urbana-Champaign, FAI-270 Archaeological Mitigation Project Report_ 24.

1981 Annual Report of 1980 investigations at the Dyroff, Levin, and BBB Motor sites. In Annual Report of 1980 investigations, pp. 40-50. Department of Anthropology, University of Illinois at Urbana-Champaign, FAI-270 Archaeological Mitigation Project Annual Report.

Finney, Fred A.
1979 Manual of field procedures and activities: excavating and recording data. Department of Anthropology, University of Illinois at Urbana-Champaign.

Fowler, Melvin L.
1974 Cahokia: ancient capital of the Midwest. Addison-Wesley Module in Anthropology 48:3-38.

1978 Cahokia and the American Bottom: settlement archeology. In Mississippian settlement patterns, edited by Bruce D. Smith, pp. 455-478. Academic Press, New York.

Fowler, Melvin L. and Robert L. Hall
1972 Archaeological phases at Cahokia. Illinois State Museum, Papers in Anthropology 1.

Harriot, Thomas
1972 A briefe and true report of the new found land of Virginia. London, 1590. rpt. Dover Publications, Inc., New York.

Hoffmeister, Donald F. and Carl D. Mohr
1957 Fieldbook of Illinois Mammals. Dover Publications, New York.

Hudson, Charles
1976 The southeastern Indians. University of Tennessee Press, Knoxville.

Jackson, Douglas K.
1980 Final report on archaeological investigations at the Sandy Ridge Farm site (11-S-660). Department of Anthropology, University of Illinois at Urbana-Champaign, FAI-270 Archaeological Mitigation Project Report 20.

Kelly, John E.

1979 1978 Annual report: Range site (11-S-47). In Annual report of 1978 investigations, pp. 16-34. Department of Anthropology, University of Illinois at Urbana-Champaign, FAI-270 Archaeological Mitigation Project Annual Report.

1980a Annual report of 1979 investigations at the Range site (11-S-47). In Annual report of 1979 investigations, pp. 18-29. Department of Anthropology, University of Illinois at Urbana-Champaign, FAI-270 Archaeological Mitigation Project Annual Report.

1980b Formative developments at Cahokia and the adjacent American Bottom: a Merrell Tract perspective. Unpublished Ph.D. dissertation. Department of Anthropology, University of Wisconsin, Madison.

Kelly, John E., Jean R. Linder, and Theresa J. Cartmell

1979 The archaeological intensive survey of the proposed FAI-270 alignment in the American Bottom region of southern Illinois. Illinois Transportation Archaeology Scientific Reports 1.

Kelly, Lucretia S.

1979 Animal resource exploitation by early Cahokia populations on the Merrell Tract. Illinois Archaeological Survey, Circular 4.

Martin, Alexander C. and William D. Barkley

1961 Seed identification manual. University of California Press, Berkeley.

Melbye, F. Jerome

1963 The Kane Burial Mounds. Southern Illinois University Museum, Archaeological Salvage Report 15.

Milner, George R.

1980 Bioanthropology. In Annual report of 1979 investigations, pp. 146-147. Department of Anthropology, University of Illinois at Urbana-Champaign, FAI-270 Archaeological Mitigation Project Annual Report.

1981a Annual report of bioanthropological investigations and excavations at the East St. Louis Stone Quarry site. In Annual report of 1980 investigations, pp. 83-89. Department of Anthropology, University of Illinois at Urbana-Champaign, FAI-270 Archaeological Mitigation Project Annual Report.

1981b Annual report of investigations at the DeMange and Turner sites (11-S-447 and 11-S-50). In Annual report of 1980 investigations, pp. 34-40. Department of Anthropology, University of Illinois at Urbana-Champaign, FAI-270 Archaeological Mitigation Project Annual Report.

Montgomery, Frederick H.
1977 Seeds and fruits of plants of eastern Canada and the northeastern United States. University of Toronto Press, Toronto.

Muenscher, Walter C.
1975 Poisonous plants of the United States. Collier Books, New York.

Munsell Color Company
1971 Munsell soil color charts. Munsell Color Company, Inc., Baltimore.

Nie, Norman H., C. Hadlai Hull, Jean G. Jenkins, Karin Steinbrenner, and Dale H. Bent
1975 Statistical package for the social sciences (Second edition). McGraw Hill, New York.

Norris, Terry
1978 Excavations at the Lily Lake site: 1975 season. Southern Illinois University at Edwardsville, Reports in Contract Archaeology Contract Series 4.

O'Brien, Patricia J.
1972 A formal analysis of Cahokia ceramics from the Powell Tract. Illinois Archaeological Survey, Monograph 3.

Panshin, A. J. and Carl de Zeeuw
1970 Textbook of wood technology Volume 1 (Third edition). McGraw Hill, New York.

Parmalee, Paul W.
1975 A general survey of the vertebrate fauna from Cahokia. In Perspectives in Cahokia archaeology. Illinois Archaeological Survey, Bulletin 10:137-155.

Phillips, Philip
1970 Archaeological survey in the lower Yazoo basin, Mississippi, 1949-1955. Harvard University, Papers of the Peabody Museum of Archaeology and Ethnology 60.

Phillips, Philip and James A. Brown
1978 Pre-Columbian shell engravings from the Craig Mound at Spiro, Oklahoma, Part 1. Peabody Museum Press, Cambridge.

Porter, James W.
1974 Cahokia archaeology as viewed from the Mitchell site: a satellite community at A.D. 1150-1200. Unpublished Ph.D. dissertation, Department of Anthropology, University of Wisconsin, Madison.

Prentice, Guy and Mark W. Mehrer
1981 The Lab Woofie site (11-S-346): an unplowed Mississippian site in the American Bottom region of Illinois. Midcontinental Journal of Archaeology 6:35-53.

Rau, Charles
1876 The archaelogical collection of the United States National Museum. Smithsonian Contributions to Knowledge, Volume 22.

Smith, Bruce D.
1975 Middle Mississippi exploitation of animal populations. Museum of Anthropology, University of Michigan, Anthropological Papers 57.

1978a Prehistoric patterns of human behavior: a case study in the Mississippi valley. Academic Press, New York.

1978b Variation in Mississippian settlement patterns. In Mississippian settlement patterns, edited by Bruce D. Smith, pp. 479-503. Academic Press, New York.

Smith, Bruce D. (editor)
1978c Mississippian settlement patterns. Academic Press, New York.

Steyermark, Julian A.
1963 Flora of Missouri. Iowa State University Press, Ames.

Swanton, John R.
1946 The Indians of the southeastern United States. Bureau of American Ethnology, Bulletin 137.

Szuter, Christine R.
1979 The Schlemmer site: a Late Woodland-Mississippian site in the American Bottom. Unpublished M.A. thesis, Department of Anthropology, Loyola University, Chicago.

Vogel, Joseph O.
1975 Trends in Cahokia ceramics: preliminary study of the collections from Tracts 15A and 15B. In Perspectives in Cahokia archaeology, Illinois Archaeological Survey, Bulletin 10:32-125.

Wagner, Gail E.
1976 IDOT flotation procedure manual. Ms. on file, Illinois Department of Transportation, District 8, Fairview Heights.

Wallace, D.L.
1978 Soil survey of St. Clair County, Illinois. Soil Conservation Service, United States Department of Agriculture, Illinois Agricultural Experiment Station Soil Report 104.

Walthall, John A.
1981 Galena and aboriginal trade in eastern North America. Illinois State Museum, Scientific Papers 17.

Woods, William F.
1978 Annual progress report #1 (15 June - 31 December 1978). Department of Anthropology, Southern Illinois University at Edwardsville, FAI-270 Archaeological Mitigation Project Report.

Yarnell, Richard A.
1972 *Iva annua* var. *macrocarpa*: extinct American cultigen? *American Anthropologist* 74:335-341.

1978 Domestication of sunflower and sumpweed in eastern North America. In The nature and status of ethnobotany, edited by Richard I. Ford, pp. 289-299. *Museum of Anthropology, University of Michigan, Anthropological Papers* 67.

Yerkes, Richard W.
1980 The Mississippian component. In Investigations at the Labras Lake site, by J.L. Phillips, R.L. Hall, and R.W. Yerkes. *Department of Anthropology, University of Illinois at Chicago Circle, Volume I - Archaeology, Part* 1. Part 1.